MONEY, SEX, and POWER

MONEY, SEX, and POWER

Toward a Feminist Historical Materialism

NANCY C. M. HARTSOCK
JOHNS HOPKINS UNIVERSITY

The Northeastern Series in Feminist Theory
Northeastern University Press
BOSTON

Northeastern University Press edition 1985

Permission has been granted to quote from the following sources:

Claude Lévi-Strauss, *The Savage Mind*. English translation
© 1966 by George Weidenfeld and Nicholson, Ltd., London, and the University of Chicago Press. Reprinted with
permission of the publishers.

Claude Lévi-Strauss, *Tristes-Tropiques*, translated from
the French by John and Doreen Weightman. Copyright
© 1973 Jonathan Cape Ltd. Reprinted with the permission
of Atheneum Publishers and Jonathan Cape Ltd.

Simone de Beauvoir, *The Second Sex*, translated and edited
by H. M. Parshley. Copyright © Alfred A. Knopf, Inc.
Reprinted with permission of the publisher.

Gayle Rubin, "The Traffic of Women," in Rayna R. Reiter,
ed., *Toward an Athropology of Women*. Copyright © 1975 by
Rayna R. Reiter. Reprinted by permission of Monthly Review Press.

Karl Marx, *Capital*, Vol. 1. Reprinted with permission of
International Publishers, New York.

Library of Congress Cataloging in Publication Data

Hartsock, Nancy C. M.
  Money, sex, and power

  (Northeastern series in feminist theory)
  Reprint. Originally published: New York: Longman,
1983. (Longman series in feminist theory)
  Includes index.
  1. Power (Social sciences) 2. Power (Philosophy)
3. Feminism. 4. Exchange. 5. Historical materialism.
6. Masculinity (Psychology) I. Title. II. Series.
[HM131.H32 1985]   303.3'3   85-5076
ISBN 0-930350-78-2 (pbk.)

Printed and bound by Malloy Lithographing, Ann Arbor,
Michigan. The paper is Glatfelter Antique, an acid-free
sheet.

MANUFACTURED IN THE UNITED STATES OF AMERICA
90 89 88 87 86   5 4 3 2

Contents

Preface

This is a book about how we do and might understand power. It is a book whose content is heavily dependent on both the political arguments within the feminist movement and the work of feminist theorists. In many ways its writing began in 1973 with my association with the staff of *Quest: a feminist quarterly*, a group of political activists who were then and are now very concerned with issues of power and leadership. In addition, I have benefited from the growing debate over the nature of a feminist sexuality.

Despite the variety of ways my writing has been influenced by activists, this remains an academic book specifically influenced by my own disciplinary background and training. While I take up theories from sociology, economics, and anthropology, my background in political science (perhaps coupled with the fact that political scientists have traditionally been among those most concerned with power) leads me to give special prominence to theories originating in that field. Thus, Chapters 3 and 4 may be of greater interest to political scientists than to the general reader. Those interested in methodology and questions of how a feminist methodology might be constituted may wish to concentrate on Chapters 5, 10, and the appendixes. These are devoted to a consideration of the methodological and epistemological issues that underlie theories of power. Earlier versions of these chapters circulated in manuscript for some time under the title "Can There Be a Specifically Feminist Historical Materialism?"

In addition to my general dependence on the state of political debate within the feminist movement, many people have contributed directly to this work. I owe a great deal to the intense, ongoing, and valuable discussions with my colleagues at Johns Hopkins: Richard Flathman, J. G. A. Pocock, and Donna Haraway (now at U.C. Santa Cruz). Each of them read and commented extensively on more than one draft of the manuscript. In addition, Isaac Balbus, Zillah Eisenstein, and Bertell

Ollman read and commented extensively and helpfully on the manuscript. I have also been helped importantly by collective discussions (some focused on sections of this book) with Annette Bickel, Sarah Begus, Alexa Freeman, and Sandra Harding. I would like to thank the following people who read and commented on chapters or sections of the manuscript: Martha Ackelsburg, Nicole Benevento, Carol Camper, Matthew Crenson, Irene Diamond, Jane Flax, Virgina Held, Alison Jaggar, Nannerl Keohane, Robert Peabody, Carolyn Projansky, Frank Romer, Jean Turner, Kathleen Weston, and Iris Young. Finally, I would like to thank Stephen Rose for his support, both material and moral, of the project, as well as his helpful comments on sections of the book at critical points in its development. All these people may find their ideas incorporated here, although not always used in the way they might wish.

Introduction

In recent decades, many of us have learned a great deal about the extent to which our society is structured by relations of domination and submission, relations constructed most importantly out of differences of race, sex, and class. Yet we lack theoretical clarity about *how* these relations of domination are constructed, how they operate, and how social theories and practices have both justified and obscured them. Due to the Marxian account of the ways capitalist domination is constructed and maintained, our understanding of class domination is the most advanced. But Marxian theory as such has had little to say about gender or racial domination; discussions of "the national question" and "the woman question" have proved unable to account for white and male supremacy. And to the extent that domination occurs along lines of race and sex, or that race and sex affect class domination, Marxian theory must be recognized as inadequate.

My particular concern here is with (1) how relations of domination along gender lines are constructed and maintained and (2) whether social understandings of domination itself have been distorted by men's domination of women. How can we develop a theory that can provide a more complete understanding both of relations of domination and of the transformations necessary to create a more egalitarian society? This book is an argument that an essential part of such a theory and practice is the critique of power relations—of the ways the exercise of power of some over others is constructed, legitimated, and reproduced.

Feminists have been more willing to focus attention on women's oppression than on the question of how men's dominance is constructed and maintained, and so over the last fifteen or so years, the subject of power has not received sustained feminist attention. Perhaps this is also a result of the effort feminists devoted to avoiding the exercise of power.[1] Feminist avoidance of exercising power took a variety of

1

forms in the early 1970s. Most typically, it resulted in the adoption of a kind of personal, structureless politics; a widespread opposition to leadership; an insistence on working collectively; and an emphasis on process, often to the exclusion of getting things done. Implicit in these strategies was the view that power was "the ability to compel obedience" or was "control and domination," the view that power was something possessed, a property possessed by an actor that enabled him to alter the will or actions of others in ways that produce results in conformity with his own will.[2] The political practice of much of the contemporary feminist movement has indicated the tacit acceptance of the view that the exercise, of power *is* the exercise of domination.[3] The effort to oppose domination, especially of course the domination of women, has taken the form of efforts to develop forms of organization (very amorphous forms) in which differences in personal attributes or differences in position within the group would not lead to differences in power—that is, small, structureless groups where there were no differences of sex, sexual preference, class, and so on.[4] The understanding of power as power over others was of course tacit and untheorized, that is, not recognized or discussed. And I do not mean to suggest that the effort to avoid power over others was necessarily wrong. I *do* mean to suggest that it is important for feminists to address questions of power more directly. There is, after all, a certain dangerous irony in the fact that both feminists and antifeminists agree that the exercise of power is a masculine activity and preoccupation, inappropriate to women or feminists, and not a subject to which attention should be directed.

Our opposition to relations of domination makes it essential for feminists to examine the exercise of power more directly. Is the exercise of power best understood as the ability to compel obedience? To what extent should power be understood as energy or ability? How should feminists understand the actions of individuals who compel others to behave in certain ways as opposed to the more impersonal force of circumstance that also compels people to particular actions? And if we look more closely at the exercise of power over others, can it really be connected with masculinity? If so, is there a way of exercising power that could be characterized as feminine or female? Are any exercises of power to be legitimate in the community we want? These are all questions a movement for social change must face if it is to succeed in transforming a society structured by domination.

A critique of theories that explain how power relations are constructed and how power is exercised can be an important resource for understanding what the construction of a more humane community would require. I argue that these theories of power can be helpful in several ways. First, theories of power are implicitly theories of community. To examine these theories of power is to involve oneself in the questions of how communities have been constructed, how they have been legitimized, and how they might be structured in more liberatory ways. Second, and related, because we live in a community structured by the domination of one gender and class, theories of power can be expected to carry both gender and class dimensions and thus provide a context in which to explore the impact of gender and class on the construction of communities.[5] Third, and perhaps most important, efforts to explain how power operates inevitably involve larger questions as well, and different theories of power rest on differing assumptions about both the content of existence and the ways we come to know it.[6] That is, different theories of power rest on differing ontologies and epistemologies, and a feminist rethinking of power requires attention to its epistemological grounding.

For this reason, both the critique of theories of power and the construction of a more adequate theory require attention to a series of questions that may at first seem only loosely related to issues of domination. These include questions such as the appropriate methods for social research, alternatives in epistemology and ontology, the relation of epistemology or theories of knowledge to human activity, historical tendencies in social development, and the relation between individual and collective capacities and actions. My focus on this set of concerns imposes a complicated logic on the book, one that requires the simultaneous pursuit of two important lines of argument. One line of argument addresses issues of community, class, and gender; the other concerns the epistemological grounding of these issues.

Power and Community: Issues of Class and Gender

The fundamental questions posed for theorists of power are these: What are the legitimate bases on which a community of actors can be organized and maintained? What are the characteristics and limits of legitimate action within a community? To what extent can relations of domination legitimately structure the human community? And to what extent is it possible to construct a human community that does not fundamentally rest on relations of domination? These questions, as we shall see, recur with surprising consistency among theorists who answer them in profoundly different ways. My own understanding of the relation of power and community leads me to argue that the form taken by the exercise of power in a community structures human interaction within that community, and so, in a community where the exercise of power takes the form of structured and systematic domination of some over others, the community itself is formed by domination. It follows that to change the practice of power is to change the structure and nature of the community.

The class and gender content of power initially becomes evident in different areas, the one in the area of economics, the other in the area of sexuality.[7] Yet, as will be seen, there are deep interconnections and definite structured relations between the two.

Class

Economic activities (especially the economic activities characteristic of men's lives) have formed the contemporary context in which the class content of theorizations of power has been explored. I argue that one can distinguish capitalist and working-class theorizations of power on the basis of the specific economic activities each takes as paradigmatic for understanding/explaining power relations. Explanations whose class content Marx would label "bourgeois" tend to privilege activities having to do with money—using it to buy things, investing it in order to increase it, banking it. "Proletarian" explanations take the activity of production as the paradigm for power relations. This is the perspective from which I approach the arguments of contemporary social scientists that power is best understood on the model provided by the function of money in the market; that power, like money, is a means of getting others to act in ways they would not otherwise act. These social scientists focus explicitly on the conflict of interests characteristic of power relationships and often take the *personae* of the buyer and seller in the market as their point of reference. Power relations, conceived on this market-oriented model, are described as similar to the relation of a buyer and seller confronting each other with differential resources.

It may not be apparent that there is a conception of community implicit here. The significance of the market model can be somewhat clarified if one reminds oneself that despite their opposing interests, the buyer and seller not only *are* associated with each other but also that the association has a certain value for each. They have created a certain sort of community. True, the fundamental gulf between buyer and seller (and, in the analogy, between parties to a power relation) persists; participants have conflicting interests and therefore can be expected to distrust each other. In addition, the community established in this way can be only partial, since it is on the one hand constituted by the common interests of participants and on the other limited by their conflict. They are engaged in a contest to determine which of them will be the dominant party to an exchange; they need in principle have only enough in common to actually engage in a competition or exchange.

The class content of Marx's theorization of power is profoundly opposed to that carried by market theories. Marx held that power is best understood on the model provided by the workers' activity in production rather than the capitalists' activity in exchange. But here one must distinguish his view of the power relations operative in the capitalist production process from those he held would operate in a communist production process, and therefore in communist society. Thus, I argue that the Marxian account of the production of surplus value by workers and its appropriation by capitalists should be read as an explanation of the mechanisms by which class domination is substituted for the more encompassing human community potentially present in workers' cooperation in production. The Marxian account of class domination, then, can enable us to recognize the real existence of a fragile and deeply unsatisfactory human community in capitalist societies. But rather than conclude that human beings are by nature isolated and interest-driven, this theory holds instead that societies need not be structured by class domination. In their place, Marxian theory holds out a vision of both power and community rooted in production. This is most strikingly described by Marx in an extraordinary passage from the *1844 Manuscripts*:

> Supposing that we had produced in a human manner; each of us would in his production have doubly affirmed himself and his fellow men. I would have: (1) objectified in my production my individuality and its peculiarity and thus both in my activity enjoyed an individual expression of my life and also in looking at the object have had the individual pleasure of realizing that my personality was objective, visible to the senses and thus a power raised beyond all doubt. (2) In your enjoyment of use of my product I would have had the direct enjoyment of realizing that I had both satisfied a human need by my work and also objectified the human essence and therefore fashioned for another human being the object that met his need. (3) I would have been for you the mediator between you and the species and thus been acknowledged and felt by you as a completion of your own essence and a necessary part of your self and have thus realized that I am confirmed in both your thought and in your love. (4) In my expression of my life I would have fashioned your expression of life, and thus in my own activity have realized my own essence, my human, my communal essence.[8]

A Marxian critique of theories of power modeled on the market, coupled with the liberatory vision carried by his account of the possibilities for community available in unalienated production, can contribute importantly to our understanding of power. Yet Marx's account of class domination, like market theorists' accounts of power relations, operates with gender-blind and therefore gender-biased categories. By ignoring the genderedness of power relations he presents an incomplete account of relations of domination and of the possibilities for a more humane community.

Gender

Perhaps because issues of power are at the same time issues about the nature of legitimate community, power seems irreducibly to involve questions of *eros* or sexuality. Both the exchange of things and the erotic fusion of sexuality bring human beings together. Both represent important experiences of the ways one person can come into contact with another. The form of the interaction may vary: It may be nurturant, instrumental or rational; it may take the form of domination, force, persuasion, bargaining, or expression of love. In every case, however, what is at stake is the very existence of a relation with another, the existence of community.

In the literature on power, social scientists have frequently alluded to the links between virility and domination. For example, one scholar introduced a book on concepts of power, influence, and authority with the statement that the first is linked with notions of potency, virility, and masculinity and "appears much sexier than the other two."[9] Or consider philosopher Bertrand de Jouvenel's note that "a man feels himself more of a man when imposing himself and making others the instrument of his will."[10] And what are we to make of Robert Penn Warren's statement that "masculinity is closely tied to every form of power in our society,"[11] or Henry Kissinger's telling but perhaps apocryphal remark, "Power is the ultimate aphrodisiac"? One must conclude that the associative links between manliness, virility, power, and domination are very strong in Western culture.

Yet while it is not news that the exercise of power has links with masculine sexuality, the theoretical content and significance of these links remains to be explored. Despite their recognition of these links, social scientists and theorists have given little analytic attention to the erotic aspect of power relations. This failure to explore the gendered linkage between sexuality and power, despite the stated recognition of its existence, typifies a surprising range of theories of power. The lacuna is perhaps most surprising and most in need of remedy in the case of Marx, given his stress on the importance of sensuous material life. The failure is important because power structures the human community, and thus the current silence about the genderedness of power forms an obstacle to the construction of a society free from all forms of domination.

The gender carried by power has, however, been explored in a quite different context, one in which the central issue is the connection of sexuality with violence and even death. Activists in the contemporary feminist movement have contended that exercises of power and domination in Western culture are systematically confused with sexual acts. There is a growing literature which argues that rape is an act of domination, an act that has to do with power and even property rather than an act growing from sexual frustration.[12] And the feminist debate about whether pornography is erotic literature or represents violence against women represents a second locus in which the relation between (or fusion of) virility and domination has been pointed out. My reading of these and other analyses leads me to argue that sexuality in our society is defined almost exclusively in masculine terms, and moreover that hostility and domination are central to the construction of masculine sexuality.[13]

This dynamic of hostility and domination structures not just the "private" world of individual action and sexuality but has a larger significance as well. It is deeply implicated in ideals for public life. One can find what is perhaps its clearest expression in a society unencumbered with market ideology, in ancient Athenian political philosophy where the public world first took theoretical form. Masculine sexuality was central to the construction of an agonal community structured fundamentally by rivalry and competition. The Homeric warrior-hero, civic ideals for the Athenian citizen, and the nature of the communities they constructed bear the marks of a hostile and aggressive masculinity.

Feminists should not simply turn their backs on the agonal communities men have constructed and have justified in political theory. Like market theories, the theorization of an agonal politics, a politics based on struggle and competition, provides important resources for a feminist rethinking of power. Agonal communities should be critically understood as expressions of a specifically masculine social experience, a masculine attempt to solve the riddle of community. If these are the power relations that both construct and are reinforced by masculine sexuality, can one envisage alternative possibilities for community present in women's sexuality?[14] The beginnings of an answer to such a question will require attention to women's lives rather than men's to determine whether women's lives provide a ground for an alternative understanding of power and community.

Power and Epistemology: Exchange, Production, and Reproduction

Because alternative theories of power rest on different epistemologies, and because the adequacy of a given theory depends on the adequacy of its epistemological base, discussions of power can enable us to open the subject of a more encompassing feminist analysis. A more encompassing analysis would be able to account for the relation of theories of knowledge to human activity, and the relation of knowledge and domination in our society. It would be able to understand the forces involved in social change and would identify the areas of social life which hold the key to development of a more humane community.

In beginning to develop an encompassing theory, Marx's analysis of class domination in capitalist society provides both an important standard for a systematic feminist theory and a series of guidelines. The depth and profundity of Marx's analysis depended on the historical materialist approach he took toward these questions, and his success stands as an implicit suggestion that feminists should adopt a historical materialist approach to understanding male supremacy. At the outset I propose to take over two of Marx's important arguments about epistemology and ontology. (One should note that the two categories collapse into each other for Marx.) First, I critically adopt his insistence that conscious human activity, or practice, has both an ontological and epistemological status, that human feelings are not "merely anthropological phenomena" but are "truly ontological affirmations of being."[15] Thus, for Marx, each mode of producing subsistence, each form of the division of mental from manual labor, can be expected to have consequences for human understanding. Thus, Marx argued that the practical activity—and therefore the world view—of capitalist and worker differed systematically because the activity of each was structured by the mental/manual division of labor. And because the activity of the ruling, or capitalist, class was structured by exchange, exchange structured not only the human community in capitalist society but also set limits to the modes in which this community could be understood. As Marx and Engels put it, the

> class which has the means of material production at its
> disposal, has control at the same time over the means of mental
> production, so that thereby, generally speaking, the ideas of
> those who lack the means of mental production are subject to
> it. The ruling ideas are nothing more than the ideal expression
> of the dominant material relationships, the dominant material
> relationships grasped as ideas; hence of the relationships which
> make the one class the ruling one, therefore, the ideas of its
> dominance.[16]

When we understand that economic categories are the theoretical expressions of the social relations of production, we recognize that data present themselves immediately, that is directly and obviously, in forms and categories that are part of capitalist society. To accept the data in this form as falling within eternal and unalterable categories is both to fail to see the underlying reality and to acquiesce in the reproduction of capitalist social relations.

Our society, however, is structured not simply by a ruling class dependent on the division of mental from manual labor but also by a ruling gender, defined by and dependent on the sexual division of labor. Control over the means of mental production belongs to this ruling gender as well as to the ruling class. Thus, one can expect that the categories in which experience is commonly presented are both capitalist and masculine. And to the extent that Marxian theory is grounded in men's activity in production and ignores women's activity in reproduction, one can expect that Marxian categories themselves will require critique.

The second point to be critically adopted is Marx's argument that the ruling ideas, because they are the ideas of the ruling class, give an incorrect acount of reality, an account only of appearances. Thus, Marx argues,

> The final pattern of economic relations as seen on the surface, in their real existence and consequently in the conceptions by which the bearers and agents of these relations seek to understand them, is very much different from, and indeed quite the reverse of, their inner but concealed essential pattern and the conception corresponding to it. [17]

These inner but concealed patterns are visible from the point of view of the proletariat, those who embody, although involuntarily, the "negative result of society." [18] Only through a process of mediation, a process of uncovering the social relations and social consequences involved even in apparently simple things, can the authentic structure of phenomena be revealed. [19]

Marxian theory holds that accounts of power based at the level of circulation or exchange provide inadequate accounts of systematic domination and inequality. In contrast, Marx argues that the social relations of capitalism generate two epistemological systems, the one at the level of appearance, and rooted in the activity of exchange, the other at the level of real social relations, and rooted in the activity of production. Yet if the institutionalized structure of human activity generates an ontology and epistemology, and if the activity of women differs systematically from that of men, we must ask whether epistemology is structured by gender as well as class. If the reality of systematic class domination only becomes apparent at the epistemological level of production, what epistemological level can allow us to understand the systematic domination of women? I argue that the domination of one gender by the other can only be made visible at a still deeper level, an epistemological level defined by reproduction. Thus, rather than argue, with Marx, that reality must be understood as bi-leveled, I am suggesting that it must be understood as three-tiered. And if at the level of production, as Marx argues, one can not only see the real relations between human beings but also understand why theories at higher levels of abstraction fail, then at the level of reproduction we should expect to develop not only a more comprehensive account of the totality of social relations but as well understand why it is that neither the level of exchange nor the level of production provides an adequate and complete epistemological ground for the theorization of power.[20] The book, then, can be seen as a kind of Wittgensteinian ladder. But whereas he held that one could ascend and then discard the ladder, my own view is that the ladder should be seen as a means by which one gradually descends to the real material ground of human existence, a ground constituted by women's experience and life activity.

Summary

Part I of the book is devoted to the move from the epistemological level of circulation or exchange to the level of production. I begin with the work of social scientists who have explicitly taken economic exchange as the privileged and prototypic human behavior. Their work can be particularly useful in spelling out the assumptions that underlie the argument that power is a circulating medium, or kind of money, in the political market. George Homans and Peter Blau present the most sophisticated versions of exchange theories. Moreover, their theories indicate with great clarity how competition in exchange can result in relations of domination, and illustrate how a community based on domination can substitute for a more fully human community. This is the subject of Chapter 1. Chapter 2 addresses the inconsistencies and inadequacies that result from using the model of exchange to understand power relations. I argue that these theories rest on an unsound and truncated theory of human nature and human sociality. In addition, I argue that they must be understood as complicated shell games by means of which coercion is presented as choice. Chapter 3 focuses on theories of power in which the market model operates in more diffuse and implicit forms. I demonstrate how the analyses of Rober Dahl, Nelson Polsby, Talcott Parsons, Harold Lasswell, and Abraham Kaplan share the fundamental assumptions of exchange theory: Individuals are assumed to be isolated and interest-driven, and to interact only on terms of their own choosing. Because they share the assumptions of exchange theory, their theories suffer from the same defects.

Those I characterize as "market theorists" have not been without their critics. Chapter 4 takes up their efforts at more adequate theories. Bachrach and Baratz's work on the importance of nondecisions, William Connolly's argument for the close relation between power and responsibility, and Steven Lukes' argument for the existence of objective as well as subjective interests help to clarify the issues a more adequate theory of class domination must face. Yet these theories fail as alternatives to market theories primarily because they have not completely abandoned the epistemological level of exchange. Chapter 5 summarizes the important features of the epistemological level of exchange as understood from the level of production. In turn this requires expanding and clarifying what it means to argue that human activity has both an ontological and epistemological status. I argue that one can understand the epistemology that constitutes the level of exchange by closely examining the human activity involved in exchange, in a sense by "reading out" the ontology and epistemology present in that activity. By understanding the problems implicit in exchange as epistemology, we can both understand the deeper problems it poses for theories of power and better avoid importing aspects of exchange into a retheorization of power. Chapter 6 takes up the understanding of power that is available if one relocates the theorization of power at the level of production and grounds an understanding of power in the workers' life activity. This theorization, it is argued, not only solves the problems faced by theories of power located at the level of exchange but can as well point beyond these relations of class domination in more liberatory directions.[21]

Part II of the book is concerned with moving the theorization of power to the level defined by reproduction and with theorizing the genderedness of power. Chapter 7 explores the association of masculinity with domination and the linkage of sexuality, violence, and death in the contexts both of psychoanalytic theory and the expression of masculine fantasies in pornography. Chapter 8 follows these associations into the public world through the medium of an examination of some ancient Athenian sources such as Plato's *Republic* and *Symposium*, Aristotle's *Politics*, and the plays of Aeschylus and Aristophanes. These sources can shed useful light on our contemporary problem since they address the genderedness of power relations much more directly, without the obfuscating model of the market. In addition, these sources underline the close connections between power and community.

In order to support my contention that power carries a masculine gender, Chapter 9 examines the work of several women who have written about power. I argue that these women do indeed understand power in systematically different ways than the men whose theories I have considered.[22] Hannah Arendt is a particularly interesting case in point, since she bases her theory explicitly on the agonal community of the ancient *polis*, the community of citizen-warriors. Yet, in her hands, this agonal ethic is transformed into a communal one. One can find similar positions in the work of the few other women who have dealt with understandings of power—Dorothy Emmet and contemporary writers with more explicitly feminist commitments have all produced strikingly similar accounts of power. Chapter 10 attempts a relocation of a theory of power to the ground of women's life experience and activity, a retheorization of power at the level of reproduction. I argue that by adopting a vantage point located in women's life activity, a feminist standpoint, one can set out a feminist (rather than simply female) theorization of power that can explain why domination has carried a masculine gender, and why masculine sexuality has been linked with violence and death. In addition, such a theory, I argue, can point beyond understandings of power as power over others. I conclude with an effort to clarify the relation of class and gender. I argue the several commonalities between the community constructed by warrior-heroes, or "agonal men," and that constructed by "rational economic men" are very suggestive. Both the exchange of commodities by rational economic men and the exchange of gifts, trophies, and women by agonal men represent the experience of one gender—an experience modeled on the opposition, distrust, isolation, and even hostility of each man to every other. And both activities carry similar dualistic epistemologies and ontologies. I have included as well an appendix analyzing the work of Claude Levi-Strauss, who has served as the vehicle by which some of the assumptions surrounding agonal man have been imported into feminist theory.

If politics is about power, and power relations in Western culture, up to the present, have carried masculine gender expressed in an aggressive sexuality, then a feminist rethinking of power can have important implications for our understanding and practice of politics. The market in power contains many similarities to the agonal politics of ancient Athens: If politics is no longer a life-and-death rivalry of agonal men, it does at least depend on the more modest and instrumental opposition of rational economic men. A retheorization of power on the basis of women's as well as men's life activity could be important in reevaluating our understanding and practice of politics. It could perhaps lead toward the constitution of a more complete and thoroughgoing human community.

NOTES

1. I have argued elsewhere that this avoidance was progressive, constructive, and important at the time, but now must be redressed. See "Feminism, Power, and Change," in *Women Organizing*, ed. Bernice Cummings and Victoria Schuck (Metuchen, N.J.: Scarecrow Press, 1980); and "Difference and

Domination in the Women's Movement: The Dialectic of Theory and Practice,'' in *The Scholar and the Feminist*, vol. 2; *Class, Race, and Sex: The Dynamics of Control*, ed. Amy Swerdlow and Hanna Lessinger (Boston: G. K. Hall, 1982). The staff of *Quest: a feminist quarterly* represented an important group exception to this, and are partially responsible for my own interest in the subject of power.

2. These definitions come, respectively, from Bertrand Russell, *Power: A New Social Analysis* (n.p., 1936), p. 35, cited by Anthony de Crespigny and Alan Wertheimer, *Contemporary Political Theory* (New York: Atherton Press, 1970), p. 22; and Talcott Parsons, "On the Concept of Political Power," in *Political Power*, ed. Roderick Bell, David B. Edwards, and R. Harrison Wagner (New York: Free Press, 1969), p. 256.

3. The definition of domination I propose to use provisionally is that put forward by Dorothy Emmet: "achievement of intended effects through coercing other people." See "The Concept of Power," *Proceedings of the Aristotelian Society* ty 54 (1954): 4. Later I hope to define domination as patterned and institutionally defined relations of domination.

4. Simply put, the feminist acceptance of the phallocratic understanding of power functioned as a justification for a series of separatist strategies. First, feminists responded to male domination by insisting that they could only work separately. The split between blacks and other minorities and whites was a similar response to a similar situation. When it became clear that heterosexual women were oppressing lesbians and trying to make them invisible within the women's movement, and that middle- and upper-class women were oppressing working-class women in the movement, the natural response was to split into smaller units. These units meant that no woman had to work with others who might be in a position—whether through class, race, or heterosexual privilege—to exercise power over her.

5. To the extent that race is one of the fundamental structural lines along which domination is constructed, power should be expected to carry a racial dimension as well. My intent here, however, is to expose the genderedness of power, and to make use of the anlysis of its class dimension to show what we should look for in terms of the genderedness of power. For an indication of one way to address the logic of the possible racial dimension of power, see note 7.

6. My point here is similar to W. B. Gallie's argument that power is an "essentially contested" concept. Power can be categorized as an "essentially contested" concept since it is appraisive, internally complex, open, and used both aggressively and defensively. Gallie, however, seems not to recognize the epistemological implications of his position. See W. B. Gallie, "Essentially Contested Concepts," *Proceedings of the Aristotelian Society* 56 (1955–56): 167–98.

7. There are some indications that the race carried by power may share the context in which power carries gender—the context of sexuality. Both the arguments of Susan Griffin and Charles Herbert Stember indicate that racial hostility is deeply connected with sexual excitement. Stember traces these connections through sociological and psychological data, to argue that sexual excitement is central to racial hostility, especially the racial hostility of white men toward black men. See *Sexual Racism* (New York: Harper & Row, 1976). Susan Griffin traces the similarities between pornography and anti-Semitism in *Pornography and Silence* (New York: Harper & Row, 1981).

8. Quoted in David McClellan, *Karl Marx* (New York: Viking, 1975), pp. 31–32.

9. David Bell, *Power, Influence, and Authority*, (New York: Oxford University Press 1975), p. 8.

10. See Berenice Carroll, "Peace Research: The Cult of Power," *Journal of Conflict Resolution* 4 (1972): 588, citing Hanna Arendt, "Reflections on Violence," *Journal of International Affairs* 23, no. 1 (1969): 12. Arendt uses the same quotation in *On Violence* (New York: Harper & Row, 1969), p. 35, where she locates it as occurring in de Jouvenel's *Power: The Natural History of Its Growth* (London: n.p., 1952), p. 110.

11. Robert Penn Warren, *Who Speaks for the Negro* (New York: Vintage, 1966), p. 292.

12. See Susan Brownmiller, *Against Our Will* (New York: Simon and Schuster, 1975); Andrea Medea and Kathleen Thompson, *Against Rape* (New York: Farrar, Strauss, and Giroux, 1974): Susan Griffin, *Rape: The Power of Consciousness* (New York: Harper & Row, 1979); Heidi Hartmann and Ellen Ross, "Comment on 'On Writing the History of Rape,'" *Signs* 3, no. 4 (Summer 1978): 931–35.

13. I use the term "masculine" rather than "male" to indicate what I take to be the fundamentally social rather than biologically given nature of sexuality and, by implication, its susceptibility to change.

14. The subject of women's sexuality is one feminists are only beginning to explore. The difficulty, historic lack of discussion, is made apparent in the fact that the syntactic equivalent of masculine sexuality—feminine sexuality— seems to be a contradiction in terms, or else to imply passive receptiveness and perhaps masochism.

15. Karl Marx, *Economic and Philosophic Manuscripts of 1844*, ed. Dirk Stuik (New York: International Publishers, 1964), pp. 113, 165, 188.

16. Karl Marx and Frederick Engels, *The German Ideology*, ed. C. J. Arthur (New York: International Publishers, 1964), p. 64. See also Karl Marx, *Grundrisse*, trans. Martin Nicolaus (Middlesex, England: Penguin Books, 1973), p. 239.

17. Karl Marx, *Capital* (New York: International Publishers, 1967), 3 : 209.

18. Karl Marx, "Introduction to a Critique of Hegel's Philosophy of Right," in *The Marx-Engels Reader*, ed. Robert Tucker (New York: Norton, 1973), p. 22.

19. Georg Lukacs, *History and Class Consciousness*, (Cambridge, Mass.: MIT Press, 1968), p. 162.

20. I should note here that my use of the category of reproduction to define an epistemological level of reality differs from several other uses, which have been rightly criticized. I am not, for example, discussing a "mode of reproduction" or a "sphere of reproduction." These expressions both indicate that there are different areas or realms of existence. They can even be used to impart a distinction between public (production) and private (reproduction) into feminist theory. In rough terms I intend the term "level of reproduction" to stand relative to the Marxian "level of production" as the "level of production" stands to the "level of circulation" or "exchange."

21. I should note here that because the theorists considered in Part I ignore issues of gender, the theories they produce are gender-biased and include only the experience of men. For this reason, the discussion in Part I uses

the "he/man" form of discussion. My intent is not to use the "neutral" man but to underline the genderedness of these theories.

22. Let me state explicitly that I do not believe this is a biological distinction at all, since a number of men (especially socialist thinkers) have put forward theories that take fundamentally similar positions. See, for example, Christian Bay, *The Structure of Freedom* (New York: Atheneum, 1968).

PART

I

*Perseus wore a magic cap
that the monsters he hunted
down might not see him.*

*We draw the magic cap
down over eyes and ears as
a make believe that there
are no monsters.*

KARL MARX, *CAPITAL*

1

Exchange Theories: Conceptions of Community

Commodity exchange in a capitalist economy has provided one of the most popular models for analysts of power.[1] They argue that if we want to understand power, we should look to functions of money in the market. Despite the fact that theorists often choose different monetary activities on which to construct their theories of power—banking, investment, buying, selling—they hold with remarkable persistence to the idea that the circulation of money in the capitalist market can give us important insights into the practice of power. My purpose in this chapter is to pursue this argument in its most rigorous form, exchange theories of social life, in order to lay bare both the assumptions on which the model rests and the unfortunate conclusions in which its use implicates the theorist.

I demonstrate that the market model leads to the conclusion that competition in exchange results in relations of domination and at the same time legitimizes this domination either by denying it or by treating it as inevitable but unimportant. Power relations as comprehended by the market model are the relations of a number of equal participants who associate voluntarily and for mutual gain. On this model one can present the "necessary evil" represented by the exercise of power in more positive terms. Indeed, one proponent of adopting such a model argued for it precisely on these grounds. Because "exchange relations ... tend to be depicted as cooperative, positive, beneficial, voluntary, and pleasant," such a focus would emphasize the relational and reciprocal nature of power relations rather than their hierarchical and asymmetrical nature and would decrease the tendency to view power relations as "conflictual, negative, and exploitative, coercive, and unpleasant from the standpoint of the one who is influenced."[2]

Thus, accounts of power based on exchange can be expected to stress the voluntary nature of power relations, their reciprocal and nonexploitative character, and even the positive benefits accruing to those over whom power is exercised. In short, they can be expected to redefine power in more consensual terms. Yet because the market model allows theories to present the systematic inequality that structures relations of domination as (at least a temporary) equality, and (at least to some extent) to transform coercion into choice, they should be read as complicated shell games that operate to conceal rather than reveal relations among people.

My argument here should not be read as an indictment of the motives of exchange theorists nor as a charge that their legitimation of relations of domination is a conscious strategy. Indeed, it often seems that the theorists' own discomfort with inequality and domination attracts them to the market model; participants there appear to be free and equal and to associate only on the basis of choice and for their mutual benefit. The theorists' desire for such a community, however, cannot protect them from the theoretical consequences of choosing the market as a model for understanding human interaction.

The basic assumptions of exchange theories are nowhere more boldly stated than by George Homans:

> Social behavior is an *exchange* of goods, material goods but also non-material ones, such as the symbols of approval or prestige. . . . This process of influence tends to work out at *equilibrium* to a balance in the exchanges. For a person engaged in exchange, what he gives may be a cost to him, just as what he gets may be a reward, and his behavior changes less as *profit*, that is, reward less cost, tends to a *maximum*. Not only does he seek a maximum for himself, but he tries to see to it that no one in his group makes more profit than he does. . . . *It is surprising how familiar these propositions are; . . . Human nature will break in upon even our most elaborate theories.* Of all our many "approaches" to social behavior, the one that sees it as an economy is the most neglected, and yet it is the one we use every moment of our lives—except when we write sociology.[3]

Homans' work and that of Peter Blau present differing versions of exchange theory, each useful for different purposes. Each of them is an important figure in sociology. And while perhaps few others would now describe themselves as exchange theorists, the economic model of social exchange they present remains widely influential and appears in social and political theory in both explicit and inadvertent forms. One can find it explicitly used as a model in such disparate locations as studies of family violence, voting behavior, sexual relations in the family, and the construction of kinship and even culture and literature.[4] And the model of exchange creeps into Marxist and feminist theories as well. A number of Marxist and neo-Marxist arguments about power are marred by some aspects of the exchange model, as is Gayle Rubin's highly influential essay, "The Traffic in Women."[5] The subject of social exchange, then, is worth detailed attention.

The best place to begin is the work of Homans and Blau, where all the assumptions of exchange as a model for social life are explicit and where the consequences of this theoretical choice are most apparent. George Homans' scheme of human exchange conforms most closely to neoclassical economic theory. In his work, the human individual operates like a capitalist firm—making investments, reaping profits, or taking losses. Homans' work is important here because it demonstrates most vividly both the fundamental assumptions of exchange theories and their close relation to economic theory. Peter Blau's more sophisticated account of social exchange attempts to differentiate social from economic exchange, yet relies on many of the same assumptions as Homans'.[6] In addition, Blau gives more direct attention to the relation between exchange and power.

My remarks here are not intended to constitute a balanced or complete analysis of the work of either, nor do I wish to involve myself in the variety of polemics about each. My interest here is simply to follow out the logic of the exchange theories they put forward in order to (1) describe the fundamental features of the market as they understand it and (2) examine the theoretical consequences the market model has for theorizations of power.

Homans on Social Behavior

Homans' account of social relations derives directly from the market. Economics, according to Homans, must be extrapolated to explain the exchange of intangibles in an imperfect market, but for him, its ultimate explanatory utility is demonstrated by the fact that men have "always" explained their behavior according to what it costs them and what it gets them.[7] Homans likens individuals to firms facing decisions about where to invest time and energy to enjoy expected future profits: Individuals (Person) enter into exchanges with others (Other) in which the "reinforcer," social approval, functions almost like money. But social approval is not precisely like money, since it is illiquid; approval gained from one person cannot be used to reward another.[8] Although he recognizes some need for translation and adaptation from economics to sociology, there remain for Homans a number of strict analogies to the economic system. Most centrally, Homans (1) begins with persons whose individual characteristics define the nature of their exchange and (2) contends that it is the laws of individual behavior that structure the laws of social behavior in the exchange setting. Indeed, Homans explicitly excludes behavior of individuals vis-à-vis a non-human entity.[9]

The transaction, then, will follow a pattern much like the following: Two individuals strike a tacit bargain as to the service each will provide, and neither will provide another kind. (This can be likened to the economists' assumption that each firm produces a single and fixed product.) In the interchange between Person and Other, the exchange of help for approval, and vice versa, yields a net psychic profit for both. Indeed, in Homans' view no exchange can continue unless both parties are profiting from it, since individuals can be counted on to distribute their time among various activities so as to achieve the greatest total profit. Thus, the very fact that an activity takes place is *prima facie* evidence that both parties profit from it.[10]

Each two-person bargaining unit develops its own rate of exchange, the social equivalent of price in economics. The rate of exchange between approval and help should equal the ratio between the value Person puts on help and Other puts on approval. Of course, the rate of exchange is affected by the fact that Other commands a scarce commodity—help, in this case. The more recently one has received quantities of a rewarding activity, the less valuable is a further unit of that activity. And the frequency with which the activity is performed bears a direct relation to the rate of profit for that activity. This is equivalent to the law of supply in economics.[11] Thus, marginal utility in the economic sphere is represented by value per unit of activity in the social sphere.[12] The question for the sociologist then becomes: How much energy is Person willing to expend to receive a unit of Other's help?

Moreover, no exchange will occur without each party receiving some reward that does not differ substantially from what both consider a "fair exchange."[13] What constitutes fair exchange is held to vary directly with the "investment" of each party—investments here including such things as age, since the older person in the exchange is held to have invested more time in living. The general rule of distributive justice or fair exchange then takes the form of an insistence that the net rewards or profits of each party be proportional to his investments, and the greater the investments, the greater the profit.[14] Given Homans' observational criteria, however, if an exchange continues at all, it *must* mean that the participants consider that the return they are receiving is proportional to their investment. And if the participants should share this opinion, the observer is in no position to come to a different conclusion.[15]

Homans holds that every activity has both a direct cost, which may be small or even zero, and a cost that becomes apparent only if one examines possible alternative activities that might have produced greater returns (i.e., an opportunity cost). Although the latter is not directly observable, it may, he claims, legitimately be inferred from the past behavior of the person in question. Thus, nearly every action has, if not a direct cost, as least an opportunity cost.[16] Logically then, for Homans, if there is no alternative, there is no cost. At least one critic has argued persuasively that Homans might better have argued that it is the very lack of alternative that is psychically costly.[17]

George Homans has taken rational economic man out of the realm of economics and molded him into man in general. He contends that if one understands the activities of rational economic men in the market, one can understand human activity in general—throughout history and across cultures.[18] Homans' account reiterates many assumptions made by neoclassical economists. He ignores the institutions in which his actors are embedded and focuses instead on the interaction between Person and Other—two individuals who meet in a disembodied transaction independent of social structure, based only on mutual desire. Because their desire is mutual, they are assumed to be equals. Indeed, when Homans considers power, he suggests that in repeated exchanges "power differences tend to disappear," thus once again reinforcing his postulate of human equality.[19]

Second, Homans' rational economic men engage only in the production and consumption of help and social approval. Even their tasks and positions in the office hierarchy are ignored. Because each individual is assumed to be equal to every other, each unit of approval is exactly equal to every other, no matter who gives or receives it. Perhaps most important, since both parties gain, no one can be said to be exploited in any reasonable sense. If they were, Homans would insist, they would refuse to participate in the exchange. Thus, exchange behavior represents an uncoerced choice. The mutual interdependence of assumption and conclusion is obvious: Exchange is voluntarily engaged in, and therefore must be mutually profitable and nonexploitative. The argument about the mutual profit of interaction is closely linked to the assumption that all exchanges are voluntary and therefore must be engaged in for gain.

Homans says he is attempting to "rehabilitate economic man." He argues that economic man needs rehabilitation because his values were too antisocial and materialistic. The new man, Homans argues, need not possess any values at all; it is required only that he maximize his satisfactions and husband his resources.[20] Homans, however, does more than simply reproduce the economists' account of market relations within the social realm. His account highlights what is taken to be the conflictual nature of human interaction and its theoretical result—the problem posed by community. As he summarizes it, "conflict lies at the marrow of our view of human behavior. . . ."[21] The situation Homans constructed between Person and Other both reveals this fundamental conflict and underscores the fact that it is inherent in the interaction based on mutual gain. Despite the interdependence of Person and Other, the latter remains Other—someone to whom Person has only instrumental and extrinsic ties and to whom he relates only to gain his own ends. Thus Homans' account of the situation emphasizes the extent to which community is problematic for him: It represents the fundamental dilemma to be resolved. His attempt at a solution, however, makes clear that the conflict between buyer and seller, the prototype for all human interaction, blocks the creation of a strong and lasting community. Homans' theory erects formidable barriers to the solution of the problem of community.

Blau on Social Exchange

Peter Blau's more sophisticated account of social exchange and the nature of power explicitly differentiates social from economic exchange. Though he relies on many of the same assumptions as Homans, Blau's expanded account of social relations as exchange and his explicit concern with power and community are important because he distinguishes social from economic exchange and argues that because only the former entails unspecified obligations, it requires more trust than the latter.[22] Thus, his analysis is not open to some of the more obvious objections that may be lodged against those who take economic behavior as the model for all human behavior. In addition, it is especially useful because he is explicitly concerned both with the creation of community and what he seems to see as the inevitably concomitant formation of patterns of dominance. He, unlike Homans, recognizes that communities have emergent properties that are not commensurate with properties of individuals. Indeed, in his view, the utility of the concept of exchange is that it directs attention to precisely this feature of social life.[23] Blau's analysis expands, strengthens, and makes more plausible the account of social relations as exchange. He moves from a simple model of individual exchange to one in which exchange and competition for scarce goods lead to class differentiation and even the accumulation of capital, a model in which one group provides continuous services to the other in return for dependence and future compliance. His work, then, can be very useful in demonstrating how the conflict and competition embodied in relations of exchange lead to the systematic appropriation of the resources of some by others.

Blau defines exchange behavior as behavior directed toward ends achievable only through interaction with other persons (rather than the natural world) and aimed at eliciting rewarding reactions. Moreover, this behavior must employ appropriate means to these ends; irrational conduct is excluded, but expressive, goal-oriented actions are included, since he characterizes social exchange as lying midway between economic exchange and the diffuse and intrinsic rewards of a love relationship.[24] In addition, exchange relations refer to social relations entered voluntarily, rather than those into which persons are born or those imposed by forces beyond their control.[25] Whenever individuals are thrown together, they will interact and form groups. Thus Blau sees exchange, a "generic social force" at work in simple as well as complex societies, as the means by which humans "establish bonds of friendship" and "establish superordination over others."[26] Exchange processes, then, bond individuals operating on their private interests in order to produce a differentiated social structure within which individuals are required to forfeit some of their interests for the sake of the collectivity.[27] To study exchange relations, then, for Blau, is to study both how associations develop and how power develops within associations.[28]

Exchange takes its most characteristic form in the face-to-face interactions of individuals, and, he argues, a study of these interactions can lay the foundation for understanding more complex associations. The initial exchange grows from attraction between individuals, an attraction based on one person's expectation that association with another will be rewarding. Thus, for Blau as for Homans, the social interaction is rooted in primitive psychological processes—feelings of attraction between separate individuals.[29] The establishment of exchange relations in this form entails what Blau refers to as "making investments that constitute commitments to the other party."[30] This primitive one-on-one process of exchange gives rise to the formation of a group and the institutionalization of exchange, since, he argues, the supplying of rewarding services to another obligates that person to furnish benefits to the first. As the exchanges continue, the profits from each exchange decrease proportional to the number of exchanges engaged in, or in more technical economic language, "the marginal utility of increasing amounts of benefits [social commodities] eventually diminishes."[31]

The individuals involved in this social exchange operate on the psychological principle of maximizing their return and minimizing costs.[32] Thus, they can be seen to have both conflicting and common interests: common interests in maintaining an association and conflicting interests as to whose investment should contribute more to sustaining it. This duality of interests leads Blau to contend that it is a generic humans condition that the first choices of participants in any social interaction conflict, but their last choices are the same—to continue the association. In this conflictual setting, each actor is assumed to profit from the association.[33]

These characteristics of social exchange appear in striking form in Blau's extraordinary discussion of the courtship market. In it, we meet isolated individuals associating on a voluntary basis for the purpose of mutual gain. Each is producer or consumer of a fixed commodity, and through their interaction for the purpose of maximizing their individual satisfactions they create a community—fragile, instrumental, and conflictual—but based in some common interest, in this case, the "interest in maintaining the other's love."[34] They might alter their interaction to maximize their satisfactions; but flexiblity, mobility, and accurate information on which to base maximizing behavior are assumed to be essential parts of this interaction.

Blau, operating of course from the masculine perspective, notes that when a man makes a decision to associate with a woman, he (somewhat unconsciously) engages in comparison shopping by comparing her traits to those of other females—their "looks, and their charm, their supportiveness, and the congeniality of their emotional makeup."[35] These are each parts of the prospective love object's market value. Blau suggests that a man measures value in part on the basis of a "love object's" popularity with other men, since popularity establishes her value (the demand for this particular commodity) publicly. As a substitute for the evidence provided by this market pricing system, he suggests good looks as *prima facie* evidence.[36]

The commodities exchanged in the "courtship market" are sexual gratification and "firm commitments" (presumably marriage). Conflicting interests are present, as in any exchange, since the girl is interested in keeping the price of her sexual favors high in order to strengthen her position, whereas the boy wants to obtain sexual gratification at the lowest possible price. She withholds sex to create a scarcity, and, assuming demand remains constant, the neoclassical economic theory most of us learned as college freshmen tells us that the price will then rise.[37] The woman, in order to safeguard the high price of her affection, must be ungenerous in expressing it; it must be a prize not easily won. Yet, if she is to "profit from their increased value," she must deliver the promised goods in return for proper payment. (Her problem is of course complicated by the fact that, unlike the manufacturer's products, her most valuable commodity can be sold only once.) Blau holds, then, that if most girls kissed boys on the first date and offered sexual favors soon afterward, they would, as he puts it, "depreciate the price of these rewards in the community, making it difficult for a girl to use the promise of sexual intercourse to elicit a firm commitment from a boy, since sexual gratification is available at a lesser price."[38] Depite conflicting interests, however, both the male and female share a common interest in commitments, symbolized differently in our culture, Blau argues, by the girl's willingness to engage in sexual relations and the boy's promise of marriage.

Blau's account of the courtship market exemplifies many features of his argument about social exchange. Although he recognizes the emergent properties of communities and claims his analysis of human behavior does not require that individuals possess perfect information, make rational commitments, or have consistent preferences, most of these features of the neoclassical economists' account of rational economic man and his world are clearly present.[39] Thus, the actors in Blau's treatment of social exchange are isolated individuals: they come together in the context of unspecified social institutions that appear to set no limits on the forms of their interactions; they join together voluntarily—indeed, Blau's definition of social exchange rules out involuntary relations—and meet in an atmosphere of mutual distrust for the purpose of maximum individual gain.

The conclusion carried by his account is clear: Humans are fundamentally isolated from each other, have deeply conflicting interests, and can associate with each other only on the basis of complementary (but conflicting) desires. Moreover, the community constructed by means of the courtship market exposes the extent to which parties to a community constructed by exchange can, assuming equal power, gain only partial satisfaction of their desires. The depressing quality of this vision of community is underlined by the fact that, especially in the context of an affectional relationship, one might hope for a less instrumental and conflictual interaction.

There are of course a number of problems with this account. The effect of Blau's disregard for the role of social institutions in shaping human interactions is clear: It makes his analysis of the courtship market an interesting period piece, which says more about Blau's insensitivity to the effects of institutions on human behavior than about the courtship market itself.[40] Blau's own two-person example, simple as it is, reflects a second sort of problem as well. Not only do institutions structure social interactions, but they also give rise to different types of social actors. The boy and girl in his courtship market are not interchangeable exchangers who might change places at will. Thus, Blau assumes that sexual gratification is worth something only to the boy, not the girl. He assumes it is a commodity she possesses and can exchange, but not he. He is the buyer, she the seller—and not vice versa. He takes it for granted that the girl's interest is only to exchange the commodity she possesses for a single other commodity possessed by the boy—a ring. (One can see the economists' assumption of the exchange of fixed commodities at work here). These assumptions reveal the effect of the institutions that regulate sexual relations and create the courtship market. But what has become of the courtship market since Blau wrote about it as a (universal?) feature of human existence? The effect of changing institutions on the courtship market is well illustrated by an ad in a major women's magazine that shows an obviously "respectable" woman stating, "I want my birth control method to be as spontaneous as I am."[41]

The Differentiation of Power

What understanding of power relations can be constructed out of the more general model of exchange behavior? It is face-to-face interactions such as those occurring in the courtship market that Blau sees as generating power. His reliance on the market as a model for understanding all social relations, however, has a number of consequences for his account of power. Most important, the market model leads him to put forward two inconsistent arguments, the one a denial of systematic inequality and domination and the other a justification for it. Thus, on the one hand, he holds that power results from unilateral exchanges; on the other, that it develops out of competition for scarce goods such as participation time in informal groups or means of livelihood in communities.[42] The one account assumes a stratified society in which already unequal resources give rise to unilateral exchanges; the other assumes equality and equal competition as the starting point for a contest in which individual capacities are rewarded. Blau attempts to avoid inconsistency by suggesting that the one account describes the exercise of power in a stratified society and is properly designated as exchange; the other describes the acquisition of power by competitors. This otherwise curious distinction between competition and exchange (or relations between equals and those between unequals) can perhaps be clarified by returning to the image of buyer and seller in the market. Competitors compete for social goods: workers with workers, firms with firms. Those not in competition may have something another wants—commodities that can be exchanged. For example, workers sell labor power to firms, and the firms sell products to their customers. The two accounts of power are intermingled in Blau's writing, but I will attempt to separate them here since they rest on differing assumptions.[43]

In the account of power relations based on the assumption of inequality, Blau defines power as the probability that one actor can carry out his own will despite resistance or can modify the conduct of another on a recurrent basis without his own conduct being similarly modified.[44] Thus, power not only contains dimensions of opposition and conflict but also of duration; the exercise of power involves the creating of ongoing relations of dominance. Despite these dominance relations, Blau argues that acts of power occur only within the context of voluntary social exchange. Punishment threatened for resistance offers a choice, and if resistance is an option, compliance, at least in principle, is voluntary. One wonders why then, without explanation, he excludes from his discussion even *threats* of physical coercion, as in the choice, "your money or your life." These would seem to fit his exchange model as well as many of the other examples he cites.[45] Finally, power is inherently asymmetrical. It depends on the *net* ability of one person to withhold rewards and to apply punishment. It requires unilateral dependence on one side and unilateral services on the other.

This situation of unilateral dependence and unilaterial service is the outcome of a process that began from an original situation of equality. Blau argues that in a newly formed group the first competition is for participation time, since this represents a "generalized means in the competition for a variety of social rewards, equivalent in this respect to profitable sales in economic competition.[46] Those who appear to advance the discussion will be allotted more speaking time, success here providing advantage in successive competitions for respect and leadership. Gradually, through competition, some come to command compliance from others, and a differentiated power structure develops.[47]

Hierarchy, then, is inevitable. Social exchange in group formation allows for the emergence of power differences based on abilities of individuals and leads to differentiation, stratification, and finally to the institutionalization of dominance.[48] Indeed, on Blau's account, one must conclude that social interaction will tend to produce oligopoly since only the victors of one contest for dominance are well positioned to participate in and win the next, and those with resources can use them as investment capital to generate greater resources. As the group becomes increasingly differentiated, social exchange relations split into exchange relations proper on the one hand and competitive interactions on the other. In complex associations several concurrent competitions exist, and exchanges occur only between those not engaged in competition. For example, high-status members of a group may assist low-status members in exchange for respect and compliance, thereby creating relations of unilateral obligations and dependence. Resources the high-status members receive from this exchange can be used in competition with others of high status, while low-status members of the group are held to gain from the competition in which they do not participate because the contributions of high-status members improve the performance of collective tasks. Thus, exchange relations develop between strata that cannot compete.[49] There is, however, no need to question social arrangements that institutionalize dominance and hierarchy, since these relations, on Blau's theory, contribute to the well-being of the community as a whole, as well as to the welfare of each individual by permitting exchanges that facilitate the separate competitions within each status group.

Blau's second account of the development of power relations highlights differential possession of or access to resources and goes against his first account. In his account of competition and the resultant differentiation and institutionalization of dominance, resources represent acquired goods or rewards for individual merit, and the equality of participants is assumed; in the account of power as unilateral exchange, a stratified differentiation is assumed. Moreover, Blau allows those who supply unilateral services to others to accumulate a capital in the form of expectations that others will comply with their wishes. Unilateral services can aid the accumulation of this capital because supplying a service obligates the receiver of the service to reciprocate. If he fails to do so or has nothing to offer, he is, Blau holds, under pressure to defer to the wishes of the person who originally provided the services; deference and compliance then become his forms of payment or currency. The compliance of those who have nothing else to offer means the supplier of services has the right to use their powers for his own ends. Thus, "by providing unilateral benefits to others, a person accumulates a capital of willing compliance on which he can draw whenever it is to his interest to impose his will upon others...."[50]

While those who play the dependent role in power relations can be expected to attempt to escape, since they experience power differences and subjection to the will of the powerholder as a hardship, the powerholder has other options. He can, if he wishes, expend his capital, or if he chooses, expand it "by profitably investing it at interest." He continues the analogy by suggesting that just as a person with much capital can live on the interest it earns without depleting it, so too a person can "live on" a superior social status that is pronounced and secure.[51] Power, then, can be expanded, like capital, by risk taking, or can be depleted by asking for the repayment of debts (since reciprocation transforms the unilateral exchanges into reciprocal exchanges).[52]

Blau argues in justification of these systematically unequal relations that they help to create stability and equilibrium in the social realm by rebalancing the social association between the powerholders and the powerless. They do so by giving the powerless a kind of currency with which to pay their debts: Their compliance is a form of reciprocity. Their own future behavior has become a medium of exchange. In sum, "unilateral services give rise to a differentiation of power that equilibrates the exchange. The exchange balance, in fact, rests on two imbalances: unilateral services and unilateral power."[53]

But by introducing the currency of compliance as a means of rebalancing unequal power relations, Blau provides a justification for perpetuation of relations of dominance between two separate and hierarchically ordered spheres (or classes). In class societies, Blau argues, exchange relations between different strata contribute to the competitive struggles within strata by adding to the store of resources available to the competitors.[54] Dominance relations in stratified society, then, must be recognized not as a necessary evil but rather as a positive good.

There are, of course, several difficulties with this account of power relations. First, one wonders why, if the exercise of power is a positive good for all concerned, Blau holds that subjugation to the will of another is a hardship. Second, his model contains no possibility of dealing with the differential possession of resources or of admitting the exploitation of some in the process of exchange. But if equals compete, and only unequals exchange, is it really possible that the exchange relation is either unproblematically voluntary or profitable in the same sense for both participants?[55] Third, Blau claims that one can understand social relations best not by examining the community as a whole but by analyzing the decisions and interactions of individuals—individuals whose roles are limited to those of buyer or seller. Organizational structures are ignored, and thus individuals are contradictorily presumed (1) to interact on the basis of equality, but (2) to enter the transaction possessing systematically differing amounts of resources. Blau fails to give an account of why it is that some have nothing to give in return, or why some have the resources to provide unilateral services.

Conclusion

Exchange theories of social life as laid out by Blau and Homans confirm my argument that power and community are closely linked. First, because exchange theorists are concerned to account for the creation of community, their analyses of exchange and the power relations it generates demonstrate that theorists of power unavoidably become involved in issues of community. The powerholder in their theories is a participant in a community with others—fragile and temporary to be sure, but present nonetheless. Second, exchange theorists' accounts of the fragile and instrumental community created by exchange underline the fact that the form taken by the exercise of power in a community represents the structure of legitimate human interaction within that community. Power relations of domination and submission are recapitulated in other hierarchies.

That the exercise of power marks the limits of legitimate action in a community emerges in the theoretical problem posed by the fact that when power is exercised by some over others, only one of the parties seems to benefit, and the participants appear to be unequals rather than equals. Yet the exercise of power is considered to be legitimate. Exchange theorists have responded to this dilemma in several ways. First, they argue that at least initially, each individual is equal to every other, is the same kind of social actor, and interacts with others in a context unstructured by institutions. Thus, there is no reason to think that anyone is coerced. Second, they assume that all interactions are entered voluntarily with a view to individual gain. Thus, if an interchange occurs at all, one *must* assume that both parties are profiting. Third, even if the individuals in the transaction can be shown to possess unequal resources, the exercise of power over some by others is held to be justifiable since the compliance of the former gives them a currency to pay their debts. Thus, relations of domination and submission must be understood as not only beneficial for the community as a whole (increasing collective output and efficiency) but also as making a positive contribution to the equality of members of the community. The Panglossian nature of this reasoning cannot be overemphasized: No matter the apparent inequality and harm occasioned by relations of domination and hierarchy, in reality all is for the best.

Despite the fact that exchange theories of social life provide deeply unsatisfactory accounts of social relations in general and power relations in particular, they contain a surface plausibility. We do live in a stratified society in which the majority of persons have few or no power resources and must mortgage their future behavior in return for such benefits as employment, a society in which the "buying" and "selling" of behaviors for "rewards" is generalized. Yet the surface plausibility reveals the deeper analytical inadequacy of the market model. It is because of this inadequacy in the model they have chosen that exchange theorists are led to conclude that dominance relations are both inevitable and a positive social good.

If these are the conclusions supported by theories of social exchange, both feminist theory and other theories that attempt to explain dominance relations and envision a more humane community must avoid using exchange models. This has, however, proved difficult, as demonstrated by the presence of exchange models in a variety of theories whose authors are committed to social change. Perhaps our theories can be improved by a clearer understanding of the logic that underlies social exchange theories. And this logic is best explored in the context of the market model constructed by neoclassical economic theory.

NOTES

1. Market models more generally are widely popular among analysts of other aspects of social life. To mention only a few examples, Anthony Downs' *An Economic Theory of Democracy* (New York: Harper & Row, 1957) and James Buchanan and Gordon Tullock's *Calculus of Consent* (Ann Arbor: University of Michigan Press, 1965) reflect this general tendency to explain politics by means of the model of the market. The latter, for example, uses an economic model of rationality. They discuss the "buying" of decisions or forms of cooperation. David Mayhew's *Congress, the Electoral Connection* (New Haven: Yale University Press, 1974) makes explicit use of the market as well. He suggests that politics is a struggle to gain and maintain power, and argues that elected officials behave like money seekers. In this analogy the vote represents a kind of deposit given to the elected official, who thereby becomes the banker. Mayhew believes a number of resources can be transformed into votes, or made into liquid assets, such as endorsements and campaign appearances. See pp. 17, 18, 39, and especially the discussion of "brand name candidates," p. 46.

2. David A. Baldwin, "Power and Social Exchange," *American Political Science Review* 72, no. 4 (December 1978): 1240–41.

3. George Homans, "Social Behavior as Exchange," *American Journal of Sociology* 62 (May 1958): 606. (My italics.) I should note that I present the theories of Homans and Blau with very little comment, in part because I feel that my commentary might slant the account and lead the reader to fail to give proper attention to these important and influential theories. My critique of them appears on p. 28. George Homans holds an eminent position among sociologists. He is professor of sociology at Harvard University and was vice-president of the American Sociological Association in 1961 and president of the Association in 1963–64. See *American Men and Women of Science: Social and Behavioral Sciences* (New York: Bowker, 1978).

4. See, for example, William Goode, "Force and Violence in the Family," *Journal of Marriage and the Family* 33 (November 1971): 624–36; Craig Allen and Murray Strauss, "Resources, Power, and Husband-Wife Violence," in *The Social Causes of Husband-Wife Violence*, ed. Murray Strauss and Gerald Hotaling (Minneapolis: University of Minnesota Press, 1980). Note the quotation from Dr. John Scanzoni's lecture "Gender Roles, Negotiation, and Marital Change," from the Program in Human Sexuality, July 22, 1977, quoted by Carole S. Vance, "Gender Systems, Ideology, and Sex Research: An Anthropological Analysis," *Feminist Studies* 6, no. 1 (Spring 1980): 135. See also the Appendix to this book in which the work of Claude Levi-Strauss is discussed. In the light of this discussion one might also review the positions taken in such works as Fredric Jameson, *The Prison House of Language* (Princeton: Princeton University Press, 1972).

5. For a discussion of these theories, see Chapters 4 and 5 and Appendix 3.

6. Peter Blau, *Exchange and Power in Social Life* (New York: Wiley, 1964), p. 114. Baldwin takes a more consensual model to argue that the mutual in-

terest of buyer and seller is likely to obscure their real conflict (Baldwin, "Power and Social Exchange," p. 1232). At least one theorist has taken Blau's more subtle analysis to separate him from Homans. See Irving M. Zeitlin, *Rethinking Sociology: A Critique of Contemporary Theory* (Englewood Cliffs, N.J.: Prentice-Hall, 1973), p. 98. Peter Blau's ideas are important ones in the discipline of sociology. His standing in the field is evidenced by the fact that he has taught at the University of Chicago and Cambridge University and is currently Quetelet Professor of Sociology at Columbia University. He spent 1962–63 as a fellow at the Center for Advanced Study in the Behavioral Sciences in Palo Alto, and served as president of the American Sociological Association in 1973–74. See *American Men and Women of Science: Social and Behavioral Sciences*.

7. George Homans, *Social Behavior: Its Elementary Forms* (New York: Harcourt, Brace and World, 1961), pp. 12–13. Significantly, he excludes from his analysis both maternal love and sexual love (ibid., p. 15).

8. Ibid., pp. 34–35, 89.

9. Ibid., p. 30. See the discussion in Zeitlin, *Rethinking Sociology*, p. 66; and Pierre Birnbaum, "Power Divorced from Its Sources: A Critique of the Exchange Theory of Power," in *Power and Political Theory: Some European Perspectives*, ed. Brian Barry (New York: Wiley, 1976), p. 22. The capacities and needs of each individual are assumed for purposes of his discussion to be immutable. Homans justified this by arguing that these are not likely to change in the short run. See Homans, *Social Behavior*, p. 48. But elsewhere, Homans refers to even a single day as "long run" (ibid., p. 69). In addition, Homans adopts the *ceteris paribus* assumption of economics, i.e., the individual will act as Homans predicts, "other things being equal."

10. Ibid., p. 62. Even the pigeon whose rewards are controlled by the psychologist, when it finds its rewards and costs imbalanced, may attempt to avoid the situation and express what Homans regards as something similar to anger when its expectations are upset. See Ibid., p. 61. Of course, Homans misses an important feature of the pigeon's situation: It cannot escape the clutches of the psychologist. It can object, but is forced, if it wants to eat, to continue to peck the trigger. Zeitlin, too, has pointed out the circularity of this argument. See his *Rethinking Sociology*, p. 69.

11. Homans, *Social Behavior*, pp. 55, 67.

12. Homans notes that qualities valued for their own sake, such as pride, altruism, or aggression, create problems for his system. See ibid., p. 45.

13. Ibid., p. 72.

14. There is additional pressure toward fair exchange in the fact that, as Homans sees it, merchants set a value on the good will of their customers. Thus, individuals are willing to forego maximum profits at times in order to continue in business (ibid., pp. 77–78).

15. See Zeitlin's similar argument in his *Rethinking Sociology*.

16. Homans, *Social Behavior*, p. 59.

17. Zeitlin, *Rethinking Sociology*, p. 70.

18. Homans has clearly committed the same error as the theorist Marx described as an "arch-Philistine," an "insipid, pedantic, leather tongued oracle of the ordinary bourgeois intelligence of the 19th century," Jeremy Bentham.

Like Bentham, Homans is taking what Marx describes as the ordinary British shopkeeper as the normal man and then applying this odd creature as a yardstick by which to measure the past, present, and future. See Karl Marx, *Capital* (New York: International Publishers, 1967), I: 609, n. 2.

19. Zeitlin, *Rethinking Sociology*, p. 78, citing Homans, "Fundamental Social Processes," in *Sociology: An Introduction*, ed. Neil J. Smelser (New York: Wiley, 1967), p. 54.

20. Homans, *Social Behavior*, pp. 67, 71. Homans claims that his individuals are not maximizers, but this only contradicts the general thesis of his account.

21. Ibid., p. 57.

22. Blau, *Exchange and Power in Social Life*, p. 315. Unlike Zeitlin, I do not hold that Blau develops the concept of exchange with a "completely different emphasis" (Zeitlin, *Rethinking Sociology*, p. 84).

23. Blau, *Exchange and Power in Social Life*, pp. 3–4.

24. Ibid., p. 5. See also pp. 95, 112.

25. These forces may be natural forces, or they may be human forces a single individual cannot control (ibid., p. 20).

26. Ibid., pp. 92, 111, 89, 20.

27. Ibid., p. 92. This, however, allows the social structure to creep into the account unnoticed, and leads to several inconsistencies. See Birnbaum, "Power Divorced from Its Sources, p. 29.

28. Although exchange is always fundamental, exchange theorists recognize that it may take different forms in different societies. Blau argues that in simple societies, the exchange of gifts serves to create bonds of friendship as well as to develop trust among peers. In addition, exchanges of gifts produce and reinforce status differences among people. Our own society has institutionalized the market rather than the gift, but both represent means by which regular exchanges occur. In addition, Blau argues that there are many similarities between our market society and primitive societies that depend on the exchange of gifts and services. He compares the apparently useless destruction and dissipation of wealth (in a potlatch society) to conspicuous consumption in our own. See Blau, *Exchange and Power in Social Life*, pp. 106, 109. Blau clearly relies on Marcel Mauss's famous essay, *The Gift*, to make this argument. One critic has correctly pointed out that Blau, in giving a psychologistic interpretation of the essay, has lost track of the structural aspect of the gift relation and has incorrectly reduced it to individual interchanges. See Birnbaum, "Power Divorced from Its Sources," p. 23.

29. See, for example, Blau, *Exchange and Power in Social Life*, pp. 13, 20, 18, 34.

30. Ibid., p. 98.

31. Ibid., p. 89.

32. They are maximizers as both producers and consumers. The circularity this introduces is evident in Blau's example of a scientist who, if he accepted a university job with a lower salary than he could obtain elsewhere, "must" be getting "psychic income" that would offset his loss in salary (ibid., p. 96; see also p. 155).

33. Blau argues that the profits are not necessarily costs to others and in addition takes the position that some costs are paid by nonparticipants while in other situations all associates benefit. These two situations arise, for Blau, in a love relation—where both parties benefit and the rejected suitor may pay the costs (ibid., pp. 15–16).

34. Ibid., p. 76. The conceptualization of women as a social commodity is strikingly endemic to exchange theories. See Appendix 1 for a discussion of another system of the exchange of women.

35. Ibid., p. 39. See also p. 35.

36. Ibid., p. 79. But see also Lévi-Strauss' argument (Appendix 1) that there are never enough attractive women and that there will always be a shortage in that market.

37. Blau argues that boys in the courtship market are both pursuing scarce goods and also competing with each other indirectly—hoping to best the others by succeeding at the game of conquest. (See Chapters 7 and 8 for my view of the social relations produced by games of conquest.) Like the female, each offers "the attractiveness of his own self on the market, so to speak, which makes success of extreme importance for his self-conception." Indeed, Blau suggests, indirect competition with other boys for conquest may be the male's primary reason for engaging in dating behavior (ibid., pp. 81–82). These themes are echoed in a quite different way in Chapters 7 and 8.

38. Ibid., p. 80.

39. See ibid., p. 18.

40. It is significant that he titles this section "An Excursus on Love." Is it love, or is it the kind of extrinsic relation he argues is best understood under the heading of exchange?

41. *Woman's Day*, February 1979. The ad goes on to note that the contraceptive container is small enough to fit easily into an evening bag.

42. Blau, *Exchange and Power in Social Life*, p. 141.

43. It is perhaps this intermingling that leads one theorist to argue that power and exchange differ in Blau's theory. He fails, however, to present any evidence supporting this contention. See Baldwin, "Power and Social Exchange," p. 1229. Jack Lively, "The Limits of Exchange Theory," in Barry, ed., *Political Power*, also finds that the two accounts of power are contradictory, but argues that this results from the fact that Blau was operating with a small-group theory in the one case and society-wide theory in the other (pp. 6–7). I hold instead that the reason for the contradiction is his reliance on the market model.

44. Blau, *Exchange and Power in Social Life*, p. 115.

45. Ibid., pp. 91, 117. I am not alone in finding his argument unpersuasive. See also Lively, "Limits of Exchange Theory," p. 8. Baldwin attempts to reformulate the threat "your money or your life" by asking whether it would be such a threat if said by a high-status person such as a doctor telling you you needed an operation to save your life. In these circumstances, he argues, it is more acceptably understood as an exchange. See Baldwin, "Power and Social Exchange," p. 1230.

46. Blau, *Exchange and Power in Social Life*, p. 125.

47. Ibid., pp. 126–27.

48. Ibid., p. 321. Lively notes that Blau assumes (incorrectly) that there is a close correlation between proper relations in small groups and in the larger society. Thus, he is led to ignore the fact that power in large groups does not depend on the personal capacities of those with power but instead is situated in a structured context. See Lively, "Limits of Exchange Theory," p. 5.

49. Blau, *Exchange and Power in Social Life*, pp. 126–27.

50. Ibid., p. 28.

51. Ibid., pp. 29, 132–43.

52. As Blau puts it, "profit, strictly speaking, is due to uncertainty and is the reward for assuming responsibility for uncertainty, that is, for risking investments whose return cannot be predicted with accuracy in advance." Blau obviously accepts the argument that profit is due to uncertainty. He argues that it is precisely when success is uncertain that it tends to be most generously rewarded. "The entrepreneur provides this security by guaranteeing his employees certain rewards for their services and by assuming the responsibility for deciding on investments under conditions of uncertainty. The profits he reaps from the enterprise are his rewards for having taken these risks." In the same way, "the increment in power the successful leader earns is his reward for having made these risky decisions and investments" (ibid., p. 137). Marx has made a case that this view depends on a faulty understanding of the nature of the economic system. See *Capital*, vol. 1, esp. pp. 186–98. While I find Marx's case persuasive, my point in this chapter is not so much to challenge the economic theory as to show the kinds of difficulties to which it leads in political and social analysis.

53. Blau, *Exchange and Power in Social Life*, p. 29.

54. Ibid., p. 141. One gets a sense of the invisible hand at work, transforming private vices into public goods. Both competitions (e.g., between experts for superior status and advice seekers for advice) are governed by supply and demand, and the two competitions adjust supply and demand by changing the rates of exchange. We can see the analogy here to competing firms with products to sell, and competing buyers of products or buyers of labor power and competing laborers. Blau argues exchange rates move toward the intersection of supply and demand curves, i.e., toward the "equilibrium price." In any situation there will be a going rate of exchange for the social commodity in question. That rate will have some relation to the "fair rate of exchange." This, Blau argues, distinguishes social from economic exchange, since in social exchange, norms of fairness intervene (ibid., pp. 152–56). One can recognize in his account of how rates of exchange are set the operation of the second major thesis pointed out by Hollis and Nell—that remuneration is proportional to productivity at the margin. See Martin Hollis and Edward Nell, *Rational Economic Man* (New York; Cambridge University Press, 1975).

55. This is a criticism I share with several others among Blau's critics.

2

Rational Economic Man and the Problem of Community

The problems of exchange theories are rooted in the theoretical construct of "rational economic man" and in the neoclassical economists' outline of the communities (markets) these men can construct. The model of rational economic man in the market involves theorists in circular reasoning, inaccuracy, and ethnocentrism. The deeper problem of which these are symptoms is the vision of community implicit in the market model—a vision of community as arbitrary and fragile, structured fundamentally by competition and domination. Despite these difficulties, I do not propose to dismiss the market model but to give it more detailed attention. While it gives us little insight into the working of actual human relations, it can reveal a great deal about what is meant by the class-specific nature of theories of power and community.

Rational Economic Man and His World

Rational economic man is most fundamentally a maximizer.[1] While we know nothing of what he wants, we do know he will maximize ruthlessly to get it. We do not know what he buys; but when prices fall, we know that he will maximize his market share or his profit. He is always at what he believes to be optimum, and is forever striking the best subjective balance between disincentive and reward. His behavior embodies the values "which would be exemplified by a perfectly rational agent" under specific conditions.[2] The market itself provides the means for bringing these independent, frequently isolated, and presumably hostile beings together. The actors in the market, rational economic men, are individuals whose very humanity is based on their independence from the wills of others, and who may dispose of their own persons and capacities freely, since they owe nothing to the community as a whole, either for who they are or for the resources they possess.[3] They enter relations only voluntarily in order to serve their own interests, and construct a community by means of developing a circulating medium they can exchange. In the market, this medium takes the form of money, though in other arenas of social life it may take the form of social approval, gifts, women, or some other "social commodity" (Blau's term). The circulating medium is the translator and bearer of the relation between the individuals involved in the exchange.

In the market, the Other's status as Other is maintained. Both solidarity and rivalry play important roles, and the community is only the *by-product* of actions directed at disparate ends. While the fundamental interests of the participants conflict, each has a common interest in maintaining the association. As Blau has tellingly put it, their last choices are identical, but the first choice of each is the second last of the other.[4] Each wants to strike the best bargain for himself, but since both want to complete the transaction, their last choices are identical. In such a community the paradigmatic connections between people are instrumental or extrinsic and conflictual; and in a world populated by these isolated individuals, relations of competition and domination come to be substitutes for a more substantial and encompassing community such as that envisioned by Marx in the passage quoted in the introduction.

The market the economists outline contains large numbers of consumers variously endowed with property and a large number of producers of each good or service, each of whom is assumed to approximate the standards set by rational economic man. Consumers purchase goods, maximizing their utility subject to the constraints of their incomes. They freely dispose of their capacity to labor, balancing disutility against expected return. Firms purchase factors of production (labor, raw materials, etc.), balancing expected productivity against cost, and sell final goods, setting quantities and prices to maximize their profits.

This simple model rests on several fundamental assumptions. First, and perhaps most important, institutional forms are assumed to be irrelevant. Each producer or consumer is assumed to take identical form—a form most commonly modeled on the capitalist firm faced with investment and consumption decisions. Two fundamental theses rest on this assumption. There is the thesis that "all market payments are exchanges in the same sense and that all market costs are costs paid for productive work in the same sense."[5] As Martin Hollis and Edward Nell note correctly, this is a very revealing thesis. It claims that markets for factors of production, such as capital and labor, and product markets work in the same way: "Potatoes have a price and so does capital."

If this is true, then, one can conclude that "in equilibrium all parties gain, and if the equilibrium is competitive, and sometimes even if it is not, no one is exploited in any reasonable sense of the term." The related thesis is that any work receiving market compensation is productive work, and "if the market is competitive, the remuneration will be proportional to the productivity at the margin."[6] And thus, once again, exploitation cannot exist.

Second, it is assumed that firms produce and sell fixed goods to consumers with fixed preferences. Moreover, the legal instant of purchase is stressed; haggling, debating, bargaining—all these do not exist for the neoclassical economist. The whole lengthy process is concentrated into the moment of decision; time is made to stand still. Third, production and consumption of goods are assumed to be the only activities that occur in the market. Thus, any individual in the market must have the perspective of either buyer or seller. Fourth, it is assumed that producers and consumers, buyers and sellers, are fundamentally equal: Each has something the other wants, and the transaction maximizes the marginal utility of both. Fifth, a series of simplifying assumptions, such as the *ceteris paribus* assumption, are made. These include assumptions that each participant possesses perfect information about the actions of others in the market, perfect mobility into and out of the market, and perfect flexibility to change products and preferences over time.

The overall Panglossian impact of these assumptions on accounts of human relations in general and power relations in particular is highlighted in Marx's sarcastic summary of the classical economists' account of relations in the market. The market "is in fact a very Eden of the innate rights of man. There alone rule Freedom, Equality, Property, and Bentham. Freedom, because both buyer and seller of a commodity, say of labour-power, are constrained only by their own free will. They contract as free agents, and the agreement they come to is but the form in which they give legal expression to the other, as with a simple owner of commodities, and they exchange equivalent for equivalent. Property, because each looks only to himself. The only force that brings them together and puts them in relation with each other, is the selfishness, the gain and the private interests of each. Each looks to himself only, and no one troubles himself about the rest, and just because they do so, do they all, in accordance with the pre-established harmony of things, or under the auspices of an all-shrewd providence, work together for their mutual advantage, for the common wealth, and in the interest of all."[7] What is wrong with this model?

The Circularity of Market Theory

Let us begin with the circularity introduced by the construct of rational economic man. Rational economic man personifies a timeless rationality exercised by the individual decision maker. Hollis and Nell present an excellent account of the circularity this creature brings to economic theory.[8] They point out that it is unclear what the behavior of rational economic man exemplifies; if predictions fail, neoclassical economists can assume either that the prediction was at fault or that the *ceteres* were not *paribus*. The latter conclusion, however, requires an understanding of which variables must be held constant and which are unimportant; yet economists have no objective bases on which to rest such a conclusion.[9] How do we know that the desire to maximize one's satisfaction motivates economic behavior? It cannot be proven *a priori* (e.g., according to positivist criteria) without making nonmaximizing behavior cease to be a subject of economics. But if this is an empirical (and therefore synthetic) claim, there seems no satisfactory way to demonstrate it while retaining the construct as a model against which theories are tested.[10] Neoclassical theory is forced to respond simply that without this assumption, many basic concepts in economics would be incoherent.

And what could refute the claim that economic behavior is motivated by the desire to maximize the satisfaction of interests? One cannot distinguish the failure of the model from the nonconformity of the agent. Each acts as the criterion for the other.[11] At this point, rational economic man becomes only a construct that determines who conforms to the prespecified model.[12] Exchange must then be by definition mutually profitable, since how, otherwise, can one understand human interaction? One may remind oneself here of Homans' and Blau's contentions that interactions *must* be profitable if they are observed to occur at all. The questions Hollis and Nell address to neoclassical economists might well be addressed to the theorists of social exchange. This leads us directly to the second area of problems with the construct of rational economic man.

The Problem of Inaccuracy

The fragile community of rational economic men falters as an account even of contemporary social relations in advanced capitalist societies because the several related assumptions on which it is based are contradicted by everyday experience. First, Blau, Homans, and economic theorists assume that individuals are fundamentally isolated from each other and that initial contacts can be presumed to be based on opposing interests. But this is unrealistic; individuals always inhabit societies. We are born helpless and begin life within a relation that can only with great difficulty and distortion be described as an exchange relation—that between mothers and infants. One can assume the presence of equal partners with conflicting and common interests only by taking rational economic man as given and by ignoring the question of why one would choose to interpret behavior in this way. Indeed, one could begin to see the outline of a very different kind of community if one took the mother/infant relation rather than market exchange as the prototypic human interaction.[13]

A second difficulty emerges from the assumption that isolated individuals participate in exchange relations voluntarily, and thus participation can be assumed to yield benefits to all parties. Through the price mechanism, which reconciles competing claims on scarce resources (or, as Blau termed it, the rate of exchange), parties are held to gain in proportion to their productive contribution. The importance of this contention for the theorist of power cannot be overemphasized, since this is what enables the theorist to reinterpret coercion as choice. On this model, for example, one could describe even the Enclosure Acts as a "popular choice for urban living."[14] Blau's view of the mutually beneficial exchange between power wielders and those who have only their compliance to offer in return for unilateral services represents a skillful attempt to recast coercion as choice. One need not look far for other examples; the "voluntary" choice made by most of us to sell our labor power is only the most obvious.

The emphasis on the isolation of each individual from every other and the inability to see association as anything other than voluntary leads to a third assumption and a third problem: Exchange theorists assume institutions are unimportant and thus refuse to recognize the ways in which institutions structure both exchange relations and the totality of relations among people. But theorists should not ignore the most significant questions about force: Who has access to it, and on behalf of which interests. They should not forget that power over others gives one the ability to enforce one's moral claims and when institutionalized can even shape the definitions of what is legitimate or moral. And they should not fail to notice how some people get control of resources, and how some things become political "assets." Peter Berger and Thomas Luckmann have gone even further when they argued that "power in society includes the power to produce reality."[15] Thus, cultural norms and institutional practices have important effects theorists ignore at their own peril; the failure of Blau's discussion of the courtship market is an excellent case in point.

In turn, ignorance of institutions leads to a misleading understanding of power as exercised only in situations structured like that between buyer and seller—two participants, the one wanting a lower price, the other a higher one—situations where the interests of the participants are in conflict but in which the conflict concerns and can be resolved by a specific decision or transaction. The failure to recognize institutions and their importance thus leads to a reduction of all social relations to a series of discrete transactions between buyers and sellers, and requires in turn that one ignore the fact that there are varieties of even economic actors, not all of whom are moved directly by the desire to maximize profit.[16]

Perhaps the most important consequence of the refusal to recognize the impact of institutions on social relations is a theoretical failure to recognize relations of domination. No distinction is made between those who own the means of production and those who simply supply labor. "The former group thus presumably find themselves facing themselves in the competitive market for services, selling to themselves what they own already. The latter are misleadingly credited with the positive power to devise their own strategy in the market, which belongs mainly to the former group. The power to withhold savings is more easily exercised than the power to withhold labour, and, unless the working households are backed by strike funds, it is disingenuous to suggest an equipoise by speaking of the 'mutual dependence' of capital and labour."[17] Moreover, in the legal arrangments of capitalism, owners choose the time, place, and methods of doing business. These elements can be neglected only if power is not fundamental in determining the structure of market exchanges and if all participants are in fact equal. The absurdity of this postulate as an accurate description of social relations has been repeatedly pointed out in both the nineteenth century and the twentieth.[18]

The market model introduces a fourth distortion of human behavior with the assumption that all events happen at a logical instant. Neoclassical transactions are completed in a flash. Yet real activities require different lengths of time and that time has a cost. Critics have pointed out that the phrase "he is buying" may encompass a lengthy ritual of inquiry, argument, delays, examinations, decisions, and so on. The legal instant of purchase is only one part of a process with a history and a future. Moreover, the whole transaction can be well done or poorly done, it can succeed or fail, it can be terminated in the middle or end in a variety of ways. The standard economic model that presents action as instantaneous, logically simple, and complete distorts a reality in which actions are in fact protracted, complex, and require effort to complete. Of the examples given by Blau and Homans, only Homans' pigeon's interaction with the psychologist comes close to this model. In other cases, such as the courtship market and the exchange of women, long ritual interchanges, advances, retreats, and haggling are clearly involved.[19]

The Community: Instrumental, Fragile, and False

Let us look at the ways these errors erect fundamental obstacles for exchange theorists' efforts to solve the puzzle of community—a puzzle they were themselves instrumental in creating, and one that grows directly from the social relations specific to capitalism, which they take as their model for all human behavior. Community, for Blau or Homans, is constituted by the variety of interactions structured by the antagonistic/complementary interests of individuals. If the human community is only a by-product of the rational search for gain, the community can only be fragile and shifting, resting as it does on the interest of each in his own private gain. The community of individuals maximizing utilities is an arbitrary community of isolated individuals who calculate their own benefits on the basis of private and arbitrary personal desires. In the prototypical transaction, the sellers of two commodities come together in the marketplace with interests based on private and arbitrary desires. One is selling something the other wants to buy. The interchange is only a brief association on the basis of this momentary conjuncture of interest. Here, desires are subjective and individual, and as far as the transaction itself is concerned, arbitrary. Who knows *why* X wants a green widget rather than a brown one? And, perhaps more to the point, who cares? The community founded on this relation can only be instrumental and arbitrary.

If to be human is to be free from dependence on the wills of others, then all human interaction must be voluntary and must rest on agreement based on the private interest of each party. And if community is based on this brief coincidence of the perceived interests of individuals who have no *intrinsic* connections to each other, these interests could change. In turn, a shift of individuals' felt interests could destroy the community, since such a shift in perceived interests could remove the mutual profit on which all interactions are presumed to be based. The community formed on this basis is fragile.

If individuals' only connection is the coincidence of arbitrary desires, for example, the desire of one for what the other is selling, and the seller's desire for money, then their fundamental isolation as individuals is not affected: Each remains fundamentally alone. But exchange theorists tell us that in society, just as in the market, the pursuit of private interest results in the greatest good for the greatest number. Blau, for example, argues that the pursuit of private interests is a good in itself, since the resultant differentiation of power creates a new currency for those without resources; they can exchange their compliance for goods and services they receive, and thereby become participants in a mutually profitable exchange. Marx puts it well: "The economists express this as follows: Each pursues his private interest and only his private interest; and thereby serves the private interests of all, the general interest, without willing or knowing it."[20] But this is hardly universal. In other cultures and at other points in history, economic systems have been embedded in social relations, rather than being independent of other relations. And distribution of goods has been done on the basis of noneconomic motives.[21] Even the provision of economic goods for individual families was a community task. *Individual* starvation was not the norm until the rise of capitalism in Western Europe because, if the community had food, it would be shared.

The interaction of isolated individuals leads not only to a fragile and arbitrary community but in the end creates a community that is fundamentally false: It cannot sustain the sociality or even the humanity of its members. The community is false because it is composed of competitors whose only commonality is their opposition to each other. The war of each against all, which Hobbes saw in the state of nature, takes the form in this community of a set of procedural rules and contracts that regulate but do not abolish the conflict. That is, the fundamental opposition of each individual to every other is embodied in a series of rights and rules for adjudicating conflict. To the extent that each operates on his own interests, individuals are profoundly separate. Each person's utilities may differ fundamentally from those of any other. Individual preferences are not comparable. While they might be similar because of common background factors, this is simply an empirical and contingent coincidence. Those who come together on this basis can form only temporary and instrumental communities—temporary because subjective interests may change and because they are only partly rational and therefore may change unpredictably. And instrumental since they are based on each individual's calculation of the utility of voluntarily joining with others. Thus, despite the insistence of contract theorists on the rationality of the contract, the community is in a fundamental sense not a rational one. It results at bottom from each individual's pursuit of private and subjective interests.

It is in such a false community that the very *social* character of activity can appear as something alien and puzzling. And individuals can appear to be subordinated to social relations "which subsist independently of them and which arise out of collisions of mutually indifferent individuals."[22] Thus the fragile, instrumental, and fundamentally false community described by exchange theorists does not provide a satisfactory account of the shape of our own community in advanced capitalist society.

The Class-Specific Roots of the Market Model

Exchange theorists have claimed that market relations not only provide the source for understanding social relations in the industrial West but in addition have claimed that this mode of behavior is universal to human interaction. They have taken exchange in a capitalist market to be the prototypic and universal human interaction. This is profoundly ethnocentric, and as one analyst has put it, has "created the delusion of economic determinism as a general law for all human society."[23] The market is an important institution in the industrialized West. But exchange theorists have failed to recognize that this is much more characteristic of the capitalist market than any other. And theorists have given the market even more importance by concluding that economic activity illustrates the workings of a real human nature and that the market truly reveals the way society works.

To adopt this form of explanation to understand all human societies simply expresses the culture-boundedness of the theorists themselves. The anthropological evidence demonstrates the culture-bound nature of the maximizer. There are a wide variety of alternative modes of social organization, and evidence that the motive of gain is neither "natural" nor universal. Indeed, there is much evidence that payment for labor is unusual in primitive societies and does not function as a motivation to work. In addition, in primitive societies, labor is often prolonged beyond the unavoidable minimum, and some have found evidence incentives to labor include important components of such things as reciprocity, the joys of work, and social approval.[24] Thus, some anthropologists have stressed the time and effort spent for aesthetic rather than utilitarian purposes; others have argued that contrary to popular belief, hunting and gathering societies were the original affluent societies.[25] Even a cursory glance at the anthropological evidence does not support the universality of rational economic man.

The ethnocentrism and limited scope of rational economic man suggests that one may find his origins in the same time and place in which capitalism developed: Western Europe during the seventeenth and eighteenth centuries. It is here that one can find the roots of this truncated and even, one might say, monomaniacal maximizer; rational economic man is unknown before the development of capitalism. Not only does one fail to find rational economic man in non-Western societies, but one would also fail to find this interest-driven creature in Western Europe much before the eighteenth century. In ancient Athens, for example, the accumulation of goods and gold was treated as shameful hoarding. The good citizen acquired goods enough to afford himself the leisure necessary for political life. But he did not further expand his fortune. His purpose was not to accumulate goods, and he was motivated much more by passions (or even *daemons*), than by an interest in maximizing profit.[26]

The eighteenth century in fact marked an important shift in taken-for-granted assumptions about human nature—a shift toward the modern understanding of men as beings for whom rationality takes the form of action on the basis of self-interest, with interests defined in a narrow, economically centered sense. At the beginning of the century, interests were seen as passions that could countervail the more danger-ous passions of ferocity, avarice, and ambition.[27] For Hobbes, for ex-ample, the aggressive pursuit of "riches, glory, and dominion" was among the passions that ought to be overcome.[28] And in the early eighteenth century, interests seemed the solution to social problems posed by passions—interests might be forces that could control ambi-tion, lust for power, and sexual lust. Greed itself was reincarnated as "interest" and if passions were "destructive and reason ineffectual," then "interests" might possibly be a force that could control the passions.[29] Interests, Hirschman argues, were in fact "the passion of self-love upgraded and contained by reason, and as reason given direction and force by that passion." The result was a hybrid whose working could substitute for true virtue by at least making actions predictable. This predictability was later termed "rational."[30] Although interests were not tied originally to economics, or money making, over the course of the eighteenth century they became associated with the new commercial classes and thereby began to acquire this connotation. As Hirschman puts it, "anyone who did not belong to the nobility could not, *by definition*, share in heroic virtues or violent passions. After all, such a person had only interests and not glory to pursue, and everybody *knew* that this pursuit was bound to be *doux* in comparison to the passionate pastimes and savage exploits of the aristocracy."[31]

Interests, then, originally provided an answer to the problem of how passions were to be managed if reason was ineffectual; only later did interests come to be tied to economics and their meaning narrowed to the pursuit of material, economic advantages. Hirschman suggests that one reason for the drift toward economic interests was the special affinity of "rational calculation implicit in the concept of interest with the nature of economic activities." He notes also that other terms had their "nonmonetary meaning driven out by their monetary one, " and suggests "corruption" and "fortune" as two other important ex-amples.[32] The increasing importance of the market, then, is correlated both with the rise of a new commercial class and with a change in the dominant conception of human nature.

It is fitting that we owe to Adam Smith the final subsumption of the desire for honor, dignity, respect, and power under the desire for economic gain. For Smith, all noneconomic drives feed economic ones. And not only did he maintain that other passions fed the economic one, but "by holding that ambition, the lust for power, and the desire for respect can all be satisfied by economic improvement, Smith under-cut the previously influential idea that passion can be pitted against passion, or the interests against the passions."[33] Hirschman notes that this line of argument takes us back to Bacon, who believed the major passions were an undifferentiated whole. It would be better, however, to see this as the intellectual result of the triumph of one class after a period of transition. Originally, the rising bourgeoisie was thought to be the solution to the problems of feudalism, especially those created by the unrestrained passions of the nobility. The period when it was believed that interests could balance passions may well represent the intellectual or ideological form of the real balance of power between the two classes. The eventual collapse of all passions into interests and the equation of passions with interests in *The Wealth of Nations* may simply have portended the increasing triumph of the bourgeoisie. But links between ideas and social relations are rarely so direct, and one cannot pretend to establish such a progression here.

Interest-driven rational economic man is, then, a social and intellectual construct based on a reduction of the variety of human passions to the desire for economic gain. It is no accident that this construction occurred over the course of the eighteenth century or that Adam Smith should have been among those responsible for the codification of this view. The rational economic man who inhabits the worlds of both classical and neoclassical economics and the exchange theories of sociology and anthropology is a radically truncated and incompleted creature, incapable of either honor or ferocity. To the extent that this flattened creature forms the basis of theories of human nature and action in general and of power relations in particular, the field of social inquiry has been greatly impoverished.[34]

Human beings are moved by more than interests; and power relations too involve more than a clash of interests or the exchange of compliance for valued goods. Despite the fact that such theories have been put forward by important social theorists and also inadvertently used by critics of domination, one cannot logically support the view that human societies are simply mechanisms for the satisfaction of interests. For exchange theorists, human beings have ceased to be creatures with diverse responses to the world involving seeing, tasting, feeling, thinking, wanting, experiencing. They have become mere creatures of utility, whose every social and interpersonal action is an effort to maximize that utility. They are rational economic men.

Exchange theorists (and for the moment I include Adam Smith as well) fail to recognize that "private interest is already a socially determined interest."[35] The relations of utility they see so clearly exist only within the social relations of private property in Western capitalist society. Marx's criticism of the bourgeoisie is applicable to the exchange theorists so far discussed. For the capitalist, "only *one* relation is valid on its own account—the relation of exploitation; all other relations have validity for him only insofar as he can include them under this one relation, and even where he encounters relations which cannot be directly subordinated to the relation of exploitation, he does at least subordinate them to it in his imagination."[36] Because the market dominates the life of the capitalist, it dominates his imagination. The effects of this domination are felt not only in the truncated and flattened vision of human nature represented by rational economic men but also in the kind of fragile and false community these beings construct.

Domination Versus Community

Given the problems and distortions the market model introduces and the narrow class and historical base to which it limits attempts to construct a universal theory of human behavior, one must ask why it has proved so attractive to social scientists. I suggest that its attractions stem from the very assumptions that lead toward a false account of reality. On the market account, we live in a world where individuals are free, equal, and able to shape their fates. Without this model, one would have to account for the unequal distribution of resources in the market and the unequal relations between the owners of property and the owners of labor. If one accepts neoclassical assumptions, social relations in market societies are not fundamentally antagonistic but represent the relations of an orderly "supermarket, where, even if the odd customer is short changed or the odd item shop-lifted, people in the long run get what they pay for and pay for what they get."[37] The operation of the assumption that social relations are fundamentally equitable and work to the benefit of all can be clearly seen in the work of the exchange theorists. One cannot fault the desire to live in such a world. Yet the possibilities for constructing such a society are undermined by the fact that the market account legitimizes (by obfuscating and concealing) relations of domination, presents coercion as choice, and ultimately justifies domination.

To understand how this obfuscates relations of dominance, we need only glance once again at Blau's discussion of the courtship market. As he describes it, the courtship market is an orderly and voluntary exchange between participants who face each other on fundamentally equal terms. Each has a fixed good the other wants; and each is both a producer and consumer of the goods in question. Blau ignores the asymmetry of the double standard for male or female behavior, and the phallocratic relations of domination this expresses—the fact that *he* could only be the buyer and *she* the seller. Second, Blau's account focuses on a transaction between two individuals, and he presumes that the important terms of their interaction are set by the individuals involved. But Blau's own analysis of the courtship market shows that this is hardly the case. Only by examining the social relations between women and men in our society can we uncover both the real relations of domination at work and the institutions that sustain these relations.

In their failure to focus on the social resources individuals bring to an interaction, and in their emphasis on individual transactions, exchange theorists neglect the interesting and important questions about power. Exchange theorists, like neoclassical economists, seem to want to avoid the unpleasant conclusions reached by classical analysts of capitalist society such as Adam Smith or Karl Marx: Labor worked and received little in return, while owners of capital took the bulk of production, and unproductive workers such as salesmen and advertisers made more money than direct producers. Those not involved in production—the money owners—did the best of all.[38]

Exchange theorists of power, like others who take capitalism and its class relations for granted, are unconscious of their roots. They see every aspect of society, including the science of society, as a replication of the interactions characteristic of the marketplace. They stress (falsely) the voluntary nature of human interaction, the exchange of equivalent commodities, and the equality of all participants. While theorists of the market do not seek to deceive their audience, the true nature of social relations is concealed as a consequence of their choice of the market model and the assumptions this model builds into their work.

Conclusion

Use of the market model, then, places a number of obstacles in the face of understanding either power or community. By claiming (falsely) that we live in a world of free and equal individuals interacting on the basis of self-interest, exchange theorists impoverish the theoretical understanding of community and present a deeply misleading account of reality. Theorization of the community in the form of a market results in the conclusion that the human community can only be fragile, instrumental, and ultimately false, composed of persons with no intrinsic connections with each other. Human beings are held to be profoundly separate and isolated from each other, lacking even common preferences and sharing little more than the most elementary needs. Human beings as these theorists understand them construct a community that cannot but replicate their own inadequacies as human beings. Rational economic men are unable to associate with each other directly and instead associate only by means of *things* they pass back and forth between them (i.e., through exchange). A community that bases itself on the self-interested passing back and forth of objects can only be an instrumental community in which exchange and competition lead directly to relations of domination.

These assumptions about the nature of humanity as well as human association are responsible for the series of contentions and conclusions about social interaction I have described in some detail in these two chapters—assumptions that there are no institutional forms that importantly structure human action, that exchanges are exchanges of fixed goods or commodities that take place at a legal instant; that production and consumption (or perhaps more precisely, *exchanges* for the purpose of production and consumption) are the only important activities that take place in the market. Finally, the operation of this set of assumptions indicates the presence of the theses that all market payments are exchanges in the same sense and that all costs are costs paid for productive work in the same sense. These theses have been shown to result in circularity, to rest on counterfactual assumptions, and finally, to conceal relations of domination by presenting them in the guise of relations of exchange between equals.

I suggested earlier that a rethinking of the nature of power could have implications for both the understanding and the practice of politics. Perhaps one can now see the ways in which the exchange theories of social life work to support a conservative politics. If we already inhabit the best possible political community—given the imperfections of human nature, and given that we all have chosen to participate (or not to participate) on the basis of the separate returns we anticipate on the investments we have made—there is no ground on which to argue for improving the lives of citizens. Exchange theories of social life, then, should be seen as complex Panglossian efforts to persuade us that we live in the best of all possible worlds.

NOTES

1. Martin Hollis and Edward Nell, *Rational Economic Man* (New York: Cambridge University Press, 1975), present a penetrating and forceful analysis of this being. They note the extent to which the construct of rational economic man is supported by a philosophy of science and an epistemology that depends on logical positivism. Thus, any alternative to rational economic man requires an epistemological critique. Although this is an important and correct observation, I have attempted to avoid epistemological questions as much as possible. Ultimately, however, these questions prove unavoidable, especially since an alternative theorization of power must rest on alternative epistemological ground.

2. Ibid., p. 55.

3. The reader will no doubt recognize the description of C. B. MacPherson's possessive individual. We will see the presence of other assumptions too,

such as "what makes a man human is *freedom* from dependence on the will of others" and "freedom from dependence on others means freedom from any relations with others except those relations which the individual enters *voluntarily* with a view of his own interest." *The Political Theory of Possessive Individualism* (New York: Oxford University Press, 1964), p. 263.

4. Peter Blau, *Exchange and Power in Social Life* (New York: Wiley, 1974), p. 114. David Baldwin uses a more consensual model to argue that the mutual interest of buyer and seller is likely to obscure their real conflict. See his "Power and Social Exchange," *American Political Science Review* 72, no. 4 (December 1978): 1232. At least one theorist has taken Blau's more subtle analysis to separate him from Homans. See Irving M. Zeitlin, *Rethinking Sociology: A Critique of Contemporary Theory* (Englewood Cliffs, N.J.: Prentice-Hall, 1973), p. 98.

5. Hollis and Nell, *Rational Economic Man*, p. 206. This, they argue, with some reliance on Marx's distinction between productive and unproductive labor, is unpersuasive. But they go on to say that the choice between the two systems cannot be made on empirical grounds since the dispute turns to a large extent on the criteria of evidence and rules for interpretation.

6. Ibid., p. 215.

7. *Capital* (New York: International Publishers, 1967), 1:176.

8. Much of their case rests quite correctly on their critique of positivist epistemology. A full critique of the problems created by rational economic man, and exchange theories of social life more generally, would require such a critique. I will not provide a complete account of this critique here, but rather refer the reader to Hollis and Nell for some of the epistemological underpinnings of my argument here.

9. Hollis and Nell, *Rational Economic Man*, p. 47.

10. Ibid., pp. 60–61.

11. Hollis and Nell trace these difficulties correctly to two sources. The first is the analytic-synthetic distinction in analytic philosophy, which makes it impossible either to apply theoretical models or to give empirical criteria of application to central economic concepts. The second is that behaviorism, into which positivism leads, prevents one from distinguishing maximizing from nonmaximizing models. They point to a number of other difficulties with rational self-interest models as well. They suggest that rationality conflicts with prediction criteria, that positivists have divided the world into analytic and synthetic, and the statement that there are rational economic men is neither sort of statement. Finally, they suggest that neoclassical economists face the problem of induction, that is, of knowing which correlations are causal and which are not (ibid., p. 64).

12. See ibid., p. 112 ff, for a more complete working out of this model.

13. In this context it is no accident that Blau contends, but does not argue, that this relation too is based on interest, and that Homans says he will not discuss this at all. For a very interesting interpretation of the psychological significance of this particular blindness, see Jane Flax, "Political Philosophy and the Patriarchal Unconscious: A Psychoanalytic Perspective on Epistemology and Metaphysics," in *Discovering Reality: Feminist Perspectives on Epistemology, Metaphysics, Methodology, and the Philosophy of Science*, ed. Sandra Harding and Merrill Hintikka (Dordrecht: Reidel, 1983).

14. Hollis and Nell, *Rational Economic Man*, p. 210. And there is of course Homans' pigeon, whose behavior exemplifies the animal kingdom's voluntary choice to engage in exchanges with psychologists and other researchers, and whose behavior, Homans tells us, indicates that rational economic man has even penetrated the animal kingdom. In addition, once one sees the inner logic of the model of exchange, Blau's exclusion of physical coercion or the threat of coercion makes little sense.

15. *The Social Construction of Reality* (New York: Anchor, 1967), p. 119.

16. Hollis and Nell, *Rational Economic Man*, pp. 211–12. The refusal to recognize institutions takes a second form in the assumption that production is highly flexible in that goods can be produced in many ways. This ignores the existence of real firms with real investments in fixed and durable goods. Moreover, maximizing of profit cannot be assumed. Some technical innovations are designed not for more efficient production but because they allow for better control of labor (ibid., p. 212). See also David Noble, "Social Choice in Machine Design: The Case of Automatically Controlled Machine Tools," *Politics and Society* 8, nos. 3–4 (1978): 313–49.

17. Hollis and Nell, *Rational Economic Man*, pp. 216–17. They note that "this leads to a view of society that has only to be seen to be disbelieved." Perhaps so, but such views are widely held.

18. See, for example, T. H. Greene, "Liberal Legislation and Freedom of Contract," in *The Political Theory of T. H. Greene*, ed. John R. Rodman (New York: Appleton-Century-Croft, 1964).

19. In short, neoclassical economics describes what Hollis and Nell have called "performances" rather than "productions." While I would choose to use different terms, the idea is a very useful one. See *Rational Economic Man*, pp. 135–37, for their case. It is a part of a larger case they make for the inapplicability of the neoclassical model even to the contemporary world. Their excellent case—much of it applicable to exchange theories of social life—rests on a series of arguments: that neo-classical economists (1) posit agents that could not endure in the market or support themselves materially (p. 224); (2) fail to recognize that change takes time and time has a fixed cost in interests; (3) fail to recognize that no rational economic man could be both rational and possess perfect market and technical information (p. 228); (4) fail to recognize the contradiction in the notion that investment is governed by considerations of marginal productivity, i.e., that while knowledge accumulates, capital goods are durable. Knowledge has a rate of interest; (5) fail to see the conflict between the assumptions of perfect rationality and perfect mobility—perfectly rational firms with perfect mobility could desert the market in a particular commodity like "startled rabbits." Mobility has a cost and thus must be imperfect (p. 230); (6) fail to see the problem of untestable models—circularity.

20. Karl Marx, *Grundrisse*, trans. Martin Nicolaus (Middlesex, England: Penguin Books, 1973), p. 156.

21. Polanyi cites a variety of anthropological evidence. See Karl Polanyi, *Primitive, Archaic, and Modern Economics*, ed. George Dalton (Boston: Beacon, 1968), pp. 23–24.

22. Marx, *Grundrisse*, p. 157.

23. See Polanyi, *Primitive, Archaic, and Modern Economics*, pp. 70–71. Ironi-

cally, it is those most opposed to Marx's vision who have become defenders of a kind of economic determinism. It is not at all apparent that when one has said that something works like the capitalist market, one has explained it.

24. See Hollis and Nell, *Rational Economic Man*, p. 51, on the culture bound-edness of the maximizer. And see Polanyi, *Primitive, Archaic, and Modern Economics*, pp. 70–71. Curiously, his sources, especially Malinowski and Firth, are those Lévi-Strauss uses to construct his exchange theory and to see primitive economic man as a maximizer (see Appendix 1).

25. See Marshall Sahlins, *Stone Age Economics* (Chicago: Aldine-Atherton, 1972).

26. See, for example, Aristotle's argument against "Chrematistic" in the *Politics*. And note also Cephalus's favorable presentation of himself as the moderate restorer of the family fortune rather than the original accumulator of the goods in Book I of Plato's *Republic*.

27. Albert Hirschman, *The Passions and the Interests* (Princeton: Princeton University Press, 1978), pp. 28–31.

28. Ibid., p. 31.

29. Ibid., p. 43.

30. Ibid., pp. 43, 50.

31. Ibid., p. 63.

32. Ibid., pp. 38–40. It is interesting to speculate on the extent to which these problems grew from the understanding of reason as passive rather than active. The ancient Greeks, for example, had no such difficulties, in part because they saw reason as an active and self-moving force. See below, Chapter 8.

33. Ibid., pp. 109–10.

34. To this extent, I agree with Hannah Arendt's position on the rise of the social and the difficulties this poses for public life. Hirschman also notes that capitalism was supported in order to create one-dimensionality, which is now believed to be its worst feature (ibid., pp. 132–35). I do not intend by my criticism to side with romantic critics of capitalism. To object to one-dimensionality is not to argue that our current difficulties grow from the fact that we lack nobility, grandeur, and passion.

35. Marx, *Grundrisse*, p. 156.

36. Karl Marx and Frederick Engels, *The German Ideology*, ed. C. J. Arthur (New York: International Publishers, 1970), p. 110.

37. Hollis and Nell, *Rational Economic Man*, p. 216.

38. See ibid., p. 49, for a concise summary of this argument.

3

The Market in Power:
Legitimating Domination

The use of the market as a model for understanding social relations is not limited to those who can be characterized as theorists of social exchange. The assumptions and contentions
that structure neoclassical economic theory have played very formative
roles in many contemporary social scientific considerations of power.
This chapter is devoted to exposing and illuminating the often implicit
aspects of the market model that structure several of the most influential
mainstream theorizations of power in political science and sociology.
The analyses of Harold Lasswell and Abraham Kaplan, Robert Dahl, Nelson Polsby, and Talcott Parsons go beyond an understanding of power
relations as exchange yet in fundamental ways remain within the market framework in which individuals are held to be isolated and interest-
driven, and to interact only voluntarily on terms of their own choosing.

Parsons, Lasswell and Kaplan, and Dahl and Polsby choose differing aspects of the market as the bases for their analyses of power relations. Parsons begins from the functions of money, Lasswell and
Kaplan from the construct of rational economic man, and Dahl and Polsby
from the interaction of buyer and seller. Without a grasp of the various
components of the market model, their theories might appear to differ
substantially. Yet familiarity with the model enables one to appreciate
the real commonality underlying these theories. I demonstrate that
each theory, precisely because it takes some aspect of the market as an
analogue for understanding power relations, tends to ignore domination and to focus instead on the voluntary (and therefore unobjectionable) decisions made by individual actors, tends to treat dominance
relations as the inevitable but unimportant outcomes of any human
interaction, or maintains both positions at once. Thus, they describe a
human community that is unavoidably fragile and ultimately false, a

world in which persons can have no deep connections with each other. While these theorists are often less enthusiastic about such conclusions than Homans or Blau, their theories of power implicitly support the position that there is no reason to be concerned about transforming social relations of domination in more liberatory directions. And it is the use of the market model that supports this outcome.

The reader familiar with these debates about power will no doubt recognize many of my specific criticisms. My purpose in this chapter is less to add new criticisms to the voluminous literature than to demonstrate how these criticisms are interrelated and how they carry an implicit critique of the market as a model for understanding human interaction.[1]

Lasswell and Kaplan: The Political Economy of Power

Lasswell and Kaplan see economics as the most advanced "science of man," and explicitly use it as a model for thinking about power. For example, they argue that "a side glance at the postulational structure of economic theory may sharpen the significance of the present concept,"[2] in order to suggest that the structure of interactions around power is the same as that of the competitive market in economic theory (that is, that there is a competitive market in power). Just as money or possession of other resources is a condition for participating in the process of exchange in our society, power, they argue, is a condition for participation in decision making in a particular case. And, like the position of a capitalist firm, the amount of power each actor holds tends to increase until limited by other powerholders. Only deviations from, rather than congruence with, this competitive market model call for comment. Thus, Lasswell and Kaplan note that *homo politicus* is an abstraction like *homo economicus*—that is, the man interested in exercising power is the same kind of creature as the man interested in accumulating capital or serving his own interests. But they are careful to state that, unlike rational economic man, "we have no record of anyone, however tyrannous and power seeking, who succeeded in transforming himself wholly into an instrument of power for the sake of power."[3] Thus, rational economic man is transformed into only partly rational political man.

In their view, the exercise of power, "the power process," is modeled on the working of the economy. In the realm of power (the arena), the relevant unit becomes an "encounter" that sets in motion "a process of focussing the activities of all concerned to the end of affecting the outcome," the outcome being a "decision" (the exchange of commodities) in which one side experiences "severe sanctions (deprivations)." They point out that this feature of power too has a market equivalent—the transaction. An "alignment" is the power ratio for and against a decision. It too has a corresponding economic analogy—prices in the market as determined by supply and demand and established in a transaction. Finally, ascendancy—the enjoyment of power—is held to be the equivalent of consumption.[4]

The market analogy as a way of understanding power brings with it a number of assumptions. Although Lasswell and Kaplan believe that their work contains "no elaboration of political doctrines,"[5] their use of the capitalist market as a means to understand the working of power relations has several (now familiar) effects and distortions of theory.

Lasswell and Kaplan hold that the situation in which power is exercised is constructed out of the subjective and private preferences of the actors, and just as transactions in the market grow out of each agent's effort to maximize his own utility, so too the agents in an arena of power interact to maximize their utilities. Although they admit that this is an abstraction for the purpose of constructing a scientific theory, they note that utilities or valuations should be understood as simple preferences. (One should remember that the utilities of rational economic man are not comparable interpersonally.)

Because *homo politicus* is modeled on rational economic man, Lasswell and Kaplan must assume that power seekers are as insatiable for that commodity as capitalists are for the accumulation of wealth in a competitive market society. Thus, although they argue that attitudes toward power are culturally defined, their reference to Zuni customs of applying sanctions to any sort of personal "aggressiveness" or "ambition" is presented in such a way that their fundamental proposition, a direct paraphrase of Hobbes, that "the amount of power tends to increase until limited by other power holders," is not called into question.[6] This, they argue, is one of the most "widely recognized" characteristics of power, and they cite with approval Michels' argument that "every human power seeks to enlarge its prerogatives. He who has acquired power will almost always endeavor to consolidate it and to extend it, to multiply the ramparts which defend his position, and to withdraw himself from the control of the masses."[7]

The desire for power, then, for Lasswell and Kaplan, is analogous to the desire for wealth in capitalist society. Powerholders, like capitalist firms, accumulate and extend power until they reach limits set for them by nature, technology, other powerholders, or even social custom. For all their stress on the differences that can be made by different cultures, it is significant that they see these differences not as fundamental modifications of the power-seeking motive or ambition but rather as the limitation of an innate drive. The parallels with and the problems of circularity introduced by the construct of rational economic man are striking. How could one counter their contention that power seeking is an innate drive? The problems posed for empirical investigation by contentions such as this are insurmountable.

In addition, this model of rational economic man transposed into political life leads to a vision of social relations as inevitably competitive and conflictual, and the assumption that the opposition of interests is a fundamental feature of human existence. This is perhaps one of the reasons Lasswell and Kaplan stress power over others as it appears in arenas defined by overt conflict and competition. "Power," they contend, "is not completely made available (shaped) until it is involved in fighting, arguing, boycotting, negotiating. . . ."[8]

The market's lack of institutional structures is replicated in their stress on the transaction itself—the isolated moment of decision to apply sanctions. Lasswell and Kaplan argue that "the subject matter of political science is constituted by power as a process,"[9] yet their dependence on the analogy to the market leads them to give pride of place to "outcomes" rather than to the shifting or stable patterns of the exercise of power over time. Their analysis leads to a focus on individual encounters that lead to specific decisions.

The related market emphasis on the interaction of equal and homogeneous participants leads Lasswell and Kaplan to overstress the voluntariness of participation in power relations, whatever the coerciveness of the particular decision. Thus, despite the coercion involved in an exercise of power as they describe it (the constraint of action by the "threat of deprivation" or the "promise of indulgence"), Lasswell and Kaplan stress the voluntariness of participation in power relations. They hold that "the fact that power, by definition, rests on coercion does not entail that the power situation itself cannot be the result, in part, of choice."[10] While this may be at least a plausible possibility, this avoids the question whether it is typical. Lasswell and Kaplan's theory that although power relations are based on coercion, they are entered by consent can be seen as a simple translation of the statement that the laws of the market—for example, the working of supply and demand —may constrain behavior but that the market itself, like the arena of power, is entered by consent. If what follows this free choice appears to disadvantage some, it remains fundamentally unobjectionable.

The transposition of the model of rational economic man into the political realm, into a situation in which, by their own admission, one side suffers severe sanctions, coupled with the contentions that follow from ignoring social institutions (voluntarism, homogeneity and equality of actors, focus on instant of transaction), has unfortunate effects. Their efforts can only help to legitimize, at least by indirection, the opposite of these relations, since upon entering individual power relations human beings do not shed their histories, their resources, or indeed their personalities. Nor do they construct power relations without regard to social institutions. Lasswell and Kaplan's account of power relations both fundamentally falsifies the real conditions of human interaction and also presents an understanding of the human community as unavoidably fragile, extrinsic, and false.

Use of the market model, in particular the attempt to transpose rational economic man from the economy into political life, results in both a vast underestimation of the strength of domination and an underrating of the possibilities for constructing a community that does not depend on domination. Lasswell and Kaplan cannot see, much less resolve, the problem of how a community might be constructed on a firmer base, and how the capitalist market might be reconstructed in such a way that persons are connected directly and intrinsically.

The Consensual Community of Talcott Parsons

Parsons carries the understanding of power farther away from a recognition of power relations as domination, that is, as the mastery and control of some by others. Once again, it is the market model— almost a metaphor in his case, which enables him to do this— although in a form different from those proposed by others considered here.[11] Use of the market enables Parsons to construct an account of power as a consensual relation. Parsons claims that power functions like money and thus has both value in itself and utility for obtaining other valued things. Like Lasswell and Kaplan, he seems unaware of the consequences of this choice of analogy.

Parsons is particularly useful, however, because he states his assumptions far more clearly than most. He argues that the concepts appropriate for the analysis of the economic and political systems of a society are parallel. His case rests on several points:

1. Each is an abstract analytical scheme that "deals with a restricted set of primary variables and their interrelations."
2. The political system is in principle a functional subsystem of a society like an economy, a system that has not been, although it could be, defined as clearly as the economy.
3. Collective action in politics is the political equivalent of production in the economy. This is so in terms of:
   a. adjustment to the conditions of "demand" by consumers of political outputs.
   b. mobilization of resources from outside the system in question.
   c. the "creatively combinatorial nature" of economic and political processes, that is, the possibility both processes

offer of producing a surplus from the resources at hand.

4. Political analysis is conceived as parallel to economics in "the sense that a central place in it is occupied by a generalized medium involved in the political interaction process, which is also a 'measure' of the relevant values."[12]

Parsons conceives of power as such a generalized medium in a sense directly parallel in logical structure to money as the generalized medium of the economic process.[13] Parsons argues that by conceiving power explicitly as money, he will be able to move beyond the problems created by other analyses of power, for example, the problem of diffuse definitions, the failure to understand the relation between the coercive and consensual aspects of power, and the problems some analysts encountered by seeing power as zero-sum. Parsons does propose solutions to these problems, but in using the categories of the capitalist market, he imports other assumptions that limit the utility of his analysis.

On Power as Money

Parsons lists the parallels between political and economic categories: land/commitment of resources to effective collective action; labor/demands or need for collective action as manifested in the public; capital/control of some part of the productivity of the economy for goals of collectivity, for example, tax revenues; organization/legitimation of the authority under which collective decisions are taken; share of income/output of power. "Specification of the properties of power," then, "can best be approached through an attempt to delineate very briefly the relevant properties of money in the economy."[14] Thus, he holds that power requires a relational system in which some commitments, either ascriptive or voluntarily assumed, are treated as binding. In such a context, Parsons argues that power is the generalized capacity to secure the performance of binding obligations by units in a system of collective organization in circumstances where obligations are legitimated with references to their bearing on collective goals and where, should persons fail to comply, one can presume enforcement by negative sanctions.[15]

Not surprisingly, this is a definition of power as it works *within* an established system. Indeed, especially when Parsons goes on to argue that power is not the ability to get compliance by threat of force (as Dahl states), it is difficult at first to see how power might differ from authority.[16] This description of power flows directly from Parsons' contention that power is like money and therefore involves confidence and requires legitimation. It cannot operate by means of the threat of force.

(Clearly, his insistence on this point reveals his own recognition of the extent to which issues of power are issues of community.) Thus, just as a monetary system resting on gold directly would be too blunt an instrument for the modern institutional state, so too, Parsons argues, power resting directly on coercion and physical force is too blunt an instrument. Our own particular society, he suggests, requires a modicum of consent to the exercise of power. Like money, the exercise of power must inspire some confidence. And, like money, it must be symbolically generalized and legitimized.[17]

Parsons' stress on the integrative importance of power highlights one of the attractions the market model holds for social theorists. The market appears to be an institution that operates with universalistic criteria, assumes the equality of participants, allows equivalents to exchange for equivalents, and requires the consent of all participants for its operation. The confidence required for the circulation of money parallels the confidence required by a political system in the Parsonian schema.

There is more to Parsons' account of power than the explicit analogy to money. There is an implicit contention that the political community is a type of capitalist firm—with employees, employers, authority, and hierarchy. This emerges most clearly in his effort to distinguish the exercise of power from authority. In the same way as employees of a business, as neoclassical economics describes them, enter into a community for mutual benefit and sustain it only so long as parties are confident their interests are being served, so also do members of a political community. We have, according to Parsons, consented to being coerced by the collectivity for our own good, since the sole purpose of the exercise of power is to mobilize resources for action by the community as a whole.

Power, properly speaking, is not exercised *within* the political system—only authority. Parsons distinguishes power from authority because authority is the legitimized *right* to use power. And authority is not a circulating medium but the institutionalized code.[18] In addition, power, like money, can be spent, is alienable, whereas authority can only be exercised and never depleted.[19] The political system circulates power between itself and what Parsons terms the integrative system (law, social control). Policy decisions are the outputs, and political support is taken in, along with demands for other action. The only way this makes sense is if the polity is conceived as organized on the model of the capitalist firm. As power circulates between the political system and what Parsons terms the integrative system (law, norms, etc.), the public invests support in order to procure binding policy decisions. The spenders of power are those members of the collectivity who have the authority to spend it.[20]

The community modeled on the capitalist firm contains clear differences of resources and capability for action. Parsons insists, however, that a universalistic value system (such as that provided by the market) will tend to overcome hierarchy. Rather than face head-on the problems of hierarchy and inequality implicit in his choice of analogue, Parsons argues that the relation between those in a position to spend the collective power and those who transfer their right of decision to them is one of equality—equality in the dual form of equality of opportunity and equality of franchise. Equality of franchise can even be seen as itself a form of power because the consequences of its exercise are binding.[21] At the same time, equality of franchise is limited by the concept of competence. Those who hold authority must, in Parsons' view, have demonstrated competence, something each person has an equal opportunity to demonstrate in the economic sphere. Thus there are some limits to equality, but the operation of the economy on the principle of equal opportunity will help to decrease the cumulative advantage of some. Overall, however, the power system is held to be hierarchical only to the extent necessary for effective collective action.[22] The conservative implications of this Parsonian position have been widely commented on.

The purpose of Parsons' distinction is to argue that the coercive element in power systems and the hierarchical aspect of the structure of systems of authority and power are not connected. The hierarchical aspect is held to be only part of the structure of power systems, one inherent in the internal structure of collectivities but one counteracted by equality of franchise and equality of opportunity. Parsons' stress on the equality of participants enlarges the area of consensus since he takes for granted that one cannot be expected to consent to an inferior position. Equality and consensus, then, are fundamental to Parsons' case against those who see power as a form of coercion or domination.

Parsons next turns to the argument that when A gains power, B loses it. We have seen that exchange theorists have used the market model to contend that all social interactions produce net profits for participants and thus that power is not a zero-sum commodity. Parsons uses the market in a more innovative way; he solves the problem of whether a gain of power by one party represents an equivalent loss by another by focusing on money in its role as capital, that is, money invested to produce more money rather than to buy goods and services for consumption. He points out that if one is budgeting a fixed income, as individuals do, one can only spend money on one thing at the expense of alternatives (opportunity costs?). But for the system as a whole, Parsons sees other alternatives. He takes as his example the creation of credit in commercial banking. Here, the whole system depends on confidence and on the bindingness of commitments (a major feature of exercises of power as Parsons understands them). This parallels his contention that power relations depend primarily on consensus and only secondarily on coercion. The banker assumes binding obligations both to depositors and to those to whom loans are made, obligations that cannot all be met at once. Thus it is only the collective confidence that makes the system work, and "the bank, as collectivity, thus enjoys a 'power position' by virtue of which it can give its borrowers effective control of certain types of opportunity."[23]

In the political realm, the position of banker is occupied by the elected political leader to whom deposits of power are made (in the form of votes) by constituents. The collectivity as a whole, through the medium of decisions by the leadership, can decide to assume new binding obligations, which, on the banking model, represent an increase in power. Moreover, the leadership has an "optional capacity" to exert influence through persuasion.[24] Thus the leaders of the collectivity operate as bankers or brokers who mobilize the commitments (deposits) of their constituents "in such a way that the totality of commitments made by the collectivity as a whole can be enhanced."[25] Parsons sees the process of power enhancement as a strict parallel to economic investment, both in terms of increased collective effectiveness and the risk taking with which neoclassical economic theory credits the capitalist.[26] Continuing the analogy, Parsons suggests that power, when operating as credit in the political system, can, like money, become overextended and result in a "deflationary spiral."[27]

Power, then, functions both as money for consumption goods and as capital in a political community modeled on a capitalist firm. The business firm, as Parsons notes, is the case where the two standards for politics and economics coincide. The firm uses its income (power) primarily to increase its productivity and, as a measure of this, its money income. Similarly, "for a collectivity specialized in political function, the primary criterion of success would be given in its power position, relative that is to other collectivities" in a competitive system.[28]

Power, then, can be invested to earn interest and thereby produce more power. Not surprisingly, Parsons is led to suggest that different kinds of power can reinforce each other. He fails to recognize that his two arguments (against those who understood power as coercion, and against those who saw power as a zero-sum phenomenon) are in conflict. In the former case, Parsons argued that equality of opportunity and equality of franchise tended to counteract hierarchical tendencies; in the latter, he gave the leaders, the bankers, the preeminent role in generating increased power. In the former, he argued that equality was increased by the equality of opportunity in the market; in the latter, that power itself can produce more power, that it functions like capital, and that it can be expanded only by the risk taking of the capitalist.

The reader will recall that these are the same two contradictory accounts of power relations as Blau put forward. He argued on the one hand that powerholders were those whose competence was rewarded and, on the other, that power was a unilateral exchange between those who possessed resources and those who had only their compliance to give in return. The fact that both Parsons and Blau were drawn into similar contradictory accounts of power gives powerful support to my argument that it is their use of the market model that leads them to give these inconsistent accounts of power and allows them to conclude that relations of domination are a positive good.

Problems with the Market as Human Community

Parsons has attempted to reduce the discussion of power relations to the question of how an institutionalized power system conceived on the model of a capitalist firm exercises power. Given his model, many of the important questions about power are unaskable.[29] Parsons' effort, that of a man who attempted to re-understand all social relations as consensual, leads to a rejection of any morality other than that of capitalist firms competing in a market. His theory ignores the possibilities for developing a broader, deeper, and more intrinsic community. Instead he presents the capitalist firm as not only the sole form but also the best possible form for human community.

Let us examine the specific ways the market model involves him in these difficulties. Parsons' argument that power is basically consensual rather than coercive, and that power relations are the outcome of voluntary choice, rests on his analogy of power to money. This allows him to claim that power not only depends on consensus but is legitimated by that consensus.[30]

Parsons gains much theoretical mileage by taking the circulation of money, rather than the specific process of exchange, as the most fundamental aspect of economic life. By basing his account on circulation, he is able to re-create that "veritable Eden of the rights of man," a system based on freedom, equality, property, and utility. Freedom to interact takes the form of consensus on the basis of mutual gain for Parsons.[31] The issue of equality is clearly a more difficult one. Even though Parsons wishes for a society in which rewards are allocated universally on the basis of individual achievement, his construction of power on the model of finance capital prevents him from theoretically moving closer to such a society. On the one hand, Parsons argues that equality of franchise and opportunity operate to decrease the hierarchy seen by critics such as C. Wright Mills. This, however, is contradicted by the real history of finance capital over the last hundred years.

Power relations, on this model, are relations entered for mutual gain on the basis of self-interest—for Parsons, the gain of the collectivity as a whole, a gain whose form is determined by the leaders (bankers) of the collectivity in question. Parsons fails to see the "literal sense in which coercion, violence, force, and all forms of might *make* right."[32]

The market, then, serves a particular obfuscatory function in Parsons' work: It hides the relations of force that underlie power relations and shunts aside the issue of how power can mold morality and can even structure a (false) consensus.[33] Parsons' use of the market as the prototype for human interaction allows him to make a far more plausible case than would otherwise have been possible simply because we are all familiar with accounts of market interaction in which human beings appear to associate only voluntarily and on the basis of self-interest for the purpose of mutual gain. Their mutual subjection to the laws of the market is ignored, as are relations of class domination. The voluntariness of interaction, and the consensus held to underlie it, is in reality the acquiescence of a population confronted with a market that works on the basis of laws that seem independent of human choice, not the false consensus of the criminal and his victim. There is a profound sense in which we do consent to the realities of the capitalist market by seeing them as inevitable.[34]

Parsons' argument against the zero-sum nature of power does explicitly allow for the production or generation of more power in a social system, but the ruling-class perspective of his view is clear. Only the leaders can generate power, since they, like bankers, are recipients of deposits of other people's power. These deposits are revocable only at election time. The implicit conclusion is that only leaders can have influence—an influence they can exercise because they are holders of deposits of power. They may indeed spend their power—by creating situational constraints for others.[35]

In sum, Parsons' theory serves to legitimize class domination. First, Parsons' argument that equality of franchise and equality of opportunity both work to decrease hierarchy in reality obfuscate the real inequalities produced by the market by, on the one hand, denying their existence or importance and, on the other, supporting them as both inevitable and a positive good. The power some exercise over others becomes instead the legitimate authority of the few who exercise power on behalf of and for the benefit of the many. Second, the analogy of power to finance capital leads to antidemocratic conclusions: If voters are depositors, and politicians are bankers, who will decide where the extra power produced by investment will go? If the banking analogy is to hold, it is the banker rather than the depositors who will decide, that is, the political leadership and not the voters. Third, if power functions like capital, the desire for accumulation must be unlimited. Thus, there is a tendency in Parsons' theory toward oligarchy in politics, modeled on the tendency toward monopoly in the economy.

Parsons fails to confront the central problem of concern to exchange theorists: How can one account for the fact that relations of equality, freely entered into, result in situations where some have power over others? Thus, he is forced to ignore the existence of binding commitments that are neither ascriptive nor voluntarily assumed. The laws of the market as they affect individuals involved in particular transactions represent just such binding "commitments." As an individual, one has very little choice about adhering to them. Parsons emphasizes those features of the market that require common interest. The conflicting interests of buyers and sellers are overlooked in favor of their common interest in money as the means of exchange. The collectivity, for Parsons, is a unitary one, a single business firm whose members have neither the conflicting interests of buyers and sellers nor the conflicting interests of different classes in a stratified society.[36]

The Pluralist Alternative: Dahl and Polsby

While the market exchanges of rational economic men do not appear directly in the work of pluralist theorists, their account rests implicitly, not on the circulation of money in the market, but on another feature of the market—the buyer/seller interaction. The pluralists, especially Nelson Polsby in *Community Power and Political Theory* and Robert Dahl in "A Critique of the Ruling Elite Model," see themselves as confronting the problem of inequality in a democracy. "That some people have more power than others is one of the most palpable facts of human existence."[37] The pluralists ask: How then can one claim that a pluralistic democracy exists? They see their task as accepting human inequality and at the same time insisting on the reality of human freedom and equality.[38] They argue against those who see the existence of a power elite; instead, they hold that each individual has an equal opportunity to engage in politics and thus to reap the rewards of political action.[39] Dahl makes the point that although citizens may have little direct influence over the powerholders in a political system, they do have indirect influence; and Polsby adds that equality is enhanced by the self-limiting of elites. Thus, despite indications to the contrary, inequality cannot be held to be a pervasive and troubling feature of the American political system.

Pluralists have been criticized on a number of grounds. Some have argued that they are improperly vague in their approaches to the concept of power: Dahl has stated simply that "A has power over B to the extent that he can get B to do something that B would not otherwise do";[40] and Polsby has added only that in cases where decisions are choices between alternate outcomes, an "actor can be said to possess a certain amount of 'power' if, by acting on others, he changes the comparative probability that these outcomes will take place."[41]

In addition, Dahl and Polsby can certainly be criticized on the grounds that their presumptions and questions have limited their theory by assuming the existence of a political structure in which holding influence is fundamentally a result of a choice to engage in political action. Third, Polsby and (to a lesser extent) Dahl impose extreme requirements on the elite theories they oppose, requirements that amount to a demand that elite theory be reformulated as a type of market theory. For example, Polsby argues that stratification theory cannot be persuasive unless it can find some unambiguous set of resources that "index" a capacity, that "predict the outcomes of conflicts."[42]

There are indeed important flaws in their work, but the more interesting issues are those that turn on the use of the market as a model for political life. I argue that the neoclassical economists' understanding of the capitalist market plays a central role in the pluralist construction of a theory to cope with the dilemma of unequal power. The market model is at the root of the pluralist focus on *"behavior* in the making of *decisions* on *issues* over which there is an observable *conflict* of (subjective) *interests,* seen as express policy preferences, revealed by political participation."[43]

What is the role played by the stress on observable behavior in making decisions, or insistence on the existence of overt conflict on public issues? Why do pluralists hold that preferences are based on subjective interests that can be revealed only by the political participation of citizens? And why stress that each issue is *sui generis,* that no connection can be assumed between one issue area and another in terms of who might be influential? I argue that the answer to each of these questions can be found in the theorists' use of the market as a model for understanding political life.[44]

The pluralist stress on overt behavior in conflict situations corresponds to the economists' focus on the conflict between buyer and seller, along with competition among buyers on the one hand and sellers on the other.[45] The stress on the centrality of decisions in understanding power relations parallels exchange theorists' stress (following neoclassical economics) on the specific transaction, in which the exchange of fixed goods is completed in a legal instant. The content of the decision itself, then, becomes the commodity for which participants in the interaction expend some of their resources. And the pluralist insistence that each interaction must be treated as *sui generis* parallels the exchange theorists' insistence that no institutions relevantly shape social interactions and that the form taken by these interactions is a result of the voluntary actions, individual preferences, and expendable resources of fundamentally equal individuals. Finally, the pluralists assume that it is the momentary coincidence of the subjective preferences (marginal utility) of the individual actors that brings and holds the community of participants together.[46]

Each of these parallels with market exchange supports the pluralists' adherence to the two basic theses of neoclassical economics: that all payments are exchanges in the same sense and that all costs are costs paid for productive work in the same sense. In pluralist theory, the first thesis takes the form of an argument that no one is altogether without the resources necessary for political participation. The parallel economic statement here is that all have at least the capacity to labor, and therefore have the necessary resources to engage in exchange. Thus, their implicit use of the market as a model leads the pluralists to exactly replicate Blau's argument that exercises of power should be understood as unilateral exchanges, with one side receiving benefits and using their future compliance as currency. The second thesis takes the form of the contention that the choice to expend one's resources on political action is a decision to engage in exchange in the same sense as the choice to buy a commodity or (in neoclassical economic theory) to sell one's labor power. The theoretical consequences of adherence to these positions, for pluralists as for other market theorists, are circularity, reliance on counterfactual claims and, most important, the presentation of relations of domination as exchanges between equals. Let us examine how these consequences emerge.

Voluntary Participation and Overt Conflict

The pluralists begin with the assumption of the equality of citizens, the proposition that "at bottom *nobody* dominates in a town."[47] This presumption of the equality of all participants requires them to search for observable indicators for the exercise of power. Thus, despite this recognition of the fact of inequality, what needs to be proved is the existence of unequal power relations. Dahl, for example, argues that without overt disagreement, one cannot tell who is on which side; one cannot tell who is ruling and who is not, and whether power has been exercised.[48] The evidence for which he is searching will allow him to discover situations in which "A has power over B to the extent that he can get B to do something that B would not otherwise do."[49] Thus the conflict and commonality that structure the relation between buyer and seller structure Dahl's definition of power. Polsby similarly builds an argument that depends on overt disagreement. He argues that the "capacity of one actor to do something affecting another actor, which changes the probable pattern of specified future events" is seen most easily in decisions. Thus the power of an actor is expressed by the magnitude of the changes he introduces.[50]

The buyer and seller appear again in the pluralist contention that citizens are not automatically participants in the political system. Just as to become a buyer or seller in the market requires a conscious choice, so too does participation in politics. Thus the pluralists' emphasis on the importance of overt participation can be traced to their implicit use of the market as a model. The pluralists' emphasis on the voluntariness of participation and the equality of participants emerges in their distinction between actual and potential influence. They suggest that having influence or power depends basically on individual choice. Political power is possible only if one makes the decision to participate in politics, that is, to expend the resources one has (and Dahl argues that no one lacks all resources) in a political direction.[51] By analogy, although a single seller (or capitalist firm) might have the capacity to corner the market in a particular commodity, if the seller does not act, the capacity amounts to nothing. Thus, although human beings are unequal in terms of the amount of resources they possess, they have at least an equal capacity to decide to expend their resources on politics.[52]

In Polsby's work, the stress on the importance of participation emerges in what he terms the "presumption that human behavior is governed in large part by inertia."[53] The possession of power or influence depends on participation, and citizens who do not choose to act should be understood to have made the choice to refrain from spending resources on this particular commodity. The distinction serves to highlight his assertion that the reason most citizens have little power or influence over public officials lies in their own choice not to expend their resources in this way.

The distinctions between potential and actual power, between those who choose to participate and those who do not, leads to a more questionable distinction between *homo civicus* and *homo politicus*, and finally to the chapter in *Who Governs* entitled "Citizenship Without Politics." Since politics is, as most of its students agree, about power, the chapter might better be titled "Citizenship Without Power." Dahl argues that a number of resources can be used to gain political power —including time, access to money, credit, control over jobs, information, and solidarity with similar people. Yet he holds that despite the unequal distribution of these resources, virtually no one lacks some resources for influence.[54] Polsby makes similar assertions. Resources are available differentially to be sure, but the pluralists argue that everyone has some resources. Dahl states that a resource is only a potential kind of power. Thus, although the rich certainly have more political resources than the poor, they cannot be said to rule unless one can demonstrate that they have actually used their power resources to further their own interests. Individuals vary in their use of potential political resources not only because of differential access to resources but, more important, the pluralists argue, because of their own decisions about probabilities of succeeding, decisions that reflect individual choices.[55]

The distinction between *homo civicus* and *homo politicus*, then, helps to resolve the pluralist dilemma of how to account for the existence of differential power relations among free and equal individuals in a democratic society. The fact that a few have far more power than others depends on the presumption stated so well by Polsby that "human behavior is governed in large part by inertia."[56] *Homo civicus* is not without resources or potential power. He *could* choose to "spend" some of these resources on politics. But for a variety of reasons, *homo civicus* chooses not to do so. Dahl seems both troubled and a bit bewildered by this. He suggests that perhaps it is due to a "political culture where individual achievement and nongovernmental techniques are assigned a high priority in problem solving." In such a culture, "men may be frustrated in their primary activities without ever turning to politics for solutions."[57]

He suggests that perhaps if politics were attached more closely to the primary activities of society, it might move from the "periphery of attention, concern and action to a point nearer the center. For most people in the United States (and probably everywhere else) this happens rarely, if at all."[58] He sees the myth of the primacy of politics as a legacy of ancient Athens reinforced by what he terms "the human tendency to blur the boundaries between what is and what ought to be"; and "by the inescapable fact that those who write about politics are deeply concerned with political affairs and sometimes find it difficult to believe that most other people are not." But perhaps most important, he takes issue with the notion that democracy can work only if citizens are concerned. This "ancient myth," he concludes, is false in the case of New Haven.[59] In any case, direct influence or control of *homo politicus* requires, according to Dahl, control over officials; and when they are elected, this means getting and maintaining control over votes.[60] Political man seeks to influence civic man directly, but civic man seeks to influence political man only occasionally.[61]

The pluralist stress on voluntary participation in situations of overt conflict, then, can be traced to the implicit use of the market as a model for understanding political life. Because the market assumes that separate, equal, and homogeneous actors voluntarily choose to interact to realize their separate interests, that they do so in a context unstructured by institutional arrangements other than those they set up for the purpose of their transaction, pluralists are led to stress the voluntary participation of essentially equal actors (though possessed of differing amounts of resources) on the basis of their subjective policy preferences in a context unstructured by institutions. But how do we know that the inactivity of *homo civicus* is due simply to free choice, particularly when the individual's assessment of his probabilities of succeeding are included as a factor in the choice? The conviction that one's actions will not make a difference provides a very different incentive to inactivity than lack of interest. Moreover, the contention that the many lack power because they choose to leads to the conclusion that the exercise of political power by some over others cannot be held to be coercive. Thus, pluralists conclude that inequality is real, but since freely chosen, unobjectionable.

Subjective Policy Preferences

The argument about the importance of participation as a way of determining whether people are in fact engaged in struggles for political power has as its corollary that they do so on the basis of subjective interests or preferences. Pluralists argue that any conflict over political power is determined by the subjective preferences of individual actors. As Polsby puts it, it is a mistake to impute any consciousness to a member of a group.[62] And one can only take an overt disagreement to be a disagreement in *preferences*.[63] Thus, not only are interests held to be subjective but all value conflicts are reduced to differences in preferences.[64] Values should be understood simply as "things or events desired by individuals and groups in society."[65] The stress on values as preferences means that individuals and societies could value almost anything and cuts away the ground for comparing what different individuals and groups value. Indeed, Polsby seems to think there are no important connections between what individuals will prefer and general cultural values. These too are likely to be so disparate that he suggests that researches need two separate indexes for determining how politics distributes values: an index that concerns getting generally valued things, and an index that concerns getting things an individual wants or prefers. This argument about subjective interests in politics is simply the replication at the level of politics of the principle of utility in economic transactions. The pluralists have given marginal utility a political form, that of subjective interests. Who can say *why* a buyer wants this or that particular commodity? And even if one could, the buyer's reasons are irrelevant to the completion of the transaction.

Polsby rejects all arguments for the objectivity of interests; he views disagreement as conflict of interests, and agreement as harmony of interests. He states that "to maintain the opposite seems perverse," and adds that if the researcher does not consider relevant information about actual behavior of groups in a community, one would have to regard the work as "metaphysical rather than empirical." Thus, an analyst's discussion of the real interests of a class simply amounts to a "false class consciousness" charge when the analyst disagrees with the group.[66] The shape of the political community, then, is inevitably arbitrary, and its persistence fragile, resting as it does on the transitory coincidence of arbitrary desires. The fundamental questions that have occupied thinkers concerned with public life for over two thousand years—issues of how to construct a good society—are ruled out of order.

Concrete Decisions in an Institutionless Setting

The influence of the market can be seen as well in the pluralist insistence that the study of concrete decisions on specific issues is the only way to discover what kind of power conflict was operative. One aspect of this argument is Dahl's and Polsby's insistence on the *sui generis* quality of each issue. The pluralist emphasis on outcomes of decisions translates the neoclassical economic focus on specific commodity exchanges into political terms. Power can then be understood as tied to issues and as nontransitive. Just as each individual purchase depends on the specific subjective preferences of the particular buyer and seller, each political decision depends on the specific resources and subjective preferences of those who choose to be actors in that transaction. This leads in turn to "the presumption that communities are likely to be less rather than more permanent in their patterns of decision-making".[67]

The context for these interactions is provided by conflict and competition. The pluralists most often model politics on the conflict between buyer and seller but occasionally use the implicit model of the capitalist firm (the competing interest groups). As Polsby puts it, the pluralists see American society as "fractured into a congeries of hundreds of small special interest groups, with incompletely overlapping memberships, widely differing power bases, and a multitude of techniques for exercising influence on decisions salient to them."[68] The focus on specific issues and the presumption and insistence that issues are *sui generis*, helps to atomize and to make any kind of class conflict invisible.[69] Polsby and Dahl argue that communities are impermanent and that it is an error to generalize from a single scope of influence. "Neither logically nor empirically does it follow that a group with a high degree of influence over one issue or scope will have a high degree of influence over another scope in the same system. It has to be determined empirically."[70] Dahl also argues that resources available to individuals are distributed on a similar principle. While any resources may be unequally distributed, individuals who are well off with regard to one resource are often badly off with respect to another.[71] Still, Dahl undermines his own case when he admits that political skills are middle-class skills and that it is difficult for persons of low social standing to exert direct influence on government officials.[72] The insistence that one must look at specific issues and that there are few if any connections between them defuses the search for a consistent group of powerholders. As for the correlative presumption that although any particular resource may be unequally distributed, there is no reason to believe that the group possessing a majority of one resource also possesses a majority of another works to undermine any assertion that socioeconomic class is an important factor in power relations, or more generally, that power relations may involve the systematic domination of one group by another.

Polsby's polemic against the "stratification theorists" is far less measured than Dahl's. Although he admits that economic positions and status vary, he argues that these variations are "in no wise" comparable to variations in power.[73] Those who have argued that power refers to the control some groups have over the "life chances" of others have failed to understand that "life chances" refer to the economic as well as political position of an individual. But Polsby finds "no reason" to think that there is a relation between power and life chances.[74] Power, he asserts, "is an empirically separable variable of social stratification" and must be ascertained by "specific, separate empirical indices by which power can be measured."[75]

Dahl carries further the fragmentation that results from focusing on individual issues. While one must also look simply at individuals or groups of individuals who have more influence than others, to find such a group need not indicate one has found an elite. One has simply found a group of individuals who have more influence.[76] Polsby himself sums up the impact of the focus on specific issues: The pluralist approach studies specific outcomes and presumes that the same pattern of decision making is unlikely to reproduce itself in more than one issue area.[77] Second, the focus on issues aids the atomizing of the public into a "congeries of hundreds of small special interest groups, with incompletely overlapping memberships."[78]

In sum, political power for Dahl and Polsby is a commodity possessed at least potentially by citizens best understood as potential participants in a series of market exchanges. They are seen to voluntarily become involved in a set of discrete and incommensurable decision-producing processes (commodity purchases or sales) on the basis of their own subjectively perceived interests. Each transaction is both *sui generis* and structured by nothing more than the preferences of the actors involved. Thus the pluralist understanding of power replicates important features of the market as understood by neoclassical economists and by the exchange theorists who relied on them. And because it does, the pluralist approach to politics both obfuscates and legitimates relations of domination.

Conclusion

The theories considered in this chapter were concerned to distinguish violence, coercion, persuasion, exercises of power, and the use of influence. Yet despite their disputes over the ways these distinctions operate, and the arguments about how particular acts should be characterized, the underlying issue all must face is how a legitimate human community can be constructed between power wielders and those who must comply. Their theoretical problem is how to justify the exercise of power by some over others—a necessity in all stratified societies. The theorists considered in this chapter present two sorts of answers. The first is to classify acts they found repugnant under the heading of coercion or violence and therefore not as exercises of power. Despite the frequent inclusion of threats as part of power-wielding behavior, one of the most frequent negative examples given is that of the thief who makes the threat "your money or your life." But as at least one commentator has pointed out, that same statement in slightly altered circumstances, for example, a doctor telling a patient that an expensive operation is necessary to save his life, would be seen by most in a different light.[79] The second common theoretical move consists of a refusal to recognize that communities of unequals that work for the benefit of only a few can exist at all.[80] That is, some theorists see communities of unequals as not only unjustifiable but inconceivable. Parsons, for example, never considers that a community might not be voluntary and consensual. Theorists exclude some situations by definition from the realm of activity they wish to term exercises of power. Their choice of this strategy underlines once again that the exercise of power involves questions of how one can construct a legitimate community.

There are, then, both implicit and explicit debates to be understood in the work of these writers. On the one hand, they are engaged in an effort to understand and distinguish coercion and violence from power, persuasion, and influence. On the other, they are committed to envisioning human relations as constructed on the basis of equality and voluntary interaction. But their choice of the market as an implicit model leads them to present coercion as choice and inequality as equality; that is, it leads them to both obfuscate and legitimate relations of domination.

It is important to stress that the poverty of community and the legitimation of relations of domination in the theories of power considered here cannot be held to be a conscious decision. The theorists do not favor such a community. In fact, most of them would oppose it. Lasswell, Kaplan, Dahl, Polsby, and Parsons are all uncomfortable with the inequalities represented by the fact that some have power over others. Indeed, it often seems that, as in the case of exchange theorists considered in Chapter 1, their discomfort with relations of inequality and domination is one source of their attraction to the market as a model, since the market appears to be an institution based on universalistic commitments to the equality of participants whose association with each other results solely from their freely given consent and cooperation.

It is the logic of the model itself, the theoretical possibilities and limitations inherent in the use of the market, that leads to a truncated and incomplete understanding of both human nature and the human community. When transposed into the realm of politics, the market model leads to a view that participation in political life, citizenship in a real sense, involves a voluntary choice that represents not merely consent but engagement. If citizens lack power, it is not because of institutional constraints such as the *de facto* property qualification for holders of most public offices or the impact of special interest groups on Congress, but because they freely chose to expend their resources in other areas than political life.

NOTES

1. For a sense of this literature, see Nelson Polsby, *Community Power and Political Theory* (New Haven: Yale University Press, 1st ed. 1962, 2nd ed. 1980).

2. Harold Lasswell and Abraham Kaplan, *Power and Society* (New Haven: Yale University Press, 1950), p. 78.

3. Ibid.

4. Ibid., pp. 80–82.

5. Ibid., p. xi.

6. Ibid., pp. 94, 96.

7. Ibid., p. 96, citing Robert Michels, *Political Parties* (n.p.: Hearst's International Library, 1915), p. 207. This search for control in capitalism, where real individual autonomy is impossible because of the overpowering of each of the laws of the market, is doomed to fail. But for that very reason autonomy must be stressed continually. Do they protest too much?

8. Lasswell and Kaplan, *Power and Society*, p. 81.

9. Ibid., p. xvii.

10. Ibid., pp. 97, 99.

11. Parsons in fact sees himself as engaged in an argument with Lasswell and Kaplan and with Robert Dahl.

12. See Parsons, "On the Concept of Power," in *Political Power*, ed. Roderick Bell, David Edwards, and Harrison Wagner (New York: Free Press, 1969), p. 252. It is perhaps just this outcome of collective action stressed by both Parsons and Arendt that no doubt leads Steven Lukes to see Parsons and Arendt as similar. Their accounts, however, are profoundly different in kind. See Steven Lukes, *Power: A Radical Analysis* (London: Macmillan, 1974).

13. Parsons, like Lasswell and Kaplan, feels it's necessary to comment only when power and money are not exactly parallel. Both use money in a capitalist economy as the standard from which the operation of power has to be distinguished in a few respects. Thus, Parsons comments that power differs from money since the former works on marginal utility terms, whereas the latter is linear.

14. Parsons, "On the Concept of Power," p. 256.

15. Ibid., p. 257.

16. I clearly differ with Gouldner's argument that Parsons' focus on legitimacy is part of his emphasis on the integrative importance of morality and is not directly derived from the analogy with the economy or with money. See Alvin Gouldner, *The Coming Crisis of Western Sociology* (New York: Basic Books, 1970), p. 291.

17. Parsons, "On the Concept of Power," p. 260.

18. Ibid., p. 265.

19. And power is distinguished from influence on the ground that influence operates to change the intentions or views of the others involved, whereas power operates to change the circumstances or situation of that person.

20. Parsons, "On the Concept of Power," p. 266.

21. Ibid.

22. Ibid., p. 270.

23. Ibid., p. 273.

24. Ibid., p. 276.

25. Ibid.

26. Ibid., p. 277.

27. McCarthyism for him represents such a spiral.

28. Parsons, "On the Concept of Power," p. 275.

29. Parsons is correct to criticize diffuse definitions of power, such as Dahl's ("A has power over B to the extent that he can get B to do something that B would not otherwise do"). But there are those who argue that the analysis of power by its nature cannot be made rigorous. They suggest that the search for a rigorous definition leads to a failure to recognize the important issues involved. See, for example, Hanna Pitkin, *Wittgenstein and Justice* (Berkeley: University of California Press, 1972), p. 279; and William Connolly's argument for essentially contested concepts in *The Terms of Political Discourse* (Lexington: D. C. Heath, 1974). See also Gallie, "Essentially Contested Concepts," *Proceedings of the Aristotelian Society* 56 (1955–56).

30. Gouldner has suggested that Parsons' view is a view from the top, one that recognizes only power as used "in, by, and for established social systems and established elites." Gouldner, *Coming Crisis of Western Sociology*, p. 292.

31. Parsons' account of power as wealth clearly depends on his assumption that he is discussing a system based on private property. Gouldner makes this point as well. See ibid., pp. 331–32.

32. Ibid., p. 293.

33. Gouldner's argument on this point is correct. The difficulty, however, is his attempt to locate the source of the error in Parsons' effort to extend the domain of morality. This may indeed be the motivational source for his effort, but its theoretical source lies elsewhere.

34. It should also be noted that I do not share Gouldner's position that power normally fails to discharge certain of its obligations. This is a misreading of Parsons. Power would be unable to meet its obligations if they all came due at once. But in the normal course of events in a stable society they do not. Thus, Gouldner's point—that there is a tension between power and morality—is invalid. Ibid., p. 295.

35. Gouldner is indeed correct that Parsons is only presenting the view from the top, and is only really talking about "establishment power." Ibid., p. 292.

36. On this same point of the unitary collective, see Lukes, *Power*, pp. 28–30.

37. Robert Dahl, "The Concept of Power," in Bell et al., ed., *Political Power*, p. 79. While Dahl has changed his positions in significant ways since he wrote the works considered here, his early views remain widely influential and so worthy of criticism here.

38. I should note that most of my criticism here is directed against the theorists Polsby has characterized as pluralists: "people who believe that for political purposes community actors may belong to groups, but in America rarely classes; that mostly people do not care about politics; that most resources in the system are not used for political purposes, etc." See Polsby, *Community Power*, pp. xiii and 195. 1980.

39. Robert Dahl, "A Critique of the Ruling Elite Model," in Bell et al., ed., *Political Power*; and Polsby, *Community Power* (1962).

40. Dahl, "A Critique of the Ruling Elite Model," p. 80.

41. Polsby, *Community Power* (1962), pp. 4–5. Parsons is the source of the critique.

42. Ibid., p. 109. And Polsby's own assumptions and the way they structure his thinking appear clearly in his confusion about how the power of a class and that of an individual are related. That is, he says that if the power position of a class is a collective property, the upper class must have more of the total amount than the lower class in every situation. He is also confused about how the power of a class a person belongs to can be revealed by his individual life chances (ibid., p. 110). The causality in fact works the other way. The individual life chances can be deduced from the power of a class.

43. Lukes, *Power*, p. 15.

44. These are not questions about the theorists' motivations but about the structure of the theories themselves, not about the theorists' reasons for stressing these features but about their origins and role in the work as a whole. My purpose here is not to add to the critique of pluralist theories, but to show their conceptual roots in the market model. These conceptual roots are sources of

both the attractiveness of pluralism for social theorists and of the contradictions and difficulties into which it leads them. Thus, on this point I am in agreement with Polsby. One should not claim that pluralist scholarship supports the positions it does because of the political beliefs of individual theorists. See Polsby, *Community Power* (1980), p. 150.

45. It is useful to recall Blau's distinction between competition and exchange as two different processes at work in the exchange theory of social life.

46. Polsby's reply to his critics makes this point more systematically and emphatically. While he does raise the important issue of how theorists can ground their contentions that the actors are not acting in their own best interests, he insists that we must believe that what individuals say they want is what their interests are—"by definition." *Community Power* (1980), p. 225.

47. Polsby, *Community Power* (1962), pp. 103–5.

48. Dahl, "A Critique of the Ruling Elite Model," p. 40.

49. Ibid., p. 80.

50. Polsby, *Community Power* (1962), pp. 3–4.

51. See Robert Dahl, *Who Governs* (New Haven: Yale University Press, 1961), p. 228.

52. Moreover, Dahl seems to assume that all decisions to expend resources on politics will have equivalent impact.

53. Polsby, *Community Power* (1962), p. 116.

54. Dahl, *Who Governs*, p. 228. It is the case, however, that the resources Dahl lists are available in far greater quantity to the well-to-do than the poor (see ibid., pp. 226–27, 233).

55. The example he gives contrasts the choices a young bachelor might make with those of an old man with dependents. Their individual stand might lead them to make different choices about expending resources.

56. Polsby, *Community Power* (1962), p. 116.

57. Dahl, *Who Governs*, pp. 279–80. Polsby doesn't seem to mind the lack of interest in politics.

58. Dahl, *Who Governs*, p. 279.

59. Ibid., pp. 280–81. But I will argue that to a large degree, we have in fact retained the myth.

60. Ibid., p. 225.

61. This leaves aside issues such as gun control, abortion, and the ERA where voters favor one policy and attempt to influence officials, but elected officials are not in fact controlled by the votes.

62. Polsby, *Community Power* (1962), p. 117.

63. Dahl, "A Critique of the Ruling Elite Model," p. 39.

64. Ibid.

65. Polsby, *Community Power* (1962), p. 99. See also the 1980 ed,. pp. 218–32, for his more recent restatement of his position.

66. Ibid., (1962) pp. 22–23.

67. Ibid., p. 116. He does not say what factors support this presumption.

68. Ibid., p. 118.

69. On this point see Isaac Balbus, "The Concept of Interest in Pluralist and Marxian Analysis," in *Politics and Society Reader*, ed. Ira Katznelson et al.

(New York: McKay, 1974), and "The Negation of the Negation" in *Politics and Society* 6, no. 1 (Fall 1972).

70. Dahl, "A Critique of the Ruling Elite Model," p. 38. See also Polsby, *Community Power* (1962), p. 116. The quotation is an extraordinarily illogical statement. And see *Who Governs* p. 163.

71. Dahl, *Who Governs*, p. 228.

72. Ibid., p. 233.

73. Polsby, *Community Power* (1962), p. 103. This contention depends on his own presumption of inertia.

74. There are problems he identifies as methodological, although they reveal more about his own political/ethical assumptions than anything else.

75. Polsby, *Community Power* (1962), p. 103.

76. Dahl, "A Critique of the Ruling Elite Model," p. 37.

77. Polsby, *Community Power* (1962), p. 113.

78. Ibid., p. 118.

79. See, for example, David Baldwin, "Power and Social Exchange," *American Political Science Review* 72, no. 4 (December 1978): 1230.

80. Some theorists recognize the existence of tendencies toward inequality within the field of power relations. The "agglutination" of power seen by Lasswell and Kaplan, and the existence of citizenship without power seen by Dahl present real problems for the theories. But in order to legitimate these inequalities, they must assume the existence of equality in other areas—i.e., those who lack power in the political world must have power in some other sphere, since that is where they have chosen to expend their resources.

4

Toward an Understanding of Domination: Critiques of Mainstream Theories of Power

The influential mainstream theorizations of power considered in Chapter 3 have been widely criticized. Among the most important critiques are Peter Bachrach and Morton Baratz's work on nondecisions, and William Connolly and Steven Lukes' connection of power with responsibility. My choice of these theorists rather than others is influenced in part by Lukes' own choices of theorists to consider in *Power: A Radical Analysis* and in part reflects my view that the concerns raised by these theorists (in the order considered here and in later chapters) move us step by step closer to a more accurate and adequate account of relations of class domination in advanced capitalist societies. While each theory fails as an adequate account, each helps clarify the important issues to be faced by a more adequate theorization of the class dimension of power and domination. Bachrach and Baratz edge closer to an understanding of the nature of domination and stress the importance of the relational aspect of power. Yet their account of power does not break decisively with the market as a model for understanding political life, and thus leads them to take a number of inconsistent positions. Lukes, relying on Connolly's linking of power with responsibility, attempts to develop an argument for the existence of objective interests. Yet he fails to present an epistemology and theory of human nature on which such an attribution of objective interests must rest.

Bachrach, Baratz, and the Problematic of the Market

Bachrach and Baratz's early critique of pluralist views is a valuable contribution to the literature of power and at the same time indicates the difficulty of avoiding the use of the market as a model for understanding social life.[1] Their stress on the importance of the nondecision-making process represents an important advance in understanding power, an advance that points beyond the limits to which they themselves were willing to go. They argue that when A devotes his energies to "creating or reinforcing social and political values and institutional practices that limit the scope of the political process to public consideration of only those issues which are comparatively innocuous to A," this actor has succeeded in preventing another from bringing up issues that might be "detrimental" to "A's preferences."[2] They argue further that without attention to the process by which this occurs, a process that has been described as the mobilization of bias, one cannot recognize important as opposed to unimportant issues in a community. Without knowing the rules of the game, the predominant values, and so on, one cannot tell which issues challenge these fundamentals and are therefore important.[3]

Using Dahl's work on New Haven, Bachrach and Baratz argue that the notables were uninterested in three of Dahl's "key decisions" and took an active interest only in redevelopment. By looking only at who initiated proposals that were finally adopted, or who most often successfully exercised a veto, Dahl concluded that the mayor and development administrator were the most influential parties. This, Bachrach and Baratz argue correctly, is too narrow a test. Rather, one should begin by asking neither who rules (as do theorists of elites such as C. Wright Mills) nor whether anyone at all has power (as do the pluralists), but by examining the particular mobilization of bias in the institution being examined.[4] Only after one has done so can one legitimately examine the dynamics of nondecision making. Although a nondecision-making situation itself will be difficult to observe, the process, they argue, is subject to observation and analysis by means of examining issues "of the type . . . usually kept submerged."[5] (The example they cite is the emergence of the civil rights movement in the South.) These issues are kept submerged by the dominant values and social institutions, and the role of the social scientist is to observe the ways in which the decision-making process "preempts the field previously occupied by the non-decision-making process."[6] In this way, one can recognize exercises of power that occur in circumstances other than overt conflicts.

Bachrach and Baratz's second important advance over the pluralists lies in their argument that power is relational rather than "possessive" or "substantive." In this of course they reaffirm the insight of exchange theorists and give support to my claim that issues of power are issues of community. They argue against ordinary language termi-nology, which suggests that a group or individual "has" power, that is, that power is a possession enabling its owner to secure desired goods and that a person's "power is measured by the total number of desires that he achieves."[7] They hold this view to be erroneous on three grounds: First, it fails to distinguish power over people from power over things when political power must involve other persons; that is, it fails to recognize the relational aspect of power. Second, simply attain-ing one's desires does not demonstrate an exercise of power because conflict is a necessary element in a power-wielding situation. Third, possession of the instrument of power is not possession of power itself. Indeed, power itself cannot be possessed at all.[8]

Although their argument for the relational character of power is confused, the point they seem to want to make is a good one. Power is a relation among persons that cannot be exercised apart from a social situation. (Parsons of course made a similar point in his analogy of power to money, and especially in his contention that the use of both depends on the confidence and even consent of the participants.) Among the relational characteristics of power, Bachrach and Baratz list conflict of interest or values (which they understand as preferences) between two or more persons or groups. In the face of this conflict of interest, an exercise of power requires a clear communication of what one party wishes the other to do. This clear communication is what gives a "rational attribute" to power relations. Bachrach and Baratz seem to mean that there is normally a communication (probably lin-guistic) in which the desires (preferences) of A are expressed to B, along with a threat of deprivation if B does not do X. They fail to differentiate relational from rational aspects and seem to see them as equivalent and interchangeable terms, thereby ignoring the reality of irrational or non-rational relations among people.

Despite the confusion of their account, both features of power are important. Their stress on the relational quality of exercises of power evidences their sensitivity to the relation of power and community, that is, their recognition that power relations necessarily construct a community. Their emphasis on the "rationality" involved in power relations grows from their recognition that power involves communica-tion (coupled with an implicit and mistaken notion that all communica-tion is rational). These two emphases, taken together, suggest that exercises of power (or compliance) involve more than the buying and selling of commodities by individuals who have no connections other than the momentary coincidence of their preferences. By stressing (even equating) the relational and "rational" features of power,

Bachrach and Baratz are suggesting that the exercise of power requires a relation between persons, a community. They are also suggesting that the community may well be founded on a deeper relation than the brief coincidence of subjective utility. The stress on the more broadly communicative aspect of power relations is further strengthened by their contention that power is exercised only if sanctions are threatened but not imposed. (In this, of course, they oppose Lasswell and Kaplan, who hold that decisions are brought about solely by the exercise of power, and that power involves the imposition of sanctions.[9])

Bachrach and Baratz's third important theoretical advance lies in the fact that their definition of power includes more features of domination than pluralist accounts. They define power as follows: "A power relationship exists (*a*) when there is a conflict over values or course of action between A and B; (*b*) B complies with A's wishes; and (*c*) he does so because he is fearful that A will deprive him of a value or values which he, B, regards more highly than those which would have been achieved by non-compliance."[10] Clearly, in their view something more than an uncoerced market exchange is involved.

Yet despite the important advances their theory represents, Bachrach and Baratz are still imprisoned by the market model. Their closer look at the human relations involved in power relations results most prominently in making their account even less consistent than those of others. While they argue strongly for the existence of imbalances in power relations, they also put themselves squarely within the confines of the market model by explicitly arguing against the assumption that there can be a stable power structure in a stratified but democratic society.[11] There are, in addition, a number of aspects of the social relations of the market in their understanding of power relations. These include the argument that nondecisions are structurally similar to decisions, that the mobilization of bias in one issue area indicates nothing about its mobilization in another, that only relational/rational interactions can be included as exercises of power, and that the exercise of power requires an observable conflict of subjectively perceived interests or preferences. These elements both indicate their adherence to the market as a model for understanding social life and introduce inconsistencies that ultimately negate the important conceptual advances they have made.

First, for all their stress on the importance of the "process" of mobilization of bias, they argue nondecisions are fundamentally analogous to decisions—so much so that the categories they suggest for analysis of decision making could be effectively used to study nondecision making.[12] They even argue that nondecisions that "confine the scope of decision-making are themselves (observable) *decisions*."[13] Yet these nondecisions may not be overt or specific to a given issue and may not even be taken to exclude challengers. Bachrach and Baratz argue that this unawareness "does not mean, however, that the dominant group will refrain from making non-decisions that protect or promote their dominance. Simply supporting the established political process tends to have this effect"[14]

To the extent that nondecisions are isomorphic with or structurally similar to decisions, Bachrach and Baratz are unable to follow through on their important modification of the definition of power. They retain a focus on a series of discrete transactions in the market. They have added the question of how some commodities are kept out of the market while others are allowed in, but their argument suggests that the (non)decision about what will become a political issue takes the same form as a decision on a political issue. They have made no case for this position, and in its absence there is every reason to believe that decisions and nondecisions take profoundly different forms on a variety of measures, for example, with regard to the conscious intentions of the actors, to mention only one obvious difference.

Second, Bachrach and Baratz argue, as do the pluralists, that different issue areas may not overlap and that the mobilization of bias in one area need not affect others. For example, in the context of their effort to distinguish power, influence, authority, force, and manipulation, they argue that one cannot say that A has power just because B does as A wishes. Power may be limited in scope and also in weight. Finally, they put forward a "rule of anticipated reactions." A may only demand actions he knows B will do.[15] In market terms, then, Bachrach and Baratz limit themselves to the study of only particular issues and the particular (non)decision-making process or (non)transactions surrounding them. Social structure and its effects disappear from view. My earlier discussion of the pluralists laid out the negative theoretical consequences of such disregard.

Third, while it is important to argue that power is a relation rather than a property (like money or capital), Bachrach and Baratz's basic commitment to pluralist (or behavioral, as Lukes terms it) analysis leads to a series of difficulties. They argue that although the distinction is not airtight, force and manipulation differ from power and influence in the fact that the former are nonrelational and nonrational. They refer to Friedrich's statement that authority is a quality of communication that has a potentiality of reasoned elaboration. This same quality, they argue, makes power relational and (therefore?) rational.[16]

Yet their stress on (an undefined) rationality in power relationships undermines their stress on the subjective nature of interests, values, and preferences—a feature of their argument central to their distinctions among force, manipulation, power, and influence. On the one hand, they argue that what makes power rational is its potentiality for reasoned elaboration. Reasoned elaboration involves a communication that is, at the least, objective in the sense of depending on intersubjective agreement on logic, language use, and so forth. Yet Bachrach and Baratz propose that its rational "attribute" exists only in the mind of the hearer. There may or may not be a "rational" elaboration possible; and indeed there may not be a clear communication (another of their requirements for the exercise of power). All that matters is that the hearer should, correctly or incorrectly, and for whatever personal or arbitrary reasons, regard it as such. The profound isolation of individuals from each other is clearly evidenced in this account. And this isolation at the same time undermines it. Is it plausible to argue for a rationality that consists simply in a hearer's perhaps irrational belief?

This conflict between rationality and subjectivity is a mark of the implicit presence of the market model. Specifically, as was made clear in Chapter 2, the subjectively defined nature of rationality is central to the construct of rational economic man. This account of the relational aspect of power in turn leads Bachrach and Baratz into other inconsistencies. At times they themselves treat power as a property or possession that can be "spent." For example, they argue that power may be lessened when it is successfully exercised: "Reserves" may "dry up."[17]

Finally, Bachrach and Baratz insist that there must be an observable conflict of interests in nondecision making as well as in decision making. But they cannot treat actors as isolated beings engaged in transactions on the basis of subjective preferences and at the same time focus on the mobilization of bias. They argue that for power to be exercised, the person threatened with the sanction must actually regard it as a deprivation and also must perceive that the threat is not an idle one.[18] They use the example of those who sat-in during the early years of the civil rights movement, and their lack of fear of physical injury, to suggest that even the Hobbesian "fear of violent death" is not a universal value. Thus they indicate that no common standards are applicable in advance of an account of the personal preferences or values of the participants. And these, they imply, may be almost anything. Lukes has stated that "whereas the pluralist considers as interests the policy preferences exhibited by the behavior of all citizens who are assumed to be within the political system, Bachrach and Baratz also consider the preferences exhibited by the behavior of those who are partly or wholly excluded from the political system, in the form of overt or covert grievances."[19]

Thus Bachrach and Baratz are simply giving a slightly new twist to the market view of individuals as essentially separate, with no comparability between the preferences of different persons. This, of course, reflects the viewpoint of a buyer or seller in the market: Neither cares what the interests of the other may be; neither inquires why the other wants X rather than Y. The focus on the transaction itself, and the stress on subjectivity as a fundamental feature of power wielding, depend on the truncated theory of human nature and human sociality on which market theories of social life depend. But Bachrach and Baratz's effort to cling to the subjectivism required by a market account, when coupled with their effort to examine issues that have "not been recognized as 'worthy' of public attention and controversy" and with their contention that these are "observable in their aborted form to the investigator" creates problems.[20] As long as Bachrach and Baratz insist that interests are subjective, as long as they focus on the subjective and individual nature of reasons for action, they have no basis other than their own subjective preferences on which to conduct their search for covert grievances and/or nondecisions. Thus, their argument that the demands of blacks in the South represent a "latent issue of the type which is usually kept submerged" is a covert and unacknowledged importation of their own standards into an area they have held to be defined by the preferences of the actors themselves. They, the investigators, are suggesting that they can see which issues the mobilization of bias has kept out of the political arena. What is the ground for their claim to be able to recognize interests which are not in overt conflict, but in some sense "should be"?[21]

Their major contribution lies in their sense that the creation of community involves more than a series of market relations, though they are silent as to what exactly these might be. Ironically, the very vision of the varieties of power really experienced in stratified societies informs both their contribution and their inconsistencies.

Steven Lukes: Power, Responsibility, and Objective Interests

Lukes has criticized both pluralist and alternative accounts of power. The pluralists, he argues, were simply "reproducing the bias of the system they were studying."[22] Bachrach and Baratz, while their work moved beyond some pluralist assumptions, confined themselves to studying situations where "the mobilization of bias can be attributed to" the decisions of individuals, and thus gave an account of power Lukes correctly describes as "both individualistic and intentional."[23]

Lukes' own contributions to the account of power are evident in his summary of the differences between the "one dimensional" view, the "two dimensional" view, and his own view, which he characterizes as "three dimensional" or "radical." He has made three contributions to the understanding of power: (1) Control over the political agenda must be taken into account; (2) latent as well as observable conflict must be included in studies of power relations; and (3) "real" as well as subjective interests must be examined. Each of these additions depends on the others, and taken together, all indicate that Lukes' major contribution to the analysis of power consists in his highlighting of the importance of social structure to power relations.

To assert that one group may control the political agenda leads to a search for conflicts that do not become overt, and the identifying mark for such conflicts lies in their relation to "real" interests. His first contribution calls attention to the fact that the power to control the agenda of political life is a result of social arrangements outside as well as within the political arena. These social arrangements include the existence of collectivities whose actions cannot be attributed in turn to the actions or decisions of individuals. Moreover, Lukes argues that the simple existence of these collectivities has effects independent of particular actions they may take, that is, that there is such a thing as the "sheer weight of institutions."[24]

To support this position, Lukes puts forward a distinction between the exercise of power in what he terms the "operative" as opposed to the "effective" sense. This distinction will, he believes, allow him to move beyond the individualistic and intentional connotations carried by the notion of exercising power.[25] Power in the operative sense refers to cases in which B's action might be a result of the actions of either A or A_1, since both of them have taken actions which would normally be sufficient to get B to do X. Although both exercised power sufficient to produce the result in question, one cannot say that either of them was actually responsible for the result. Lukes proposes the term "effective" exercise of power to contrast this case with a situation in which A really does make a difference in the result.[26]

This distinction allows Lukes to argue that an attribution of the exercise of power involves a double claim: (1) A acts in a certain way, and (2) B does what he would not otherwise do (think, feel, want). The counterfactual implied is "but for A, B would not have done X."[27] Overt conflict provides the relevant counterfactual. But, using Matthew Crenson's study of activity on issues of air pollution in Gary and East Chicago, Lukes suggests that there may be other grounds for using the counterfactual. That is, conflict may be latent rather than overt because a few groups or corporations control the political agenda.

The distinction between operative versus effective exercises of power functions in his argument to link the issue of latent conflict with control of the political agenda by separating the clear case in which A's action produces the desired result from cases in which, although the desired action was produced, it cannot be clearly attributed to the intentional actions of individuals. The distinction helps to support Lukes' contention that the agenda of politics may be controlled by forces other than the overt actions of identifiable individuals or groups. The "effective" exercise of power helps disconnect the action of A from the action of B, since one does not know why B acted as he did. In a sense, Lukes' distinction represents an expansion of the questions Bachrach and Baratz were asking. He asks: How can we know that the reason B did X was because A did (or threatened) Y?

The issue of latent conflict is linked with Lukes' desire to examine "real" as well as subjective interests. Lukes correctly argues that the liberal conception of interests is a very narrow one that stresses what people actually prefer and relates their interests to their policy preferences as manifested by political participation. He suggests that the reformist relates persons' interests to what they prefer, but also "allows that they may be revealed in more indirect and sub-political ways."[28] The radical, however, as Lukes describes himself, maintains that "wants may themselves be a product of a system which works against their [human] interests, and, in such cases, relates the latter to what they would want and prefer, were they able to make the choice."[29] As a criterion for the discovery of real interests, Lukes relies on William Connolly's suggestion that the real interests of an individual are represented by the policy he would choose were he to experience the results of several alternative policies.[30] The real interests of an individual, then, are defined by the researcher's judgment about what the individual would choose under conditions of relative autonomy.

There are a number of problems with the account he puts forward. Lukes continues to refer to "preferences" of individuals.[31] But the values and needs of individuals, as Lukes' own account of the important difference autonomy might make demonstrates, cannot be reduced to simple preferences. His use of "preferences" represents an incongruous holdover from the market theories of power he has criticized.[32] In addition, Lukes notes but fails to take sufficient account of the individualist and intentional language surrounding the use of the concept of power. He notes that the language of exercising power carries "the suggestion that the exercise of power is a matter of individuals consciously acting to affect others," and argues that this assumption should be abandoned since what is built into our language "provides no reason for adopting such assumptions."[33] Surely this is too facile, especially when he later uses linguistic evidence to support his own views.[34] Connolly gives a much better justification for a similar position when he argues that he does not accept ordinary language as the final court of appeal here, since an atomistic view of human nature continues to infect talk about interests.[35]

The most important difficulty with Lukes' "radical analysis" of power grows from his use of "real interests" as the criteria for uncovering latent conflict, and it is here that the limitations of his self-designated radical, but not explicitly Marxist, views make themselves most apparent. Lukes argues that persons may not express their real interests and may not even be conscious of these interests.[36] At the same time, he argues that these interests can ultimately be identified on the basis of empirically supportable or refutable hypotheses and that any adequate account of power must include attention to real interests. It is clear that Lukes' idea of real interests depends in important ways on his own sense of human requirements, such as, for example, the need for autonomy and choice. He does not, however, include a statement of his views on what autonomy means or requires, and thereby leaves his argument unsupported.

The attribution of "objective interests" can only be supported by an understanding of human nature and social life that can satisfactorily account for a systematic failure to perceive and act on one's own interests. Such an account is not simple, and a very general and cursory argument for the autonomy of individuals provides inadequate support. Marx gives a complex account of both human nature and human sociality, on the basis of which one could support an attribution of objective interests, and perhaps this is the model Lukes has in mind. But allusions to the need for autonomy are no substitute for a careful working out of the way alienated labor is constructed and surplus value extracted, both of which describe the means by which the systematic domination of the many by the few takes place. Failing such a systematic exposition, one cannot support the concept "objective interests."

The problems with Lukes' argument for the existence of objective interests are compounded by his search for latent conflict. Lukes himself recognizes several difficulties: The exercise of power may involve inaction rather than action; it may even be unconscious; and it may be exercised by collectivities.[37] Each of these possibilities poses problems for the researcher, and Lukes addresses each in turn. First, inaction is often difficult to judge, but it can, Lukes argues correctly, have specifiable consequences. While it may be difficult in practice, he suggests that at least in principle it is possible to see where inaction by an important party can lead to the nonappearance of an issue in the public arena.[38] Second, Lukes addresses the question of how power can be exercised without the exerciser being aware of his impact. He notes that an individual or organization may be unaware of their real motives, of how others interpret their actions, or finally, of the consequences of their action or inaction. Thus, identifying an unconscious exercise of power may in practice be very difficult but poses no difficulties in principle.[39] For example, can A be said to exercise power over B where knowledge of the effects of his action is not available to A? The issue, as Lukes sees it, turns on the question of *why* A did not know.

Presumably, if A did not know because of a lack of interest or refusal to find out, the judgment of his actions would differ from what it might be if the information were genuinely unavailable.[40]

The third difficulty Lukes sees in the idea of "latent conflict" is that it may blur the distinction between the intentional and voluntary connotations of power (as the term is used in ordinary speech) and structural determinations involved in actions of collectivities.[41] Lukes argues that the problem which arises when attributing exercise of power to collectivities is that some social causation should be characterized as an exercise of power, whereas other kinds of causation are more properly labelled "structural determinations."

He sees the debate between Nicos Poulantzas and Ralph Miliband as a contribution to the resolution of this issue in the context of Marxist theory. He cites Poulantzas' argument that Miliband treats individuals as agents who exercise political power when in reality they are merely the bearers of a structural determination. Poulantzas argued that class relations are "at every level relations of power. Power, however, is only a concept indicating the effect of the ensemble of the structures on *the relations of the practices of the various classes in conflict.*[42] Miliband, in response, argued that Poulantzas had stressed objective relations in such a way as to suggest that state action is wholly determined by the "objective relations," and that he had substituted the notion of objective relation for the notion of a ruling class. Their debate, as Lukes correctly points out, marks a real tension within Marxist theory, one which can be denoted in shorthand form by the label "voluntarism/determinism."[43] Lukes is correct to argue that to assimilate power to structural determination obscures class distinctions and class struggle, and his presentation of the problem points to several important issues raised by this debate.

Lukes suggests that the choice is not one between objective structural determinations and the motivations of individual actors; instead, collective political action must be included in an understanding of power. Moreover, Lukes argues that the debate itself points to an important conceptual connection between power and responsibility.[44] Thus, in Lukes' view, Poulantzas has lost track of the fact that it is in the exerciser's power to act differently and that to attribute power to someone is also to attribute responsibility for consequences held to flow from the action or inaction of certain specifiable agents. More succinctly, Poulantzas has lost track of the distinction between power and fate, that is, events that are beyond the control of "any circle or groups of men."[45] Thus Lukes proposes to restrict the concept of power to situations in which individuals or collectivities, through action or inaction, are responsible for outcomes. Where they cannot be held responsible, Lukes proposes the concept of "fate." This is a very curious resolution of the problem of voluntarism/determinism, one that is no resolution at all. The distinction between power (responsibility) and fate (structural determination) simply replicates the opposition Lukes diagnosed in the Marxist theories of Miliband and Poulantzas.

Lukes' account, however, moves us closer to an understanding of power based on systematically differing interests and possession of resources and farther away from the market theories of the pluralists. He recognizes the need (and the defects of his own work reinforce the point) for an alternative account of both human nature and human sociality as a base for developing a theory of real interests and of collective action. But he himself remains trapped in the vocabulary and outlook of those he wishes to argue against. He remains imprisoned in the market as a model for understanding power relations. Like Poulantzas and Miliband, he has not broken free of the language of interests, and thus carries the linguistic baggage of individualism and intentional actions into the heart of his theory. He retains conflict of interests as one of the central identifying features for an act of power, although he does modify the ways in which the conflict may be discovered. Lukes is attempting to put forward a concept of real human interests, but fails because he bases it only on a brief assertion of the importance of personal autonomy.

Despite these inadequacies in his argument, Lukes has made two major contributions to an adequate theorization of power and class domination in advanced capitalist society. He has demonstrated the importance of questions of social structure by emphasizing the effects of control over the political agenda, latent conflict, and real interests. And his presentation of the problems posed by structural determination versus individual action (or responsibility and fate) for Marxist understandings of political domination has opened up important avenues for further exploration.

Conclusion

The alternatives to market theories of power considered in this chapter encountered difficulties around the relation between structural determination and individual action, that is, the issue of the effect of control over the political agenda and the importance of latent as opposed to overt conflict. In addition, they have been shown to be unable to provide an adequate ground for an attribution of "real" rather than subjectively held interests. And finally, these alternatives to market theories have failed to address the question of why community should have been such a puzzle for social theorists.

These theories, unlike those previously considered, do not lead us to the Panglossian conclusion that relations of domination are either inevitable but unimportant or represent a positive social good. Yet, if we tend to regard either of these claims with suspicion, the theorizations of power considered in this chapter give us little help in turning our suspicions into a well-grounded analysis and critique of domination. Many of my specific criticisms of the theories of power considered to this point have been anticipated by others. My argument must, however, be distinguished from theirs. Despite the fact that the theories of Bachrach and Baratz, Lukes, Miliband, and Poulantzas point to the major issues to be resolved by an adequate theorization of class domination, these issues themselves must be seen as symptomatic of a deeper disorder. We cannot resolve them or even fruitfully address them without first understanding how questions of power involve questions of epistemology.

I suggested in the Introduction that theorizations of power are intertwined with theories of knowledge and that the adequacy of any understanding of power is determined by the epistemological level at which it operates. Both the problems the theorists considered in this chapter have named and have failed to resolve, and the contradictions and inconsistencies in their own work, are rooted in their theoretical reluctance to abandon the epistemological premises on which the market model rests. Only by taking up the question of the epistemological underpinnings of the market model can we put ourselves in a position to understand such issues as the relation between structural determination and individual action, between the choices individuals may make as opposed to the choices available to social groups and classes, between real and subjectively held interests. This epistemological discussion is the task of Chapter 5.

NOTES

1. They include Lasswell and Kaplan in the pluralist "school." Their critique is both substantive and methodological. For a similar and more systematic and complete argument, see Richard Bernstein, *The Restructuring of Social and Political Theory* (New York: Harcourt Brace Jovanovich), 1976; and Martin Hollis and Edward Nell, *Rational Economic Man* (New York: Cambridge University Press, 1975).

I share with Bachrach and Baratz the criticism that the pluralists' assumptions about the unreality of unmeasurable elements predetermined their findings and conclusions. See their "The Two Faces of Power," in *Political Power*, ed. Roderick Bell, David Edwards, and Harrison Wagner (New York: Free Press, 1969), p. 99. In addition, they are correct that a sound understanding of power cannot be developed on the assumption that power is completely embodied in concrete decisions and activity which is part of the process of making those decisions (ibid., p. 95). Finally, they are correct that the pluralists are unable, by their own criteria, to distinguish between key and routine political decisions due to their failure to recognize the importance of control over the agenda of politics—the mobilization of bias (ibid., p. 96).

2. Ibid., p. 95.

3. Ibid., p. 97.

4. Ibid., pp. 99. This strategy would seem to lead directly toward the disclosure of power elites.

5. Peter Bachrach and Morton Baratz, "Decisions and Non-Decisions," in Bell et al., ed., *Political Power*, p. 109.

6. Ibid.

7. Ibid., p. 101.

8. This assertion can, once again, be understood on the model of money: Possession of money is not, after all, possession of the commodities one values, but only a means to attain those values.

9. Bachrach and Baratz, "Decisions and Non-Decisions," p. 108.

10. Ibid., p. 102.

11. This of course reiterates the pluralists' contention.

12. Bachrach and Baratz, "Decisions and Non-Decisions," p. 109.

13. Steven Lukes, *Power: A Radical Analysis* (London: Macmillan, 1974), p. 18. Polsby, too, noted this difficulty. See Nelson Polsby, *Community Power and Political Theory* (New Haven: Yale University Press, 1980), pp. 210–11.

14. *Power and Poverty* (New York: Oxford University Press, 1970), p. 50, cited in Lukes, *Power*, p. 18.

15. Bachrach and Baratz, "Decisions and Non-Decisions," p. 103.

16. Ibid., p. 105.

17. Parsons in fact puts forward a clearer and more consistent account of the ways in which power analyzed on the model of the capitalist market can be both a property and a relation among people.

18. Bachrach and Baratz, "Decisions and Non-Decisions," p. 102.

19. Lukes, *Power*, p. 20.

20. *Power and Poverty*, p. 49, quoted in Lukes, *Power*, p. 20.

21. Lukes' criticism of Bachrach and Baratz misses this point and seems to find their argument here unexceptionable, no doubt in part because he repeats their error. See Lukes, *Power*, pp. 16–20.

22. Ibid., p. 36. Clearly I find this to be a simplistic evaluation.

23. Ibid., p. 39.

24. Ibid., pp. 22, 38.

25. Ibid., p. 39.

26. Ibid., p. 40.

27. Ibid., p. 41.

28. Ibid., p. 34. By "reformist" he means theories such as Bachrach and Baratz's work.

29. Ibid.

30. Ibid., citing Connolly, "On 'Interests' in Politics," *Politics and Society* 2 (1972): 472. See also Polsby, *Community Power* (1980), p. 223, who characterizes

Lukes' argument in a similar way, though from a profoundly different perspective than mine.

31. Lukes, *Power*, p. 33.

32. Lukes also takes a peculiar view of the theories of Parsons and Arendt. He fails to recognize the affinities Parsons' account has with other accounts based on the market, as well as failing to see the ways Arendt's work grows from an entirely different tradition. He sees both as participants in the debate about the coercive/consensual nature of power and argues that by stressing the consensual nature of power, both are putting forward rationally defensible conceptualizations of power that are redefinitions of power that are "out of line with the central meanings of 'power' as traditionally understood and with the concerns that have also centrally preoccupied students of power." In particular they focus on "power to" rather than "power over." Ibid., pp. 30–31. Parsons and Arendt take very different positions on power. True, both deal with the consensual aspect of power. Yet, the presuppositions from which they begin differ profoundly. Moreover, both theorists describe power as more than an interplay of coercion and consent. See Chapter 9 for a more complete discussion of Arendt's contribution.

33. Lukes, *Power*, p. 39.

34. For example, he argues that the language of power marks out the fact that to speak of power is to speak of "human agents, separately or together, in groups or organizations, through action or inaction, significantly affecting the thoughts or actions of others (specifically, in a manner contrary to their interests)." Ibid., p. 54.

35. William Connolly, *The Terms of Political Discourse* (Boston: D. C. Heath, 1974), p. 80.

36. Lukes, *Power*, p. 25.

37. Ibid., pp. 50–53.

38. Ibid, p. 51. His argument is clearly closely related in form to Bachrach and Baratz's idea that nondecisions take forms similar to decisions.

39. Ibid.

40. See also Connolly, *Terms of Political Discourse*, p. 105, on the problem of intentionality.

41. Lukes, *Power*, pp. 52–53.

42. Ibid., p. 55, citing Nicos Poulantzas, *Political Power and Social Classes* (London: New Left Books, 1975), p. 101. (Italics in original).

43. I do not mean to use these labels for either participant in the debate.

44. Lukes, *Power*, p. 54. Connolly makes a similar point when he notes that attributions of power often function as accusations. See his *Terms of Political Discourse*, p. 1.

45. Lukes, *Power*, p. 56.

5

The Market as Epistemology:
The Exchange Abstraction in
Theories of Power and
Domination

Because my discussion of the epistemology carried by the market model rests on the Marxian contention that human activity has both an ontological and epistemological status, I should outline briefly what I mean by such a claim. Most fundamentally, I propose to take seriously Marx's injunction that "all mysteries which lead theory to mysticism find their rational solution in human practice and in the comprehension of this practice."[1] Marx states the issue most generally when he asks, "What is life, but activity?"[2] For him the concept of praxis, or human work, defines what it is to be human—a striving first to meet physical needs and later for the realization of all human potentialities.[3] The concept of praxis in a more general sense refers to the idea that one can only know and appropriate the world (change it and be changed by it) through practical activity. Marx argues not only that persons are active but that reality itself consists of "sensuous human activity, practice."[4] Thus Marx can speak of products as crystallized or congealed human activity or work and can state that even plants, animals, light, and so forth constitute theoretically a part of human consciousness, and a part of human life and activity.[5]

While human beings do not create the world from nothing, human activity does produce existence differentiated into individuals, species, and all the categories we take as given, categories and concepts that respond to specific problems posed for us by social life. At the same time, however, consciousness is itself a social product. Human consciousness and the shape of human society depend on each other.

What can be appropriated (constructively incorporated into human consciousness) varies with the practical forms of human activity. The production of the linked processes of consciousness and material existence is directed by human attempts to satisfy physical needs, a process that leads in turn to the production of new needs. These efforts, however, are more than the simple production of physical existence. They form for Marx a "definite *mode of life*." Marx goes on to state: "What [individuals] are, therefore, coincides with their production, both with *what* they produce and with *how* they produce. The nature of individuals thus depends on the material conditions determining their production."[6]

My purpose in this chapter is to endorse and adopt these general positions to examine the epistemological effects of commodity production for a capitalist market in a class-divided society. Most centrally I attempt to support the contention that the exchange theories considered in Chapter 1 and the presence of the market model in the theorizations of power considered in Chapters 3 and 4 rest on the epistemology implicit in the life activity of the capitalist. As such, they replicate his experience and express his class perspective. This I suggest is the reason why adopting the market model involves one in a logic of domination that carries the variety of antisocial consequences outlined in Chapter 2.

Exchange as Epistemology: The Capitalist Experience

Let us recall the simple two-person example presented in Chapter 2—the capitalist purchasing labor power, as seen from the perspective of the capitalist, a being whose life is fundamentally structured by his participation in commodity exchange. (See p. 40.) From the perspective of the capitalist, the buying and selling of labor power, as with any other commodity, is voluntary, since each party is constrained only by his own free will; equal, since each has a commodity to exchange with the other; respectful of private property, since each exchanges only what he owns; and based on the subjective utility of the participants.

The capitalist enters the market as money owner rather than possessor of labor power. The world of the capitalist is constituted by the series of transactions marked by buying commodities from A and selling them to B, and the buying of fresh ones from A. The process of setting these commodities to work in order to produce more commodities for sale is a process in which the capitalist as capitalist or money owner does not engage.[7] (To the extent that the capitalist does so, himself performing the labor of supervising production, his opposition to the natural processes involved in production is intensified, since qualitative aspects of the process and the changes in the natural states of objects—ripening, rotting, and so on—are not things to be simply ignored as immaterial but things to be actively overcome. In addition, the passage of time is not something that can be ignored, but a real barrier, a clock against which the capitalist as supervisor works.)

Commodity exchange, then, structures the practice of the capitalist, is expressed at the level of epistemology, and in consequence, structures his thought. Its conceptual consequences have been characterized as the exchange abstraction.[8] The exchange abstraction is related to but broader than what Marx termed the fetishism of commodities. Commodity fetishism refers to the process by which people come to believe that social relations among people can take place only by means of things. In its extreme form, commodity fetishism holds that relations between people can be seen (and understood) only as relations between the things they own; it is the "mist by which the social character of labor appears to us to be an objective character of the products themselves."[9] If human knowledge depends on human action, capitalist understandings can only be constructed on the model provided by commodity exchange. What are the fundamental features of this model, and in turn, of the capitalist understanding of social life?

Commodity exchange is fundamentally tied to the structure of the commodity itself, and Alfred Sohn-Rethel has claimed that "the formal analysis of the commodity holds the key not only to the critique of political economy, but also to the historical explanation of the abstract conceptual mode of thinking and the division of intellectual and manual labor, which came into existence with it."[10] My claim here is less controversial—only that a formal analysis of the commodity and the activity of exchanging commodities can allow us to understand the sources for the partial character of bourgeois thought and for its inadequacy as a base for social theory.

Sohn-Rethel points out that the most fundamental feature of a commodity is its duality, a duality that reverberates through the transaction as a whole, and in which exchange, as such, brings only one side of the dualism into play. The dualism takes several important forms: (1) the opposition of quantity to quality and the related separation of exchange from use; (2) the separation of nature and interchange with nature from society and social interaction; (3) the opposition of the persons who are participants in the transaction; and (4) the division of mind from body, ideal from material (most particularly in the counterfactual assumption that the commodity does not deteriorate on the market). Yet exchange provides a medium for social synthesis, a synthesis that can only be partial because exchange as such takes place on only one side of these dualities, and because the community itself is only a by-product of a relation between strangers. These are the dualities that appear in other forms in Marx's distinctions between circulation and production, appearance and essence, and ideology and science (to be considered below). Clarity about the nature of commodity exchange can thus move the discussion a long way toward clarity about a number of epistemological questions.[11]

For exchange to operate, the specific products of an individual's labor must be transformed into commodities—that is, they must be given values that make them commensurable, exchange values, in addition to the value specific to each object, its use value. The former is abstract in contrast to the latter, since only quantity is important to its determination. Thus, the very concept of exchange value is characterized by an absence of qualities and differentiation of commodities only according to quantity. It is just this qualitylessness that gives commodities their reality in exchange, their concrete and specific uses at that point being only "stored in the minds of people."[12]

Commodity exchange cannot take place, however, unless this constructed duality, the separation of exchange from use, is strictly observed. Neither exchange nor use can take place at the same time as the other. And the purely social character of exchange results from this stringent separation of exchange from use. While exchange, especially its money form, has no meaning apart from the social relations in which it is embedded, use covers "all the material processes by which we live as bodily beings on the bosom of mother earth, so to speak, comprising the entirety of what Marx terms 'man's interchange with nature' in his labour of production and his enjoyment of consumption."[13]

The opposition of the persons who are participants in the transaction replicates the duality contained in the commodity itself and in the transaction. As each commodity owner approaches the market, each recognizes the other as an owner of private property. That is, there is a reciprocal exclusion of ownership concerning two sets of commodities. In addition, each move made by one participant is countered by the other. In exchange, the needs, feelings, and thoughts involved on both sides are polarized on the basis of whose they are. Not "*what* two people need or feel or think but *whose* need, feeling or thought will prevail is what shapes the relationship." Sohn-Rethel concludes: "Thus one can justifiably say that commodity exchange impels solipsism between its participants."[14] It is, fundamentally, a relation between strangers who during the transaction need share only their common interest in the transaction. The motives, needs, feelings, and desires of each are his own and not the other's. Indeed, if their needs were the same, exchange would become impossible, and the transaction could not take place.

The need for a series of counterfactual assumptions that remove the commodity from time and space and from their effects on it is symptomatic of the artificiality of this series of constructed dualisms. In the market, the processes of nature must stand still. Commodities are considered to be immutable while their price remains unaltered. From the perspective of commodity exchange, nature in the marketplace is a force both totally separate from and opposed to the human sphere. Nature "is supposed to abstain from any ravages in the body of [the] commodity and to hold her breath, as it were, for the sake of this social business of man."[15] Whereas time and space are intrinsically involved with human activity in the use of objects, exchange empties time and space of any material contents and instead gives them contents of purely social significance, which depend only on the social relations of people—most fundamentally, the relation of ownership. Time and space take on a character of "absolute historical timelessness and universality which must mark the exchange abstraction as a whole and each of its features."[16] The assumption of exemption from material changes is a conceptual fiction by means of which the reality of material change over time is simply assumed away. As Marx summed up the deeply immaterial nature of commodity exchange: "Not an atom of matter enters into the objectivity of commodities as values; in this it is the direct opposite of the coarsely sensuous objectivity of commodities as physical objects. We may twist and turn a single commodity as we wish; it remains impossible to grasp it as a thing possessing value."[17]

Despite the fact that the coarsely sensuous objectivity present in the use of commodities is absent from the activity of exchange, this sensuous objectivity remains in the minds of the commodity exchangers, "occupying them in their imagination and thoughts only."[18] In exchange, then, mind and action part company and go in different directions, the one private, the other social. The separation of mind from action, then, lies at the heart of commodity exchange. This split between the two leads toward a kind of necessary false consciousness, a false consciousness that denies the importance of the bodily, that gives great weight to purely quantitative differences, and that, basing itself on the experience of exchange, treats the private activities of mind or imagination as profoundly different entities than those engaged in by means of overt (sensible) activities.[19]

Despite the duality and solipsism inherent in commodity exchange, it remains the source of a social synthesis, a synthesis established by the network of exchange rather than use—by buying and selling rather than production. The community created in this way is itself abstract because the producers do not come into social contact with each other except by means of the exchange of their products.

Thus the real social and historically determined character of the labor of each only appears in the form it takes during the act of exchange. That is, the specificity of the labor of each (whether construction or sculpture) is apparent to the other only in its objectified commodity form.[20]

Sohn-Rethel concludes that the formal analysis of the commodity form and its consequences for the activity of exchange reveal the act of exchange as "abstract movement through abstract (homogeneous, continuous, and empty) space and time of abstract substances (materially real but bare of sense-qualities) which thereby suffer no material change and which allow for none but quantitative differentiation (differentiation in abstract, non-dimensional quantity.)"[21] The community that emerges from the exchanging agents practising their solipsism against each other is likewise abstract and universal in the sense of being emptied of space and time, a community that is a by-product of actions and intentions aimed at purposes other than the creation of a community.

The categories of thought embodied in the activity of exchange express the exchange relation and as such do not penetrate but only express the mystery of the commodity form as it is experienced in exchange: the dependence on quantity, the duality and opposition of nature to culture, the rigid separation of mind and body. From the perspective of exchange, where commodities differ from each other only quantitatively, it seems absurd to suggest that labor power differs from all other commodities. Exchange is concerned only with labor power's *quantitative* relation to other commodities, and thus envisions its sale and purchase simply as a contract between free agents, in which "the agreement [the parties] come to is but the form in which they give legal expression of their common will." It is a relation of equality, "because each enters into relation with the other, as with a simple owner of commodities, and they exchange equivalent for equivalent. . . . The only force that brings them together and puts them in relation with each other, is the selfishness, the gain and the private interests of each." Exchange structures the entire existence of the capitalist—the buyer of any commodity and the seller of all but one. Perhaps because it is not his own life activity that changes hands (as is the case with the worker), the capitalist can successfully maintain that the formal symmetry of the situation is a real symmetry. Here, then, is the real, material source for the thesis discussed in Chapter 2, that the prices of potatoes, capital, and labor power have a fundamental equivalence; now we can begin to understand why and to whom such a claim might have a surface plausibility. The formal symmetry of the transaction can appear to be a real symmetry only for the capitalist, but given the dominance of capital, can be made plausible to all parties.

The Exchange Abstraction, Exchange Theories, and the Fetishism of Commodities

This discussion of the importance of activity can form the basis for reunderstanding the use of the market model as a basis for theories of power as an outgrowth of that peculiar phenomenon of the level of circulation in capitalist societies: the fetishism of commodities. On this basis we can understand not only the inadequacy of the market as a model for social life but also why such social theories have seemed so widely attractive, and why the problem of community has proved so puzzling for social theorists. The theorizations of power and the difficulties they encounter are directly rooted in the capitalist experience of a life structured by the exchange of commodities. The abstractness inherent in all commodity exchange lays the basis for the more thoroughgoing fetishism of societies fundamentally structured by commodity exchange. The theoretical choices made by individual writers come to appear more as choices deeply reflective of the social activity of one particular class. Thus, one can see how the exchange theories of social life considered in Chapter 1 and, to a lesser extent, the market theories of power considered in Chapters 3 and 4 simply trace the outlines of the commodity itself as it exists in the process of exchange. As a result, social relations between people are understood to be not only conducted by means of things but as the reverse of what they really are: "Commodities," in a curious reversal, writes Marx, "appear as the purchasers of persons."[22]

The exchange abstraction, the epistemological form of human activity in commodity exchange, has marked theories modeled on the market in specific, though varied, ways. Thus they cannot be held to be entirely determined by the categories of commodity exchange, yet one finds that each theorist has to a large extent followed the implicit epistemological directions of commodity exchange in theorizing power. The influence of the qualitylessness of the commodity exchange led theorists of power to attempt to develop similarly qualityless but formally equivalent categories: Blau and Homans' category (commodity) of "social approval" (purchased with "help"); Lasswell, Kaplan, Dahl, and Polsby's "decisions" (purchased with expenditures of effort or exercises of power); Parsons' equation of power with money (to be spent for a variety of social commodities or invested at interest). All these represent what Marx termed the way a social relation between two persons can take the form of a relation between two separately produced commodities, a relation characterized by the dominance of abstract quantity. Thus, just as Marx described the basis of the fetishism of commodities as located in the fact that each produces in private and confronts the other only by means of the interaction of products, this relation has been elevated to the status of a fundamental structure of social interaction.

The opposition of participants in commodity exchange appears clearly in Blau's statement that the first choice of each participant in social exchange is the next to last choice of the other, and in Lasswell and Kaplan's argument that decisions grow out of the opposed efforts of individuals to maximize their own powers. It appears as well in Polsby's and Dahl's atomization of political participants and their insistence that groups are not the relevant unit of analysis: Groups *may* form temporarily on the basis of the private and subjectively held preferences of individuals, they hold, but no intrinsic connections among persons should be sought.

The most prominent forms taken by the several counterfactual assumptions and contentions required by commodity exchange are the assumptions that social actors exchange or expend their resources for fixed commodities (e.g., help, social approval, sexual services, firm commitments, outcomes, decisions) in contexts structured only by the current preferences (subjective utilities) of the actors. (The falsity of these contentions was demonstrated in Chapter 2.) The removal of the transaction from time and space is evidenced as well by the claims to the universality of this mode of social interaction; we can now understand something of the material roots of Homans' assertion that men have "always" explained their behavior in terms of profit and loss. Such a statement simply confirms Marx's charge that commodity exchange, understood only at the level of circulation rather than production (i.e., from the point of view of the capitalist) is seen to be natural, universal, and ahistorical.[23]

The separation of mind and action in commodity exchange (coupled with the solipsism of the participants) appears most commonly in market-influenced theories in the form of an insistence that interests may only be understood as individual and subjectively held preferences, fundamentally inaccessible to the observer. Their content is held to be private and analytically irrelevant except insofar as it is expressed in overt and observable actions. Here one should remember Lasswell and Kaplan's stress on the importance of overt threats or promises for marking the occurrence of an exercise of power, or Polsby's and Dahl's insistence that overt behavior in conflict situations is essential if the analyst is to discern an exercise of power. Subjective states and overt actions are by implication not only incommensurable but also have no necessary connections. One might even hold that this disjunction forms a source for the pluralist distinction between potential and actual power, the one available to anyone, the other to only a few; the one a state of mind, the other a result of overt action; in all cases, the solipsism inherent in commodity exchange defines community as a problem for the theorists. The depth of the isolation of individuals from each other is nowhere more clear than in Blau's discussion of the courtship market. There, solipsism invades even the relation between potential lovers. The intentions and goals of the participants have in common only their interest in completing the exchange of sexual services for firm commitments. Otherwise their interests are polarized along the dimension of whose interests and intentions they are.

In addition to situating exchange theories of social life as instances of the fetishism of commodities and providing an answer to the question of why community should pose such problems for theorists transfixed by exchange, we can now deepen the criticism of the market as a model for understanding social life. In Chapter 2 I argued that the use of the market carried a number of unfortunate consequences, among them circularity, inaccuracy, and important but often implicit justifications of domination. Moreover, I argued that the market was not universal but had certain historical and class-specific roots. We have now managed to locate these problems and class-specific roots in the acitivity of commodity exchange and to trace the epistemological consequences of this activity when it is elevated to the organizing principle of social life. The inadequacy of this class-specific understanding of power relations can now be seen to be rooted in the partial and inadequate character of the human activity the theorists have chosen as their model.

If one recognizes the use of the market as a model for social life as an expression of the fetishism of commodities, one can understand the reasons why community has posed such a problem for the theorists considered in Chapters 1, 3, and 4. In a society modeled both in fact and in theory on the exchange of commodities, the attainment of a complex and deep-going series of relations with others is indeed difficult. Community itself is only a by-product of activities directed at other ends, and thus the social synthesis that results from exchange is one in which persons are in opposition to each other and associate with each other only indirectly, by means of the exchange of things passed back and forth on the basis of self-interest. On the basis of the analysis presented here, it is no surprise to find an early theorization of this kind of community in the work of Adam Smith, nor that it was the eighteenth century that marked both the development of the concept of interest and important advances in capitalist development. In addition, one can see the deep and implicit ways in which the market as epistemology can pose problems for the unwary theorist, however committed to social change she or he might be. The critics of market theories considered in Chapter 4 present interesting and instructive cases in point. (See also Appendixes 1–3).

I argued that their efforts to construct an adequate theory of power had failed. But to understand both their usefulness and why they ultimately fail as alternatives we must return to the second claim I have taken over from Marx: that the class that controls the production of goods and services controls mental production as well. Thus, "the ruling ideas are nothing more than the ideal expression of the dominant material relationships, the dominant material relationships grasped as ideas; hence of the relationships which make the one class the ruling one, therefore, the ideas of its dominance."[24]

Critics of Mainstream Theories of Power

Despite their real efforts to move beyond the class perspective that denies the reality of social institutions in structuring and limiting the choices of actors, the theorists considered in Chapter 4 have not escaped from the separation of mind and action inherent in exchange. The effects of this failure are most prominent in their ability to name but not resolve the problems centered on the relation of latent vs. overt conflict, real vs. subjectively held interests, or power vs. fate. These dualities have posed problems for Marxist theory as well, and the Marxian form of this debate, structural determinatism vs. methodological individualism, can provide a setting in which these issues can be addressed in their most complex and pointed forms.

Lukes has argued that the problem underlying the Miliband/ Poulantzas debate is one of identifying collective responsibility and determining where "structural determination ends and power and responsibility begins." He insists, however, that the purpose "of locating power is to fix responsibility for consequences held to flow from the action, or inaction, of certain specifiable agents."[25] The problems posed for Marxists are really more complex than he allows. The argument between determinism and individualism is too broadly drawn. Yet Lukes has named one of the major issues for Marxist theory, an issue that remains unresolved in either Miliband's *The State in Capitalist Society* or Poulantzas' *Political Power and Social Classes*.

The failures of these efforts, however, differ profoundly, and an examination of these twin (and in a sense obverse) failures can be important in both documenting the theoretical effects of commodity exchange and in setting out the powerful account of the nature of class domination Marxist theory can provide once it is epistemologically relocated. The more recent work of both Poulantzas and Miliband coupled with a return to Marx's own work can demonstrate both the real contributions and important limitations of the Marxist problematic. This account will in turn be important in constructing an alternative and more encompassing theory of power, one that can theorize gender as well as class. The debate about power (or, in more Marxist terms, the organization of class domination) has been situated within the field generally defined by theories of the capitalist state. Here, I attempt to avoid the wide variety of issues raised by this large and growing litera-ture by concentrating only on the work of Miliband and Poulantzas as it contributes to an understanding of power.[26]

Miliband describes his purpose as arguing against the view that power in Western societies is "competitive, fragmented and diffused: everybody, directly or through organized groups has some power and nobody has or can have too much of it."[27] He is arguing instead that this view is "in all essentials wrong—that this view, far from providing a guide to reality, constitutes a profound obfuscation of it."[28] He claims Marxist theory as the locus of his investigation, although he is nowhere more specific about the nature of this Marxism than to point out, quite correctly, that Marxism lacks a theory of state power.[29] To fill this void, Miliband sets out, first, to demonstrate that an economically dominant class exists, one that controls both wealth and the major institutions of society. They are, he argues, the personnel who staff the institutions of the state.[30] He then proceeds to show that this economically dominant class (whether owners or high-level managers) has important ties to and controlling interests in the institutions of representative govern-ment and in the administration and the police, and possesses veto pow-er over most public policy decisions. He goes on to discuss their influ-ence over political socialization and communications, and takes up the role of ideology in obtaining the population's consent to the continua-tion of capitalism.

On the basis of the evidence he has presented, Miliband concludes that "the most important political fact about advanced capitalist societies, it has been argued in this book, is the continued existence in them of private and ever more concentrated economic power. As a result of that power, the men—owners and controllers—in whose hands it lies enjoy a massive preponderance in society, in the political system, and in the determination of the state's policies and actions."[31] This unequal economic power in turn produces political inequality.

While it supports the argument against the pluralists by demon-strating the existence of a group of people who are in positions to con-trol most of the institutions of public life, the book is profoundly flawed. The source of the difficulties stems, ironically, from what has been generally agreed to be the book's greatest strength: its direct engagement with market theorists. In attempting to confront the plur-alists on their own ground, Miliband remained trapped within their problematic and therefore gave far too much emphasis to the intention-al actions of individuals. He therefore treated societal causation too much in terms of the strategies and actions of individuals and groups. As one group of critics put it, the "formation of state policy seems to be reduced to a kind of voluntarism on the part of powerful people."[32] As a result of his concentration on the acts of so few powerful figures, Mili-

band downplays the possibilities of reform, especially reform from below, and concludes the book with a very pessimistic argument that no
action by the Left is likely to make much difference.[33]

In addition, by putting himself on the terrain of bourgeois
theories, or within what has been called the "problematic of the subject," he fails to understand that "it is never possible simply to oppose
concrete facts to concepts, but that these must be attacked by other
parallel concepts situated in a different problematic. For it is only by
means of these new concepts that the old notions can be confronted
with 'concrete reality.'"[34] That is, Miliband's work (like that of Lukes)
fails to address the need for epistemological underpinnings for an
alternative theorization of power. Hollis and Nell pointed clearly to the
epistemology that supported neoclassical economic theory and to the
need for an epistemological critique. And now that we have located the
epistemology of market theories in commodity exchange, we can see
that this same epistemology underlies Miliband's stress on the voluntary actions of powerful individuals. The theoretical consequences of
Miliband's failure to relocate his theory have been well stated by
Poulantzas: "To transpose this problematic of the subject into Marxism
is in the end to admit the epistemological principles of the adversary
and to risk vitiating one's own analyses."[35]

By taking individuals, or even aggregations of individuals, as the
relevant actors, Miliband failed to give proper attention to the structural limits on individual and intentional action. Poulantzas is correct that
Miliband fails to recognize that individuals are not the "origin of *social
action*" and that explanations should not be "founded on the *motivations of conduct* of the individual actors."[36] The search for a series of
powerful individuals, whatever their common social origins, does violence to the Marxian understanding of class as fundamentally rooted in
the relations of production. Despite Miliband's demonstration that a
small group of owners and managers control the relevant institutions
of representative government, bureaucracy, media, and so on, their
theoretical status remains contingent. Miliband leaves unanswered the
question of why it is this group rather than another that holds power.
On his account it might be a historical accident and not an arrangement
intrinsic to a particular organization of the economy.[37]

I do not of course mean to argue that Miliband's theory tells us no
more about domination than do theories modeled explicitly on the
market. Nevertheless, his stress on the motivations for the conduct of
powerful individuals gives evidence that he has not fully relocated his
theory on an epistemological base other than commodity exchange.
And since there, mind and action go in opposite directions, to choose
to stress the one is to fail to understand the importance of the other.

Poulantzas attempts to move the analysis of class domination away from the intentional action of individuals, the "problematic of the subject." He sees his purpose as providing a theory of domination, one that "implies the possibility of demarcating a clear line between the *places* of domination and subordination," and argues that the concept of power has reference only to class struggle and therefore can be traced from the structures of society.[38] In addition, his analysis is meant to counter a simplistic economic determinism. Success at these tasks would represent an important contribution to theories of power, yet Poulantzas' account is marred by a variety of difficulties: His confused analysis leads on the one hand toward structural functionalism, and thereby a form of determinism, and on the other toward a replication of some features of the pluralist arguments considered in Chapter 3.

Poulantzas argues that power "specifies the effects of the ensemble of [levels of the structure] on the relations between social classes in struggle. *It points to the effects of the structure on the relations of conflict between the practices of the various classes in 'struggle.'*"[39] Power, then, is an effect, and economic power in particular is an "overdetermined effect." At the same time, Poulantzas proposes a second understanding of power, that it "designate[s] *the capacity of a social class to realize its specific objective interests.*"[40] Given the structure of class society, power must relate to conflict, since the capacity of one class to realize its own interests is in opposition to the capacity and interests of other classes.[41] And because Poulantzas hopes to develop a Marxist theory of domination totally devoid of psychological connotations, he argues that "the concept of power cannot be applied to 'inter-individual' relations or to relations whose constitution in given circumstances is presented as independent of their place in the process of production, i.e., in societies divided into classes, as independent of the class struggle."[42] Thus Poulantzas takes up a position on the side of the mind/action duality that excludes mind altogether.

There are several problems with these formulations, among them, vagueness, confusion, and contradictory definitions. But these problems are merely in turn symptoms of more serious epistemological failure. Poulantzas restricts power relations to the narrow arena of class struggle on the basis of his attempt to link the concepts of class and power through the argument that the concepts of "class and power are akin" because both are "constituted" in the field "bounded by social relations."[43] An argument such as this could link any concept in the field of social relations with any other; it cannot support his restriction of power relations to class relations. Second, Poulantzas' definitions reflect his confusion of effect with ability, or domination with capacity.

The distinction between the two, coupled with the recognition of the specific roles of both, is important to Marxist theory, but Poulantzas presents one definition following the other as though he had failed to recognize the distinct role of each concept.[44]

Third, Poulantzas fails to present an adequate account of the concept of interest, even within the Marxian problematic. His efforts to purge it of "psychological connotations" point toward a location of objective interests in the structures that constitute class, but he attempts to draw back from this (as a part of his rejection of simple determinism) and insists on the one hand that "the concept of interest can only be related to the field of practices" and on the other that "this does not mean that interests consist of behavioral motivations." Poulantzas' effort to locate interests in a vaguely defined field of "class practices" ("a concept which covers not behavior but an operation carried on within the limits imposed by the structure") compounds the confusion. Poulantzas' efforts to combat determinism fare no better. Miliband has argued that Poulantzas' work terminates in a kind of determinism. My own reading suggests that both determinism and, contradictorily, a return to the pluralist or even Parsonian model are involved. Poulantzas' adoption of the structuralist model of Althusserian Marxism is clearly at work here.[45]

In order to combat a simplistic reading of power relations directly from economic relations, Poulantzas argues that the powers of a class must be "characterized by the specific autonomy of the levels of structures and practices, and of the respective class interests." This done, one can see the distinction between economic, political, and ideological power.[46] The "autonomy" of political and economic domination is an important theme in Marx's theory, while their radical disjunction into separate spheres is much more characteristic of Althusser's revision of it. Yet because Poulantzas is operating on the latter model, he pictures the spheres not as autonomous but independent.[47] Thus he stresses the fact that a class may have the capacity to realize its economic interests (something to which he refers by the term "trade unions") without having the capacity to realize its political interests, and vice versa.[48] This stress on the intransitivity of power across spheres suggests that we have returned to the pluralist position: Power in one area provides no indication of power in any other. In consequence, this theoretical move undermines Poulantzas' own stated assumption that there is such a thing as a dominant class. Yet he nowhere makes a case for the existence of such a class, and the division between different spheres leaves his claim of systematically asymmetrical class relations unsupported.

Poulantzas' failure to account for class domination is accompanied by the introduction of a more sophisticated determinism. He argues that despite Marx's own interchangeable usage of the terms "social relations of production" and "relations of production," structures and social relations must be differentiated. Social relations, as designated by concepts such as "class," are simply the "effects" of the structures.[49] As Clarke has pointed out, on this model, relations of domination are effects of the structure at the level of social relations. "The dominance of the dominant class can, therefore, only be explained by reference to technical features of the process of production itself, and specifically to an implicit technically necessary dominance of the means of production over the labour process."[50] Poulantzas, then, excludes motivational considerations altogether from his account of class domination. He has chosen to stress only the "structural determination" side of the duality.

These failures of both Miliband and Poulantzas demonstrates the strength of commodity exchange as a model for understanding social relations. There is a sense in which one might say that Miliband and Poulantzas have replicated the dual conclusions carried by exchange theory but simply reversed their valuation. Exchange theorists concluded that relations of domination were inevitable but unimportant, or alternatively that they resulted from the voluntary actions of individuals and were therefore socially beneficial. Miliband's failure to break with the problematic of the subject links him with those who argue that relations of domination result from the actions of individuals. He, however, clearly considers these a social harm rather than benefit. Poulantzas' position that relations of domination are simply effects of the structures links him with the other conclusion: Relations of domination are inevitable, however difficult and troubling they may be.

The errors of both sides in the debate about the importance of intentional action as opposed to structural determination illustrate the wrongheadedness of Lukes' argument that one must attempt to draw a line between power and fate. Such an effort is not simply difficult but theoretically unhelpful. The attempts of both Miliband and Poulantzas to draw such a line in Marxist theory obscure the roles both of structural features of society and of intentional actions by individuals and groups. Neither theorist brings us close to an understanding of the meaning of Marx's own statement that "political power is precisely the official expression of antagonism in civil society."[51]

The problem here is that as long as one remains at the epistemological level defined by or even influenced by the exchange of commodities, mind and action are not only incommensurable but analytically impossible to link. The deep problem is the theorization of social life in any of the terms provided by the commodity form. While theorists who base their accounts on the market simply expressed the relationships implicit in this form, their critics demonstrate that the dominant material relations, while they cannot be said to totally determine theories of social life, do have important effects.

If the ruling class controls not only the means by which goods are produced but also the means of mental production, then one should not be surprised by the real difficulties faced by any theories that attempt to oppose themselves not only to the ideas of the ruling class but to the real social relations that express this dominance, and in which all members of society have no choice but to participate. These effects can vitiate much of the critical force of alternate theories. Thus, just as the problems I pointed to in the theories of those who used the market as a model for understanding social life were symptomatic of deeper problems at the level of epistemology, so too the difficulties encountered by their critics (for example, being able to name but not resolve problems centered on the relation between structural determination and individual action, or their failure to account for why community should pose such problems for social theorists) are symptoms of their failure to break with the market model at the level of epistemology, and the concomitant failure to base their theories in a more encompassing form of human activity.

This discussion of the difficulties caused for Marxist theory by the failure to relocate the theory at a different epistemological level stands as both warning and advice to theorists attempting to understand gender as well as class domination. It is possible to construct an account of class domination that can avoid the pitfalls encountered by the theories considered to this point. And although Miliband and Poulantzas' early work serves more as warning than as model, their more recent work can be valuable in the construction of a Marxist account of class domination that rejects the duality of individual action and structural determination, or power vs. fate. We must begin again by laying out the epistemological foundation on which the theory of class domination should be relocated, a task that those of us attempting to explore the systematic domination of one gender by the other should find very instructive.

NOTES

1. Eighth Thesis on Feuerbach, in Karl Marx, "Theses on Feuerbach," in Karl Marx and Frederick Engels, *The German Ideology*, ed C. J. Arthur (New York: International Publishers, 1964), p. 121.

2. Karl Marx, *Economic and Philosophic Manuscripts of 1844*, ed. Dirk Stuik (New York: International Publishers, 1964), p. 111.

3. Here I will use praxis as the most general reference to human self-

realizing activity. Marx often refers to this activity as "work" and sometimes even as "labor." There are, however, some distinctions that can be made among these concepts. See, for example, Bertell Ollman, *Alienation: Marx's Conception of Man in Capitalist Society* (New York: Cambridge University Press, 1971), pp. 99–105; and Marx and Engels, *The German Ideology*, p. 94.

4. Marx, "Theses on Feuerbach," p. 121.

5. Marx, *1844 Ms.*, p. 114.

6. Marx and Engels, *The German Ideology*, p. 42.

7. See Marx's fascinating discussion of how it is that only labor is capable of transforming itself into capital. *Capital*, trans. Ben Fowkes (Middlesex, England: Penguin, 1975.), 1:994–95. Hereinafter cited as *Capital* (Penguin ed.).

8. Alfred Sohn-Rethel, *Intellectual and Manual Labor: A Critique of Epistemology* (London: Macmillan, 1978).

9. See, for comparison, Marx's discussion of fetishism in *Capital* (New York: International Publishers, 1967), 1:70 ff. Hereinafter cited as *Capital* (International ed.). The quotation is from p. 74.

10. Sohn-Rethel, *Intellectual and Manual Labor*, p. 33.

11. I should note that my analysis both depends on and is in tension with Sohn-Rethel's. Sohn-Rethel argues that commodity exchange is a characteristic of all class societies, one that comes to a head in capitalism or takes its most advanced form in capitalism. His project, which is not mine, is to argue (a) that commodity exchange, a characteristic of all class societies, is an original source of abstraction; (b) that this abstraction contains the formal element essential for the cognitive faculty of conceptual thinking; and (c) that the abstraction operating in exchange, an abstraction in practice, is the source of the ideal abstraction basic to Greek philosophy and to modern science. See ibid., p. 28.

In addition to analyzing the commodity for a different purpose, I should indicate several major differences with Sohn-Rethel. First, he treats the productive forces as separate from the productive relations of society, and ascribes too much autonomy to them. (See, for example, his discussions on pp. 84–86, 95.) My own position is closer to, though not identical with, that articulated by Stanley Aronowitz, *Insurgent Sociologist*, 8, nos. 2–3 (Fall 1978), that the distinction between the two is better seen as an analytic device than a feature of the real world. Second, Sohn-Rethel characterizes the period preceding generalized commodity production as primitive communism (see p. 98). This is, however, an inadequate characterization of tribal societies given such studies as those of Claude Lévi-Strauss, *The Savage Mind* (Chicago: University of Chicago Press, 1966); and Mary Douglas, *Purity and Danger* (London: Routledge and Kegan Paul, 1966). See below, Appendix 1, for a discussion of the former.

12. Sohn-Rethel, *Intellectual and Manual Labor*, pp. 52, 19, 46. See also *Capital* (Penguin ed.), 1:137. As Sohn-Rethel lays it out, the most abstract form of exchange value is money—commensurable to any commodity and consisting of nothing but the form detached from the use-value of the commodities. What makes it money, he points out, has nothing to do with anything felt or perceived by the five senses (Sohn-Rethel, *Intellectual and Manual Labor*, p. 2). He puts forward a very entertaining example differentiating what a dog, as opposed to a human, understands about the role of money and an exchange of commodities more generally in the form of a joint trip to a butcher shop (ibid., p. 45).

13. Ibid., p. 27.

14. Ibid., p. 41.

15. Ibid., pp. 25, 55.

16. Ibid, p. 49; see also p. 48.

17. *Capital*, (Penguin ed.), 1:138.

18. Sohn-Rethel, *Intellectual and Manual Labor*, p. 36.

19. Consider, for example, the lengthy Wittgensteinian dispute about the privacy of sensations such as pain.

20. Marx, *Capital* (International ed.), 1:74.

21. Sohn-Rethel, *Intellectual and Manual Labor*, p. 53.

22. Marx, *Capital* (Penguin ed.), 1:1003.

23. Marx, *Capital* (International ed.), 1:73–77.

24. Marx and Engels, *The German Ideology*, p. 64.

25. Steven Lukes, *Power: A Radical Analysis* (London: Macmillan, 1974), p. 56, relies strongly on William Connolly's working out of the links in *The Terms of Political Discourse* (Lexington: D. C. Heath, 1974).

26. The debate has been both extensive and international and to date has led toward the production of both national differences and cross-national tendencies such as those denoted by the labels "instrumentalist," "structuralist," "Hegelian-Marxist." There have been a number of contributions to the debate: Louis Althusser, "Ideology and Ideological State Apparatuses," in *Lenin and Philosophy and Other Essays* (New York: Monthly Review Press, 1971); Isaac Balbus, "Ruling Elite Theory vs. Marxist Class Analysis," *Monthly Review* 23, no. 1 (1971); Etienne Balibar, *The Dictatorship of the Proletariat* (London: New Left Books, 1977); Amy Bridges, "Nicos Poulantzas and the Market Theory of the State," *Politics and Society* 4, no. 2 (1974); G. William Domhoff, *Who Rules America?* (Englewood Cliffs, N.J.: Prentice-Hall, 1967); David Gold, Clarence Lo, and Erik Olin Wright, "Recent Developments in Marxist Theories of the Capitalist State," *Monthly Review* 17, no. 56 (October and November 1975); J. Holloway and S. Piccioto, *State and Capital* (Austin: University of Texas Press, 1979); Ralph Miliband, *The State in Capitalist Society* (New York: Basic Books, 1969); Ralph Miliband, "The Capitalist State—Reply to Nicos Poulantzas," *New Left Review* 59 (1970); Ralph Miliband, "Poulantzas and the Capitalist State." *New Left Review* 82 (1973); Ralph Miliband, *Marxism and Politics* (New York: Oxford University Press, 1977); James O'Connor, *The Fiscal Crisis of the State* (New York: St. Martin's Press, 1973); Claus Offe, "Advanced Capitalism and the Welfare State," *Politics and Society* 2, no. 4 (1972); Claus Offe, "The Abolition of Market Control and the Problem of Legitimacy," *Kapitalistate* 1–2 (1973); Nicos Poulantzas, "The Problem of the Capitalist State," *New Left Review* 58 (1969); Nicos Poulantzas, *Political Power and Social Classes* (London: New Left Books, 1973); Nicos Poulantzas, *State, Power and Socialism* (London: New Left Books, 1978); Goran Therborn, *What Does the Ruling Class Do When It Rules?* (London: New Left Books, 1977); Alan Wolfe, "New Directions in the Marxist Theory of Politics," *Politics and Society* 4, no. 2 (1974); Alan Wolfe, *The Limits of Legitimacy* (New York: Free Press, 1977).

27. Miliband, *State in Capitalist Society*, p. 2.

28. Ibid., p. 4.

29. Ibid., pp. 5–6.

30. Ibid., pp. 63 ff. He notes that although working-class people do sometimes succeed in attaining these positions, those who succeed are often most ready to adopt upper-class attitudes and values.

31. Ibid., p. 265.

32. Gold, Lo, and Wright, "Marxist Theories of the Capitalist State," p. 35.

33. Miliband, *State in Capitalist Society*, pp. 265–77.

34. Poulantzas, "Problem of the Capitalist State," p. 69.

35. Ibid., p. 71.

36. Ibid., p. 70.

37. It should now be evident why C. Wright Mills' work on the power elite has been absent from my work. Not only was he engaged in a search for powerful individuals but he also explicitly rejected the linking of economics and politics. His analysis, then, while descriptively interesting, has little theoretical significance. See Mills, *The Power Elite* (New York: Oxford University Press, 1959), p. 277. See also Poulantzas, *Political Power and Social Classes*, pp. 103, 117–19.

38. Poulantzas, *Political Power and Social Classes*, pp. 105–7.

39. Ibid., p. 99.

40. Ibid., p. 104.

41. Poulantzas recognizes the problems posed by the concept of interests, but himself fails to give any adequate account of this troublesome concept and in the end leaves his meaning implicit. I hope to avoid the issue of interests, whether objective or subjective. There has already been a great deal written on the subject, both within and without Marxist theory. See, for example, William Connolly, "On Interests in Politics," *Politics and Society* 2 (1972); Isaac Balbus, "The Concept of Interest in Pluralist and Marxian Analysis," in *The Politics and Society Reader*, ed. Ira Katznelson, Gordon Adams, Philip Brenner and Alan Wolfe (New York: McKay, 1974); Isaac Balbus, "The Negation of the Negation," *Politics and Society* 3 (1972); Theodore M. Benditt, "The Concept of Interest in Political Theory," *Political Theory* 3, no. 3 (August 1975); Felix Oppenheim, "Self-Interest and Public Interest," *Political Theory* 3, no. 3 (August 1975); Richard Flathman, "Some Familiar but False Dichotomies Concerning 'Interests': A Comment on Benditt and Oppenheim," *Political Theory* 3, no. 3 (August 1975).

42. Poulantzas, *Political Power and Social Classes*, p. 106.

43. Ibid., p. 99.

44. On the importance of "powers" in Marxist theory, see, for example, Ollman, *Alienation*, esp. pp. 75–95.

45. See my "Louis Althusser and the Unity of Science and Revolution" (Mimeo), and Simon Clarke, "Marxism, Sociology and Poulantzas's Theory of the State," *Capital and Class* 2 (Summer 1977), for critiques of this model.

46. Poulantzas, *Political Power and Social Classes* , p. 113.

47. Arguing against this structuralist reading, Clarke points out that rather than look for spheres, it would be better to see that the "economic, political and ideological are forms which are taken by the relations of production." Clarke, "Marxism, Sociology," p. 10 (italicized in original).

48. Poulantzas, *Political Power And Social Classes*, p. 114.

49. Ibid., pp. 62–67.

50. Clarke, "Marxism, Sociology," p. 16 (italicized in the original). For an explicit and very careful working out of the connections between structural-functionalism and determinism in Marxist theory, see G. A. Cohen, *Marx's Theory of History: A Defence* (Princeton: Princeton University Press, 1978). Cohen argues both for a technical determinist reading of Marx and for a reading of Marx as a structural-functionalist.

51. Karl Marx, "*The Poverty of Philosophy*," in Karl Marx and Frederick Engels, *Collected Works* (New York: International Publishers, 1976), 6:212.

6

Power and Class Struggle:
Toward a Marxist Theory
of Class Domination

In order to provide a foundation for an account of class domination that avoids the difficulties into which both market theorists and their critics have fallen, one must move the discussion beyond the dichotomies of power/fate, intentional action/structural determinism. The significance and nature of such a move is perhaps best brought to a head by the question, "Are capitalists responsible for the fact that capitalism continues?" To answer this question a Marxist would have to work out the complex connections between two (layered) relations. First, one would need to examine the relation between the general constraints on individual action imposed by class society (such as the laws of tendency of capitalist development—the falling rate of profit, increasing organic composition of capital, the tendency toward monopoly, crisis, etc.) and the choices available to and made by those individuals (the specific reasons why each capitalist chooses—is forced by competition—to invest in more machinery and to increase, as an individual owner, the intensity and sometimes the hours of labor of his employees). That is, one would have to examine the ways the general laws of capitalist development articulate with, motivate, and even undermine the intentional actions of individuals.

Marx's own work illustrates the tension. In the preface to the first German edition of *Capital*, in defense against those who had criticized him for not portraying capitalists as personally evil, he wrote, "I paint the capitalist and the landlord in no sense *couleur de rose*. But here individuals are dealt with only in so far as they are the personifications of economic categories, embodiments of particular class-relations and class-interests. My standpoint, from which the evolution of the econo-

115

mic formation of society is viewed as a process of natural history, can less than any other make the individual responsible for relations whose creature he socially remains, however much he may subjectively raise himself above them."[1]

A close examination of the relation between Marx's account of the laws of capitalist development and the effects of individual action as these appear in the production and extraction of surplus value can help us to understand the extent to which circumstances that from the perspective of a single individual appear as "fate" may be intentionally altered by collectivities. In this way, Lukes' arguments that an analysis of power must take into account the effects of control over the political agenda, latent as opposed to observable conflict, objective as opposed to subjective interests, can all be supplied with firmer foundations.

In order to properly understand the relation between individual and collective actions, we must take up this relation in its epistemological form: the relation between the level of circulation (in which individual actors interact intentionally, exchange goods and services, exercise powers) and the level of production (in which collectivities are the relevant actors, and the real relations of domination that structure and limit the intentional actions of individuals are revealed). Specifically, we must counterpose to the epistemology implicit in exchange the very different epistemology rooted in production, the one that defines the standpoint of the proletariat. In this task, the Marxian disjunction between appearance and reality, and the stress on the standpoint of the proletariat as the only adequate vantage point on the social relations of capitalism, represent differing forms taken by the Marxian insistence that the perspective of those who rule (the power wielders) and that of the ruled differ profoundly and that the latter can provide a more complete and accurate vision of social relations.[2]

I argue that this epistemological relocation of the theorization of power can enable us not only to resolve the difficulties inherent in any effort to dichotomize power and fate but also, by exposing the systematically inhuman relations between human beings and locating their source in the production process, to begin to put forward an account of power that points beyond the present in more liberatory directions.

Putting forward a detailed discussion of Marx's account of the production process and of the concept of the standpoint of the proletariat can prepare the ground for a feminist theorization of power. In setting out the conceptual basis for locating epistemologies on the levels of production as opposed to exchange, I hope to lay the basis for developing the groundwork for a specifically feminist historical materialism that can build on the power of Marx's method but transcend the specific conclusions he reached.

Circulation, Production, and the Standpoint of the Proletariat

Let us begin with a discussion of what is meant by the levels of circulation and production in Marxist theory and how they relate to the standpoint of the proletariat. The distinction between appearance and essence, or in the historial terms appropriate to our own era, between circulation and production, is fundamental to Marx's argument that these dual levels of reality are linked with the theoretical forms appropriate to and generated by each—bourgeois ideology on the one hand, and scientific understanding on the other.[3]

We have seen that the level of circulation is the theoretical home of the bourgeois world view and expresses the categories within which the capitalist lives his life. Indeed, Marx argued that liberation, from the perspective of the bourgeoisie, was competition itself, a social relation that in the eighteenth century did provide for the freer development of individuals.[4] Moreover, Marx recognized that the effort to portray competition and exchange as universal features of human existence, and thereby to portray one particular set of class relations as universal (e.g., exchange theories), resulted not from a desire on the part of a few to deceive the many, but followed from a real necessity faced by each new ruling class—the need "to represent its interest as the common interest of all members of society, that is, expressed in ideal form: it has to give its ideas the form of universality, and represent them as the only rational, universally valid ones."[5]

The epistemology implicit in the activity of the worker, that which defines the level of production, is both different and more complex than that of the capitalist. Unlike the experience of the capitalist, the experience of the worker provides the ground on which a standpoint, a specific kind of epistemological device, can be constructed. The concept of a standpoint structures epistemology in a particular way. Rather than a simple dualism, it posits a duality of levels of reality, of which the deeper level or essence both includes and explains the "surface" or appearance and indicates the logic by means of which the appearance inverts and distorts the deeper reality. In addition, the concept of a standpoint depends on the assumption that epistemology grows in a complex and contradictory way from material life.

The concept of a standpoint, then, is complex and includes a series of related claims. Perhaps most fundamentally, a standpoint carries the contention that there are some perspectives on society from which, however well intentioned one may be, the real relations of humans with each other and with the natural world are not visible. This general claim can be sorted into a number of distinct epistemological and political claims:

1. Material life (class position in Marxist theory) not only structures but sets limits on the understanding of social relations.
2. If material life is structured in fundamentally opposing ways for two different groups, one can expect both that the vision of each will represent an inversion of the other and the vision of the ruling class will be partial and perverse.
3. The vision of the ruling class structures the material relations in which all parties are forced to participate, and therefore cannot be dismissed as simply false.
4. In consequence, the vision available to the oppressed group must be struggled for and represents an achievement that requires both science to see beneath the surface of the social relations in which all are forced to participate, and the education that can only grow from political struggle.
5. Because the understanding of the oppressed is an engaged vision, the adoption of a standpoint exposes the real relations among human beings as inhuman, points beyond the present, and carries a historical and liberatory role.

The Opposed Vision of Capitalist and Worker—Production

We can begin to understand the standpoint based in the process of production by reformulating Lukács' analysis in "Reification and the Consciousness of the Proletariat" from a more materialist perspective. While there are a number of valuable insights in that essay, Lukacs himself has admitted to a number of errors. Among the most important for our purposes are (1) his separation of the natural and social worlds, leading to his view of Marxism as social philosophy but not theory of nature; (2) his Hegelian equation of objectification with alienation; and (3) perhaps most fundamentally, his failure to ground his argument against the contemplative attitude of bourgeois thought in the activity of labor.[6]

Lukács notes that it is "in line with such philosophical misconceptions that *History and Class Consciousness* should begin its analysis of economic phenomena not with a consideration of work but only of the complicated structures of a developed commodity economy." Let us take his advice, then, and begin again, this time exploring in more detail Marx's injunction that the solution to all mysteries lies in human practice and in the comprehension of this practice. Marx holds that the source both for the proletarian standpoint and the critique of capitalism it makes possible is to be found in practical activity itself. The epistemological (and even ontological) significance of human activity is made clear in Marx's argument not only that persons are active but that reality itself consists of "sensuous human activity, practice."[7]

The concept of praxis, or human work, defines what it is to be human—a striving first to meet physical needs and later for the realization of all human potentialities.[8] If reality itself consists of "sensuous human activity, practice," Marx can speak of products as crystallized or congealed human activity or work, of products as conscious human activity in another form.[9]

The production of the linked processes of consciousness and material existence is directed by human attempts to satisfy physical needs, a process that leads to the production of new needs. These efforts, however, are more than the simple production of physical existence. They structure the totality of social existence. As Marx and Engels put it:

> As individuals express their life, so they are. What they are, therefore, coincides with their production, both with *what* they produce and with *how* they produce. The nature of individuals thus depends on the material conditions determining their production.
>
> This sum of productive forces, capital funds and social forms of intercourse . . . is the real basis of what the philosophers have conceived as "substance" and "essence of man." . . .[10]

Marx is arguing here that individuality must be understood as a social phenomenon, that human existence in whatever forms it takes must be seen as the product of human activity rooted in but not confined to the process of production.

This starting point has definite consequences for Marx's theory of knowledge. If humans are not what they eat but what they do, especially what they do in the course of production of subsistence, each means of producing subsistence should be expected to carry with it both social relations and relations to the world of nature that express the social understanding contained in that mode of production. And in any society with systematically divergent practical activities, one should expect the growth of logically divergent world views. That is, each division of labor can be expected to have consequences for knowledge. Capitalist society, according to Marx, does produce this dual vision in the form of the ruling-class vision and the understanding available to the ruled—the one at the level of circulation or exchange, the other at the level of production.

We have analyzed the epistemology carried by commodity exchange. Let us now leave the sphere of circulation in which people are brought together only by their individual greed and self-interest and follow the buyer and seller of labor power into the world of production. As Marx puts it, "on leaving the sphere of simple circulation or of exchange of commodities . . . we can perceive a change in the physiognomy of our *dramatis personae*. He who before was the money-owner, now strides in front as capitalist; the possessor of labour power follows as his labourer. The one with an air of importance, smirking, intent on business; the other timid and holding back, like one who is bringing his own hide to market and has nothing to expect but—a hiding."[11]

Let us follow the capitalist and worker into this other world, the one defined by production. Only by following the two into the realm of production and adopting the point of view available to the worker was Marx able to uncover the process by which surplus value is produced and appropriated by the capitalist and the means by which the worker is systematically disadvantaged. Marx describes the process of production of surplus value in capitalism in a way that demonstrates very clearly the roles of both compulsion and freedom. His account of the extraction of surplus value depends on his development of a labor theory of value, and this in turn rests explicitly on an understanding of the nature of humanity.[12]

The theory of surplus value is for our purposes best thought of as a description of the source of profits in capitalist society. Marx argues that profits arise, not from the risks taken by individual capitalists, but rather depend on the fact that labor power, the human capacity for work, while not itself value, becomes value when embodied in the form of objects.[13] The process of extracting surplus value from workers is set in motion by the intentional decisions of individuals to buy or sell labor power—its price being the wages received by the worker. Marx argues that the exchange value of labor power, like that of any other commodity, is the cost of its production, and that labor power, in common with all other commodities, has not only an exchange value but also a use value. The latter represents the value of a commodity as it is used, or put to work. But labor power is distinguished from all other commodities by the fact that its exchange value and its use value can be measured as two different magnitudes along the same dimension; the differential between the costs of its production and the value it creates when put to work represent the source of surplus value.[14]

As Marx describes the process leading to production, the individual capitalist buys all the necessary commodities at their value. He pays the laborer the amount it would cost to reproduce his labor power, and pays the full value of the labor time embodied in the other commodities as well. While Marx recognized that all commodities, including labor power, sometimes sell either above or below their value, and also that the cost of reproducing labor power varies spatially, temporally, and with the skill of the worker, his simplified model excludes these considerations.[15]

Following on the sale, the seller of labor power realizes its exchange value and parts with its use-value. In this he differs not at all from the seller of any other commodity. "The use-value of labour-power, or in other words, labour, belongs just as little to its seller, as the use-value of oil after it has been sold belongs to the dealer who has sold it. The owner of the money has paid the value of a day's labour-power; his, therefore, is the use of it for a day; a day's labour belongs to him." Marx constructs an example in which the sustenance of labor power requires half a day's labor. At the same time, however, he points out that the very same labor power can work through a whole day. Thus the value its use creates during one day is twice what the capitalist has paid for it. Marx is careful to point out, however, that "this circumstance is, without doubt, a piece of good luck for the buyer, but by no means an injury to the seller." Equivalent has been exchanged for equivalent: The capitalist paid the full value of each commodity he purchased, and then, as do the purchasers of all commodities, he consumed the use value.[16]

Most fundamentally, then, the capitalist is able to realize more than his initial outlay of money because the products of the day's labor are his and because he extends the working day past the point where production suffices to reproduce the workers, while paying the workers wages that express, not the value of their product, but the cost of their reproduction. At the end of the day, the gap between the monetary power of the worker and capitalist has been increased; the one has no more than at the beginning of the day, while the other possesses products that embody twice as much labor as he paid for.[17]

The worker who has sold labor power, then, has by the sale of that particular commodity, and that one only, entered into a situation in which he will of necessity fare less well than the capitalist. The fact that he will be the loser is independent of the goodwill or individual intentions of the actors; it results not from any foul play but follows from the exchange of equivalents by formally (though not really) equal individuals. Were exchange theorists correct that humans can be expected to enter only transactions profitable to them, one could not expect the sellers of labor power to continue to participate in the exchange. In fact, however, sellers are forced by external circumstances to participate—lacking free food, savings, or other resources that could provide alternative sources for maintenance.[18]

Given this discussion of the production and extraction of surplus value, and Marx's demonstration that all commodities are not the same, perhaps we are now in a position to better understand his sarcastic dismissal of the contention that in exchange, the participants "in accordance with the pre-established harmony of things, or under the auspices of an all shrewd providence, work together to their mutual advantage, for the common wealth and in the interest of all."[19] And we now see more clearly what is implied in the Marxian image of the capitalist striding in front of the worker, the former with an air of importance, smirking, intent on business; the other, timid and holding back.[20]

The Alienation of Labor

The "hiding" involves a loss deeper than the appropriation of several hours of labor without payment, a loss whose significance stems from the importance of labor, or more broadly, work, in Marxist theory. Work is for Marx the real human life activity, the activity through which the human creation of human beings is accomplished.[21] Work is "human action with a view to the production of use-values, appropriation of natural substances to human requirements; it is the necessary condition for effecting exchange of matter between man and Nature; it is the everlasting Nature-imposed condition of human existence, and therefore is independent of every social phase of that existence, or rather, is common to every such phase."[22]

Human activity, then, the human production of human life, is at the core of Marx's world view. However, Marx argues that human work, the creation of real individuals, has been perverted. In capitalism, work has become a means to life rather than life itself. It has become a barrier to self-creation: Human work has become alienated labor; and as a result, because of the ontological character of activity, humanity itself is alienated.[23]

Marx understands alienation or estrangement to be founded upon estranged activity. It is constituted, first, by the fact that in capitalism, labor is external to the worker, that it "does not belong to his essential being; that in his work, therefore, he does not affirm himself but denies himself, does not feel content but unhappy, does not develop freely his physical and mental energy but mortifies his body and ruins his mind."[24] Through this activity, objects are produced. But because, for Marx, products are simply human activity in another (physical) form, and because the objects are expressions of the life of the species itself, the objects produced through alienated activity can only confront the worker as alien powers. The worker's relation to these objects represents what Marx sees as the second aspect of alienation—the worker's relation "to the sensuous external world, to the objects of nature, as an alien world inimically opposed to him."[25] Third, alienation refers to a separation from the life of the human species. That is, estranged labor makes "the *life of the species* into a means of individual life. First it estranges the life of the species and individual life, and secondly it makes individual life in this abstract form the purpose of the life of the species, likewise in its abstract and estranged form."[26] Thus the life activity of the workers separates them from their human potential; it makes them work only to satisfy needs for survival rather than for the joys of the work itself. Finally, estranged labor leads to a separation from other human beings. "What applies to a man's relation to his work, to the product of his labor and to himself, also holds of a man's relation to the other man's labor and object of labor."[27]

For Marx, then, the worker's own activity destroys what he could become, separates each human being from all others, and creates the domination of the nonproducer over the product. The market in labor power in capitalism leads people to participate in the separation of their life activity from themselves and makes them confer that activity on strangers. Marx's writing in *Capital* must be understood, then, as an analysis of the workings of private property. As such, it functions at the same time as a statement of the laws governing the systematic perversion and theft of the worker's humanity. Marx's account of the extraction of surplus value, coupled with his understanding of alienation, form the basis for his vision of capitalist society as structured by fundamental antagonisms. Systematic domination and conflict extend far beyond the relations of production in which Marx argues they are based, but the structural antagonism manifested in these relations is formative of social relations more generally. As we shall see, this contention structures the Marxian account of class domination.

Because the worker's own life activity becomes a commodity in capitalism, he can take up the perspective available to the commodity which recognizes itself *both* as a commodity and as a human subject denied humanity, a human being who embodies within himself the inhumanity of the social order. The worker's own life activity is at once both the means by which the human creation of human beings is accomplished and the force that destroys what he himself might become and separates him from all other human beings. From this perspective, the mechanisms of capitalist development become visible as mechanisms for the progressive destruction of humanity itself. This doubled experience, the doubled experience of being both a commodity and an active human subject, form the basis for the recognition of double levels of determination.

Production as Epistemology: The Worker's Perspective

The Marxian treatment of activity as epistemology suggests that there is a specific relation to both the social and natural worlds implicit in the activity of the worker. The epistemology we must now attempt to read out of this activity is more spatially and temporally specific than is the general Marxian claim that work is the means by which humans are constituted as social human beings. The life activity of the worker, unlike that of the capitalist, is profoundly structured by production, that is, by the use of labor power rather than the buying and selling (exchange) of labor power along with other commodities.

Following the sale of labor power, the worker (but not the capitalist) inhabits a world in which the emphasis is on change rather than stasis—both the transformation of some commodities into others in production and the natural changes (deterioration, ripening, etc.) of the commodities themselves. It is a world in which interaction with natural and concrete substances (the various commodities and capital equipment supplied by the capitalist) is central, and in which the particular qualities of things used in and by the production process, rather than their quantitative equivalence, is important. Within the labor process, commonality and cooperation with others is required; the workers engaged in a joint enterprise have only common interests (unlike the situation in exchange where the conflicting interests of parties rather than their common interests are predominant). There is as well a unification rather than separation of mind and action inherent in the labor process itself.

The specific organization of the labor process in capitalism represents a series of efforts to break apart these unities and commonalities of head and hand, human and natural worlds. In addition, one can see a series of attempts to undermine cooperation among workers and minimize the experience of transforming one series of commodities into another.[28] Yet, despite these efforts, and despite the distortion and damage that result from alienated labor, the life activity of the worker contains echoes of a rich, concrete, and quality-laden world, a world in which the objects he produces, the crystallization and objectification of his human activity, might represent not the theft of his humanity but its expression. This is so because the process of production itself cannot take place in the absence of attention to change (both natural and human), concrete qualities, and cooperation. If one takes seriously Marx's claim that existence produces consciousness, the understanding available to the producers can be expected to manifest these features.

Because I have centered my account of the standpoint of the proletariat on labor and production in capitalism, there are several obvious differences from Lukács' formulation. Interchange with nature, a dialectical unity of human and natural worlds, lies at the heart of a nondualist vision and practice. Interchange with the natural world is central to production, though not to exchange. Whereas in exchange, the focus is on the purely social change of status the object undergoes, in production the materials themselves experience no social change of status. They remain throughout this process the property of the capitalist, while their form, shape, and even chemical composition change with and because of the activity of the worker.

Objectification, in my analysis, unlike that of Lukács, need not be in and of itself alienated. On my reading of Marx, objectification has to do with an affirmation of the existence of the material world. As Marx puts it,

> *to be* objective, natural and sensuous, and at the same time to have object, nature, and sense for a third party, is one and the same thing. *Hunger* is a natural *need*; it therefore needs a *nature* outside itself, an *object* outside itself, in order to satisfy itself, to be stilled. . . .

To take the simplest possible relation, Marx suggests that

> the sun is the *object* of the plant—an indispensable object to it, confirming its life—just as the plant is an object of the sun, being an *expression* of the life-awakening power of the sun, of the sun's objective essential power.[29]

When the objective world confirms essential human powers, all objects become the objective forms of ourselves, objectifications that "confirm and realize" individuality. Human beings are then "affirmed in the objective world not only in the act of thinking, but with *all* [their] senses."[30]

Despite the perversion of these relations in alienated production, the worker's activity retains possibilities for objectification in the form of unalienated production. The potential form it takes even in capitalism—the residual but real engagement of both mind and body in labor—is one source for both the liberatory role embodied in a standpoint and an alternative theorization of power. Thus, my account of the vision available to the worker, unlike Lukács', stresses the unity of social and natural worlds, does not equate objectification with alienation, and is grounded directly in the activity of labor.

On the basis of the standpoint of the proletariat, one can understand market theories of social life as ideological refractions of the experience of the capitalist. This is not meant to suggest that the economic realities of one's situation totally determine analyses. One need only look to the exchange theories of power that take every aspect of the market as a model for social life; even there one sees important variations. These are reflective of the autonomy (not independence) of the political and ideological realms. For example, the circularity contained in the concept of rational economic man, the assumption that to be rational is to maximize one's own utilities, can now be recognized as a statement from the perspective of the capitalist that it is inconceivable that one could act in any other way. And of course, it is a materially defining feature of the existence of the capitalist firm that it must seek to maximize utilities (profits) or go out of business. The isolation of individuals from each other in a world structured by institutions can now be understood as rooted in the experience of exchange, and the inadequate account of human community that results from such an understanding must be seen as replicating at the level of theory the real poverty of communities constructed by exchange. The distinction between the levels of circulation and production in Marxist theory, then, can be seen to structure epistemology in terms of a duality of levels of reality; the deeper level or essense both includes and explains the "surface" or appearance, and indicates the logic by means of which the appearance is an inversion of the deeper reality.

The Marxian contention that material life structures the understanding of social relations required the explication of the epistemological consequences of the model of exchange as opposed to production, the former resulting in a dualism based on the separation of exchange from use, and the positing of exchange as the only important part of the duality. The epistemological result is a series of opposed and hierarchical dualities—mind/body, ideal/material, social/natural, self/other—replicating the devaluation of use relative to exchange. The valuation of use over exchange on the basis of involvement in the process of production results in a dialectical rather than dualist epistemology: the dialectical and interactive unity (distinctions within a unity) of human and natural worlds, mind and body, ideal and material, and the cooperation of self and other (community).

To the second claim of a standpoint, that each understanding inverts the other, we must add that the one is not merely an inversion of the other, but in addition is both partial and fundamentally perverse. The real point of the production of goods and services is, after all, the continuation of the species, a possibility dependent on their use. The epistemology embodied in exchange, then, not only occupies only one side of the dualities it constructs but also reverses the proper ordering of any hierarchy in the dualisms: Use is primary, not exchange. And no matter how often it may appear to be the reverse in capitalism, it is in reality persons who purchase commodities.

Let us look at the theorization of power possible on the epistemological ground provided by production rather than exchange, and the contributions this account can make to solving the problems posed by the dichotomies of power/fate, intentional action/structural determination, individual/group. These problems can best be addressed in the context of the Marxian theory of the extraction and appropriation of surplus value. There we can see the working out of the real relation between capitalist and worker, one not visible at the level of circulation, where human interaction is dichotomized into either individual and intentional action or action determined entirely by structural forces to which individual intentional action is antithetical.

Class Antagonism and Domination

An account of power relations constructed on this fundamentally antagonistic model would take very different form from theories constructed on the model of exchange found in neoclassical economic theory. One cannot, in addition, deduce it directly from the economic model. Still, one can see that on the Marxist account, the working of society does not flow from a bargaining process between parties who accept the principle that they can and want to live together harmoniously.[31] The opposition between the interests of the worker and capitalist differs profoundly from the opposition of buyer and seller in the market. The latter have both conflicting and common interests; the former, only conflicting interests, since one party is forced to participate in a series of transactions in which he is the consistent loser.

This contrast can be marked by the images of society discussed in Chapters 1 through 4. Does the human community resemble an orderly shopping center, frequented by buyers and sellers on the basis of mutual interest, or is it a battlefield where the interests of some are irrevocably opposed to those of others? This is not to say that relations of domination are simple reflections of economic class relations, or, in more Marxist terms, that the superstructure is simply an appendage of the base. Rather, one must see the political structure as both an outgrowth of the economy and as an autonomous structure operating in different ways to serve specific ends, which are, however, supportive of the maintenance of capitalistic control.[32]

What kind of understanding of relations of domination is generated by the claim that social relations of production mark the location of fundamental conflict? First, in part because the analysis is rooted in the *process* of production, a process that rests fundamentally on transformation, the account of domination sees class domination not as a simple instantaneous fact but as a process—a point both Miliband and Poulantzas have come to support in their later writing. Miliband, for example, had described this domination as a "continuing endeavour on the part of the dominant class or classes to maintain, strengthen and extend, or defend, their domination."[33] Second, just as the production of surplus value grows out of a specific *relation* between capitalist and worker, the concept of power, too, names a relation and a field of struggle.[34] Poulantzas' similar argument that "the field of power . . . is strictly relational" is meant to point implicitly to both these aspects. "Power," he argues, "is not then a quality attached to a class 'in-itself,' understood as a collection of agents, but depends on, and springs from, a relational system of material places occupied by particular agents."[35]

The process of class struggle, then, has primacy over structure, since power understood as a relation then becomes for Poulantzas the capacity of a class to realize its interests in a particular field of struggle. The interesting question becomes not who *has* exercised power over others but rather, given a particular configuration of forces, who has the capacity to maintain or extend dominance.[36] Thus power can be defined as a "relation between struggles and practices (those of the exploiters and the exploited, the rulers and the ruled)."[37]

If power is a relation, then institutions as such should be seen as social relations. For example, the concept of class as a social relation refers to and is in turn defined by an ongoing interaction between capital and wage labor. The focus is not on the individuals, but on the pattern and process of their activity. Their interrelatedness and interaction have been elevated to the same plane of reality as what is called their physical existence.[38] In the context of the state, the institution that organizes the power of the ruling class as a whole, the significance of understanding institutions as social relations, emerges in Poulantzas' argument that one should refuse to regard the state as an "intrinsic entity," and his rejection of theories that see that state as either a "thing" or a "subject." This, he argues, leads to the mistaken understanding of the relation between the state and social class as an "external relation."[39] The state itself must be seen as a relation of forces, or, as Poulantzas describes it, "the material condensation of such a relationship among classes and class fractions, such as this is expressed within the state in a necessarily specific form."[40] Miliband makes a similar point when he argues that the organs of government are instruments of the ruling class not only because state personnel have ties to business but, finally, because of a structural dimension of "objective and impersonal kind"; because, given its position within the capitalist mode of production, it cannot be anything else.[41]

These theorizations of the state as a locus for systematic conflict structured *both* by "objective and impersonal" forces *and* by the intentional actions of individuals and groups can be read as efforts to theorize at the level of politics a relation similar in structure to the relation described by surplus value at the level of the economy.[42] They are attempts to work out the real tension between structural determination vs. intentional action, to lay the basis for examining compulsion vs. freedom within Marxist theory.

Just as the coherence of Marx's theory of surplus value depends on understanding the structures that define, limit, and give significance to action, as well as the individual action itself, so too an understanding of political domination requires attention to both structural and intentional aspects of class struggle. Marx's theory of surplus value illuminates the contention that the individual capitalist, *as individual actor*, is not so much guilty of exploitation as the beneficiary of a piece of "good luck." Nor is the individual worker compelled to sell his labor power to any particular capitalist. The individual capitalist, *as individual*, may well be guilty of exploitation in forms such as failing to provide adequate safety or proper equipment. The point is that the individual capitalist is not *necessarily* guilty but instead profits from a situation not of his own making. Yet capital *as a whole* is responsible for the systematic exploitation of a whole class of people, persons who *as a class* are compelled to sell their labor power because they own no means of production.

While, for the individual capitalist or worker, the structural features that determine that the one shall profit at the other's expense appear as natural laws (or fate), at the level of the collectivity or society these appear as social relations subject to human control, social relations of class domination subject to change through intentional efforts.[43] An account of political domination on the model provided by the theory of surplus value, whether in the generic field of class struggle or in the specific condensation of relations designated by the state, describes a social relation in which one side is systematically disadvantaged.

The key to the proper theorization of the tension between structural determination and intentional action lies in a careful distinction between the capacities and options of individuals as opposed to groups. This tension is key as well in clarifying and supporting Lukes' effort to provide a structural dimension to analyses of power, that is, his argument that an adequate theory of power must account for control over the political agenda, latent as well as observable conflict, and must recognize "real" as well as subjectively understood interests. The Marxian account of political domination, constructed on a model structurally similar to the form taken by relations defined by surplus value, can clarify these two levels of analysis. It can, for example, help specify the means by which the political agenda is controlled. It is neither a matter of a few powerful men intentionally directing the course of events in class society for their own benefit nor an inevitable result of the working out of the laws of capitalist development.

Rather, the shape of the political agenda at any point in time expresses the relation between the struggles and practices of the exploiters and the exploited, taken as groups rather than individual actors. And the state itself, in all its variety of institutional forms, represents the material expression of these relations. The political agenda, then, is controlled on the one hand by the structural relations of social classes as expressed in Marx's account of the extraction of surplus value from the one by the other. On his account, class relations in capitalist society express systematic inequality and domination because they are most fundamentally based on this extraction. As the same time, just as the extraction of surplus value from a class proceeds by means of individual and intentional actions, so too does the shape of the political agenda depend on intentional actions to achieve conscious goals—that is, on class struggle. Indeed, class struggle, according to Marxist theory, can, for example, reduce the surplus extracted from the consumption of labor power by means of raising its price (though not its value). This can be accomplished through such means as the organization of trade unions.[44]

Second, the Marxist account of class domination allows for specification of the loci within which one should expect latent conflict. These loci may go well beyond the confines of the state in the traditional sense and may exist in areas such as the family, church, and even theoretical and ideological struggles. Marx's account of the nexus of class domination in the relations of production is the source of his account of class society as structured by irrevocably opposed interests. These opposed interests grow (though not in any simple way) from the class relations of production, and form criteria for the identification of "latent" conflicts. These criteria are part of an understanding of the structure of society as a whole, and depend on a vision of human nature that is far more worked out and well supported than Lukes' postulation of a need for personal autonomy. In the context of such a theory, the identification of issues about which conflict "can be expected to occur" need not be reduced to an individual scholar's own sense of what circumstances "would be" changed, or what issues "should become salient."

Finally, Marx's theory of surplus value, when coupled with his explicit theory of human nature and the alienation resulting from the sale of labor power, can rescue Lukes' argument for the existence of "real" as well as subjectively held interests. On the basis of his account of the extraction and appropriation of surplus value, the "real" interests of the worker and capitalist can be seen to be opposed, *whether or not* either understands the mechanisms by which the one profits at the expense of the other.

No philosophical system argues that the systematically disadvantaged should accept their lot. Indeed, a vast amount of philosophical energy has gone toward demonstrating that those who may appear to be disadvantaged are instead the beneficiaries of a system that gives them little. To take only one of the most obvious examples, Aristotle's arguments for slavery were supported by his contention that the lot of the natural slave, whose own capacity to reason was severely limited, was in fact *improved* by his enslavement.[45] The exchange theories considered in Chapter 1 represent more modern attempts in this same tradition: No one can be presumed to be systematically disadvantaged in contemporary capitalism if all social relations are entered and continued on the basis of reasonably anticipated profits or benefits.

Marx is arguing instead that the workers are systematically disadvantaged by the facts that labor power can be bought and sold and that the products of the labor of the many can be appropriated by the few. The real interests, then, of the workers require the abolition of these social relations. Their real interests demand an alteration of the political agenda, a raising to public consciousness of conflicts that have previously been only latent. These latent conflicts can include such widely separable issues as increased public transportation, workplace safety, increased political representation, and the more general issue of revolution itself. Because any theory of real interests, or even subjective interests, rests on a particular understanding of human nature and a theory of social relations, an encompassing alternative, such as Marx provides, is required to support an understanding of interests that goes beyond subjectively held utilities.

A Marxist account of class domination, then, rooted explicitly in Marx's theory of human nature and in his understanding of the extraction of surplus value, can adequately support the points Lukes quite correctly wishes to make. The account of class domination Marx's theory makes possible can thus resolve the series of problems that marred the efforts of those who attempted both to criticize and to put forward alternatives to market theories of power.

In addition, the Marxian account of class domination can advance the argument beyond simply providing support for the points Lukes wished to make. By providing a place to examine the relation between individual and collectivity in its less apparent form, that is, in the form of the relation between the levels of circulation and production, Marxian theory can enable us to understand the importantly differing perspectives available to different classes in capitalist society. In the process of examining the relation between the analytical levels of circulation and production and the corresponding epistemological categories of appearance and reality, one can discover the important opposition in Marxist theory between the perspective of the powerholder and that of the person who complies, an opposition characterized by the relation competition/domination. That is, Marx's theory can allow us to explore both the effects of class divisions in capitalism on the theorization of power and the possibilities for theorizing power in terms of class relations. It can put exchange theories of social life and market theories of power in their proper context, and can demonstrate that the vision of social relations they provide is both partial and pernicious. In so doing, we can begin to understand why community poses such a puzzle for social theorists, and can demonstrate both the extent to which the theorists of exchange were in fact pointing to a real problem and the extent to which their reluctance to face the questions posed by class domination led them to give an inadequate account of the social relations of domination.

Science, Mediation, and the Achievement of Understanding

The epistemological understanding made available by a standpoint contributes to an understanding of theories of power in a third way as well, one named in the third claim implicit in the concept of a standpoint. By positing a duality of levels of reality, one can understand how, despite the perverseness and perniciousness of the ruling group's vision, it can be *made real* becaue of the power of the ruling group to define the terms for the community as a whole. In Marxian analysis, this power takes the forms both of control of ideological production and of the real participation of the worker in exchange. Thus, exchange epistemology and market theories more generally should not be dismissed either as simply false or as relevant to only a few; the worker as well as the capitalist engages in the purchase and sale of commodities, and if material life structures consciousness, this cannot fail to have an effect. This leads into the fourth claim implicit in the concept of a standpoint—that it is achieved rather than obvious, a mediated rather than immediate understanding. Because the ruling group controls the means of mental as well as physical production, the production of ideas as well as goods, the standpoint of the oppressed represents an achievement both of science and of political struggle on the basis of which science can be constructed.

The understanding that grows from and expresses the vision structured by production rather than exchange insists that *"everything appears reversed in competition."*

> The final pattern of economic relations as seen on the surface, in their real existence and consequently in the conceptions by which the bearers and agents of these relations seek to understand them, is very much different from, and indeed quite the reverse of, their inner but concealed essential pattern and the conception corresponding to it."[46]

A surface account of capitalist development would see the development of methods for raising the social productivity of labor as progress, pure and simple, without recognizing that "... *all means for the development of production transform themselves into means of domination over, and exploitation of, the producers"*; therefore, "accumulation of wealth at one pole is, therefore, at the same time accumulation of misery, agony of toil, slavery, ignorance, brutality, mental degradation, at the opposite pole, i.e., on the side of the class that produces its own product in the form of capital."[47] It was, then, Marx's adoption of the standpoint of the working class that enabled him to discover that phenomena contain their opposites within themselves in tension, and to recognize the fetishized (or reified) forms of capitalism as such.

The uncovering of these inner patterns, the discovery of oppositions contained within phenomena, is neither simple nor automatic. Commodity exchange, because it structures the vision of the ruling class, structures the self-understanding of society as a whole. This occurs in part because "the ruling ideas are nothing more than the ideal expression of the dominant material relationships, the dominant material relationships grasped as ideas; hence of the relationships which make the one class the ruling one, therefore the ideas of its dominance."[48] It should, then, come as no surprise that theories of social life in capitalism frequently take exchange and competition to be fundamental and see the relation of buyer and seller as the prototypic form of social interaction. These are indeed the dominant material relations for at least the capitalist class, and, through their dominance, of society as a whole.

The ruling-class vision of the centrality of competition and exchange structures society for all in a second way as well. The producers as well as the owners do *engage* in exchange—most importantly in the sale of their own labor power. While the separation and opposition to nature in exchange is at odds with nature as experienced in the labor process, in the worker's role as an agent of the market he is as divided from nature as the other commodities on the market.[49] Thus, once exchange governs life, the activity of the individual producer acquires a twofold character: On the one hand it must satisfy a want, but it can satisfy the wants of the producer only to the extent that all kinds of useful private labor are exchangeable.[50] Thus, what Marx termed the "verbal masquerade" of capitalist ideology cannot be dismissed as simple deception.[51] The distinction to be made is that these appearances constitute the totality of reality for the capitalist, but represent only part of the worker's reality. The analytical point is best made by a clear vision of different levels of determination, within which appearances are neither accidental nor self-evident.[52] Appearances, then, must be recognized as "real" and must not be dismissed because of their partial and misleading character. Perhaps their designation as "surface," or as confined to the realm of circulation, is more accurate.

Thus, the forms of *immediacy* are the same for both the working class and the bourgeoisie, but the vantage point of the working class, the perspective located in the process of production, is such that it discloses a fundamentally different reality. Through mediation, "the proletariat is capable of the transformation of the immediately given into a truly understood (and not merely an immediately perceived) and, *for that reason*, really objective reality. . . ."[53] For example, "immediate" accounts such as the exchange theories of social life see the development of methods for raising the social productivity of labor as progress, pure and simple, without recognizing that these developments are at the same time the development of new means for the mutilation of human life. Only through a process of mediation, a process of uncovering the social relations and social consequences involved even in apparently simple things, can the authentic structure of phenomena be revealed.[54]

The process of mediation, defined, following Lukács, as the effort to go beneath the surface of things, involves both scientific analysis and political struggle. The need for both, and their interdependence, results from the historical and materialist character of Marxist theory. As Lucio Colletti has put it:

> ... Marx—utilizing an aspect of *reality*—overthrows the arguments of the economists and points to the overthrow of capitalism itself. Marxism is therefore science. It is an analytical reconstruction of the way in which the mechanism of capitalist production works.
>
> On the other hand, as well as being a science, Marxism is revolutionary ideology. It is the analysis of reality from the viewpoint of the working class. This in its turn means that the working class cannot constitute itself as a *class* without taking possession of the scientific analysis of *Capital*."[55]

The process of building an analysis on the basis of the experience of the worker, then, requires both the generalization of proletarian experience and the gradual sharpening of class antagonisms and development of class consciousness through protacted struggle. This process, if one takes Marx's work as the measure of the development of a full-scale analysis of capitalism from a proletarian perspective, took from fifty to seventy-five years. It required the real advance (and false starts) made by the utopian socialists and anarchists; it required the conspiracies of Babeuf and Blanqui; and it rested fundamentally on the working-class struggles of the Luddites, the Chartists, and the Lyons weavers. The historical character of the analysis produced by these dual yet unified means is embedded within the central concepts of Marxist theory, and thus the concepts themselves have a historical character. This historical character, and the continuing struggle required to maintain a mediated and revolutionary understanding in the midst of capitalist social relations, are illustrated by the difficulties encountered by the critiques of the market model discussed in Chapter 5. In each case, the failure of the critiques could be traced to the failure to successfully relocate the theory of power on the epistemological ground of production. Yet the problems encountered in particular by the Marxist critics serve as an indication of the real difficulties of both accomplishing and maintaining such a relocation.

The Liberatory Potential Embodied in a Standpoint

Because of its historical character, the appearance/essence relation in Marxist theory takes the form of the tension between "authentic potentiality and immediate existence,"[56] between what something could be but is not and what it might become. It is "reality in a 'bad' form," but includes the promise that "this transformation *can* be accomplished. This is what makes the possibility real."[57] That is, Marxian concepts contain both an accusation and an imperative.[58] Thus the historical and liberatory role of the proletariat is anchored in the relation between appearance and essence, once this has been reformulated specifically in historical terms as defining the tension between potentiality and actuality. The specific content of this tension emerges in Marx's claim that the proletariat is the first class in human history to possess the potentiality for creating a classless society because it is the first class in history whose interests do not depend on the oppression of other classes. Marx can make this claim because of his faith in the possibility of abundance capitalism creates. Thus, the poverty of the proletariat must be recognized as artificially produced, and the class-wide loss of humanity as unnecessary.[59] The epistemological position defined by a standpoint is inseparable from historical role: The standpoint of the working class as described by Marx is a position that does not require the generation of justifications for the maintenance of inequality, poverty, and domination. Only from this perspective, the perspective of a class that has the capacity to create a society free from class domination, could Marx avoid the necessity of creating justifications for the unjustifiable through the concealment of real social relations, that is, through their presentation as static and eternal relations between things. The standpoint of the working class, then, is both an analytic tool and a perspective that, at the same time, embodies such distress, such dehumanization, that it requires a solution. It is, as Marx puts it, a class that contains in its own existence the "effective dissolution" of the existing social order, since "when the proletariat demands the *negation of private property*, it only lays down as a *principle for society* what society has already made a principle for the proletariat. . . ."[60] That is, by generalizing its own condition, by making all of society a propertyless producer, the proletariat has the possibility of creating a classless society.

Objectification, Alienation, and Community

The historically liberatory role Marx saw for the proletariat involves the possibility for a different construction of power and thereby of community, the possibility of transforming an existence deeply structured by antagonism and domination into the authentic potential-ity it contains for a more complete and complex human community. The dual nature of the Marxian understanding of objectification and objec-tified labor is central to this possibility. Objectification is for Marx another form of the description of the production process, one that encompasses both alienated and unalienated labor (Lukács to the con-trary). Objectified labor in capitalism is represented by commodities, means of production, and capital—all products that embody (objectify) definite acts of labor.[61] In these forms, however, labor is only impor-tant in the form of general social labor or undifferentiated socially necessary labor, that is, living labor in the sole form of "value creating factor."[62] Objectified labor in these forms is alienated and abstract, and the community constructed on the basis of this labor is the inadequate one-sided community we have described in the initial chapters, a com-munity that rests fundamentally on domination.

Yet labor has a second aspect: its character as concrete use values specific to each commodity, that is, the labor peculiar to each object. This aspect of labor is the source for the lived proletarian experience of a world structured by change, interaction with natural substances, the centrality of concrete qualities, commonality, and cooperation, and thereby for the possibility of constructing a community on a different model. Thus, despite the damaging forms taken by objectification in capitalism, the centrality of labor in Marx's analysis makes it clear that on the one hand, domination is produced by the activity and actions (though not by choice) of the dominated themselves, and that on the other, the nature of their activity itself contains the outlines of another possible theorization of power, one that rests on capacity and ability and that includes interaction with both the natural and social worlds in order to give specific form to human powers. This aspect of labor enabled Marx to put forward a vision of society in which production was unalienated. It is so unusual that it is worth quoting again here in full:

> Supposing that we had produced in a human manner; each of us would in his production have doubly affirmed himself and his fellow men. I would have: (1) objectified in my production my individuality and its peculiarity and thus both in my activity enjoyed an individual expression of my life and also in looking at the object have had the individual pleasure of realizing that my personality was objective, visible to the senses and thus a power raised beyond all doubt. (2) In your enjoyment of use of my product I would have had the direct enjoyment of realizing that I had both satisfied a human need by my work and also objectified the human essence and

therefore fashioned for another human being the object that met his need. (3) I would have been for you the mediator between you and the species and thus been acknowledged and felt by you as a completion of your own essence and a necessary part of yourself and have thus realized that I am confirmed in both in your thought and in your love. (4) In my expression of my life I would have fashioned your expression of life, and thus in my own activity have realized my own essence, my human, my communal essence.[63]

This account of a more human manner of production has several important features. It indicates that objectification could take the form of making the individuality of each person present in the form of objects available to the senses and to other persons. In addition, Marx's stress on the importance of bodily existence and the human relation to the natural world indicates that specifically human nature is at once part of the natural world, and the external world of nature can be viewed as the "inorganic body" of human beings. The source of this unity with nature is, once again, the labor process. As Marx puts it, the "much renowned 'unity of man with nature' has always existed in industry and has existed differently in every epoch according to the lesser or greater development of industry." Marx's account of humane production rests on the reintegration of exchange and use. If use were primary, he is suggesting, the production of objects would not of necessity divide persons as it does under capitalism but would bring them together as social and cooperative beings.

The Marxian account of the process of production, then, implicitly contains two accounts of power—the one a description of relations of domination in the present form of society, the other an indication of the possibilities inherent in human activity. This second account of power points beyond relations of domination and allows for a reformulation of power (both in theory and in fact) as not simply power over others but as competence and effective action in dealing with both the natural and social worlds.

The community produced by the exercise of human power in the form of objectification and sharing one's individuality with others is clearly very different from that produced by the solipsistic interaction of equal possessors of commodities to be exchanged, or by the systematically unequal interaction of the buyers and sellers of labor power. The community Marx is suggesting as a possibility is one in which persons relate to each other directly, their products operating as an expression rather than denial of their individuality, and as a means of connecting rather than separating them both from each other and from the world of nature.

Conclusion

This chapter marks an important progression toward the project of this book: the construction of an adequate theory of power, one that can understand the gendered as well as class nature of power. I hope I have made clear the ways a Marxist account can resolve many of the problems posed by other theories of power, most particularly the issues of how the political agenda is controlled, why one should expect conflict to arise at some structural points rather than others (e.g., points defined by class differences), and how one can understand the relation between structural constraints and individual actions. I do not pretend to have given a complete account of the operation of class domination in advanced capitalism, but I have attempted to put forward the outlines of Marx's views of the extraction of surplus value, the operation of alienation, and the effects of existence on consciousness.

My major purpose here was less to defend and argue for the Marxian theorization of power relations as relations of class domination than to show how such a theorization can meet the objections raised against theorizations of power that fail to give adequate attention both to individual, intentional action and the effects of social structure. In addition, rather than put forward a developed account of the operation of class domination in capitalism, I have been more concerned to work out the overall shape such a theorization of power should take, that is, to concentrate on the methodological issues an adequate theory must confront and the pitfalls that await the unwary.

Several objections can be leveled at my attempt to both criticize and build on Marxist accounts of power. First, some may object that while Marx may have produced an adequate account of nineteenth-century capitalism, his theories cannot explain the economic forms of the late twentieth century. The debate has been waged both by anti-Marxists and by others who consider themselves to be Marxists. A number of theorists have pointed to a variety of changes—the rise of joint stock companies (Eduard Bernstein), the introduction of professional managers (A. A. Berle and Gardiner Means), the increase in the importance of professional and technical workers (Andre Gorz, Herbert Marcuse). They have been answered by others who argued that joint stock companies did not represent a spreading of ownership (Rosa Luxemburg), that professional managers' roles do not differ importantly from that of nineteenth-century capitalists (Paul Baran, Paul Sweezy, Ralph Miliband), that the major growth of "technical workers" has been the growth of low-paid clerical and service workers (Harry Braverman), that knowledge itself could not be understood as a productive force (Harry Braverman), and that the rise of living standards of the industrial working class was less dramatic than had been thought (Richard Sennett, Jonathan Cobb, and Lillian Rubin). Rather than defend my own positions here, I should note that I have found the arguments of the latter group more persuasive, and refer the reader directly to their arguments.[64]

Marxian theory, however, because it fails to take account of or analyze the genderedness of power, fails as an encompassing theorization of power. The specific problems feminists have pointed to will be summarized in the next section. Here, we should note only their general effect: Marx's theory is useful more as a methodological guide to the feminist theorist than as an adequate theorization of domination. It contains, however, several important injunctions. Among the most important set of charges to the theorist of power are (1) the necessity for constructing/exposing the epistemological bases on which theories of power rest, and for recognizing that any alternative theorization of power must rest on an alternative epistemological base; (2) the need to recognize the achieved and mediated character of theories of power that can describe social relations accurately, as they are rather than as one might wish them to be; and (3) the need to recognize the liberatory potential (as well as the conservatizing potential) carried by theories of power. That is, Marxist theory underlines the direct practical and political importance of theories about the operation of power in society. I take up each of these injunctions as I attempt to work out the meaning of the genderedness of power.

NOTES

1. *Capital* (New York: International Publishers, 1967), 1:10. Hereinafter cited as *Capital* (International ed.).

2. These issues raise an immense number of epistemological questions, only some of which I hope to address here. I intend to focus my discussion on the consequences of these distinctions for the theorization of power. Within the general context of Marxist theory, these issues have been helpfully addressed by William Connolly, "Appearance and Reality in Politics," *Political Theory* 7, no. 4 (November 1979); Henri LeFebvre, *Dialectical Materialism*, trans. John Sturrock (New York: Viking Press, 1968); Lucien Goldmann, *The Human Sciences and Philosophy*, trans. Hayden White and Robert Anchor (New York: Viking Press, 1968); Herbert Marcuse, "The Concept of Essence," in *Negations*, trans. Jeremy Shapiro (Boston: Beacon Press, 1968); and Ralph Miliband, *Marxism and Politics* (New York: Oxford University Press, 1977), pp. 28–32.

3. I leave aside for the moment the argument that Marx's account of social relations is an improvement over those of the exchange theorists because it

does not justify domination and inequality. In any case, Marcuse was correct to point out that the truth of Marxist theory is "indeterminate" and can only be established by historical action. He says, perhaps more precisely (and more obscurely), "its concretion can thus result only *post festum*" ("The Concept of Essence," p. 73). It should also be clear that the questions of appearance and reality touch on the issue of the Marxist concepts of ideology and science. I shall attempt to avoid these issues too, except insofar as they bear directly on the central subject matter. For more general treatments of the issue of ideology and science in Marxist theory, see Alex Callinicos, *Althusser's Marxism* (London: Pluto Press, 1976); Lucio Colletti, *From Rousseau to Lenin* (New York: Monthly Review Press, 1972); Martin Seliger, *The Marxist Conception of Ideology* (New York: Cambridge University Press, 1977); John McMurtry, *The Structure of Marx's World View* (Princeton: Princeton University Press, 1978), Chap. 5; and Ernest Mandel, *Late Capitalism* (New York: Monthly Review Press, 1975), Chap. 16. Bertell Ollman has pointed out to me that my claim here is perhaps too strong. While these may be the two major class positions, other positions do exist. He is correct, and the reader should keep this point in mind throughout the discussion. Nevertheless, I have chosen to write as though there are only two classes in order to underline the importance of these two.

4. Karl Marx and Frederick Engels, *The German Ideology*, ed. C. J. Arthur (New York: International Publishers, 1964), p. 111.

5. Ibid., pp. 65–66.

6. George Lukacs, *History and Class Consciousness*, (Cambridge, Mass.: MIT Press, 1968), pp. xvii, xxiv, xviii respectively.

7. Marx, "Theses on Feuerbach," in *The German Ideology*, p. 121. Conscious human practice, then, is at once both an epistemological category and the basis for Marx's conception of the nature of humanity itself.

8. Here I use "praxis" as the most general reference to human self-realizing activity. Marx often refers to this activity as "work" and sometimes even as "labor." There are, however, some distinctions that can be made among these concepts. See for example, Bertell Ollman, *Alienation: Marx's Conception of Man in Capitalist Society* (New York: Cambridge University Press, 1971), pp. 99–105; and Marx and Engels, *The German Ideology*, p. 94.

9. Marx, "Theses on Feuerbach," in *The German Ideology*, p. 121. See also Marx, *Economic and Philosophic Manuscripts of 1844* (New York: International Publishers, 1964), p. 112. Nature itself, for Marx, appears as a form of human work, since he argues that humans duplicate themselves actively and come to contemplate themselves in a world of their own making (*ibid.*, p. 114). On the more general issue of the relation of natural to human worlds, see the very interesting account by Alfred Schmidt, *The Concept of Nature in Marx*, trans. Ben Fowkes (London: New Left Books, 1971).

10. Marx and Engels, *The German Ideology*, pp. 42, 59.

11. *Capital* (International ed.), p. 176.

12. Marx argues that human beings "begin to distinguish themselves from animals as soon as they begin to *produce* their means of subsistence, a step which is conditioned by their physical organization" (Marx and Engels, *The German Ideology*, p. 42).

13. *The Marx-Engels Reader*, ed. Robert Tucker, 1st ed. (New York: Norton, 1973), p. 212. There have been a variety of attacks on this concept, and I cannot hope to defend it here. Mandel cites one of the classic attacks, which can be found in Eugen von Böhm-Bawerk, *Karl Marx and the Close of His System* (New York: n.p., 1949). Another is by Vilfredo Pareto, in *Marxisme et économie pure* (Geneva: n.p., 1966). For a defense, see Roman Rosdolsky, *The Making of Marx's Capital* (New York: Humanities Press, 1977), pp. 626–40. Ernest Mandel, "Introduction," *Capital*, vol. I, trans. Ben Fowkes (Middlesex, England: Penguin, 1975) (hereinafter cited as *Capital* [Penguin ed.]) summarizes the debate, pp. 40 ff. Marx's own refutation of the "vulgar economist's" position is highly amusing (see *Capital* [International ed.], 1:191–92). Recall that this position was argued by Blau.

14. See *The Marx-Engels Reader*, p. 245.

15. But see *Capital* (International ed.), 1:197.

16. Ibid., pp. 193–94.

17. Marx terms the simple form of surplus value produced by prolongation of the working day "absolute surplus value." The surplus value arising from the curtailment of the necessary labor time and from the corresponding alteration in the respective lengths of the two components of the working day he calls relative surplus value. Relative surplus value arises from lowering the cost of subsistence for workers by cheapening products through technological innovations that act to increase productivity. See Mandel, "Introduction," p. 51; *The Marx-Engels Reader*, pp. 265–67. I should note as well that my continued use of the masculine pronoun is meant to underline the fact that Marx focused on men's and not women's lives.

18. Mandel has pointed out that when such alternatives have been available, juridical compulsion was frequently required (see "Introduction," p. 48). Marx has documented the draconian measures which produced a work force with few resources (see *Capital*, [International ed.], vol. I, Chaps. 26–28).

19. *Capital* (International ed.), 1:176.

20. Ibid.

21. See Herbert Marcuse, *Studies in Critical Philosophy*, trans. Joris de Bres (Boston: Beacon Press, 1973), p. 14.

22. *Capital* (International ed.), 1:183–84.

23. Marx, *1844 Ms.*, p. 137.

24. Ibid., p. 110.

25. Ibid., p. 111.

26. Ibid., pp. 112–13.

27. Ibid., p. 114.

28. These efforts have been ably documented by Harry Braverman, *Labor and Monopoly Capital* (New York: Monthly Review Press, 1976).

29. Marx, *1844 Ms.*, p. 181.

30. Ibid., p. 140.

31. See also Miliband, *Marxism and Politics*, p. 17.

32. Although this is a general point in Marxist theory, see Nicos Poulantzas, *State, Power, Socialism* (London: New Left Books, 1978), p. 17. He even suggests that political power is the "primordial" form. Zillah Eisenstein has

impressed on me the importance of differentiating my argument here from a reductionist "reflection theory" by stressing the relative autonomy of the state.

33. Miliband, *Marxism and Politics*, p. 18.

34. For an explication of the significance of the concepts of process and relation in Marxist theory see, for example, George Lukács, "What is Orthodox Marxism?" in *History and Class Consciousness* (Cambridge, Mass.: MIT Press, 1968); Karl Marx, "Introduction," *Grundrisse*, trans. Martin Nicolaus, (Middlesex, England: Penguin, 1973); and Ollman, *Alienation*.

35. Poulantzas, *State, Power, Socialism*, p. 147.

36. See ibid., pp. 147, 151. My own reading of the Marxist understanding of capacity suggests that this concept is to be explicated through an examination of the complexities of the concept of labor power.

37. Ibid., p. 151.

38. On the importance of this elevation, see Lukács, *History and Class Consciousness*, p. 154. This formulation clearly marks Poulantzas's evolution away from Althusserian Marxism.

39. Poulantzas, *State, Power, Socialism*, pp. 127, 131. While he simply dismisses the error, his formulation does state concisely the problematic that has led on the one hand to structural determination, and on the other to the difficulties of the problematic of the subject.

40. Ibid., p. 128; see also p. 131. This, along with my own understanding of the nature of Marxian theory, is much closer to Bertell Ollman's explication of "Relations." See Ollman, *Alienation*.

41. Miliband, *Marxism and Politics*, pp. 68–73. See also Poulantzas, *State, Power, Socialism*, p. 155.

42. It should be said that the "state" in Marxist theory refers to a variety of institutions which go far beyond ordinary notions of government to encompass the church, schools, etc.

43. My account at this point is oversimplified in the same way as Marx's account of the extraction of surplus value. Individual capitalists may and indeed often do more than simply benefit from the differential between the use value and the exchange value of labor power. Indeed, their position as competitors forces them to intensify labor, extend the hours of work, etc. But these factors remain peripheral to their role as structured by their participation in the purchase of labor power. In addition, one cannot see the working class's lack of means of production as an absolute: small businesses and various craftspeople, for example, *do* possess means of production. My point here is to emphasize the dominant features of social life in Western industrial societies.

44. There are limits to this process in capitalism, however. Too high a price for labor power may destroy the capitalist's surplus and put him out of business.

45. See Aristotle, *Politics* 1254a–1255b.

46. Marx, *Capital* (International ed.), 3:209.

47. Marx, *Capital* (International ed.), 1:645, italics in original. See also Marx, *1844 Ms.*, pp. 148–49, and Marx, *Grundrisse*, p. 107, for similar arguments.

48. Marx and Engels, *The German Ideology*, p. 64. See also Marx, *Grundrisse*, p. 239.

49. Alfred Sohn-Rethel makes this point. See his *Intellectual and Manual Labor: a Critique of Epistemology* (London: Macmillan, 1978), p. 55.

50. Marx, *Capital* (International ed.), 1:73.

51. See Marx and Engels, *The German Ideology*, p. 10; see also Marcuse, "The Concept of Essence," p. 72.

52. See Mandel, "Introduction," p. 21.

53. Lukacs, *History and Class Consciousness*, p. 150.

54. Ibid., p. 162. Thus, Marx can argue that although commodities at the level of circulation appear to be simple, even trivial things, a correct understanding demonstrates that they abound in "metaphysical subtleties and theological niceties" [*Capital* (International ed.), 1:71.] Marx's account of commodities in the first seventy pages of *Capital* makes clear that when any relation in the process of capitalist (re)production is grasped, that is, appropriated in its mediated form, one can "unravel" from it (or use it as a vantage point from which to understand) the totality of capitalist social relations. Lukács, for example, cites Marx's letter to Engels in arguments that "these gentry, the economists, have hitherto overlooked the extremely simple point that the form: *20 yards of linen* = *1 coat* is only the undeveloped basis of 20 yards of linen = £2, and that therefore the *simplest form of a commodity*, on which its value is not yet expressed as a relation to all other commodities but only as something *differentiated* from the commodity in its natural form, contains *the whole secret of the money form* and with it, in embryo, of *all the bourgeois forms of the product of labour*" (Letter of June 22, 1867, *Selected Correspondence* [Moscow: n.p., n.d.], p. 228, cited in *History and Class Consciousness*, note 30, p. 218). This statement is an excellent example of Marx's views on method. See also Marx, *Grundrisse*, pp. 101–5.

55. Colletti, *From Rousseau to Lenin*, p. 235. I should note that in traditional empiricist terms, a statement such as this misunderstands both science *and* revolution. Social scientists have become familiar with arguments that the student of politics needs some detachment from political activity and commitment. Many have argued that while values have a legitimate role in the selection of research problems, they play a less legitimate role in the identification of fact, in the assessment of evidence, and in the working out of conclusions. Marx's vision of science differs fundamentally from this. In his theory, the sciences of economics and politics have become the basis for a theory of revolution, a revolution implied by Marx's own analysis and included in the analysis from the beginning. Marx escapes the duality of observation and action by beginning from a world view founded on acting and feeling human beings. His stress on human activity (in the various forms of "praxis," "work," "labor") as the core of human existence forms the basis for his unification of observation and outrage.

56. Marcuse, "The Concept of Essence," p. 85. Marcuse carries the argument too far when he argues that the concepts themselves "belong to two levels; some deal with phenomena in their reified form, as they appear immediately, and others aim at their real content, as it presents itself to theory once its phenomenal form has been transcended." Thus he holds that there are two sets of concepts within Marxist economic theory—some corresponding to

the immediate appearance, the level of circulation or exchange, others to the level of production. This, however, locates the opposition between essence and appearance within Marxist theory itself rather than between Marxist theory and the categories of bourgeois life.

57. Ibid., p. 83. See also p. 74.

58. Ibid., p. 86. This formulation seems to contradict Marcuse's earlier formulation (n. 57 above) that there are two kinds of concepts in Marxist theory.

59. Marx, "Introduction to a Critique of Hegel's Philosophy of Right," in *The Marx-Engels Reader*, pp. 21–22.

60. Ibid.

61. "Appendix," *Capital* (Penguin ed.), 1:993.

62. Ibid, pp. 993–94.

63. Quoted by David McClellan, *Karl Marx* (New York: Viking, 1975), pp 31–32.

64. See Eduard Bernstein, *Evolutionary Socialism* (New York: Schocken Books, 1961); Rosa Luxemburg, "Reform and Revolution," in *Selected Political Writings*, ed. Dick Howard (New York: Monthly Review, 1971); A. A. Berle and Gardiner Means, *Modern Corporation and Private Property* (New York: Macmillan, 1932); Daniel Bell, *The Coming of Post-Industrial Society* (New York: Basic Books, 1973); Jurgen Habermas, *Toward a Rational Society* (Boston: Beacon Press, 1970); André Gorz, *Strategy for Labor* (Boston: Beacon Press, 1967); Herbert Marcuse, *One-Dimensional Man* (Boston: Beacon Press, 1974); Paul Baran and Paul Sweezy, *Monopoly Capital* (New York: Monthly Review Press, 1966); Ralph Miliband, *The State in Capitalist Society* (New York: Basic Books, 1969); Braverman, *Labor and Monopoly Capital*; Richard Sennett and Jonathan Cobb, *The Hidden Injuries of Class* (New York: Vintage Books, 1973); Lillian Rubin, *Worlds of Pain* (New York: Basic Books, 1976).

PART

II

*Compared to feminism,
communism is child's play.*

TI-GRACE ATKINSON, *1971*

The use of Marxian theory was able to advance the discussion by demonstrating how market theories represented the codification of the experience of the ruling class in capitalism. Thus, we were able to see both why certain theoretical moves had been made and how one might solve the problems these moves posed for the theorization of power. We have now to address the issue of how power carries gender as well as class. Both the criticisms laid out in Part I and the positive contributions of the Marxian account can be of help, the latter most importantly as a source of methodological precepts and a model for the construction of a set of charges to the theorist of power. Yet on the specific question of the ways power is gendered, I believe Marxian theory can be of little direct help.

This may seem an unjustified conclusion about the work of a man who called for the abolition of the family and argued that the status of women in capitalism was at bottom a system of public and private prostitution, a man who held that the status of women was so important that on the basis of the relation of women and men one could "judge man's whole level of development."[1] Yet, despite his concerns about what he and other Marxists termed the emancipation of women, Marx (and most Marxists following him) failed to analyze the work of women and their specific relations to the process of capitalist production, and failed to recognize the importance of social conflicts other than class conflict. Thus Marx's critique of private property fails to recognize that this property is in fact in male control.[2] The Marxian reluctance to face questions of gender, sexuality, and sexual domination means that Marxist theory provides inadequate accounts of the genderedness of power relations feminists work to understand, most particularly those connected with sexuality, the family, and what had been defined as "personal life."[3]

Many feminists share my belief that the contradictorily gender-blind and gender-biased nature of Marx's categories is a major theoretical source for the inadequacy of Marxist theory. As Marx himself admits, "We set out from real, active *men*, and on the basis of their real life-process we demonstrate the development of the ideological reflexes and echoes of this life-process."[4] While one might argue that this usage simply replicates the use of the neutral "man," Marx's procedure was in fact to set out from men's labor and to ignore the specificity of women's labor.

One can see the effects of these gender-blind categories in a number of places where questions related to women's labor arise and could have been attended to. For the feminist theorist, one of the most intriguing occurs in *The German Ideology*, where Marx and Engels take up the division of labor. They note that the family was in the beginning the only social relationship. And similarly, that the first division of labor was the sexual division of labor—even, originally, the "division of labour in the sexual act." Yet they avoid consideration of the significance of this fact by labeling the relations within the family and the sexual division of labor as "natural."[5] And they manage to dismiss this division of labor with the statement (unsupported by any argument) that the "division of labour only becomes *truly such* from the moment when a division of material and mental labor appears."[6] Thus Marx and Engels recognize the existence of the sexual division of labor, but at the same time fail to devote analytic attention to its significance.

Women's Labor and the Production of Surplus Value

Marx's inattention to the specifics of women's labor and to the ways such attention might affect his analysis affects the very heart of his theory, his account of how surplus value is produced by the worker and appropriated by the capitalist. Let me call attention to an important feature of the discussion of surplus value in the last chapter. There I stated that Marx argues that the value of labor power is equivalent to the means of subsistence necessary for the production of labor power. If we look more closely at the passage from *Capital*, however, we find both some inconsistencies and a blindness to the significance of women's labor. Thus Marx adds that the necessary means of subsistence include the means necessary to produce children who can later replace the worker.[7] And here one might expect some note to be taken of the role of the childrearer. But Marx passes over this point and indeed takes the position that only the *commodities* required by the laborer and *his* children are to be counted. He states that the minimum limit of the value of labor power is determined by the value of only those means of subsistence that are the *commodities* required daily for the production of labor power.[8] It should be said, however, that Marx adds a third formulation, which he seems to see as not inconsistent with the preceding ones, a formulation that could allow for attention to women's labor. Thus he states: "The value of labour-power resolves itself into the value of a definite quantity of the means of subsistence. It therefore varies with the value of these means or with the quantity of labour requisite for their production."[9] But despite the fact that this formulation allows the incorporation of nonwaged labor, Marx gives attention only to wage labor and commodities.

Given the overall positions taken by Marx, one can conclude that for him the value of labor power depends only on labor power incorporated into commodities; no attention is given to the value of labor power consumed directly or incorporated into use values. Women's labor as such vanishes in this theoretical move, since both when Marx wrote and today an important percentage of women's labor power takes the form of use values consumed in the home. Both the production of use values in the home and the labor required to consume commodities brought home are disproportionately done by women.[10] And this labor is not included in Marx's formulation of the value of labor power. Perhaps because of his blindness to women's labor, Marx sees no need to give analytic attention to issues such as the sex segregation of the labor market, the limitation of women workers to only a few job categories, or the income differential between women and men in similar jobs—this despite the fact that evidence for these phenomena is clear in *Capital* itself.[11]

Perhaps because of this inattention, much of Marx's discussion of the labor of women both groups it together with the labor of children and centers the discussion not on women's labor but on the moral effects of their employment. Marx argues that the worker had previously been a free agent who sold his own labor power, but because of the employment of women and children, he now sells his wife and child as would a slave dealer.[12] Thus the labor of the wife and children is held to belong to the man (though perhaps this comment is better taken as a sarcastic presentation of the social relations of capitalism). And Marx notes what he sees as the enormous mortality of the children of operatives as being due, he says, to the employment of mothers. He cites the finding that where the employment of women is low, so is the child death rate, and concludes that the problem is the "moral degradation" caused by the capitalist exploitation of women and children.[13] Marx's concern for the moral depravity of women and girls caused by their employment in wage labor shows up in other places as well—indeed, even affects his vision of the future. In the "Critique of the Gotha Programme," Marx seems to question whether communism should abolish the sexual division of labor because some branches of industry are especially unhealthy for the female body or morally objectionable for the female sex.[14]

All this can be traced to the fact that because Marx gives no attention to the gender of the "worker," the worker is presumed to be male. It can of course be objected that in volume I of *Capital*, Marx was concerned with a simple two-class, two-man model, one that ignored such major factors as the complexity of class structure in industrializing societies, the effects of imperialism, and the tendencies toward monopoly. Moreover, it could be claimed with justice that his real contributions to the understanding of capital were due to this theoretical simplicity. But this means that Marxist theory gives us little help in constructing a theory that can account for the genderedness of power.

The consequence of Marx's use of gender-blind categories such as "human labor power" and "class" is that he gives a gender-biased account of social production and an incomplete account of the real life-processes of human beings. In Marxist terms, one might argue that with regard to women's labor, he has fallen into a kind of abstractness, that is, he has given the kind of partial account characteristic of market theories.

Gender and Class

The gender-blind character of Marxian theory has a second result, one that emerges in understandings of the nature of class. Many Marxists have claimed that all societal conflicts can be understood as "directly or indirectly derived from or related to, class conflicts," and have argued that other societal conflicts, such as those arising from racial or sexual domination, are derivations of class conflict.[15]

While they have included women in the list of the oppressed and exploited, then, Marxists have failed to recognize that women's specific relationships to the means of production do not fit the models Marx developed out of an examination of men's situations. Engels' analysis of the role of women has been definitive for many Marxists: Monogamous marriage is an essential condition for the development of industrial capitalism, and since monogamous marriage in Western industrial society grew out of the institution of private property, the abolition of private property would relieve women's oppression. Engels expected that even if the institution of monogamous marriage did not disappear, major changes would occur. Since in his view both the supremacy of the man and the indissolubility of the marriage contract resulted from the economic situation, these would disappear with the restructuring of the economic base.[16]

Marxist theory bears other marks of this blindness. For example, as a result of the focus on the life activity of men and not women, Marxist theory has been led to treat relations within the family and outside the family in a contradictory fashion. Zillah Eisenstein has pointed out that when Engels discusses the family, he notes that within it the man is in the position of the bourgeoisie and the woman, the proletarian. But when he discusses relations outside the family, this analogy disappears, and people are treated only as ungendered agents of the process of production.[17] And Heidi Hartmann notes that when Marxists do take up the position of women, they discuss the relation of women to the system of production rather than the relation of women to men.[18]

Perhaps more important, attention to women's life activity as well as men's might well require a re-examination of such basic and seemingly gender-blind categories as class. Class in Marxist theory is a category based on men's experience, a category that mistakes men's experience for the general human experience. Marx himself, for example, argues that women and children are "supplementary" wage labor, and Engels sees the world of paid employment—from then to now a predominantly masculine world—as the sphere in which women's problems can be solved. More recently, writers such as Nicos Poulantzas in his *Classes in Contemporary Capitalism* totally ignored those persons without paid employment and by implication suggested that they had no class position. He seems to have imagined the working class to be composed of blue-collar factory workers, and has argued that clerical and service workers (mostly female) were part of the *petit bourgeoisie*, a "penumbra" of wavering elements around the periphery of the stalwart blue-collar working class.[19] One of his critics pointed out that by the definition he was using, only 14.6 percent of even the economically active females (working 20 hours a week or more) could be considered part of the working class, as opposed to 22.7 percent of the economically active men.[20] This is a curious reversal of Engels' suggestion that within the family the wife occupies the position of proletarian. Now she is the representative of the *petit bourgeoisie* in the heart of the family. What does it do to this kind of class analysis that a large percentage of female clerical and service workers are married to skilled, semiskilled, and unskilled blue-collar workers?[21]

My point in raising this issue is not to enter the immensely controversial and complicated analysis of the specifics of class distinctions in advanced capitalism. Rather, I want to point to the kinds of issues that might arise for Marxist theory if attention were directed to women's lives and to the theoretical problems that have resulted from inattention.[22]

Toward a More Adequate Theory

Despite their problems with Marxist theory, many feminists have held that feminism and Marxism "inhabit the same space," that they are "at once incompatible and in real need of each other," and that "each theory deals with important issues which the other slights."[23] Among feminists interested in taking up the insights of Marxist theory but dissatisfied with its narrow focus on class, attention has been centered on the possibilities for extracting or taking over Marx's method.[24] The power of Marx's critique of class domination underlines the need for a theory that can put individual and intentional action in the context of structural constraints, including gender and race as well as class, and can explain how what seem on the surface voluntary interactions between equal participants are in reality deeply and structurally unequal.

We need to begin again to construct a theory of women's oppression and exploitation which is both materialist and historical:

1. The theory would be materialist in the sense of explaining the relations and factors that structure women's lives.
2. It would be historical in the sense of examining both the changes and the concrete regularities that have persisted over time.

What is needed, in sum, is a thoroughgoing feminist historical materialism that can explain the structural mechanisms and the laws of tendency by which the capitalist form of patriarchy operates.[25] The danger of attempting to rest such an effort on Marx's analysis has been pointed out: The very power of the Marxian method can lead the relation of feminism to Marxism to be that of the traditional husband and wife in English common law: "Marxism and feminism are one and that one is Marxism."[26]

While I recognize the importance of developing a feminist historical materialism, my effort here is much more modest. Here I attempt to work out only what a feminist historical materialist epistemology can allow us to discover about the genderedness of relations of domination. To do this I develop the concept of a feminist standpoint and use this as a basis for understanding the sexual or erotic form taken by gendered power relations. I propose to expand and modify Marxian analysis in order to understand the gender as well as class dimensions of relations of domination. This of course is only one part of a collective effort to construct an account of women's oppression from the ground up, having taken what we can from Marxist theory.

Part II takes a form similar to that of Part I. I begin by focusing on questions of how *eros* has structured community, and how *eros* and power have been connected. I argue that in the contemporary Western world, the gender carried by power associates masculinity with domination and by means of this connection fuses sexuality, violence, and death. The gender carried by power is evidenced in the ideology and institutions of "normal" heterosexuality. In addition, I argue, these associations, understandings, and practices characterize not only the "private" world of individual action and sexuality but are more tellingly found in the ideals of public life put forward in ancient Athenian political philosophy. Moreover, the public sphere and ideals for political action first took theoretical form in an all-male community. My argument for the genderedness of current understandings of power gains additional support from the fact that when women (not necessarily feminists) write about power, they put forward accounts that are both strikingly similar to each other and strikingly different from those of the men considered in this book. Indeed, one can almost argue that there is a separate and distinct women's tradition of theorizing power. I argue that these gender differences have implications for an adequate theory of power and suggest that gender and class may have similar epistemological consequences.

What is needed is a transformation of our understanding of sexuality, or, more broadly, *eros* along lines similar to the transformation Marxian theory makes in the theorization of power. Such a transformation can be accomplished by a relocation of theory onto the epistemological terrain defined by women's lives. But whereas Marx relocated power onto the epistemological ground of production, I argue that women's lives provide a related but more adequate epistemological terrain for understanding power. Women's different understanding of power provides suggestive evidence that women's experience of power relations, and thus their understanding, may be importantly and structurally different from the lives and therefore the theories of men. I suggest that, like the lives of proletarians *vis-a-vis* capital, women's lives make available a particular and privileged vantage point not only on the power relations between women and men but on power relations more generally. The construction of a more complete and adequate account of power relations on the basis of women's perspective requires the articulation of an epistemology that grows from women's life activity. The task requires the same kind of effort as was laid out in Chapter 6.

On the basis of an examination of women's life activity in contemporary capitalism, I describe the world view available from the adoption of a feminist standpoint. Such a standpoint (and I mean to refer to all five of the claims the concept carries) can form the ground for an explanation of why the erotic dimension of power has taken the form of domination, and why women theorists have understood power in such different ways than most men. It can also aid in the transformation of the meaning of *eros*. In addition, such a standpoint, by exposing a level of reality beneath that defined by production, one that can be characterized as the epistemological level of reproduction, can allow us to begin to understand the theoretical relations between gender and class, and to recognize the epistemological level defined by exchange as the expression not only of a capitalist vantage point but also a masculinist one.

NOTES

1. See, respectively, Karl Marx and Frederick Engels, "The Communist Manifesto," in *The Marx-Engels Reader*, ed. Robert Tucker, 2nd ed. (New York: Norton, 1973), pp. 488, 83.

2. This is a point many feminist theorists have made. See, for example, Roberta Hamilton, *The Liberation of Women: A Study of Patriarchy and Capitalism* (London: Allen and Unwin, 1978), p. 13; Lorenne Clarke, "Introduction," *The Sexism of Social and Political Thought* (Toronto: University of Toronto Press, 1979); Zillah Eisenstein, "Developing a Theory of the Capitalist Patriarchy," in *Capitalist Patriarchy and the Case for Socialist Feminism*, ed. Zillah Eisenstein (New York: Monthly Review Press, 1978), p. 11; Heidi Hartmann, "The Unhappy Marriage of Marxism and Feminism: Toward a More Progressive Union," *Capital and Class* no. 8 (Summer, 1979): 1–2. The classic Marxian statement on the causes and solutions of the oppression of women is of course Frederick Engels, *The Origin of the Family, Private Property and the State* (New York: International Publishers, 1942). The contradictions in his theory have been pointed to by Jane Flax, "Do Feminists Need Marxism?" in *Building Feminist Theory* (New York: Longman, 1981).

3. The Marxian lack of theoretical attention to these issues had a practical effect as well. See, for example, the discussion of the role of women and personal life in the Communist party. Ellen Kay Trimberger, "Women in the Old and New Left: The Evolution of a Politics of Personal Life," *Feminist Studies* 5, no. 3 (Fall, 1979); Karen Margolis, "The Long and Winding Road (reflections on *Beyond the Fragments*)," *Feminist Review* 5 (1980); and Sheila Rowbotham, "The Women's Movement and Organizing for Socialism," *Radical America* 13, no. 5 (September–October 1979).

4. Karl Marx and Frederick Engels, *The German Ideology*, ed. C. J. Arthur (New York: International Publishers, 1964), p. 47.

5. Ibid., p. 49. One should note that Marx and Engels often use the term "natural" as a synonym for "spontaneous" in Part I of *The German Ideology*, or as a way to indicate that "this is how X happened." My point is not so much to accuse them of biological reductionism as to point to the ways they moved away from an analysis of the significance of the sexual as opposed to the mental/manual division of labor, which could as easily have been classified as natural, in one of several of the senses in which they used the term. See also Karl Marx, *Capital* (New York: International Publishers, 1967), 1:351, 420, and 519 for other usages.

6. Marx and Engels, *The German Ideology*, p. 51; my italics.

7. Marx, *Capital*, 1:172.

8. Ibid., p. 173; my italics.

9. Ibid., p. 172.

10. See Batya Weinbaum and Amy Bridges, "The Other Side of the Paycheck," in Eisenstein, ed., *Capitalist Patriarchy*; and Heidi Hartmann, "The Family as the Locus of Gender, Class, and Political Struggle: The Example of Housework," *Signs* 6, no. 3 (Spring 1981).

11. See for example his references to the "natural division of labor" in *Capital* (International ed.), 1:351, 420, 519. See also his sense that the value of labor power should be calculated on the basis of the price of subsistence for a nuclear family including two parents and children. He holds that "the value of labour power was determined, not only by the labour time necessary to maintain the individual adult labourer, but also by that necessary to maintain his family. Machinery, by throwing every member of that family onto the labour market spreads the value of the man's labour over his whole family. It thus depreciates his labour-power" (ibid., p. 395; see also pp. 519, 568). And note too that Marx includes widows in the lowest stratum of the surplus labor force, along with those industrially injured (ibid., p. 649) and that he recognizes the difficult position of married females with dependent families (ibid., p. 402). In addition, Marx argues that capital for its self-expansion "has usurped the labor necessary in the home of the family" (ibid., p. 395).

12. Ibid., p. 396.

13. I owe this insight to Lisa Rofel.

14. I am indebted to Alison Jaggar for this point.

15. See Ralph Miliband, *Marxism and Politics* (New York: Oxford University Press, 1977), p. 19, for the quotation. That this is not altogether universal is indicated by the fact that theorists such as Nicos Poulantzas have been willing to at least recognize that power relations not only extend beyond issues of the state but beyond class questions to those which include the issue of phallocratic domination. See his *State, Power, and Socialism* (London: New Left Books, 1978), p. 43.

16. Frederick Engels, *Origins of the Familiy, Private Property and the State*, pp. 73, 148.

17. Eisenstein, "Developing a Theory," pp. 14–15.

18. Hartmann, "Unhappy Marriage," p. 2.

19. Nicos Poulantzas, *Classes in Contemporary Capitalism*, trans. David Fernbach (London: New Left Books, 1975), esp. Part III, secs. 3, 4, 6, 9.

20. Erik O. Wright, *Class, Crisis, and the State* (London: New Left Books, 1978), pp. 56–57. See also Erik O. Wright, "Varieties of Marxist Conceptions of Class Structure," *Politics and Society* 9, no. 3 (1980).

21. To be more precise, 44.8 percent of the wives of skilled blue-collar workers are clerical and sales workers. And 38.2 percent of these wives are in unskilled blue-collar (primarily service) jobs. For male unskilled blue-collar workers, the figures for wives' employment are 33.1 percent and 45.7 percent respectively. See Stephen J. Rose, *Social Stratification in the United States: An Analytic Guidebook* (Baltimore: Social Graphics, 1979).

22. There are a number of issues apart from class which would have to be re-thought on the basis of attention to women's lives. Among these are the Marxian periodization of history. Joan Kelly-Gadol has pointed out the importantly differing experiences of women and men in "Did Women Have a Renaissance?" in *Becoming Visible: Women in European History*, ed. Renate Bridenthal and Claudia Koonz (Boston: Houghton Mifflin 1977). In addition, an area of Marxist theory feminists have been concerned to critique is humankind's relation to nature. Communism, as Marx understood it, rested on the "mastery of nature," the bending of nature to human will. Marx's stress on human work as the basis for human community, and on the creative and sensuous possibilities for humanized work, however, suggests that a feminist rereading/rewriting of Marx might put forward a very different account of the possible relation to nature. While Marx himself often referred to the mastering of nature, I question whether a fully liberatory society could depend on the mastery of anything— one's "base" instincts or appetites, as Plato held, another person or class of persons, or "nature." The question of the human relation to nature bears directly on the issue of whether human work can ever be a sensuous delight, or whether it is only in freedom from necessary labor that one can become fully human. My own reading (or perhaps revision) of Marxist theory would lead me to contend that domination and liberation are fundamental contradictions and that, particularly when analyzing women's labor, the pair freedom/necessity provides very poor analytical categories. See below, Chap. 10, for a more complete argument. See also Isaac Balbus, *Marxism and Domination* (Princeton: Princeton University Press, 1982).

23. Sheila Rowbotham, *Women, Resistance, and Revolution* (New York: Random House, 1972), p. 246; Hamilton, *Liberation of Women*, p. 77. Rowbotham is responsible for the first two quotations.

24. See, for example, the different kinds of arguments put forward in Zillah Eisenstein, "Some Notes on the Relations of Capitalist Patriarchy," in Eisenstein, ed., *Capitalist Patriarchy*; Hartmann, "Unhappy Marriage"; Nancy Hartsock, "Feminist Theory and the Development of Revolutionary Strategy," in Eisenstein, ed., *Capitalist Patriarchy*; Juliet Mitchell, *Woman's Estate* (New York: Pantheon, 1970).

25. It should be noted that I take the position that the oppression of women must be understood to be structural rather than ideological or attitudinal, and thereby part company with many Marxists and a number of Marxist feminists.

26. Hartmann, "Unhappy Marriage," p. 1.

7

Gender and Power: Masculinity, Violence, and Domination

Power irreducibly involves questions of *eros*. I put this claim forward both as a logical point (*eros* and power both involve questions about fusion and community) and a commonplace observation (many social scientists have noted that power is linked with notions of potency, virility, and manliness). There is more to my claim than this, however. Like power relations, relations structured by *eros* involve the establishment of relations with others. They, like exercises of power over others, or like the objectification of being Marx foresaw in unalienated production, represent the creation of community. This community may be fragile and instrumental or deep-going and intrinsically valuable to its members. The form of the community depends fundamentally on the shape of the human nature and human sociality it expresses, and thus on the mode of interaction or practice of power within it. To the extent that either sexual relations or other power relations are structured by a dynamic of domination/submission, the others as well will operate along those dimensions, and in consequence, the community as a whole will be structured by domination. This chapter, then, addresses the nature and character of *eros* in our culture and its significance for both structuring and understanding human community. Particularly in the context of the current debates about sexuality, I cannot pretend to have put forward a complete account. Rather, my purpose here is to focus on the association of sexuality with power.

Sexuality and Society

One of the first questions to be addressed is what is meant by sexuality. Definitions of what is to be included often cover many aspects of life. For example, Freud included but did not clarify the interrelationships among such various things as libido, or the basic tendency toward being alive and reproducing, the biological attributes of being male or female, sensuality, masculinity and femininity, reproductive behavior, and intense sensations in various parts of the body, especially the genitals.[1] And Jeffrey Weeks, summarizing our culture's understanding of sex, argues that in our society "sex has become the supreme secret," which is at the same time the "truth" of our being. It defines us socially and morally. Moreover, the common understanding of sexuality treats it as a "supremely private experience," which is at the same time "a thing in itself."[2]

My own reading of the literature suggests that in contrast to these definitions, we should understand sexuality not as an essence or set of properties defining an individual, nor as a set of drives and needs (especially genital) of an individual. Rather, we should understand sexuality as culturally and historically defined and constructed. Anything can become eroticized, and thus there can be no "abstract and universal category of 'the erotic' or 'the sexual' applicable without change to all societies."[3] Rather, sexuality must be understood as a series of cultural and social practices and meanings that both structure and are in turn structured by social relations more generally. Thus, "sex is relational, is shaped in social interaction, and can only be understood in its historical context. ..."[4]

Because a number of theorists have argued for this position in several different contexts, it seems unnecessary to go into detail here, but to indicate that I subscribe in a general way to their arguments.[5] At the same time, because sexuality is commonly seen as rooted in an unchanging human nature and biology, it is relevant to add here a reminder about the continuing significance of my assumption that human activity or practice has both an ontological and an epistemological status. Thus, human activity constructs a historical and constantly changing human nature, and with it a set of historically specific and changing sexual relations. It is worth reiterating this point here since in much of the literature on sexuality, possibilities both for systematically changing and socially constructed human nature and for changing dynamics of sexual excitement remain unaddressed. One wonders about the extent to which many theorists may hold to a view of a sexuality either rooted in human nature or a human nature that, while socially constructed, does not change in this area.[6]

Hostility and Sexual Excitement

If sexuality is a social and historical construction, how has contemporary Western culture shaped sexuality? There is a surprising degree of consensus that hostility and domination, as opposed to intimacy and physical pleasure, are central to sexual excitement. In attempting to understand these connections, the work of Robert Stoller is central.[7] Stoller contends that in our culture, "putting aside the obvious effects that result from direct stimulation of erotic bodily parts it is hostility—the desire, overt or hidden, to harm another person—that generates and enhances sexual excitement." Thus, erotic excitement must be understood as only one component of sexual excitement; others are "triumph, rage, revenge, fear, anxiety, risk."[8] Moreover, he contends, "the same dynamics, though in different mixes and degrees, are found in almost everyone, those labeled perverse and those not so labeled."[9] He suggests as well that if researchers of sexual excitement look closely they will discover that "permutations of hostility will be found far more frequently than is acknowledged today" and to underline this point, we should note that he states that he chose the term hostility, rather than power or aggression, to indicate that "harm and suffering" are central to sexual excitement.[10]

As Stoller outlines it, the mechanisms that construct sexual excitement rest most fundamentally on fetishization and on the dehumanization and objectification of the sexual object. And these are associated with debasement of the object and the construction of mystery, risk, illusion, and a search for revenge. The sexual object is to be stripped of its humanity; the focus is on breasts, buttocks, legs, and penises, not on faces. Or an inanimate object, an animal, or a partial aspect of a human such as a breast or penis is given the personality taken from the object. These are the ways fetishization as a means for creating sexual excitement can go far beyond the clinical cases in which the fetishism is obvious. It is present in the widespread practice of treating people as though they were only organs or functions.[11]

Despite our dismay at such formulations, we should note that these practices are so ubiquitous that they have been enshrined in ordinary language. One has only to glance at the popular or vulgar language surrounding sexual activity. In each case, human reality is reduced to its most mechanical dimensions. Thus, one philosopher cites the reduction of the term for testes (from the Latin term suggesting witnesses) to "balls" and the reduction of the female partner as a whole to a "skirt," "broad," "chick," "pussy," or "piece."[12]

Given our stated cultural ideals, one would not expect to find hostility at the center of sexuality. Why not intimacy, warmth, or physical pleasure? But Stoller is not alone in finding hostility in sexual excitement. A wide variety of theorists have commented on the relation of hostility and anger to sexual excitement. For example, Kinsey noted that "the closest parallel to the picture of sexual response is found in the known physiology of anger."[13] Or consider a psychologist's note that sex can be a power weapon and that "in general it has far more intimate relationships with dominance feeling than it has with physiological drive."[14] And Kate Millett has commented that in some literary sources "the pleasure of humiliating the sexual object appears to be far more intoxicating than sex itself."[15]

Nor are references to the relation of sexual excitement and hostility limited to passing comments. These links are at the center of philosopher/pornographer Georges Bataille's theory and fiction. As he describes it, "sexual activity is a form of violence." And the desire of the "potential killer in every man" to kill relates to the taboo on murder in the same way that the desire for sexual activity relates to the various prohibitions on it. Killing and sexual activity share both prohibitions and religious significance. Their unity is demonstrated by religious sacrifice since the latter

> is intentional like the act of the man who *lays bare*, desires and wants to penetrate his victim. The lover *strips* the beloved of her identity no less than the bloodstained priest his human or animal victim. The woman in the hands of the assailant is *despoiled* of her being ... loses the firm barrier that once separated her from others ... is *brusquely laid open* to the violence of the sexual urges set loose in the organs of reproduction; she is *laid open* to the impersonal violence that overwhelms her from without.[16]

Note the use of the terms "lover" and "assailant" as synonyms and the presence of the female as victim.

Issues of sexuality and hostility appear as well in the context of analyses of racism. Thus one writer notes that the practice of linking apes, blacks, and Jews with mythological satyrs "reveals that there are sensitive spots in the human soul at a level where thought becomes confused and where sexual excitement is strangely linked with violence and aggressiveness. ..."[17] And another writer, in the context of an argument about the connections between racial hostility and sexuality, makes a fairly detailed case that "the gratification in sexual conquest derives from the experience of defilement—of reducing the elevated woman to the 'dirty' sexual level, of polluting that which is seen as pure, sexualizing that which is seen as unsexual, animalizing that which is seen as 'spiritual.'"[18]

In the context of these statements it is not surprising to encounter a common-sense view that sex is dangerous and violent.[19] Nor should we be surprised to find this violence deeply ingrained in language itself: The best known of the vulgar sexual verbs comes from the German *flicken*, meaning "to strike"; similar violent verbs are present in Latin, Celtic, Irish, Gaelic, and so forth; and consider other contemporary English terms, such as "screw" or "bang."[20]

The hostility Stoller analyzes is fueled in part by danger and the construction of risk. Childhood traumas, frustrations, and dangers are turned into risks where there is a more clearly calculable outcome, where the degree of risk can be carefully controlled. This risk, then can be experienced as excitement, the childhood trauma re-created as adult sexual script. But this can happen only if the risk is simulated and the danger not too extreme.[21]

The dynamic of undoing childhood traumas and frustrations is, Stoller argues, central to the construction of sexual excitement. And while hostility is embedded in a number of social institutions and practices (e.g., humor), Stoller argues that the hostility in sexual excitement grows out of traumas and frustrations intimately connected with and threatening to the development of masculinity or femininity. He has, of course, much company in his position that these practices are continuing attempts to undo childhood traumas and frustrations that threatened the development of masculinity or femininity.[22] He concludes that sadomasochism has to be seen as a central feature of *most* sexual excitement and that the desire to hurt others in revenge for having been hurt is essential for most people's sexual excitement all the time, but not all people's excitement all the time.[23]

Some feminists have criticized Stoller's argument. Kathleen Barry states that his argument about how hostility is infused into sexuality removes responsibility from the actors, who are in most cases males. As she sums up his position, he is arguing that the fetish is created to right past wrongs, so when a woman is being raped, the rapist is not really raping her but rather is fetishizing her to right the past wrongs of being denied sexual intercourse with his mother. One can see, she adds, how this explanation plays into myth that black men rape to right the wrongs of racial injustice, or lower-class men to right past or present wrongs of poor working conditions.[24] Moreover, Stoller's work leads to the conclusion that "sexual violence simply can't be helped— it's nature—as said Sade, as said Freud, now says Stoller...."[25]

There are really two issues here: the responsibility of those who commit violent acts against another, and the question of whether sexual violence is inevitable. On each point, Stoller's writing gives some support to Barry's reading, yet I think her dismissal of his insights goes too far. As I read him, Stoller is analyzing a cultural tradition of violence he neither endorses nor supports. While he puts far too much responsibility for producing "normal heterosexuals" on the mother, I have difficulty reading him as saying that rapists should not be held responsible for their acts. In addition, he explicitly raises the question whether hostility is a real universal or is simply ubiquitous, that is, whether gross hostility is not necessary but only usual.[26] He argues as well that it is probably not inevitable, even if universal, that people debase their sexual objects. And he proclaims himself disappointed that sexual pleasure in most people depends on neurotic mechanisms. Finally, he suggests in a hopeful tone that perhaps there is a continuum toward less use of hostility in sexual excitement. Especially in the range of "the normative," Stoller believes there may be both hostility and affection and capacity for closeness. At the far end of the continuum, he suggests, there may be a small group of contented and secure people who are not so frightened by intimacy that they must fetishize the other person.[27] Still, Barry's view that Stoller sees the dynamic of hostility as inevitable does gain support from the fact that Stoller seems to see no way to avoid the dynamic of hostility, does note that his views put him at odds with those who see sex as a cultural and historical phenomenon (although from the text it is unclear what he means by this), and does title his last chapter "The Necessity of Perversion."[28]

Andrea Dworkin objects to Stoller's work on other grounds. She accuses Stoller of arguing that sexual sadism is manifested in both males and females. Women too are sadists, she quotes Stoller as saying. Thus he is justifying men's abuse of women because women are "formidable" sadists too, "despite the fact that it is not socially or historically self-evident."[29] As she puts it, "The sexual philosophers, like the pornographers, need to believe that women are more dangerous than men or as dangerous as men so as to be justified in their social and sexual domination of them."[30] Moreover, she argues, Stoller mistakes female suffering for female triumph. Belle's fantasies (Belle is the pseudonym of the female patient on whom Stoller bases much of his theorization of sexual excitement) are those in which she is ostensibly in the control of brutal, powerful men who try to dominate her but in Stoller's view cannot enslave her. He should have seen these sexual images as symbolic of a larger sexual reality in which she is "used, trapped, humiliated, angry, and powerless to change the values of the men who devalue her." Instead, Stoller holds that Belle chooses "sexual masochism because through it she triumphs over men whom ultimately she controls because she is the provocation to which they respond. This is an expression 'of her own oversexed nature.' She wants it, they all do."[31]

Once again Stoller's text lends support to Dworkin's charges. He is clearly unaware of the lack of choices available to most women and far too unquestioning of the cultural institutions and cultural apparatus of male supremacy (e.g., he takes the cultural meanings of the penis for granted, and describes it as "aggressive, unfettered, unsympathetic, humiliating").[32] There may, however, be a deep theoretical disagreement between Dworkin and Stoller. The latter sees not just female masochism, but all masochism as from another point of view expressing sadism and power.[33] The correctness of Stoller's account receives support from an interesting quarter: A very similar position is taken by lesbian feminists who practice sadomasochism. As they describe the dynamics of sadomasochism among lesbian feminists, it is the masochist, or "bottom," who retains control.[34] Whatever their differences on this point, Stoller's work seems to imply a conclusion very similar to Dworkin's own: "Antagonism is established in male sexual thought as a key element in sexual excitement."[35]

Dworkin's position that Stoller attempts to assimilate male and female sexual behavior misses what I found to be one of the most intriguing and interesting aspects of his work: He highlights the existence of important but admittedly unexamined gender differences in sexual behavior and sexual excitement, differences that allow me to read Stoller as supportive of my own contention that what is culturally defined as sexuality for us is a masculine sexuality that does not grow from or express the lives of women. The area in which these differences emerge for him is in what he terms perversion.

Masculinity, Perversion, and Normality

I should note that Stoller would probably not agree with the use I have made of his arguments. In particular we part company over the meaning to be attached to, and the behaviors to be described as, perversions. Despite the great prevalence of the practices he would characterize as perverse, he wants very much to keep the term as a way to characterize deviance.[36] He defines perversion as "the erotic form of hatred," a fantasy either acted out or restricted to a daydream of doing harm. It is a fantasy motivated by hostility—the wish to do harm—not by simple aggression or forcefulness.[37]

He adds that "the more gross the hostility, the less the question that one is dealing with perversion. Murder that sexually excites, mutilation for excitement, rape, sadism with precise physical punishments such as whipping or cutting, enchaining and binding games, defecating or urinating on one's object—all are on a lessening scale of conscious rage toward one's sex object, in which an essential purpose is for one to be superior to, harmful to, triumphant over another. And so it is also in the non-physical sadisms like exhibitionism, voyeurism, dirty phone calls or letters, use of prostitutes, and most forms of promiscuity."[38] It is interesting to note here that the psychological dynamics of perversion do not differ importantly from those Stoller has identified as typical of sexual excitement. Hostility, fetishization, and dehumanization figure centrally in both perverse and "normal" sexual excitement.[39] He attempts to distinguish variant sexual practices from perverse ones on the basis of whether or not the "aberrant" practice is or is not primarily motivated by hostility.

Stoller found two puzzles in his work on perversion. First, he continually ran into the problem that by his definition, where hostility was central to perversion, a great deal, perhaps even most, of contemporary "normal" heterosexual sexual activity must be labeled perverse. Thus he himself notes that we risk finding that there is very little sexual behavior that might not have a touch of the perverse. He attempts to draw back from this position, however: Wouldn't this ruin the meaning of the term perverse, he asks? And he complains that "the idea of normality crumbles" if one notes the ubiquity of sexual pathology in heterosexuals who are supposed to be the "normals."[40] One must deal with behavior that is not in a statistical sense aberrant. Stoller is not alone in finding this difficulty; the scholars at the Institute for Sex Research found something similar. Dworkin calls attention to a statement from Sex Offenders: An Analysis Of Types: "If we labelled all punishable sexual behavior as a sex offense, we would find ourselves in the ridiculous situation of having all of our *male* histories consist almost wholly of sex offenders . . . . The man who kisses a girl [sic] in defiance of her expressed wishes is committing a forced sexual relationship and is liable to an assault charge, but to solemnly label him a sex offender would be to reduce our study to a ludicrous level."[41]

This quotation points toward the second puzzle Stoller found in his work but did not analyze. Why, he asks, is perversion (i.e., gross hostility or eroticized hatred) found more in males?[42] And he raises several other important and related questions: He wonders whether "in humans (especially males) powerful sexual excitement can ever exist without brutality also being present." He asks, "Can anyone provide examples of behavior in sexual excitement in which, in human males at least, disguised hostility in fantasy is not a part of potency?" And given that psychoanalysis explains why women are as perverse as men, why has it not explained why they are not?[43]

His own analysis in Sexual Excitement follows this pattern; as he himself notes, he has not dealt with the issue of how women are unlike men rather than like them in the construction of sexual excitement.[44] In addition, Stoller wonders why women neither buy nor respond to pornography as intensely as men (he defines pornography by the presence of a victim; see p. 168) and begins to ask whether the question itself is wrong. Women, Stoller argues, do buy "masochistic" but "romantic" and "unsexual" stories, and thus, he suspects, the definition of pornography hinges on what is pornography for men.[45] The romantic, masochistic stories women buy raise another problem as well for Stoller: Why, he asks, given these fantasies, do so few women practice sadomasochism?[46]

These gender differences indicate that the account we have of sexual excitement works better for men than women. In addition, I take these differences to suggest that what we treat as sexuality and sexual excitement is a gendered masculine sexuality and masculine sexual excitement.[47] This masculinity can be strikingly confirmed in a variety of areas; evidence is present in such varied areas as ordinary language and popular assumptions, social psychology, and literature. I need give only a few examples here.

The language that describes the institution our society places at the center of acceptable human sexuality, heterosexual intercourse, focuses exclusively on the experience of the man. As Janice Moulton has put it, "sexual intercourse is an activity in which male arousal is a necessary condition, and male satisfaction, if not also a necessary condition, is the primary aim . . . [whereas] female arousal and satisfaction, although they may be concomitant events occasionally, are not even constituents of sexual intercourse."[48] While the polite language is one of symmetry, the vulgar language presents a quite different picture (e.g., "if he fucked her, it does not follow that she has fucked him").[49] And the conceptual baggage of even the polite language is such that intercourse formally begins when the male's primary focus for sexual stimulation is inserted in the vagina and ends with male orgasm. Given this conceptual baggage, Moulton is led to wonder why "anyone ever thought the female orgasm had anything to do with sexual intercourse, except as an occasional and accidental co-occurrence." As she notes, "sometimes the telephone rings, too."[50]

The assumptions embedded in ordinary language take more explicit forms as well. Feminist writers have commented widely on the popular assumptions that what is referred to as sex drive is a male sex drive.[51] And feminists have also noted that "it was not very long ago that the notion of being sexual *and* being female was outrageous." Others have lamented the "total lack of images of women being motivated by sexual desire."[52] These assumptions appear as well in more professional contexts populated by sex researchers, educators, clinicians, and social workers. One feminist report from such a conference noted that "sex" was the term for heterosexual sex, and "sex" required "genital contact, male erection, and penetration."[53]

Sociological studies support both the fundamental masculinity of "sex-drive" ideas and their connections with dynamics of hostility and domination. One study of "corner boys" indicates that the "maximization of sexual pleasure clearly occurs for these boys when there is a strong component of conquest experience in the sexual act," and goes on to suggest that without the conquest, the act is less gratifying.[54]

Kate Millett, analyzing the work of Norman Mailer, finds similar dynamics. She argues that sex for Mailer is a 'thrilling test of self" (the self defined as an "athletic 'hunter-fighter-fucker'"). "Little wonder," she states, "that Mailer's sexual journalism reads like the sporting news grafted onto a series of war dispatches." On reading the work of Henry Miller, she concludes, "the pleasure of humiliating the sexual object appears to be far more intoxicating than sex itself."[55] And Charles Stember underlines her point that indeed, "for men it is a vital part of the sex act, not an added attraction."[56]

We can, then, state with some confidence that the culturally produced dynamics of hostility that structure sexual excitement correspond to a masculine sexuality that depends on defiling or debasing a fetishized sexual object. Thus we are dealing with a gendered power relation based in what our culture has defined as sexuality. In turn, this cultural construction of sexuality must be understood to express the experience of the ruling gender. This of course is to be expected. We should recall the significance of the second assumption I have taken over from Marx: The ideas of the ruling class express the dominant material relations in the form of ideas. Thus, what our culture has made of sexuality expresses the dominance of men over women in the form of ideas. But just as the ideas of the capitalist class are at once the ideas that express its experience and its dominance and also those that structure social relations for other classes, so too we can expect that because of masculine cultural hegemony, these sexual dynamics typify some women. (Note that the patient with/on whom Stoller worked out much of his theory of sexual excitement was a woman.) This does not change the fact that these dynamics are more typical of men than women and correspond to men's rather than women's experience.

Sexuality, Power, and Hostility

If these are the dynamics of "normal" heterosexual excitement, we can begin to understand both the existence of rape and rape fantasies and the depiction of violence against women for purposes of arousing sexual excitement. At the same time, this analysis of the culturally constructed dynamics of sexual excitement suggests that we re-examine the current feminist debates about rape and pornography. In both cases, one can interpret the lines of debate as drawn between the myth that sexual excitement should be centered on intimacy and physical pleasure, and the reality that in our culture it depends on hostility and domination.

Feminist theorists have been concerned to expose the relations of power and domination that define rape and have argued strongly that rape is not a sexual act but an act of domination and humiliation.[57] Susan Brownmiller has suggested that rape, once put "within the context of modern criminal violence and not within the purview of ancient masculine codes," will be seen to fall "midway between robbery and assault."[58] Rape, as she understands it, has been essential to the process of establishing male power throughout history; it has been a part of a "conscious process of intimidation by which *all men* keep *all women* in a state of fear."[59] Brownmiller has highlighted the extent to which power and domination are central to rape, but at the same time has ignored the specifically sexual aspect of rape.

This move was important both theoretically and as a political strategy for responding to the widespread view that rape is either the act of an ordinary man strangely overcome with lust or that of a maniac continually subject to excessive lust. On the latter view, rape is often seen as an unavoidable part of human behavior, due to men's overwhelming sexual desires.[60] Opinions such as this appear in more sophisticated academic garb as well. For example, Edward Shorter, in a critique of Brownmiller, suggested that while rape today may have become a political act, at least in the "three or four centuries before the French Revolution," rape can be charged to "sexual frustration," since there were few means of sexual release available for men in that period other than rape.[61] This "huge, restless mass of sexually frustrated men" (existing, he admits, in a social system that maximized male domination) led to rape.[62] On this view, in contrast to Brownmiller's, the focus is on issues of sexuality, and hostility and domination drop from view. The fact that such a debate could take place (in part in the pages of a major feminist periodical) is symptomatic of the cultural confusion of sexuality, violence and domination.

The question whether pornography is simply erotic literature or whether it involves systematic domination and degradation revolves around similar issues. Some feminists have protested the violence much pornography shows directed at women: Images of women in chains, being beaten, or threatened with attack carry the social message that "victimized women are sexually appealing" and that "the normal male is sexually aggressive in a brutal and demeaning way."[63] They have objected strongly to the prominence of "snuff" films (in which the pornographic action consists largely in what is claimed to be the "on camera" dismemberment and death of a woman).[64] What does it mean, they ask, "when men advertise, even brag, that their movie is the 'bloodiest thing that ever happened in front of a camera?'"[65] Pornography, it is argued, is "about power and sex-as-weapon" and thus "not really about sexuality at all."[66] Other feminists, however, have argued that pornography demystifies sexuality and enables women to move beyond a "sexually deprived condition." And given the power relations involved in everyday heterosexuality, they ask, "Can we really expect the realm of fantasy to be free of the residues of that power struggle?"[67]

An analysis such as mine leads to the conclusion that arguments about whether pornography is erotic or depends instead on degradation are fundamentally insoluble. What *is* sexually exciting in Western culture is hostility, violence and domination, especially but not necessarily directed against women.

What is the theoretical significance of the association of sexuality and power for a liberatory understanding of power? If the sexual dimension of power implies a masculinity structured by violence and domination, how could a movement for liberation that included the liberation of women *both* understand *and* practice power differently? Should feminists conclude that sexuality is inseparable from violence against women, that in some sense sex *is* violence? If hostility is so omnipresent—for men, and given our culture, women too—is there any escape?

The Nature of *Eros*

In order to move the discussion onto new and I hope more productive ground, I propose to reformulate issues of sexuality under the heading of *eros*. Such a reformulation can both clarify some of the central dynamics of sexuality and allow me to put forward a broader understanding of the variety of forms taken by sexuality in our culture. It will enable me to include the sexual meanings of issues and institutions which are not explicitly genitally focused, such as fusion with another, sensuality and bodily pleasure, and creative activity. By shifting the terms of the discussion to *eros*, I hope to escape the traps laid by the specifically masculine definition of sexuality that is so widespread in our culture. In addition, such a move can be of use in an effort to transform the meaning of *eros* in more liberatory directions, to develop a cultural construction of sexuality that need not depend on hostility for its fundamental dynamic. Most important, refocusing the discussion in this way can highlight the relation of sexuality to issues of power and community.

Three distinct though not necessarily separate aspects of *eros* emerge from my reading of the psychological literature.[68] The first is represented by Freud's definition of *eros* as the "aim of making one out of many."[69] This desire may take narrowly genital form or may appear in other, sublimated forms. Freud suggests that the inhibition of the direct aims of sexual impulses and their subjugation to the control of "the higher mental operations," that is, the repression of *eros*, is required for the development of civilization.[70] And thus one should expect to find a number of sublimated forms of *eros*.

The second aspect of *eros* turns on the role given to sensuality and bodily concerns in social life. Historically, various societies of Western civilization have found little place for this aspect of *eros* in public life as traditionally understood. Plato, for example, was one of the first to reject it as unworthy of the citizen's concern due to the bad effects of uncontrolled appetites—likened in the *Republic* to being at the mercy of "a raging and savage beast of a master." He argued that if the soul were properly ordered, the body would be well taken care of, and therefore was due no special concern.[71]

Creativity and generation—whether intellectual creativity in philosophy and art, physical work on the substances of nature, or the generation of children through sexual relations—emerge as the third aspect of *eros*. Some psychologists have pointed to the pleasure in the "effortful achievement of purpose" as fundamental to what makes us human. They have suggested that only when these pleasures take pathological forms can sublimation (and the civilization on which it depends) occur.[72] Freud concurs at least to some extent when he argues:

> Laying stress upon the importance of work has a greater effect
> than any other technique of living in the direction of binding
> the individual more closely to reality; in his work he is at least
> securely attached to a part of reality, the human community.
> Work is no less valuable for the opportunity it and the human
> relations connected with it provide for a very considerable
> discharge of libidinal component impulses, narcissistic, aggressive
> and even erotic, than because it is indispensable for subsistence
> and justifies existence in a society. . . . [This is true especially]
> when through sublimation it enables use to be made of existing
> inclinations, of instinctual impulses that have retained their
> strength . . . . And yet as a path to happiness work is not
> valued very highly by men."[73]

Marx's great achievement, from this perspective, was to open the possibility of a society in which the majority of people need not be driven to work only under the press of necessity. This is the society to which Marcuse refers when he suggests the posibility of "non-repressive sublimation."[74] In this case, sexuality would not be blocked or deflected from its object, but rather, in attaining its object, transcend it to others. Under these conditions, Marcuse argues that sexuality could tend to grow into *eros* in a broader sense through what he terms the resexualizing of work. He argues that this may become a real possibility, thus eroticizing the body as a whole. These, then, are some important features of the third aspect of *eros*, the pleasure derived from acting in the world.[75]

The making of one out of more than one, sensuality in a broad sense, and finally the pleasure of competent activity—all represent aspects of *eros*. I hope to show how an expansion of the terms of the debate such as this can aid efforts to examine the effects of *eros* on the organization and construction of community. By recasting *eros* in these terms, we are in a better position to trace the associations of masculinity with power and violence, and to see the variety of ways our society puts *eros* into the service of violence and even death. In the area defined by each aspect of *eros*, the cultural choice of violence and hostility erects profound barriers to the construction of a humane community.

In a world of hostile and threatening others, each aspect of *eros* can take a repressive rather than liberatory form—one that points toward death rather than life. For example, the desire for fusion with another can take the form of domination of the other. Sensuality and bodily pleasures can be denied, and the third aspect of *eros*, creativity and generation, can also take forms of domination both in the world of work, where creative activity becomes alienated labor, or in reproduction, in which the creation of new life becomes either disembodied or recast as death.

The industry of pornography provides a locus in which each of these repressive and negative dynamics can be fruitfully examined. There we find erotic scripts intended to produce sexual excitement fantasized in detail. In addition, because it is such an extensive industry, we can treat commercial pornography as recording the choices of the ruling gender as a whole about what is erotic, and thus can see this literature as expressing what our culture has defined as sexually exciting. The fact that these are choices made by society as a whole means that they cannot successfully be challenged by individual action or objection. Rather, these societal choices must be understood to structure and limit the erotic scripts individual men or women may produce.

To raise the issue of pornography is to immediately confront questions of definition. Here I propose to use as a working definition Robert Stoller's useful statement that pornography requires hostility and the presence of a victim. For Stoller, no victim, no pornography. In addition, nothing is pornographic until the observer's fantasies are added. And with the addition of these fantasies, several hostile dynamics may take place; voyeurism is the most apparent, sadism is the second, and masochism, or identification with the depicted victim, is the third.[76] All pornography has in common a construction of risk and an evocation of danger surmounted. Thus, for Stoller, there is no non-perverse pornography, that is, "sexually exciting matter in which hostility is not employed as a goal." Moreover, pornography will be "loathsome" to the person responding to it. Stoller here refers not only to forbidden sensuality but also to the observer's fears that hostility will be released.[77]

The fantasies of sexual excitement that appear in pornography so defined are most importantly structured by the dynamic of reversal/revenge. As a result, each aspect of *eros* takes repressive forms that point toward violence and death. The specific dynamics of reversal/revenge rest on infant and childhood experience, since the traumas of childhood are memorialized in the details of sexual excitement; the fantasies that produce sexual excitement re-create the relationships of childhood trying to undo the frustrations, traumas, and conflicts.[78] The traumas re-created in sexual excitement are, Stoller hypothesizes, memorials to childhood traumas aimed at sexual anatomy or masculinity or femininity—at gender identification. Moreover, he suggests, sexual excitement will occur at the moment when adult reality resembles the childhood trauma—the anxiety being re-experienced as excitement.[79]

Reversal/revenge (my term) is the major shift that allows anxiety to take the form of pleasure, that is, a reversal in the positions of the actors in order to convert the trauma into revenge. In men, Stoller suggests, this dynamic of reversal/revenge leads to perversion (and, in the light of his later work, to sexual excitement more generally) constructed out of rage at giving up the early identification with the mother and concomitant ecstasies of infancy, the fear of failing to differentiate oneself from the mother, and a need for revenge on her for putting one in this situation.[80] This dynamic of reversal/revenge rooted in childhood trauma means that revenge fantasies can be expected to be most often directed against the mother. And Stoller notes that to the degree that a child feels it has been debased, it will as an adult reverse this process in fantasy to create sexual excitement.[81] The sexual fantasies of pornography, then, can be read as patterned reversals of the traumas of childhood and as adult (male) revenge on the traumatizer. These dynamics structure each aspect of *eros* in specific ways. Some are clearest in pornography itself. Others emerge with greater clarity in the work of those Dworkin has termed the sexual philosophers such as Mailer or Bataille.

Fusion, Community, and the Death of the Other

In pornography the desire for fusion with another takes the form of domination of the other. In this form, it leads to the only possible fusion with a threatening other: The other must cease to exist as a separate, opposed, and for that reason, threatening being. Insisting that another submit to one's will is simply a milder form of the destruction of discontinuity in death, since in this case one is no longer confronting a discontinuous and opposed will, despite its discontinuous embodiment. This need to destroy the other is directly connected with childhood experience. Stoller has argued that sexuality and intimacy can threaten "one's sense of maleness or femaleness" and that this risk is at the same time a source of sexual excitement.[82] Pornography, then, must reduce this danger to a titillating risk if sexual excitement is to be created.

In order to reduce the danger of fusion or intimacy, pornography substitutes control. Susan Griffin in her analysis of the major themes that motivate what she terms "the pornographic mind" argues that the idea that a woman might reject a man appears at the heart of the culture of pornography.[83] The problem, she notes, is that when a woman rejects a man, he must face the reality that he does not control her. Thus, in pornography, issues of control are central to the creation of sexual excitement. One finds the importance of controlling women repeated at length: The woman is controlled, mastered, and humiliated.[84] One can remark as well the consistency of advertisements for sexual dolls in men's magazines. The makers argue that their products are better than real women because they will never say no. The dynamic of conquest and the thrill of overcoming a resistant will are epitomized in the figure of Don Juan, for whom excitement and gratification come not from sensual pleasure and intimacy but rather from overcoming the resistance of a woman: "Easy women do not attract him."[85] Kathleen Barry has commented on more extreme forms of this dynamic and cites passages from several stories in which women are "bound, gagged and tied into positions which render them totally vulnerable and exposed."[86]

Fetishism is a second and related move to avoid fusion and intimacy with another. Rather than concentrate on the pleasure of overcoming the will of another, fetishism avoids confronting the will by fantasizing the other as a thing rather than a human being, treating a body part as a substitute for the person, or even dispensing with the human being altogether.[87] Woman's "thingness" can also be created through her reduction to an image. The mildest of heterosexual male pornography is represented by a massive industry producing photographs of nude women that reduce the real woman to an image on the page, "imprison" her on paper, and therefore render her powerless to threaten the viewer.[88] One should view Griffin's account of Hugh Hefner's own practices in this light. Hefner, she argues, was fascinated with images as opposed to experience. He lived in a world made up of images he could control, and Griffin suggests that his control over the images allowed him both to keep a safe distance from reality and real women and to believe that he could control this reality.[89]

The reality of women as fellow human beings can also be avoided by forbidding them to speak. Griffin notes that "a morbid fear of female speech" is central to pornography, and comments that "even the sexual action, in pornography, seems to exist less for pleasure than to overpower and silence women."[90] And her analysis of *The Story of O* takes note that the heroine is silenced: One of the first rules at Roissy is not to speak to another woman, and then later, not to speak at all.[91]

The dynamics of control and fetishization are both well illustrated by the photograph "Beaver Hunters," described by Andrea Dworkin. The naked woman in the picture, tied like a dead animal to the front of a jeep, has been hunted, subdued (the caption states that the hunters "stuffed and mounted their trophy as soon as they got her home," thus playing off and highlighting the suggestion that the woman was killed), and is displayed as a trophy of conquest.[92]

Third, erotic fusion and intimacy take forms structured by reversal/ revenge. And here the infantile roots of the fear of intimacy are more clearly visible. Griffin points tellingly to the importance in pornography of the image of

> a woman driven to a point of madness out of the desire to put a man's penis in her mouth. So that finally, by this image, we are called back: this image reminds the mind of another scene, a scene in which the avidity to put a part of the body into the mouth is not a mystery. Here is a reversal again. For it is the infant who so overwhelmingly needs the mother's breast in his mouth, the infant who thought he might die without this, who became frantic and maddened with desire, and it was his mother who had the power to withhold.[93]

The dynamic of reversal/revenge occurs in a variety of cultural myths as well, in which a man struggles against dangerous women. One finds this struggle between Samson and Delilah, about which Griffin argues, "not only is male freedom based on female silence, but a man's life depends on the death of a woman." She finds this theme in the modern novel as well—Norman Mailer, who in *An American Dream* describes the protagonist as the victim who acted in self-defense when he killed his wife. "It was as if killing her, the act had been too gentle, I had not plumbed the hatred where the real injustice was stored."[94] And of course this is not just fiction. Lawrence Singleton, convicted of raping and cutting off the hands of a teenage girl, considered that it was he, not she, who was kidnapped and threatened. In his mind the roles were reversed, and he was the victim. "Everything I did," he wrote, "was for survival."[95] Given this kind of hostility, ability to reverse roles, and deep needs for revenge, one can begin to understand why watching a woman tortured or dismembered on camera could be sexually exciting. Perhaps she should be seen as a sacrificial victim whose discountinuous existence has been succeeded in her death by "the organic continuity of life drawn into the common life of the beholders."[96]

Shameful Sensuality: The Denial of the Body

The second aspect of *eros*, too, can take a repressive form: the denial of sensuality and bodily pleasures. While this may initially strike the reader as an odd claim to make about literature and photographs intended to produce sexual and thus presumably physical excitement, the generation of this excitement relies on the experience of the body as shameful. And the source of this shame can be found in childhood experience. One psychologist has commented that "the loathing and disgust that we feel for what we cannot help being interested in is our homage to the reasons we had for burying the interest."[97]

In pornography, the body—usually a woman's body—is presented as something that arouses shame, even humiliation, and the opposition of spirit or mind to the body—the latter sometimes referred to as representing something bestial or nonhuman—generates a series of dualities. Griffin captures the essence of this experience of the body when she argues that "speaking to that part of himself [the pornographer] wishes to shame, he promises, I'm going to treat you like something that crawled out of the sewer."[98] Pornography is built around, plays on, and obsessively re-creates these dualities. The dichotomy between spiritual love and "carnal knowledge" is re-created in the persistent fantasy of transforming the virgin into the whore. She begins pure, innocent, fresh, even in a sense disembodied, and is degraded and defiled in sometimes imaginative and bizarre ways.[99]

Transgression is important here: Forbidden practices are being engaged in. The violation of the boundaries of society breaks its taboos. Yet the act of violating a taboo, of seeing or doing something forbidden, does not do away with its forbidden status. Indeed, in the ways women's bodies are degraded and defiled in the transformation of the virgin into the whore, the boundaries between the forbidden and the permitted are simultaneously upheld and broken.[100] Put another way, the obsessive transformation of virgin into whore simply crosses over and over again the boundary between them. Without the boundary, there could be no transformation. And without the boundary to violate, the thrill of transgression would disappear.

The sexual excitement striptease produces can be viewed as similar in form. It only "works" to produce sexual excitement because the exposed body is considered shameful and forbidden. The viewer is seeing something he is not entitled to see, something forbidden, and moreover, something potentially dangerous because it might have the power to change or transform him. Griffin suggests that our culture believes that the sight of a woman's flesh can turn a man into a rapist, and presumably do other things as well.[101] One finds the same view of the (female) body as loathsome, humiliating, and even dangerous in a stripper's comment that one of several styles of producing sexual excitement in striptease is "hard," that is, exphasizing the dark, hard lines of constraint provided by women's clothing, constraint of an aggressive female sexuality: "It is as if the notion of sexual woman were so overwhelming that she had to be visibly bound."[102]

Loathing for the body, in the sense that bodily needs and desires are humiliating, appears in another way in pornography in the form of the contrast between the man's self-control and the woman's frenzied abandon. It is consistently a woman who is, as Griffin puts it, "humiliated by her desire, her helplessness, and materiality."[103] These issues of control and humiliation are clear in *The Story of O*. The speech O is given her first night at Roissy is one in which the men are portrayed as fully in control of their bodies. Thus, she is told that while their costume "leaves our sex exposed, it is not for the sake of convenience . . ." and that what is done to her is "less for our pleasure than for your enlightenment." Thus they make clear that while they make use of her, they are independent and do not need her.[104] This insistence on independence and control on one side and a victim humiliated by her own desires on the other appears frequently.[105] The presence of a victim, one who submits in fact, requires another who remains in control, who, one author suggests, establishes selfhood by controlling the other.[106] The fact that it is the woman whose body is in the control of another, and the woman who is humiliated by her desires and materality, expresses and records the reversal/revenge of infant and childhood experience.

The theme of succeeding by ignoring/overcoming the feelings of the body is related to the fear and loathing of the body. Thus Griffin can argue that Don Juan, the "femme fatale," and de Sade share the quality of being unfeeling, an unfeelingness that allows them to be "powerful and free," yet leads at the same time to feelings of numbness.[107] In pornography, feeling is conquered by projecting emotions onto the victim who is humiliated by bodily appetites, by reducing the woman to the status of a feeling body, and in "snuff" films to a literal corpse.

Thus, sensuality and bodily concerns, the second aspect of *eros*, take repressive form. They become entangled with and point toward death—what Griffin has termed the death of feeling as well as the death of the body. Griffin is right to point out that the denial of the body is in part due to the fact that it is a reminder of mortality and therefore of death.[108] Indeed, as she argues in her excellent and innovative analysis of the Oedipus myth, knowledge of the body *is* knowledge of death. She holds that Oedipus' association with flesh comes from the fact that he grew up away from his father (and therefore, Griffin claims, closer to nature and the body). More important, though, his knowledge of the body represents knowledge of his mortality. It was this which allowed him to answer the riddle of the sphinx: "What walks on four legs in the morning, two in midday, and three in the evening?" As Griffin points out, he could answer the riddle, "Man," because he knew that he was once a vulnerable infant and would one day require a cane to aid him in old age.[109]

Generation, Creativity, and Death

The third aspect of *eros*, that of creativity and generation, can also take the form of domination and death. We have noted how each aspect of *eros* as constructed by pornography involves death: fusion with another requires the death (or at least submission) of the other; bodily feelings are denied because the fact of existence as embodied beings reminds us that we are mortal. In this context, it should not surprise us that issues of creativity, generation, and reproduction are reformulated in ways that link them to death.[110] These linkages appear to some extent in pornographic stories and photographs but are more clearly stated by those Dworkin has identified as sexual philosophers.

Dworkin has described an instance of these links in a genre she terms the "pornography of pregnancy." She argues that this pornography, both in pictures of pregnant women and in the accompanying text, stresses the "malevolence" of the female body, "its danger to sperm and especially its danger to the woman herself." In this vision, the "pregnancy is the triumph of the phallus over the death-dealing vagina." She notes as well that the transformation of the virgin into whore is present as well, since the pregnancy is evidence of lack of virginity.[111] Thus, reproduction comes to be linked with danger and even death. Historically, of course, reproduction did have important connections with death. It is perhaps significant that a writer such as Norman Mailer recognized these connections when he noted that sexual intercourse had lost its gravity (in part?) because pregnancy had ceased to be dangerous.[112]

French philosopher/pornographer Georges Bataille makes even clearer connections between *eros* and death and even reformulates reproduction itself as death. He argues that there is a "profound unity of these apparent opposites, birth and death." (Bataille is in good company: Aristotle made the similar point that whatever comes into being must pass away.) Yet, despite their unity, Bataille gives primacy to death and argues that one must recognize a "tormenting fact: the urge towards love, pushed to its limit, is an urge toward death."[113] Moreover, reproduction is connected to continuity, but the continuity is defined by death. Indeed, "death is to be identified with continuity, and both of these concepts are equally fascinating. This fascination is the dominant element in eroticism."[114] Reproduction itself, seen from this perspective, is better understood as death: The new entity formed from the sperm and ovum bears in itself the "fusion, fatal to both, of two separate beings."[115] One can see here the traces of some of the roots of this view in childhood experience, and the threat to identity posed by fusion: The erotic fusion of the sexual connection not only threatens death but indeed requires it. The danger is not simply a risk to be run but is, at some level, inevitably fatal.

The separation of generation and reproduction from life takes a second, more indirect form: Sexuality and sexual activity are portrayed in pornography as profoundly distanced from the activities of daily life. The action in pornography takes place in what Griffin has termed "pornotopia," a world outside real time and space, where no one worries about doing dishes or changing diapers, and women enjoy rape, bondage, and humiliation. The distance from the real world structured by daily necessities is aptly symbolized by Griffin's description of Hugh Hefner's house: "His house has no windows. Nothing unpredictable or out of his control can happen to him there. Sunrise makes no difference. . . . Food emanates from a kitchen supplied with a staff day and night. . . . [And] as if one layer of protection [or distancing] were not enough, his bedroom contains another self-sufficient and man-made world, with a desk, and food supplies, and a bed which is motorized so that it not only changes positions but also carries him about the room."[116]

This transformation of creative activity and generation into negative forms is not of course limited to sexuality but occurs in other areas of society as well. Some of the clearest examples occur in the world of work. There, what could have been empowering and creative activity in conjunction with external nature becomes alienated labor in industries that pollute and destroy both their natural surroundings and the minds and bodies of those who labor, not a development of physical and mental capacities, but a destruction of both. As Freud so clearly pointed out, persons must either sublimate the erotic joys of creativity in work or must be driven to work by the force of necessity. And as for the external world of nature, to the extent that it is seen not as a means of affirming the actor but as a threat to his/her continued existence, then that relation too must take the form of domination.

Conclusion: The Gender-Specific Roots of the Agonal Model of Community

We are now in a position to begin to say something about the theoretical content and significance of the association of power with virility and masculinity, that, is, about the gendered connections between sexuality and power and their consequences for community. Put another way, we can now begin to understand the significance of describing contemporary Western social relations as a capitalist patriarchy. Beneath the polite language of sexual reciprocity we have uncovered not only one-sided relations of domination and submission but also dynamics of hostility, revenge, and a fascination with death. The negative forms taken by *eros*, forms that in our culture define masculinity, pose profound difficulties for the creation of a humane community.

Intimacy and fusion with another pose such deep problems that they require the domination of the other or control of the actions of the other, reducing the presumably threatening person to a nonentity with no will of its (her) own. Fetishism provides a second solution to the problem of intimacy: The other who presents the possibility (or threat) of erotic fusion produces such fright that she (and in most cases it is a woman) must be reduced to two-dimensional images or even a set of body parts to make it safe enough to pleasurably fantasize her victimization. And even in fantasy she must be silenced, reduced to a being without feelings or speech. Yet this "solution" to the problem of intimacy and fusion is profoundly unsatisfactory on its own terms. Jessica Benjamin has analyzed the problematic nature of the search for control in the context of *The Story of O*. O's complete submission and her complete domination by her lover make her incapable of granting the recognition her lover wants. As Benjamin puts it in the case of O, complete domination of the other means that the master may find himself alone because the other has ceased to be a person at all.[117]

The second aspect of *eros*, the role of sensuality and the body, in its negative, masculine form raises further barriers to the creation of community. Our existence as embodied beings does not open possibilities for sensual and physical connections with others but comes to stand as a loathsome reminder of our mortality, which must be excised as much as possible from existence. Virility, or the masculine gender carried by power, requires the denial of the body and its importance, whether this takes the form of control of the body of another or the portrayal of the man in heterosexual male pornography as complete master of his own body and the woman as totally at the mercy of her own desires. The third aspect of *eros*, too, is given negative form. Creativity and generation become instead a fascination with death, and even reproduction is reformulated as concerned with death rather than life. Issues of daily life and necessity, as reminders of mortality and materiality, must be avoided.

For each aspect of *eros*, the centrality of hostility, the wish to do harm, marks a fascination with death—the death of the other as a separate being, the denial of one's own body in order to deny one's mortality, and the recasting of even reproduction as death. These, then, are the outlines of the community structured by a masculine *eros*, a community that expresses the life activity and experience not of the ruling class but the ruling gender.

The masculine gender carried by power intensifies the tensions of community and leads to the construction of an even more conflictual and false community than that formed by means of exchange. It is a community both in theory and in fact obsessed with revenge and structured by conquest and domination. The opposition of men to women and perhaps even to other men is not simply a transitory opposition of arbitrary interests, but an opposition resting on a deepgoing threat to existence. Rather than an interaction in which parties have both conflicting and common interests, where the first choice of each is the second last of the other, the participants in the agonal community structured by a masculine *eros* have no common choices. The community emerges only through conquest, struggle, and even the potential death of its members. These dynamics of conquest and domination mean that the gain of one participant can come only at the expense of the other's submission, humiliation, or even death.

Intimacy and fusion with another pose problems too deep to be resolved by postulating an artificial community of formal equals who interact, by mutual agreement, through the exchange of objects. The other (the woman) must be completely controlled, must be made into a thing rather than a trading partner, sometimes even made into an object to be traded. Fetishism operates here in even more harmful and direct ways than in the fetishism of commodities. There, life and movement are attributed to things; here, living beings are made into things. Whereas in exchange the will and feelings of the other, though inaccessible and irrelevant, were recognized to exist, in the community constructed by a masculine *eros*, the will of the other must be conquered and destroyed over and over again.

Likewise, problems of the relation of mind to body, of the existence of whole human beings, take insoluble form. Mind and body part company in the act of exchange, yet the mind of at least one participant in the exchange is occupied with the sensual and bodily satisfaction to be obtained in the future consumption of the commodity being purchased. But in the community structured by a masculine *eros*, bodies and their appetites and desires are given no legitimate place. The body and its desires are treated as loathsome, even inhuman, things that must be overcome if a man is to remain powerful and free. To meet the cultural standards of masculinity, individuals must separate themselves from and conquer the feelings and desires of the body.

Perhaps these more extreme forms taken by domination are rooted in the fact that, unlike the experience of the ruling class, where persons seem to relate only indirectly through the medium of things (rational economic men exchanging their commodities), the experience of the ruling gender is one in which participants confront each other directly, share no common interest, and experience each other as threats to continued existence. Because sexuality is a social construction, individuals as individuals are not free to experience *eros* just as they choose. Yet just as the extraction and appropriation of surplus value by the capitalist represents a choice available, if not to individuals, to society as a whole, so too sexuality and the forms taken by *eros* must be seen as at some level open to change.

In addition, we re-encounter in the context of gender as well as class the fact that the experience of the ruling group cannot be dismissed as simply false. This experience, because of the hegemony of that group, sets the dynamics of the social relations in which all parties are forced to participate—women as well as men, unmasculine as well as masculine men. Because the social relations that construct masculinity depend on these negative forms of *eros*, a community grounded on a sexuality structured by violence, domination, and death are made real for everyone.

I argued earlier that market theories attempted to solve the riddle of community by giving an account of how fundamentally separate human beings could come to be associated with each other through the medium of exchange. Their accounts of exchange led them directly toward a substitution of rational economic man and relations of exchange (and the resultant relations of domination) for a more complete and well-rounded human individual, and a more encompassing human community. The relations of domination in current Western understandings of sexuality, too, represent a substitute for a more complete form of community. Both exchange and the erotic fusion of sexuality can bring human beings together. Both represent important experiences of the ways one can come into contact with another. The form of the interaction may vary: It may be nurturant, instrumental, or rational; it may take the forms of domination, force, persuasion, bargaining, or expression of love. In every case, however, what is at stake is the very existence of a relation with another. The community based on the negative form of *eros*, then, both differs importantly from the community based on momentary conjunction of arbitrary interests, and at the same time replicates some of its important features. Most fundamentally for my analysis here, the possibilities for community itself become even more of a problem: The community created through conquest and domination, the community defined by *eros* is both more deep-going than the social synthesis constructed by exchange and more deadly.

NOTES

1. Robert Stoller's restatement of Freud, in *Perversion* (New York: Pantheon, 1975), pp. 12–14.

2. Jeffrey Weeks, *Sex, Politics, and Society* (Essex, England: Longman, 1981), p. 12.

3. This argument is made in much more depth by Robert Padgug, "Sexual Matters," *Radical History Review*, no. 20 (Spring-Summer 1979) quoted material from p. 11. I should note that while his case is similar to mine, he does not focus as much as I do here on the effects of structured social relations. Nor am I using his definition of *praxis* as "language, consciousness, symbolism and labor," since that strikes me as too compartmentalized.

4. Weeks, *Sex, Politics, and Society*, p. 12. Weeks gives a series of factors that should be taken as guidelines in studying sexuality: He includes the kinship and family system, economic and social changes, changing forms of social regulation, the political moment, and the existence of cultures of resistance.

5. See especially Weeks' discussion of the different strategies of investigating sexuality in *Sex, Politics, and Society*, pp. 1–18; *Radical History Review*, special issue on Sexuality, no. 20 (Spring-Summer 1979); Sherry B. Ortner and Harriet Whitehead, "Accounting for Sexual Meanings" in their *Sexual Meanings: The Cultural Construction of Gender and Sexuality* (New York: Cambridge University Press, 1981), pp. 1–27; Adrienne Rich, "Compulsory Heterosexuality and Lesbian Existence," in *Signs* 5, no. 4 (Summer 1980); Ann Ferguson, Jacquelyn Zita, and Kathryn Pyne Addelson, "On Compulsory Heterosexuality and Lesbian Existence: Defining the Issues," *Signs* 7, no. 1 (Autumn 1981).

6. One can find these assumptions, for example, in Amber Hollibaugh and Cherrie Moraga, "What We're Rolling Around in Bed With," *Heresies* no. 12, (1981); Paula Webster, "Pornography and Pleasure," *Heresies*, no. 12 (1981). Webster does state that masculinity and feminity are social constructions but at the same time argues that the images one gets in pornography are at least demystifying and that our fantasies can be used to map the zones of arousal, thus accepting unquestioningly the erotic conventions of our culture. See also Barbara Lipschutz, "Cathexis," in *What Color Is Your Handkerchief?* (Berkeley, Calif.: Samois, 1979), p. 9. One of the basic problems in much of this feminist literature is that while authors state that they see sexuality as a cultural creation, they often go on to argue in ways that suggest that changing sexuality is an impossibility: One must simply accept it. But if sexuality is a social relation and is culturally and historically specific, then those of us who are committed to changing other social relations must include sexuality as one of the dimensions of our existence open to change.

7. I should note at the outset that I have many difficulties with the positions he takes and I note them here in part to indicate that the points I take from him and use are just that and not an endorsement of the system of thought he puts forward. In particular, I oppose his unquestioning acceptance of the existence of the vaginal orgasm (Robert Stoller, *Sexual Excitement: The Dynamics of Erotic Life* [New York: Pantheon, 1979], p. 88; and *Perversion*, p. 23); his stress on the centrality of maternal responsibility in producing "normal" heterosexuals (*Perversion*, pp. 138, 154, 161), and his account of how people become homosexuals (e.g., *Perversion* p. 153). Nor do I share his concerns: I do not believe homosexuality should be considered either a perversion or a diagnosis, nor am I interested in the psychological origins of gender identity (see *Perversion*, pp. xvi, 199 f). At times as well, Stoller's discussion is marred by a male-centered understanding of the world, e.g., his statement that "it is hard to imagine a little girl, confronted with this task, who would not envy boys and their aggressive, penetrating, hedonistic, arrogant, unfettered, God-granted, antisocial, unsympathetic, humiliating penis" (*Sexual Excitement*, p. 74). Thus he seems to accept without question the social and cultural meanings associated with the penis.

8. Stoller, *Sexual Excitement*, p. 26.

9. Ibid., p. 6.

10. Ibid., pp. 23, 6.

11. See Stoller, *Perversion*, pp. 8, 59; idem., *Sexual Excitement*, p. 8.

12. Barbara Lawrence, "Four-Letter Words *Can* Hurt You," in *Philosophy and Sex*, ed. Robert Baker and Frederick Elliston (Buffalo, N.Y.: Prometheus Books, 1975), p. 32.

13. Andrea Dworkin, *Pornography: Men Possessing Women* (New York: Putnam's, 1979), p. 182, quoting Alfred C. Kinsey, Wardell B. Pomeroy, Clyde E. Martin, and Paul H. Gebhard, *Sexual Behavior in the Human Female* (Philadelphia: W. B. Saunders, 1953), p. 705. She adds that the reference indicates that this physiology is true of both males and females. Her own style of presentation suggests that she does not believe this to be true.

14. A. H. Maslow, "Self-Esteem (Dominance-Feeling) and Sexuality in Women," *Journal of Social Psychology* 16 (1942): 291, quoted by George Herbert Stember, *Sexual Racism* (New York: Harper & Row, 1976), p. 145.

15. Stember, *Sexual Racism*, p. 150, quoting Kate Millett, *Sexual Politics* (New York: Doubleday, 1970), p. 304.

16. Georges Bataille, *Death and Sensuality* (New York: Arno Press, 1977), p. 90. The italics in the text are mine.

17. O. Mannoni, *Prospero and Caliban* (New York: Praeger, 1964), p. 111, quoted by Stember, *Sexual Racism*, p. 164.

18. Stember, *Sexual Racism*, p. 149. The gender dimensions of this statement are not accidental, nor is the notion of pollution.

19. See discussion immediately following this argument in Deirdre English, Amber Hollibaugh, and Gayle Rubin, "Talking Sex: A Conversation on Sexuality and Feminism," *Socialist Review*, no. 58 (July-August 1981): 52

20. Lawrence, "Four-Letter Words," p. 32.

21. Stoller, *Perversion*, pp. 7, 105–9; idem., *Sexual Excitement*, pp. 18–21.

22. Stoller, *Perversion*, p. xii. This is a common psychoanalytic position,

but see also Ann Snitow, "Mass Market Romance: Pornography for Women Is Different," *Radical History Review*, no. 20 (Spring/Summer, 1979): 153.

23. Stoller, *Sexual Excitement*, p. 113.

24. Kathleen Barry, *Female Sexual Slavery* (New York: Avon Books, 1979), p. 230.

25. Ibid., p. 233.

26. Stoller, *Sexual Excitement*, pp. 23, 33 respectively.

27. Ibid., pp. 13, 35, 31 respectively.

28. See also Stoller, *Perversion*, p. 208.

29. Dworkin, *Pornography: Men Possessing Women*, p. 135.

30. Ibid., p. 136.

31. Ibid., p. 151.

32. Stoller, *Sexual Excitement*, p. 74.

33. See Stoller, *Sexual Excitement*, p. 124. See also *Perversion*, p. 58, where Stoller argues that the masochist is never really a victim because she or he never really relinquishes control.

34. See Pat Califia's statement that the bottom is the superior in "A Secret Side of Lesbian Sexuality," *The Advocate*, December 27, 1979; or Pat Califia, "Feminism and Sadomasochism," in *Heresies*, no. 12 (1981): 31, who notes that the "stubbornness and aggressiveness of the masochist is a byword in the S/M community."

35. Dworking, *Pornography*, p. 158.

36. Stoller, *Perversion*, p. 97.

37. Ibid., p. 4.

38. Ibid., p. 56.

39. One can compare Barry's definition of perversion as "not just that which is wrong, bad, or evil, but that which distorts, devalues, depersonalizes, warps, and destroys the person as she or he exists in time and space. It involves destruction of the human being in fact. Accordingly . . . sexuality that is fostered through the arrested male sex drive which objectifies, forces, and violates, whether it is heterosexual or homosexual, is perversion." Objectification itself, she argues, is perversion (see Barry, *Female Sexual Slavery*, p. 266).

40. See Stoller, *Perversion*, pp. 97, xvii respectively.

41. Paul Gebhard, John H. Gagnon, Wardell B. Pomeroy, and Cornelia V. Christenson, *Sex Offenders: An Analysis of Types* (New York: Harper & Row, 1965), p. 6, cited in Dworkin, *Pornography*, p. 52; italics mine.

42. Stoller, *Perversion*, p. 9.

43. Respectively, Stoller, *Perversion*, p. 88 and pp. 135 ff, 98.

44. Stoller, *Sexual Excitement*, pp. 220–21.

45. Stoller, *Perversion*, pp. 89–91.

46. Stoller seems to subscribe to the idea/argument that sexuality is a social construction when he notes that female masochism should be expected to be related to women's power in a particular culture, and states that masochism should not at all be considered a biological drive (*Sexual Excitement*, pp. 119, 122 respectively).

47. This in and of itself should not be surprising. McClellan's work on need for achievement, since redone to take account of women's differences by Matina Horner, or Lawrence Kohlberg's work on the stages of moral develop-

ment, since redone by Carol Gilligan and Susan Freeman, provide two important examples of other areas of social research in which this has been true.

48. "Sex and Reference," in Baker and Elliston, eds., *Philosophy and Sex*, p. 36.

49. Ibid.

50. Ibid.

51. See Barry, *Female Sexual Slavery*, pp. 255 ff, who cites a number of authors in support of her point.

52. Amber Hollibaugh, et. al, "Talking Sex," p. 46. Dierdre English takes this position (ibid., p. 53).

53. Carole Vance, "Gender Systems, Ideology, and Sex Research: An Anthropological Analysis," *Feminist Studies* 6, no. 1 (Spring 1980): 133. See also Weeks, *Sex, Politics, and Society*, who notes that among those who see sex as a driving force, it is held to be basically male, and to have a firmly heterosexual orientation (p. 3).

54. William F. Whyte, "A Slum Sex Code," *American Journal of Sociology* 49 (July 1943): 27, cited in Stember, *Sexual Racism*, p. 146.

55. Millet, *Sexual Politics*, p. 327, cited in Stember, *Sexual Racism*, p. 146.

56. Stember, *Sexual Racism*, p. 150.

57. Susan Griffin, *Rape: The Power of Consciouness* (New York: Harper & Row, 1979); Andrea Medea and Kathleen Thompson, *Against Rape* (New York: Farrar, Strauss and Giroux, 1974); Heidi Hartmann and Ellen Ross, "Comments on 'On Writing the History of Rape,'" *Signs* 3, no. 4 (Summer 1978).

58. See Susan Brownmiller, *Against Our Will* (New York: Simon and Schuster, 1975), pp. 423–24.

59. Ibid., p. 5. She notes that Margaret Mead and other anthropologists have discovered the use of gang rape in a number of cultures as a control mechanism (p. 315), and documents the extensive use of rape in war as a policy of intimidation of the conquered.

60. See, for example, Medea and Thompson, *Against Rape*, p. 32. See also Brownmiller's conversations with reporters in Vietnam, in *Against Our Will*, pp. 87–118.

61. Edward Shorter, "On Writing the History of Rape," *Signs* 3, no. 2 (Winter 1977): 471–82.

62. Ibid., p. 474.

63. Women Against Violence Against Women Newsletter, June 1976, p. 1.

64. "Snuff" films not only claim to depict a woman's death and dismemberment, but one of the selling points of the advertising is that the actress is really killed on camera. See Beverly La Belle, "Snuff—The Ultimate in Woman-Hating," in *Take Back the Night*, ed. Laura Lederer (New York: Morrow, 1980).

65. *Aegis*, November/December 1978, p. 3.

66. Gloria Steinem, "Erotica and Pornography: A Clear and Present Difference," in *Take Back the Night*, p. 38; or see Helen Longino's definition: "verbal or pictorial material which represents or describes sexual behavior that is degrading or abusive to one or more of the participants *in such a way as to endorse the degradation.*" Longino, "Pornography, Oppression, and Freedom: A

Closer Look," in Lederer, ed., *Take Back the Night*, p. 43. See also Dworkin, *Pornography*, pp. 199–202.

67. Paula Webster, "Pornography and Pleasure," *Heresies*, no. 12 (1981): 49–50. Webster is not alone in such positions. Positions somewhat similar to this have been taken by writers such as Amber Hollibaugh, Deirdre English, Gayle Rubin, Ellen Willis, and Pat Califia.

68. I should note that my definition of *eros* here differs from that of others who have used the term. Stoller uses the term as a narrower reference than "sexuality." Thus, he argues that most of what we label sexual excitement has many different parts, only one of which can be characterized as erotic excitement. The others include triumph, rage, revenge, fear, anxiety, and risk (*Sexual Excitement*, p. 26). In contrast, I take *eros* to be the more inclusive term. Nor is my definition the same as that put forward by Susan Griffin who states: "The very force of eros, the very brilliance of vitality, the irrepudiability of feeling, that eros cannot be reasoned out of existence . . ." (*Pornography and Silence*, p. 77).

69. Sigmund Freud, *Civilization and Its Discontents*, trans. Joan Riviere (Garden City, N.Y: Doubleday, 1958), p. 57. Freud, however, does not recognize the possibility of making one out of more than two.

70. Ibid., pp. 42–43.

71. Plato, *Republic* I: 329c. and III: 403d, respectively, in Paul Shorey, trans., *The Collected Dialogues of Plato* (Princeton: Princeton University Press, 1978). All references to dialogues are from this collection unless otherwise noted. In this context, the uniqueness of Marx's contribution to political thought is marked by the centrality of the place given to human sensous experience, one indicating a respect for rather than a devaluation of the body —with all its needs and failings. What could be more explicit than his critique of Feuerbach's materialism for not conceiving of reality itself as "human sensuous activity"? See "Thesis I," in Robert Tucker, ed., *The Marx-Engels Reader*, 1st ed. (New York: Norton, 1973), p. 143.

72. See Dorothy Dinnerstein, *The Mermaid and the Minotaur* (New York: Harper & Row, 1976), p. 140. Note her discussion of Norman O. Brown's *Life Against Death* (Middletown, Ct.: n.p., 1959), pp. 135–51. See also Herbert Marcuse, *Eros and Civilization* (Boston: Beacon Press, 1955).

73. Freud, *Civilization and Its Discontents*, p. 21.

74. Marcuse, *Eros and Civilization*, p. 211.

75. Ibid., pp. 220, 222. I differ with him on the possibilities for a "resexualized work" since it seems that the pleasure of acting on the world is in itself an "erotic" one.

76. Stoller, *Perversion*, p. 64–65.

77. Ibid., pp. 86, 91 respectively.

78. See ibid., pp. 4, 80; Stoller, *Sexual Excitement*, p. 77.

79. Stoller, *Perversion*, p. 105.

80. Ibid., p. 99. I should note that Stoller makes this point in the context of an argument that perversion "may be a gender disorder in the development of masculinity." On this point, see below, the argument of Chapter 10.

81. Ibid., p. 119; Stoller, *Sexual Excitement*, p. 13.

82. Stoller regards this as a tentative hypothesis (*Sexual Excitement*, p. 21).

He notes in *Perversion* that the perversion is a fantasy that is a defensive structure raised to preserve pleasure and that perversion arises as a way of coping with one's gender identification (pp. xiv, xii respectively).

83. See Griffin, *Pornography and Silence* , p. 144. I have relied heavily on her description of the major themes to be found in contemporary pornography. But I have many fundamental and important disagreements with her. I do not believe that the problems we face can be traced to the pornographic *mind*. Nor do I believe that pornography endangers our lives because action begins in the mind and then moves to reality. Rather, I hold that what endangers our lives is the same social structure that produces pornography as well as other attacks on humanity. Griffin misses the importance of institutions, in part because she focuses on the mind. Thus, she can hold that the pornographer cuts off the heads of nature, and others grow, and for this reason the violence must accelerate. In addition, I am not concerned, as Griffin is, to address questions whether the pornographer is a revolutionary of the imagination or whether pornography is catharsis—worthy subjects, but not my own. I do not think pornography is fundamentally rooted in religion (as she claims, p. 16). Nor do I share the mysticism that invades her work, e.g., her references to the "sacred image of the goddess, the sacred image of the cow, the emblematic touch of divinity in the ecstasy of the sexual act" (p. 71). I find her elevation of the "heart" as an organ between mind and appetite difficult to accept (p. 81). Why not the liver? I found myself asking. The "heart" as a model for feeling is a cultural, not a universal construction. I list this variety of disagreements to indicate my various difficulties with her analysis and to indicate that, as with Stoller's work, only specific points are being taken over and used in my own framework of analysis. I should note in addition that I found it extremely difficult to translate Griffin's account into my own terms. Thus the footnote references to *Pornography and Silence* should be seen as references to the place in her work where I found the material I make use of, and to places where her work highlighted issues for me, not as references to arguments she has made, unless clearly indicated as such.

84. Ibid., p. 34.

85. Stoller, *Perversion* p. 57.

86. Barry, *Female Sexual Slavery*, pp. 208–9.

87. See Griffin, *Pornography and Silence*, pp. 49, 41; Stoller, *Perversion*, p. 133.

88. Stoller, *Perversion*, p. 133.

89. Griffin, *Pornography and Silence*, pp. 122–23.

90. Ibid., pp. 89, 90.

91. See Griffin's chapter on Silence, Ibid., pp. 201–50.

92. Dworkin, *Pornography*, pp. 25–26.

93. Griffin, *Pornography and Silence*, p. 61. Griffin's point here is echoed by Stoller, who underlines that the major way for looking to be sexually exciting is for the man to believe he is acting sadistically and revengefully on an unwilling woman (*Perversion*, pp. 108–9).

94. Griffin, *Pornography and Silence*, p. 91, quoting *An American Dream* (New York: n.p., n.d.), p. 9.

95. See Amanda Spake, "The End of the Ride," *Mother Jones*, April 1980. The quotation is from p. 40.

96. Bataille, *Death and Sensuality*, p. 91. See pp. 91ff for a more complete account of the commonalities of sexual activity and ritual sacrifice.

97. Dinnerstein, *Mermaid and Minotaur*, p. 135.

98. Griffin, *Pornography and Silence*, pp. 24–28, 59.

99. For an analysis of how this works, see Angela Carter, *The Sadeian Woman* (New York: Pantheon, 1978), pp. 38–77; and for a very different analysis more similar to that put forward here, see Griffin, *Pornography and Silence*, pp. 21–25. See also Dworkin's synopsis of Bataille's *Story of the Eye* with the (to me) odd centrality of egg fetishism—a proof, if one is needed, that anything can be eroticized (*Pornography*, pp. 167–75).

100. See Jessica Benjamin, "The Bonds of Love: Rational Violence and Erotic Domination," *Feminist Studies* 6, no. 1 (Spring 1980): 154.

101. Griffin, *Pornography and Silence*, p. 30. See also the discussion of the power dynamics of striptease from the stripper's point of view, where when the show is going well, the stripper is in complete control. Seph Weene, "Venus," *Heresies*, no. 12 (1980): 36–38.

102. Ibid., p. 37. The other types she mentions are "soft and powerless," "not-a-woman," and "rich." It is interesting to note that each of these ways of producing sexual excitement rely on a move away from dailiness.

103. Griffin, *Pornography and Silence*, p. 64.

104. Benjamin, "Bonds of Love," p. 157. The quotation she takes from *The Story of O*, by Pauline Réage, trans. S. d'Estree (New York: Grove Press, 1965), pp. 15–17.

105. Griffin gives a number of examples in *Pornography and Silence*, pp.64–66, 68.

106. Benjamin, "Bonds of Love," p. 155.

107. Griffin, *Pornography and Silence*, pp. 56–58. Griffin analyzes *The Story of O* as an account of how O "unlearns all the knowledge of her body" (p. 219 ff). But it should, I believe, rather be read as a series of ever-increasing attacks on the body, and more precisely, on the will of another.

108. Ibid., p. 29.

109. See ibid., pp. 132–38.

110. Griffin makes a similar-seeming but different point. She argues that pornography contains three levels of death—the links of death with sex, the fear of the body, and the death of self-image. See *Pornography and Silence*, p. 32.

111. Dworkin, *Pornography*, p. 222. The account of the photographs and stories appears on pp. 217–23.

112. Ibid., p. 54, citing Mailer, *Prisoner of Sex* (Boston: Little, Brown, 1971), p. 126.

113. Bataille, *Death and Sensuality*, p. 42. While Adrienne Rich acknowledges the sometimes violent feelings between mothers and children, she quite clearly does not put these at the heart of the relation. See *Of Woman Born* (New York: Norton, 1976).

114. Bataille, *Death and Sensuality*, p. 13.

115. Ibid., p. 14. See also p. 101.

116. Griffin, *Pornography and Silence*, p. 123. She uses this description to make the point of the obsessive need for control.

117. Benjamin, "Bonds of Love," pp. 158–59, 163 respectively.

8

The Erotic Dimension and the Homeric Ideal*

The association of virility and domination carried by the gendered aspect of power has a larger significance than may be apparent from the analysis of the last chapter. While the genderedness of power emerges in the modern world in the "private" realm of sexuality, one finds very similar dynamics in a different context at another point in history. The negative forms of *eros* are strikingly prominent in a number of the central works of ancient Greek political philosophy. There, competition for dominance of others, the denial of the importance of the body, and a struggle to cancel death were presented as the ideals for which the political actor, or citizen, should strive. Power is intimately connected with (and indeed becomes an aspect of) masculinity in the person of the warrior-hero as he appears in the *Iliad*. He later takes the theoretical form of the good citizen who engages in rhetorical competition.[1] Yet, given the importance we still attribute to these ideals for political life, we should not conclude that attention to the nature of the Athenian political community holds only antiquarian interest. To the extent that contemporary understandings of politics and power are rooted in these ideals, our own political life too must be understood to be structured by a masculine *eros* closely associated with violence and death.

Ancient texts such as the *Iliad*, the *Oresteia*, and Plato's *Republic* and *Symposium* can contribute importantly to the discussion of the genderedness of power. First, because they are explicitly concerned with the collectivity as a whole, these works allow us to see the effects of a

---

* This chapter should be taken as a promissory note for the more detailed analysis of these works to be undertaken in *Sexuality and Politics: The Barracks Community in Western Political Thought* (forthcoming).

masculine *eros* on the shape of a larger group of people than one commonly finds in contemporary sexual stories and photographs. In addition, because ancient Greece was a society not structured by market relations, a society in which public life did not center on production and exchange, the significance of arguing that power carries gender as well as class can be seen with greater clarity. Finally, these texts, the theoretical records of an all male political community, directly contribute to our understanding of the gendered dimension of power through such things as their insistence that female existence (but not male) is defined by the body, and their presentation of mythic female forces as fundamental threats to the political community.

I argue that as presented in these works, the Greek understanding of politics and power rested more directly and explicitly than ours on the division between women and men, between the household, a private and apolitical space, and the *polis*, a public and political space. This division was, moreover, a division between a realm of necessity and a realm of freedom, a realm held to be characterized by inequality and a realm seen as populated by equals, a realm described as dominated by the body and a realm where the soul or intellect was held to be dominant. All of this both rested on and reinforced a profound misogyny. The result was a theorization of politics and political power as activities that occurred in a masculine arena characterized by freedom from necessary labor, dominance of intellect or soul, and equality among the participants, in which political power rested on heroic action defined by courage in war and courage in speech, a world defined exclusively in masculine terms.[2] It rested on, depended on, but at the same time opposed another world—a world where necessity was held to rule, where inequality and hierarchy were seen as central, bodily needs as opposed to those of the soul or intellect were described as dominant, a world in which heroic action was not even a possibility, a world of women—the household. I argue that the refracted impact of these dualities still structures our thinking.[3] Let us begin by pursuing the *eros* of this community to its literary source in Homer, where it :akes the form of a community of warriors, or, more precisely, of warrior-heroes.

The Homeric Warrior-Hero

The Homeric epics set the stage for a dichotomous (and precarious) political community. In the *Iliad*, the battlefield is the stage on which the action takes place. It is inhabited solely by men, and heroism is the supremely masculine role. The purpose of each man there is less to win battles than to achieve undying fame through a demonstration of masculine virtue (almost a redundant phrase, since the Latin root of virtue refers to manliness). Whether the hero's courage results in glorious victory or glorious death matters little; the point is the achievement of immortality, of a reputation for honor. A classical scholar has underlined the importance of this reputation for honor: When moderns read the *Iliad*, he states, they may note that Achilles is never charged with public irresponsibility for refusing to fight; the ancient Greeks understood that honor, rather than the battle, was central.[4]

Achilles himself is given a clear choice. He is told that he carries two destinies:

> If I stay here and fight beside the city of the Trojans,/my return home is gone, but my glory shall be everlasting;/but if I return home to the beloved land of my fathers,/the excellence of my glory is gone, but there will be a long life/left for me, and my end in death will not come quickly.[5]

The primacy of honor is memorialized in Achilles' choice to stay and fight. The conflict between what the hero must do for honor as opposed to even life itself is replicated in other ways in the hero's situation.

In the role of the hero, one finds the prelude to the tensions and conflicts that structure the *polis* in later centuries. The political community *as community* exists only on the battlefield, where the collective good can be the primary concern of the hero.[6] The community both sustains and provides for the warrior-hero and sends him to possible death. Because of the warrior's role on the edge of the community, one scholar argues that the warrior stands on the "frontier between culture and nature."[7] Because of this privileged position, culture appears for the warrior in what is perhaps its true form—a "translucent screen against the terror of nature."[8] Yet the warrior-hero was also the head of a household made up primarily of women and was a carrier of the private and particular interests of that household. The ethic of warrior and householder conflict: The warrior-hero must be prepared to achieve fame undying through glorious victory or glorious death; the householder must preserve or perhaps cautiously expand his property. There is a conflict between loyalty to the community and to the family. To meet the first set of obligations, the warrior-hero must be ready to die, but to meet his obligations as a householder, he must survive.[9]

In addition to the dichotomies between nature and culture, household and political community, the warrior-hero experienced the conflict between the collective good as an end in itself, and as an instrument of his own glory and honor. The highest good for the warrior-hero is not, as Socrates/Diotima point out in the *Symposium*, a quiet conscience, but the enjoyment of public esteem, and through this esteem, immortality. Honor, or *timē*, is central. Thus, Achilles can ask, "Why should I fight, if the good fighter receives no more *timē* than the bad?"[10]

Just as the warrior-hero faced the conflicts between community and nature in extreme form on the battlefield, so he faces this dualism in extreme form within his own being. He fights to win reputation, as well as to preserve the community. It is perhaps the importance of public reputation that leads to the externalization of emotions. If to "lose face" is unbearable because it is to lose moral identity, how then can one explain actions one would be ashamed to acknowledge as one's own? E. R. Dodds has suggested that in such circumstances, the society may well allow individuals to project these feelings and actions onto some divine agency. The dichotomy is so extreme in Homer that the emotions are seen as detached entities responsible for *atē*, a kind of temporary insanity or clouding of the normal consciousness in which the hero behaves in ways he can give no good account of. Significantly, of the three agencies to which *atē* is ascribed, two are female. Zeus is the primary source, but the female figures of the Moerae and the Erinyes are also capable of inducing *atē*.[11] The hero must struggle against these female forces, but with little hope of victory. They are stronger than he. The dualism, then, between male and female *within* the person of the warrior-hero is externalized and made into a dichotomy between the person himself and supernatural and alien forces, which may overcome him from time to time.

In the case of the warrior-hero, then, each aspect of *eros* takes negative form. Relations with others take the form of the struggle for victory in battle, a struggle for dominance that requires the other's submission or even his death. The alternatives of victory versus death or dishonor preclude reciprocity. Hector and Achilles have no choices in common. The second aspect of *eros*, too, sensuality and bodily concerns, takes negative form. The body and its needs, even for life itself, are held to be irrelevant. The warrior-hero must risk death if he is to gain a reputation for honor. And even the emotions are held to be not his own, but are treated as produced by detached entities responsible for creating temporary madness. Finally, creativity and generation, issues centering on life, are replaced for the warrior-hero by a fascination with death, a longing to undo death. Ironically, however, physical death most often provides the means for attaining undying fame. The rejection of life takes indirect form as well. The world in which heroic deeds are done exists in a space totally apart from daily life activity. To gain and preserve his honor the warrior-hero must show himself to be "above" concerns of necessity and daily life.

The Homeric warrior-hero, then, contained within his person and situation many of the contradictory forces that would take attenuated form in the life of the Athenian citizen. But the citizen and the hero are not one and the same. The transition from the tribal or clan-based world portrayed in the Homeric poems to the world of the *polis* is marked in poetic and mythological terms by the *Oresteia* of Aeschylus in the fifth century B.C., a series of three plays that can be most instructive for our purposes.

The Founding of the *Polis* in Poetry and Philosophy

The transition required was a great one, from what was basically a stratified tribal society to a settled, class-divided community. These plays can be read as a fifth-century representation of a mythic founding of the *polis* and (in the process) an important development of Western understandings of politics and power. Most fundamentally, the establishment of the *polis* takes place through a process of domesticating and subordinating the dangerous and threatening female forces that surround what is to become the political community. Where, for the warrior in battle, these were the forces of a hostile "nature," the forces responsible for *atē*, or human enemy seen in that guise, now they have taken on distinctly female shape.

As Aeschylus tells the story, Agamemnon, in order to get good winds and victory in battle, sent home for his daughter Iphigenia, with a promise that he had arranged for her marriage, only to sacrifice her when she arrived, "heedless of her tears" because "her judges valued more their glory and their war" than the life of a woman.[12] The glories to be had in combat and the willingness to pay almost any price for them is a recurring theme in both the heroic poems and the political ideals whose birth they attended.

When Agamemnon returned from the war, Clytemnestra, his wife, killed him in vengeance, and their son, Orestes, killed his mother in revenge. In Aeschylus' play, Orestes is urged to do the deed by Apollo, the god of light, and the mythic representation of the male principle.[13] Orestes, after killing his mother, justifies the deed by saying that he belongs to his father, not his mother. His mother is a "treacherous web" that killed his father, a "pollution,"[14] and therefore Orestes argues that he has committed no sin. But the Furies, the avengers of infractions in the tribal code of vengeance, come after him. They are female figures of darkness and chaos from beneath the earth. Orestes describes them in terms that the more psychoanalytically oriented might characterize as primitive masculine fears. Their purpose is to "hound matricides to exile."[15] They are

> Not women, I think I call them rather gorgons, only/not
> gorgons either, since their shape is not the same . . . no/wings,
> that could be seen; they are black and utterly repulsive, and
> they snore with breath that drives one back./From their eyes
> drips the foul ooze, and their dress is such/as is not right to
> wear in the presence of the gods'/statues. . . .[16]

The Erinyes are avengers of matricide; for them, Clytemnestra's crime in killing her husband is a lesser offense than Orestes' crime in killing his mother. Since she was Orestes' blood relation, and no relation to Agamemnon, the latter's death must be a lesser crime. Through the intervention of Apollo, the god of light and order, Orestes, pursued by the Erinyes, flees to Athens with the promise that he will be delivered from his difficulties. Both parties present themselves to Athena for judgment, and she calls the Athenian jurors into session.

Apollo himself presents Orestes' defense, a statement of the new and patriarchal code of the city-state as opposed to the more ancient tribal laws. Apollo argues that Agamemnon's death was awful. He was a king and a woman killed him; worse, it was not an Amazon who killed him in battle, but his own wife who killed him at home. It was not a manly death. Apollo goes on to argue against the matrilineal rules defended by the Erinyes. He argues that the mother is not the real parent of the child but only a "nurse who tends the growth of the young seed planted by its true parent, the male."[17] So "if fate spares the child, she keeps it as one might keep for some friend a growing plant."[18] And then he offers the following: "And of this truth / that the father without mother may beget, we have / present as proof, the daughter of Olympian Zeus: / one never nursed in the dark cradle of the womb." This is of course a reference to the myth that Athena sprang from Zeus's forehead. The jurors are deadlocked, and significantly, while they wait for the verdict, Orestes prays to "bright Apollo," and the Furies pray to "mother night." Finally, Athena makes the judgment in favor of Orestes: Because of her own position as motherless, she says she will support "the father's claim / and male supremacy in all things."[19]

The finding in favor of male supremacy enrages the Furies, who threaten vengeance on Athens. But Athena calms them, promises them a home, a cavern of their own, and a role in the city. *Their* task will be to dispose of all *mortal* ways and to help households prosper. That is, they are to concern themselves with daily life, with the household realm of production, with tasks traditionally within the sphere of women. They are not to concern themselves with issues of immortality, philosophy, or war—the sphere of men and divine virgins in the new state.

The *Oresteia* has held continuing interest for a number of theorists. Simone de Beauvoir and Kate Millett have seen it as the mythic rendering of a patriarchal takeover.[20] Philip Slater has used it to uncover the psychology of the Greek mother/son relation. George Thomson, from a Marxist perspective, has seen it as a mythic account of the beginnings of Greek democracy, which, based as it was on a system of private property, required the subjection of women.[21] Froma Zeitlin argues that while Thomson and Slater are correct to focus on the problem of justice in the *Oresteia*, although from very different perspectives, the more important issue is the way the male/female conflict is transformed into a struggle between the new and progressive male world and the old and reactionary female world.[22]

My reading of these plays indicates that any male takeover involved a number of complex social changes and conceptual shifts, many of which were central to the theoretical construction of the political community. The outcome of Orestes' trial suggests that Athens as a *polis*, a political arena, depended in a vital way on the domestication of female forces of disorder—forces whose symbolic sources are the earth and the night, forces seen as deeply connected with fertility, sexuality, and reproduction. The danger these female forces presented to the *polis* is accentuated by Aeschylus' complex presentation of the dangers the female presents to the community.[23]

The unruly female threatens the fragile male community in several ways. One can see some of these threats in the figure of Clytemnestra. She functions in the plays as the representative of the older, clan-based order that operated on the ethic of the blood vendetta. As such she is not only out of place in the new world of law where decisions are made by the jury, but also an indication of how disruptive the old ways may now be. And even within the context of the clan system, the fact that she has killed her husband indicates that a woman's responses to provocation can be expected to exceed the proper (here read masculine) response, and lead to disequilibrium. It can even bring society to a halt.[24] The figure of Clytemnestra holds yet another threat to the political community. She is a sexual creature who has demonstrated her ability to act on her own by taking a lover while her husband was away at war.

The dangers female forces present to the political community appear in slightly different form in the case of the Furies. They appear as elements of the archaic "old religion." It is characterized as primitive, lawless, regressive, and tied to the forces of earth and nature, while the male, "bright Apollo," is seen as leading toward the future —law abiding, orderly, and by implication part of the world of reason. Because of the danger the female presents to the male world, the plays can be read as a statement of the importance fifth-century Athenians gave to domesticating the forces of disorder. Failing this domestication, they feared, the male community could not survive.[25]

The *polis* is mythically founded on the new, explicitly patriarchal religion of the Olympian gods; the meaning of the transition to this new religion is made clear in the images of the opposition of light to darkness, Apollo to the Furies. The Athenian jury that decides Orestes' fate is the institution that replaces the blood feud. The conflict between Orestes and Clytemnestra, the Furies and Apollo, and by implication between Zeus and the Moerae, can be seen as a poetic restatement of the real historical process of moving from tribe to state.[26] More is involved, however, than the transition from tribe to class society. The patriarchy has, in a sense, increased its control through the double means of the Athenian jury, a group of the wisest citizens (the future Council of the Areopagus), and Athena, a benevolent female figure without whose intervention Orestes (and by implication even Apollo) could not have won the trial.

The disorderly, sexual, and earthy female figures are presented as so powerful that even a man aided by a god cannot control them. They require the aid of another female figure, a virgin goddess. In contrast to Clytemnestra and the Furies, Athena's distance from sexuality, fertility, and reproduction is extreme. She is a virgin, yet she is even less a sexual being than other virgin goddesses because her birth was not ordinary; she sprang not even from the body of a god but rather from his head.[27] Yet the end of the *Eumenides* implies that the *polis* cannot exist without these unruly female figures. Unless the Furies can be persuaded to accept a role in the community, they might destroy it.[28] On the other hand, because the *polis* is constituted as a *political* body through its conflict with the female forces of disorder, these female forces cannot be given a role in the *polis* itself. Despite the fact that they are essential to its existence and proper functioning, the fragile masculine political community must create a safe and separate space for itself. At the same time, it cannot ignore its own need for continuance, and indeed cannot ignore the forces of life represented by women.

There is yet another aspect of the *Oresteia* that deserves mention. The *polis* is established not only in opposition to unruly female forces but in opposition to nature. Just as the Homeric warrior-hero lived on the boundary between nature and culture, and confronted nature as a hostile force, so the *polis* draws its boundaries against a hostile (and female) nature, which must be subdued. The Furies, for example, are explicitly associated with the earth and fertility. Moreover, the nature to be subdued is both internal and external. Not only must the outside world be defended against, but the inner nature of each individual must also be controlled. Freud recognized the importance of this opposition to nature when he noted that the founding of the *polis*, especially the turning from mother to father, "signifies a victory of intellectuality over the senses." Thus he puts himself on the side of those who argue that civilization itself depends on controlling the forces of disorder within the individual.[29] The *Oresteia*, then, can be read as an account of the establishment of a harmonious and unitary political whole, a whole in which the different parts take their proper place and in which female is subordinate to male, body to soul, and emotion to reason.

In such a reading, the *Oresteia* can be seen as describing an alteration, though not a transformation, in each aspect of *eros*. Thus, the domination that characterizes relations with others ceases to require that one take revenge on one's enemies by killing them: Opponents instead may take part in a rhetorical competition before the Athenian jury. Rather than risk the literal death of the body in combat and rather than externalize the emotions, the *Oresteia* suggests that the subordination of bodily appetites and sexuality to the rule of reason is sufficient.

The alteration in the third aspect of *eros*, a move away from the requirement that one die a glorious death to gain immortality, appears in another important text. The transition from warrior-hero to citizen is memorialized in the speeches of Plato's *Symposium*. The speakers in this competition *cum* dialogue replicate in at least rough form the evolution from the Homeric hero through the role of the citizen in the founding of the *polis*, to the final repression/sublimation of *eros* in the philosopher's love of beauty.[30] They present an excellent view of the changing but continuing association of manliness with the negative forms of *eros*, of the continuing efforts to subjugate what are conceived to be female forces, and of the creation of a ritualized and disembodied *eros* between citizens. At the same time, the vision of the *Symposium* is one that attempts to move *eros* away from the disorderly realm of the physical and toward reason, away from bodily concerns and toward those of the soul (ultimately toward the divine). Only when it is cleansed of enough of its bodily impurities can *eros* take its place as an honorable tie between citizens.

The dialogue takes place at a communal feast, one that usually included a drinking contest. (In this particular instance, the participants swear they will not repeat their exploits of the night before.) The conversation turns to love, and each participant is required to make a speech on the subject which will improve on those that went before.

Phaedrus and Pausanius begin the discussion—both taking up the dualism of reason and desire, mind and body, describing love as a kind of possession by an alien invader. In addition, they stress the importance of reputation, a concern clearly in tune with the values of the ancient heroes.[31] Phaedrus stresses the links between *eros* and military virtue, or courage in battle. He argues, for example, that the lover would be unable to bear that his beloved should find him in an inglorious act, or worse, in submission to "ill-usage." He turns directly to the military possibilities in this, and suggests that if a city or army were composed of none but lovers and beloved, they might well conquer the world. "For the lover would rather anyone than his beloved should see him leave the ranks or throw away his arms in flight."[32] He makes explicit the relation of *eros* and the warrior-hero when he argues that Homer's statement that some god "breathed might" into one of the heroes is in reality a reference to the power of love in the heart of the lover. Moreover, Phaedrus is impressed not only with the willingness of the lover to die for the beloved but also with his wish to avenge him. *Eros*, then, takes the form first of wishing to distinguish oneself in the eyes of the beloved by dominating others, but then is transformed more directly into an agent of death.

This speech is followed by that of Pausanius, who, although he presents the appearance of disagreeing (perhaps in order to distinguish himself), carries forward the argument Phaedrus had begun. His contribution focuses on the dualism of mind and body and the proper ordering of the two in the worthy lover, an ordering that rejects sensuality in favor of submission to another only in search of wisdom or other virtue. Pausanius suggests that there are two sorts of love. There was the heavenly Aphrodite, who represents a higher sort of love, and the common Aphrodite, who represents a common sort of love. Common love is described as the love that inferior men feel, a love that works at random. They may "love firstly women as well as boys; next, when they love, they love bodies rather than souls." The association of manliness with mind and reason and the rejection of sensuality or bodily concerns is clear in this passage.[33]

Common Aphrodite is described as much younger than the other goddess and as having had a share of both male and female in her birth. The share of the female is responsible for the sensual, bodily orientation of this kind of love. The other love, the higher goddess, had no share of the female but only the male. She is the elder, and does not inspire violent passions. Those inspired by this goddess feel affection for boys who have shown signs of intelligence, signs which usually appear with the first growth of beard.[34] The *Symposium* can be read as an account of how *eros* can be incorporated into public life of the *polis*. But the *eros* that has a place in politics rejects the body in favor of the soul, rejects the material and not lasting in favor of higher things. Those things associated with the bodily and with the female world are seen as subordinate to the things associated with maleness and the higher world. Love of bodies interferes with and disrupts the pleasures of the soul.

The *Symposium* progresses through Eryximachus' and Aristophanes' development of the theme of harmonization, reconciliation of opposites, and the search for fusion with another. Both speeches form the basis for the sublimation and final disembodiment of *eros* in the speech of Socrates/Diotima. Eryximachus accepts the dichotomy of love as described by Pausanius, but argues that love is a kind of harmony, or resolution of conflict. If this is so, he suggests, then the creation of such harmony is an art. Thus, such things as medicine, his own art, or music are "under the sole direction of the god of love."[35] Aristophanes, once again claiming to take the argument in a different direction, both reinforces the argument about the dichotomous nature of love and develops the idea of harmony (mediation and reconciliation) with his story of the original three human sexes. The original male, female, and mixed-sex creatures, each now sliced in half by Zeus, "attempt to reintegrate our former nature, to make two into one, and to bridge the gulf between one human being and another." This fusion is a weak reflection of the dream of being a single and harmonious whole with one's beloved.[36] Yet the fusion itself carries the mind/body hierarchy: Only the original male creatures are capable of the highest love.

Agathon and Socrates/Diotima move the consideration of *eros* toward the disembodied love of truth or wisdom, and the vision of *eros* as the reconciler of ignorance and truth, the mediator between human and divine worlds. Agathon contributes an argument that love, however heroic, is a poet versed in all creative arts.[37] It is, he argues, longing, desire, and lack that have led to the development of all the arts. Socrates carries the case still further. *Eros* is a mediator between mortal and immortal. He can fulfill this role through his longing for the beautiful, a longing apparent in all the arts because the longing for the beautiful and the good, is, as well, a longing for immortality.[38] Reproduction, creativity, and generation, then, the third aspect of *eros*, take only disembodied form.

The material interactions with real objects involved in creative physical work are rejected in favor of a longing for immortality, a desire to cancel death. Significantly, Diotima states that this longing for immortality takes the forms both of procreation and a desire for "eternal mention in the deathless role of fame."[39] "For the sake of fame they will dare greater dangers, even, than for their children; they are ready to spend their money like water and to wear their fingers to the bone, and, if it comes to that, to die." Moreover, she adds, those who hope for this endless fame are more noble than others because they are "in love with the eternal."[40] Only some men are capable of achieving this latter kind of immortality. Here the discussion once again supports the dichotomous vision of male and female, soul and body, reason and appetite, and strikingly reinforces the hierarchical relation between them and the rejection of the latter.

The rejection of the body takes most striking form in the argument that all men are pregnant in both body and soul. Those who are pregnant in body turn to women, and raise a family, in the hope that they are securing immortality, memory, and happiness. In contrast, those who are pregnant in soul conceive and bear such things as wisdom and all her sister virtues. This group can attach themselves to others (beautiful in both body and soul) and bear more beautiful and immortal children than others; and as Socrates/Diotima says, "who would not prefer such fatherhood to merely human propagation, if he stopped to think of Homer, and Hesiod, and all the greatest of our poets. Who would not envy them their immortal progeny, their claim on the admiration of posterity."[41] The real activity of reproduction is thus replaced by the mental activity of achieving wisdom and immortality. Once again sensuality and bodily pleasures are rejected.

The Pythagorean and Aristotelian accounts of paternity are clearly at work here. There is an opposition of creativity to fertility—the one a male capacity, the other a female property. In the *Symposium* the male begetting offspring is involved in an art. Even the common lover who begets mortal children is involved in a creative act. But the pregnancy of the women is of the body in a literal sense.[42] Socrates/Diotima simply take the argument further and add that just as the soul is the proper ruler of the body, the creations of the soul are more beutiful than the creations of the body. Here, the citizen becomes disembodied. Procreation involves only the spirit; the flesh is irrelevant.

What does all this say about *eros*, community, and the fusion of virility and domination, first in the person of the warrior-hero in the Homeric poems and later in ideals for the Athenian citizen? The *Symposium* can be read as a philosophical restatement of the shift in the *eros* of the community from one appropriate to a clan-based society to an *eros* more appropriate to a class state, the *polis*. But because the political community continued to be deeply structured by masculinity, the fundamental concerns remain unchanged. Fusion or community with another continues to operate through the effort to subordinate and control the other. But whereas for the warrior-hero this effort took the form of combat, for the Athenian citizen a ritualized rhetorical competition (such as takes place in the *Symposium*) can substitute. Loathing for the body and a denial of its needs no longer requires the disregard for the body to be demonstrated by risking death. Instead, the good citizen must allow his reason to rule over violent passions, should sublimate sensual and bodily love into the love of truth or wisdom, a translation perhaps, of sexuality into philosophy. Creativity and generation too continue to take negative form. But Plato retheorizes the effort to achieve immortality by dying a glorious death in terms more closely connected to reproduction. Immortality can now be achieved by begetting immortal children in the forms of art, poetry, and philosophy. The effort to cancel death thus now focuses more directly on efforts to associate reproduction with manliness.

The Nature of the Athenian Community

The *eros* of the community lies at the heart of its life as a community; the forms taken by *eros* indicate the fundamental structure of the community itself. As presented in theoretical form, the ancient political community is both fragile and unsatisfactory. The community is fragile in part because the warrior-hero is a brittle and fragile creature, not only threatened on all sides by those against whom he fights, but also in danger from the natural world, especially from the world of women. The sources of these threats must be subjugated. From this perspective, the *polis* represents the community built to protect the warrior-heroes from these threats—a community based on its maleness (even, perhaps, *machismo*). It segregates the female forces, both material and figurative, and also splits off the female forces within each man, represented traditionally by the bodily and the appetitive parts of their humanness.[43]

The forces that hold this fragile community together are the same as those that threaten to destroy it. The *eros* that holds it together may break it apart unless it is disembodied and sublimated; and competition for dominance must be ritualized, lest it become the all-out war of each against all. Thus, the *polis* both carried on the heroic ideal in which the virtues of citizenship required valor in battle in wartime and courage in rhetorical competition in peacetime and attempted to reconcile and ritualize the conflicts to which this gave rise.

Fame and honor and glory in both situations were to be gained at the price of another losing *his* fame, honor, and glory.[44] The continued importance of military imagery in the political vocabulary is striking. The centrally important terms of commendation for the Athenians were *aretè* and *agathos*. Both were terms that commended military bravery and success in war. To be *agathos* is above all to be independent of the constraint of another—due, it is implied, to one's military success. As daily life moved away from the battlefield, the nature of the combat among citizens changed, but retained its character of competition or contest, the object of which was to achieve as much recognition as possible especially among the group of fellow citizens who could be considered contestants in the same game.

If the object is to win more public prestige or fame than all the other "players," one can do so through victorious participation in wars, through threats, or through inducing others to enter into situations where their performance may be compared to one's own. The amount of fame the citizen-warrior can win depends importantly on the ranking of his fellow contestants. The greater the rank of the loser in any competition, the greater the value of a victory over that man. The point, to the citizen-warrior, is not to increase his own fame in a general sense, but to increase the difference between his fame and glory and that of his equals, his competitors.[45]

The. fundamental dualism of the Homeric poems continued to structure political life. The opposition of *polis* both to nature and to female forces continued to dominate thought, though not necessarily in such overt forms. The shape of this opposition in the ideals for the city-state is once again apparent in the *Symposium* when Agathon and Socrates/Diotima move the discussion toward the definition of *eros* as the disembodied love of truth and beauty, and the mediator between mortal and immortal. Even Plato's concept of reason acts to disembody the good citizen by means of aiding in the proper ordering of the soul. The good citizen will be a being on whom bodily needs, appetites, and emotions cannot intrude, a being not dependent even on his own body.

One can now begin to see some of the possible significance of both the association of reason with the male and of the particular Platonic (and to a lesser extent Aristotelian) conception of reason. Plato views human beings as materials the planner must work against rather than with—materials on which the planner must impose himself, since they are disorderly and chaotic.[46] When Plato constructs a just community in the *Republic*, he does so according to the dictates of reason—a reason associated with the need to control and master the world, to dominate natural objects and bend them to human will. The community he creates is both ordered and perfect. Yet the description of the process of degeneration (significantly a degeneration set in motion by women) in Book VIII of the *Republic* makes it clear that even the perfect community established in the best possible way has tendencies toward disorder.

Plato also, Gouldner suggests, views the division of objects into classes as an important aspect of control. As he points out, *nomos, moira*, and reason are all dividers and allocators. The core assumption is that classification aids control.[47] One can note as well that for Plato order itself is equated with hierarchy. In this world in which reason takes the form of a combative agent of domination through its role in classification and naming, Plato mistrusts the senses and suggests that they may corrupt reason both in the city and in the individual. This, after all, is one of the points of the massive education of the senses in the *Republic* where music and exercise are to be used along with other techniques to ensure the rule of reason in the lives of the guardian class.[48]

Even Plato's conception of reason itself is infected with the essential hierarchical quality of his outlook. Reason, for him, is not simply another human faculty; it is the master of all of them, the only one with a legitimate claim to command. Reason can be either the master of the passions or appetites or their slave; no other relation than domination and submission is possible. The two are profoundly alien. Aristotle, too, uses the analogy of the authority of man over slave and the different authority of man over wife to construct the account of the superiority of the soul over the body, and reason over appetite.[49]

As to the subduing of inner as well as external nature foreshadowed in the *Oresteia*, both Plato and Aristotle are explicit about the proper ordering of the human soul. Indeed, the only respect Socrates gives what might be termed the irrational side of his own soul occurs in his accounts of his *daemon*. And Socrates externalizes this aspect of his being by calling it a *daemon*. He never acknowledges it as a part of himself, and, in part due to this refusal, never accepts the passions and appetites of individuals as creative, energetic, and fundamentally enriching aspects of the human character.[50] In this of course he is part of the tradition that goes back at least as far as Homer's invocation of the madness of *atē* as an explanation for the actions of the heroes.

The basic polarity in Plato's view of social thought and action, then, is the opposition of emotional or appetitive to rational behavior. Plato is seeking to assimilate the rational and divine, in part through the role both have in the mastery of nature (both external and internal nature). This serves to heighten the opposition between the rational and the appetitive. The rational faculty arranges things, and by naming, imposes order on the world. The divine then becomes pure mind, and as a result, the excellent citizen is almost disembodied. In contrast to the divine, the natural tendency toward disorder is there in all other things, especially in their bodily or material forms. For Plato, the nondivine is, then, both disorderly and a thing of necessity.[51] The fear that the material will contaminate the divine shows clearly in Plato's refusal to allow the guardian class to have any property other than what is absolutely necessary, and his insistence that they live in common and share possessions. Were they to get land, they would become householders and farmers instead of guardians. That is, they would have become contaminated by the realm of necessity.[52] The human population of the disorderly realm of necessity, even in Plato's *Republic*, is disproportionately composed of women and slaves.

Gouldner argues that this view of order versus disorder reflects the impact of the experience of slavery on the Greek mind. I see it, however, as a result of the sexual division between women and men in Greek society. The fact that we find these dualisms so comfortable simply speaks to the persistence of those same divisions in our own society. But the effects of this vision seem to be remarkably similar in structuring the understanding of power as the domination of alien, disorderly, hostile, and dangerous forces.

The warrior and the guardian class, in contrast to women and slaves, must exercise the cardinal virtues: courage, temperance, justice, and wisdom.[53] To exercise these virtues, the citizen must be free of the necessity to labor. Thus Aristotle finds it appropriate to discuss in the *Politics* the property necessary to support a life of political activity. In this he follows Plato, whose guardian class rules in part through its separation from the demands of necessity. And Plato argues, even more clearly than Aristotle, that a city based on necessity alone is a city of pigs.[54] One might suggest that the citizen, in order to exercise the cardinal virtues, must be free of the demands of the body in order to allow his soul, or rational part, to rule. It is a fascinating commentary on the Greek view of the relative strength of the soul and body that the soul seems to have no chance of ruling if necessary labor intrudes into the citizen's life. The only way to protect the soul of the citizen is to wall it off as much as possible from necessity, and thus from the female.[55]

The warrior-hero and his citizen successor share many important qualities. Yet the *polis* is not a battlefield. The citizen is continually caught between the freedom of political competition and the necessity of household management; demands of the two worlds conflict, yet entrance to the higher realm requires membership in the lower. It is here that *eros* can play a role as mediator and reconciler of oppositions. The community of competitors threatens to destroy itself—to degenerate into the war of each against all—unless the competition for dominance is ritualized and regulated. *Eros* too could take a destructive form, but it can also serve to protect the community.[56] *Eros* can help to ritualize the competition, and to direct it away from dangerous competitions. The community must incorporate *eros*, including its explicitly sexual dimensions, to develop ways for the many to become one. It accomplishes this through the *eros* of male citizens for each other.[57] There is, of course, a contradiction between competition as their way of life on the one hand and the maintenance of the community through their *eros* for each other on the other, a conflict never satisfactorily resolved, which becomes a contributing factor to the fragility of the political community.

The community as a whole, the *polis*, exists for the purpose of, or in Aristotle's terms, has as its end, the arranging of competition among its citizens to show that they are worth loving or (the same thing within the Athenian context) to show that they are worth dominating. That is, the citizen-warrior must show that a victory over him is significant enough to make his vanquisher preeminent among citizens, a victory that will mean the achievement of honor and glory.

The political community is an exclusively male community, one in which power and sexuality are intertwined, a community in which the exercise of political power involves rule over equals, over those who are worth loving, over those who might be able to turn the tables. In this community, only through dominating those worth dominating can one achieve glory and honor.

Necessity and Opposition

The point I have attempted to make is that *eros* and power are deeply connected, and when *eros* takes negative, masculine forms that point toward death rather than life, the community as a whole will be structured by those dynamics. The political community that rests on negative forms of *eros* can now be seen to be structured by a deeper and more thoroughgoing hostility than that constituted by exchange. On the basis of this reading of ancient sources, the masculine political community emerges as more problematic than the fragile, arbitrary, and fundamentally false community of exchangers. It is contradictorily both essential and deeply impossible to maintain. Its participants are not simply strangers to each other but enemies.

If we look at the forms taken by each of the three aspects of *eros*, we can see the differences (though shared problematical nature) between the community structured by *eros* in a negative form and the community understood on the model provided by (I would prefer to say overlaid by) exchange. The ancient sources indicate that the first aspect of *eros*, the search for reciprocal fusion with another, takes the essential form of the search for the death of the other, or for his ceasing to exist as a separate and discontinuous being. At the least there is an effort to conquer the other's will. The combination of conflicting and common interests of buyer and seller in the market in these sources take forms that indicate only conflicting needs. Where the buyer and seller each left the market (even after the purchase or sale of labor power) with something they did not possess before the transaction (money or commodity), in the competition for mastery the one competitor could only gain what the other lost. The opposition of victory to death or dishonor does not represent a situation in which one can argue that both sides gain, even if they do not gain equally. Yet each combatant needs the other. Their dilemma anticipates the dilemma of O's lovers: Recognition grows from the death struggle (or rhetorical competition) with a worthy opponent. At the same time, however, the death of the other, especially his heroic death, negates the recognition of the power of the victor, and his humiliation or dishonor makes him unfit to confer recognition on the prowess of the victor. Thus the need for recognition of one's mastery in competition carries with it a number of contradictory requirements.[58] One should recall Benjamin's account of the dilemma of the master: Complete domination is both necessary and results in the masters' being left alone because the other is not a person at all.

The second aspect of *eros*, sensuality and bodily concerns, takes the negative form of the denial of the importance of the body and of mortality. The denial of mortality takes the forms of valuing the risking of physical death in favor of legendary immortality, giving great weight to the organizing powers of reason rather than real work in the material world, and subjugation of the sensual and appetitive parts of the soul to the rational aspect—the disembodying of the good citizen. Plato's refusal to allow the guardian class in the *Republic* to own property can be seen in this context as an indication of the extent to which he feared contamination by the realm of necessity.

The third aspect of *eros*, too, creativity and generation, in these ancient sources takes the form of a rejection of the importance of any creative work other than disembodied mental activity and a devaluing of the real children born to women in favor of the children that can be born to the minds of those not contaminated by the concerns of necessity or the body.

The result is that power appears as domination not only of others but of parts of oneself—domination both internal and external—and the community itself rests on dualism and contradiction. Power is domination of those outside the community. It requires an attempt to dominate material nature, women, slaves, and barbarians. Second, within the community, each citizen strives for mastery or preeminence. And third, it requires the attempt to dominate the appetitive and irrational part of the self. The fear of and contempt for the bodily, the irrational, the appetitive, and ultimately the female, are all part of the same pattern. These then are the forms of *eros* central to the ancient texts that still influence our thinking about politics.

What emerges from all this is an understanding of the political community that rests on dualism and contradiction, in which the two realms are in opposition and in which the higher world depends on the lower world. Just as in the individual, the higher part should rule the lower part, so too in the community, the best should rule. But in the literal way the *Republic* takes the analogy of the nature of the individual to the community, the existence of the ruler (soul, reasoning part) depends on the survival of the ruled (or body), and yet can be distorted and corrupted by the demands of the ruled. The contradictory nature of the community emerges in several areas. First, the *eros* of the citizens, which holds the community together, is constantly threatened by their competition with each other. Their efforts to distinguish themselves at someone else's expense create a situation in which the existence of the community is constantly threatened. The *polis* might disintegrate into a battlefield. Even the *eros* of citizens is invaded by this competition: there it takes the form of wishing to distinguish oneself in the eyes of the beloved, wishing to dominate others for the sake of the beloved, and thereby showing oneself capable of taking only the most worthy as lover.

Second, the realm of politics, the public realm, both depends on and exists only in opposition to the private realm, that is, the household. One can be a citizen only by being the head of a household.

Third, the realm of freedom and leisure inhabited by citizens depends on the existence of a realm of necessity populated by women, slaves, and laborers—but defined in essence by its female nature. Fourth, there is an opposition between a realm in which political rule is possible—rule over equals, which involves the constant possibility of changing from ruler to ruled; and a realm defined by the rule of master over servants—a rule over unequals, where the ruled can never become rulers. The citizen must be involved in this realm of unequals to qualify to enter the public realm. The *polis*, Aristotle argued, must be understood as an association of households. He lays out in systematic form the ways *oikos* and *polis* are interdependent but in tension with each other.[59]

The comedies of Aristophanes further demonstrate this tension between the *oikos* and *polis*, a tension rooted in the situation of the Homeric hero in battle. The fact that it remained a fundamental problem is highlighted by the reliance on this tension as a major source for humor. The comic situations in both the *Lysistrata* and the *Congresswomen* rely on the breakdown of the disjunction between the *polis* and *oikos*, and most especially on women's breaking away from their traditional roles—with catastrophic results for the political community. In the *Lysistrata*, it is the *eros* of the household—common or physically inspired love—that takes over the public space. The *Congresswomen* uses a similar comic strategy, where it is the organization of the household that takes over the *polis*. For Aristophanes, to put women in charge of the city is to transform it. The plays make it clear that a public role for women would inevitably involve the destruction of the *polis* itself.

The community based on the negative form of *eros*, then, both differs importantly from the community based on momentary conjunction of arbitrary interests and at the same time replicates some important features. Most fundamentally, for my analysis here, the nature of community itself remains a problem. On the basis of the ancient sources one can conclude that the question of how individuals come to associate with each other is not at issue; the other with whom one competes for mastery is clearly necessary.[60] The all-male political community of the ancients, the community created by rivalry, combat, and competition, is both more direct and deep-going than the social synthesis constructed by exchange and more deadly.

NOTES

1. One might argue that this being is most recently reincarnated in the capitalist entrepreneur who competes in the market for victory or death—now termed, somewhat more prosaically, "going out of business."

2. Once again it is worth reminding the reader that my use of the term "masculine" is intended to refer to the social construction of gender.

3. I should stress that my case here is based on the theoretical congruence of the sources with the dynamics (or, perhaps, metaphysics) of contemporary pornography. I am not presenting the kind of historical and sociological evidence that could fully support my claim that the ideas in these sources are rooted in a sex-segregated and male-dominant society. Rather, I rely here and in the next chapter on the weight of suggestive, though indirect, theoretical evidence. Others have attempted the kind of analysis with regard to class relations that could perhaps be attempted here with regard to gender.

George Thomson and Alvin Gouldner, for example, have instructively attempted to link some features of Greek life to their social relations. Thomson, for example, suggests that the Pythagorean doctrine of the fusion of opposites in the mean was generated by the rise of the middle class to act as a balance between the landowners and the peasants. The aristocracy and common people were balanced by the wealth of the new middle class. What Hesiod had understood as a struggle without the possibility of victory in this life, by Pythagoras' time had become a possible cessation of the struggle. See George Thomson, *Aeschylus and Athens* (London: Lawrence and Wishart, 1941), pp. 214–19.

Gouldner, in contrast, calls attention to the relation of social life to thought in another way. He suggests that Plato's world view is structured by a covert analogy with slavery. Plato's views about slavery, the state, the individual, and the cosmos all follow a single hierarchical pattern. Because Plato's world view has the master-slave relation at its heart, Plato sees the orderly world constructed/imposed by the master as constantly threatened by the disorder of a slave, who lacks *logos*. Gouldner argues that disorderliness is always experienced in relation to one's own ends. The behavior of the slave only seems disorderly and unpredictable from the point of view of the master's (and not the slave's) ends. See Alvin Gouldner, *Enter Plato* (New York: Basic Books, 1965), pp. 351–55.

One could look as well at the argument by N. Wood and E. M. Wood that political theory represents practical proposals concerning political and social institutions and actions in *Class Ideology and Ancient Political Theory* (Oxford: London, 1978), p. 3. My purpose here is not to defend these particular theses; indeed I tend to differ with these arguments. Rather, I hope to call attention to the implications of the argument I put forward—to stress the importance of dualism in the lives and thought of a number of important political thinkers, and to remember that the most fundamental dualism experienced by the ancient Greeks was the sexual division between women and men.

4. M. I. Finley, *The World of Odysseus* (Baltimore: Penguin, 1979) ,p. 117.

5. *Iliad* IX: 411–16, trans. Richard Lattimore (Chicago: University of Chicago Press, 1951).

6. One can see the links with Arendt's concept of power as action in concert, and some of the attendant problems. But, as James Redfield has pointed out, the community can be secured only by combat, which is, after all, the negation of the community.

7. James Redfield, *Nature and Culture in the Iliad: The Tragedy of Hector* (Chicago: University of Chicago Press, 1975), p. 101. See also Finley, *The World of Odysseus*, pp. 74–85.

8. Redfield, *Nature and Culture*, p. 103. Redfield does not touch on the question of why nature should be so terrifying. That he can fail to do so is an important statement in and of itself about the extent to which we share the Greek world view.

9. Ibid., pp. 124–25.

10. See E. R. Dodds, *The Greeks and the Irrational* (Berkeley: University of California Press, 1951), pp. 17–18, citing *Iliad* ix: 315 ff.

11. My discussion owes much to Dodds, *The Greeks*, chapt. 1. He argues that *moira* in this context refers to portion rather than to the Fates. Still, the female connotations should not be ignored. Dodds also notes the intellectual form given to explanations of behavior. One is said to "know" not only technical things, but also things concerning moral character. From this perspective, the Socratic paradoxes such as "virtue is knowledge" are the culmination of an ingrained pattern of thought (see p. 17).

12. Aeschylus, *Oresteian Trilogy*, trans. Philip Vellacott (Baltimore: Penguin Books, 1956), p. 50. There are, however, some important fifth-century additions to the story, noted by both Thomson and Slater. What was for Homer a simple fight about the succession becomes a story of women out to kill their husbands. In addition, one should note that Slater reports that if attention given to a dramatic character is a measure of his popularity, Orestes was by far the most favored figure of fifth-century Athens. He might better have said that in the few surviving plays, Orestes is one of the most important characters. See Thomson, *Aeschylus and Athens*, p. 248. See also Philip Slater, *The Glory of Hera* (Boston: Beacon Press, 1968), p. 162.

13. But note that in the version of Euripides, *Electra*, it is she who urges him to do the deed. He is so weak he is almost incapable of any act without the assistance of a god or a woman or even, as we will see, both. See Slater, *The Glory of Hera*, on this point.

14. *Oresteian Trilogy* (Penguin ed.), p. 141.

15. Ibid., p. 154.

16. Ibid., trans. Richard Lattimore (Chicago: University of Chicago Press, 1953), p. 136.

17. *Oresteian Trilogy* (Penguin ed.), p. 169.

18. This is of course a restatement of the influential Pythagorean view, and also of the Aristotelian view. See Thomson, *Aeschylus and Athens*, p. 288; Marilyn Cline Horowitz, "Aristotle and Woman," *Journal of the History of Biology* 9, no. 2 (Fall 1976): 194, on the plant analogy, and pp. 198–202 on the vision of the female as a multilated male.

19. *Oresteian Trilogy* (Penguin ed.), p.172. Significantly, she makes one exception to this support of male supremacy—the giving of herself in marriage. One could spend a great deal of time on the mythic role of Greek virgins. See for example, Thomson, *Aeschylus and Athens*, pp. 282–83.

20. Simone de Beauvoir, *The Second Sex*, trans. H. M. Parshley (New York: Knopf, 1953), p. 73; Kate Millett, *Sexual Politics* (Garden City, N.Y.: Doubleday, 1970), pp. 111–15.

21. Thomson suggests that this consequence was recognized even by contemporaries of Aeschylus; both Aristophanes and Plato saw that the abolition of private property would involve the emancipation of women. See Slater, *The*

Glory of Hera, pp. 161–93; Thomson, *Aeschylus and Athens,* p. 288, Winspear makes a different argument and sees Pythagoras as an aristocrat. But Thomson argues that the later Pythagoreans were reactionaries (p. 291). See also Alban Dewes Winspear, *The Genesis of Plato's Thought* (New York: S. A. Russell, 1940).

22. She argues that the two spheres must be assimilated before male can triumph over female. My own reading, however, suggests that these two spheres are never assimilated. See Froma Zeitlin, "The Dynamics of Misogyny: Myth and Mythmaking in the *Oresteia,*" *Arethusa* 11, nos. 1, 2 (Spring and Fall 1978).

23. Philip Slater makes this case in "The Greek Family in History and Myth," *Arethusa* 7, no. 1 (Spring 1974).

24. Zeitlin, "The Dynamics of Misogyny," p. 156.

25. Zeitlin puts it well: "The pacification of the Erinyes becomes the ideological effort to solve the dilemma of the inextricable connection between female fertility and female sexuality, between female beneficence and female malevolence . . ." (ibid., p.159). The problem of female duality has had important impacts on thought and social structure, most recently documented by Dorothy Dinnerstein in *The Mermaid and the Minotaur* (New York: Harper & Row, 1976).

26. Thomson argues that this is the beginning of the reign of law. I would argue it represents a mythic representation of a change in a mode of production from tribal society to a class state. See Thomson, *Aeschylus and Athens,* p. 289.

27. Can one say that these dual types of female figures in some way anticipate the opposition between virgin and whore in more contemporary contexts?

28. It is interesting to compare this solution to the Pythagorean doctrine of the fusion of opposites in the mean.

29. Sigmund Freud, *Moses and Monotheism,* (New York: n.p., 1958), p. 145, cited in Zeitlin, "The Dynamics of Misogyny." She also presents a useful tabulation of the male/female polarization in Greek thought—a polarization that put reason and the appetites in opposition to each other, that associated reason with the male and appetites with the female, and that required the stronger of the two opposing forces should control the weaker. Ideally, reason should control the appetites (see esp. p. 171).

30. Although this progression may sound a bit extreme, another commentator has suggested that in reading the *Symposium,* one should replace the term "lover" with "hero." See Stanley Rosen, *Plato's Symposium* (New Haven: Yale University Press, 1968), p. 52.

31. See Finley, *The World of Odysseus;* see also Dodds, *The Greeks and the Irrational.* Dodds sees far more of a transformation from shame to guilt culture than I do. Interestingly enough, these same themes appear prominently in the *Phaedrus* as well.

32. *Symposium,* trans. Michael Joyce in *The Collected Dialogues of Plato,* ed. Edith Hamilton and Huntington Cairns (Princeton, N.J.: Princeton University Press, 1961), 179:a

33. Ibid., 180b–182c. The association of the two was also shared by Aristotle. See his discussion of human reproduction in *De Generatione Animulium.*

34. Ibid., 181d.

35. Ibid., 187a.

36. Ibid., 192e.

37. Ibid., 196d.

38. Ibid., 207a. See also Ibid., 204c–205d.

39. Ibid., 208c.

40. Ibid., 208e.

41. Ibid., 209d.

42. Aristotle codifies the view that even in the creation of human children, women provide the matter for the creation and men provide the form. It is the man's soul that contributes form to the child. See Horowitz, "Aristotle and Woman," p.197.

43. One can find enormous amounts of support for this claim in the works of Plato and Aristotle. See also Elizabeth V. Spelman, "Metaphysics and Misogyny: The Soul and Body in Plato's Dialogues" (unpublished manuscript available from the author, Department of Philosophy, Smith College, Northampton, Massachusetts).

44. Slater notes that one is struck repeatedly by the zero-sum nature of Athenian competition; the "twin delicacies of daily life were to achieve revenge and to arouse envy." See Slater, "The Greek Family," pp. 25, 35–36; see also Gouldner, Enter Plato, pp. 48–50.

45. Gouldner, Enter Plato, pp. 48–53, documents this feature of Greek life.

46. The following discussion owes much to Gouldner's discussion.

47. Gouldner, Enter Plato, pp. 327–29.

48. Although Plato includes women in his guardian class, they are detached from the world of necessity and nature. They participate not as females but as inferior and mutilated males. On the issue of reason and domination, see Plato, Republic V. 439e–441d. The theme of the weakness of males confronted by female forces appears in the Republic as well, in the form of Plato's real skepticism about the strength of the soul when confronted by the overpowering demands of the body or the emotions.

49. See Aristotle, Politics, trans. Ernest Barker (New York: Oxford University Press, 1962), I. 5:1254b. 2–9. I. 13:1260a. 4–8; see also Horowitz, "Aristotle and Woman," p. 210.

50. See, for example, the passage in the Republic where he says that the soul not ruled by reason would be unable to act because the passions would oppose it at every turn. Hamilton and Cairns, ed., Collected Dialogues, IV. 352a. See Gouldner, Enter Plato, p. 337. But see especially the role of the daemon in the Apology, Crito, and Phaedo.

51. Republic VIII. 550.

52. Ibid. III. 415e–420a.

53. Ibid. IV. 427e–432d.

54. See, for a different view of the significance of the city of pigs imagery, Arlene W. Saxonhouse, "Comedy in Callipolis: Animal Imagery in the Republic," The American Political Science Review 72, no. 3 (September 1978): 888–901.

55. Slater cites Erich Neuman, The Great Mother (Princeton: Princeton University Press, 1963), p. 215, as an example of the powerlessness and fragility of male forces. Perseus is barely able to kill the Medusa with two gods helping, magic implements, a sleeping enemy, and a goddess guiding his hand. This

buttressing reflects for Slater the brittleness of masculine self-confidence among the Greeks. See Slater, "The Greek Family," p. 40.

56. See for example, the first half of *Phaedrus*.

57. The institution of Greek homosexuality has been usefully discussed by Kenneth J. Dover in *Greek Homosexuality* (New York: Random House, 1980).

58. Jessica Benjamin, "The Bonds of Love: Rational Violence and Erotic Domination," *Feminist Studies* 6, no. 1 (Spring 1980): 158–59.

59. Aristotle, *Politics* I.

60. Interestingly, the public world constructed by the *eros* of citizen-warriors is more overtly and directly a setting for the playing out of relations of domination and submission. The erotic dimension of power is less overlaid than other aspects of power by an ideology that attempts to present coercion as choice, or inequality as equality. Perhaps this is because neither the domination of women by men (whether sexually or otherwise) nor the fact that erotic relations took forms of domination/submission has been open to question until very recently. In contrast, the commitment to human equality characteristic of political theorists from the sixteenth century on was integral to the generation of accounts of social relations that took human freedom and equality as unquestioned givens, and proceeded to give accounts of social life that argued that visible relations of inequality and bondage were illusory.

9

An Alternative Tradition:
Women on Power

The public world constructed by the *eros* of citizen-warriors took the form of competition for dominance and resulted in the creation of a community of men based on dualism and contradiction. The community that grows from the negative, masculine forms of *eros*, when translated into the context of the modern world, underlies the reality of rape, sexual murder, and pornography. This is the social reality representative of the negative forms of *eros*. The only fusion possible occurs through the death or submission of another; sensuality is denied/repressed; and creativity and generation are sublimated or take forms that point toward death. The gender carried by power in the modern world, as in the ancient, leads to the domination of others, domination of external nature, and domination of one's own nature. Or perhaps more precisely, the repression/denial of *eros* in a male-controlled society underlies the redefinition of both sexuality and power as domination.

Yet this is only half the story. A community structured by forms of *eros* that express women's experience might take quite different form. This suggestion is supported in an interesting way by the fact that theories of power put forward by women rather than men differ systematically from the understanding of power as domination. While few women have theorized about power, their theories bear a striking similarity both to one another and to theories of power recently characterized as feminist understandings of power. My several cases clearly constitute only suggestive evidence for my argument. Yet I believe it is significant that I was unable to discover any woman writing about power who did not stress those aspects of power related to energy, capacity, and potential.

210

Hannah Arendt's Reconstitution of the Public Realm

My reading of the deep connections among power, *eros*, and domination in the ancient sources opposes that put forward by Hannah Arendt, who explicitly makes Athenian democracy the basis for her own theorization of politics, power, and community. She represents a very interesting and important challenge to my argument that the political community constructed by the ancient Athenians has little in the way of a liberatory vision to offer contemporary theorists of power. On the basis of the account I have given of the ancient political community—an account of which one can find more than a few elements in Arendt's theory—one could certainly echo the protest Hanna Pitkin lodged against her own construal of Arendt's theory in these directions:

> What a contemptible doctrine, that denies the possibility of freedom, of a truly human life, even of reality, to all but a handful of comfortable males who are willing and able to dominate all others and exclude them by violence from privilege. And when the excluded and miserable do occasionally insist on entering history and asserting their humanity, Arendt condemns them for their rage, their failure to respect the "impartiality of justice and laws." Impartiality! Justice! Where were these fine principles when that immense majority was relegated to shame and misery? . . . [It] can make one prefer hell with those who labor and suffer in the dark, to a heaven of light and free action among the exploiters.[1]

Others, too, have found her theory both shocking and perhaps allowing a justification of immoral action. George Kateb has argued that in disallowing moral judgment of action and insisting that action must be judged only by its greatness, Arendt seems to be "siding with Alcibiades." He objects to her contention that "greatness has its own morality" and holds instead that "she is playing with fire."[2]

My own reading of Arendt leads me to suggest that despite the fact that she has used the ancient Greek sources as the foundation for her theory, she reads them and incorporates them into her own theory in ways that systematically reduce the conflictual nature of the oppositions between necessity and freedom, intellect and body, and social and natural worlds. As a result, she is able to put forward a vision of power and community surprisingly akin to Marx's references to the kind of social relations possible in a communist society.[3] Arendt's rehabilitation of the public realm can be shown to rest on several specific theoretical moves. First, she takes the antagonistic dualisms that structured the *polis* and reformulates them as arguments that the mode of life characteristic of one side of the duality makes that of the other possible. The two are therefore necessary to each other, but not opposed. Second, she translates the radical alterity that characterized the life of the warrior-hero into plurality (almost into individuality itself). Third, and related, Arendt redefines the nature of heroic action and agonal politics itself. In her theory, agonal politics is not the zero-sum game commented on by other students of Athenian politics, in which the submission of the other is essential to distinguishing oneself, but rather, heroic action becomes the establishing of one's uniqueness as an individual. Fourth, she reinterprets the nature of community to argue (1) that the *polis* is not simply an instrumental community, an audience to applaud the performers of great deeds and speakers of great words, but rather provides an answer to individual futility by holding out the possibility of immortality, and (2) that the public life of the *polis* operates to decrease rather than increase inequality.[4]

Let us begin with an examination of Arendt's reworking of the series of dualisms that occupied us in the last chapter. As Arendt formulates the relation between public and private, the distinction between necessity and freedom is central. The public sphere is constituted by equals who neither rule nor are ruled. Its purpose is to foster individuality and excellence. It is free of necessity, and thereby free from labor or from any useful activity; and it has as its content only two kinds of activity: action and speech (*praxis* and *lexis*).[5] As Arendt summarizes it: "Although the distinction between private and public coincides with the opposition of necessity and freedom, of futility and permanence, and finally, of shame and honor, it is by no means true that only the necessary, the futile, and the shameful have their proper place in the private realm."[6] Her point is that some activities should be hidden, while others can exist only in public. Arendt mourns the loss of the genuine public sphere inhabited by citizens of ancient Athens and Rome and regrets as well the loss of the need to cross the gulf between the public and private and "rise" into the realm of politics.[7] She argues that one of the problems of the modern age is that it has brought into the open things that should better be hidden. And it is not only the activities that should be hidden but, one senses, the people who perform these activities as well. From the beginning of history to the modern age, she notes, it has always been the "bodily part of human existence that needed to be hidden in privacy." And so, "hidden away were the laborers who 'with their bodies minister to the [bodily] needs of life' and the women who with their bodies guarantee the physical survival of the species." Both groups were hidden because their lives were laborious, and therefore concerned with necessity and the body.[8] Thus the very activities performed in the private realm differ from those performed in public. The two realms differ in another important way as well: Force and violence are appropriate in the private world, since they are "the only means to master necessity."[9] The gulf between the two worlds must be crossed by the citizen who lives in both of them. This crossing requires courage because in order to gain admittance to the fellowship that transcends "mere togetherness," one must demonstrate that one has mastered necessity by demonstrating a willingness to risk one's life.[10]

The outlines of the ancient dualism are clear in Arendt's discussion. At the same time, she argues that the two spheres ought not to be seen as opposed; rather, the one should be seen as the precondition for the other: "And if there was a relationship between these two spheres it was a matter of course that the mastering of the necessities of life in the household was the condition for freedom of the polis."[11] Moreover, she approvingly notes that, unlike the Greeks, the Romans never "sacrificed" the private to the public but instead understood the necessity for the two to coexist.[12] One gets a sense of two modes of action, each in its appropriate sphere of existence, the lower making the higher possible, but not deeply in conflict with or opposed to it. In contrast, my reading of the ancient sources suggests that the political community existed most fully when farthest separated from the household—on the battlefield.[13]

Arendt's treatment of the opposition between intellect, or soul, and body is closely linked to her discussion of freedom and necessity. She explicitly rejects Plato's argument that the body is merely a shadow of the soul. This, she contends, reverses the (proper) Homeric world order.[14] Her treatment of the relation of body to soul indicates, then, that she is attempting to go back to, and draw her model of politics from, that world. She seems to see an overconcern with inwardness as equally as bad for political action as overconcern with the body.[15] Thus she is led to distinguish the "time-honored resentment of the philosopher against the human condition of having a body" from the "ancient contempt for the necessities of life"[16] and to argue that in retrospect she sees her failure to give central enough place to embodied action rather than contemplation as the main flaw in *The Human Condition*: "The moment you begin to act, you deal with the world, and you are constantly falling over your own feet, so to speak, and then you carry your body—and, as Plato said: 'The body always wants to be taken care of and to hell with it!'"[17]

In addition, Arendt alone among the political theorists on whom she bases her work begins her discussion of the human condition not simply with *mortality* but with *natality*. I read this as symptomatic of a greater acceptance of mortality. To be born means that one will die. The fact that the discussion in Plato's *Symposium* turns on giving birth and pregnancy of the soul strikes me as very telling. The participants discuss giving birth—an experience they do not have—as opposed to the experience they do have—that of being born. The point of the analogy in the *Symposium* makes its importance clear: Giving birth is discussed as a means to immortality; having been born sentences one to death, unless one can find other means to immortality.[18]

Arendt is far more respectful of the body than Plato or Aristotle in part, but only in part, because of her admiration for the Homeric tradition. Arendt, unlike Plato, does not argue for the suppression/repression of the body, but only for the exclusion of bodily concerns from the public realm, whether in the form of labor or in the form of the urge for individual survival. It is in fact the overcoming of this innate urge that marks for her a characteristic central to the political—that of being no longer bound to one's biological body.[19] The dualism, then, between body and soul is not the antagonism between the two that characterizes most of ancient Greek philosophy. What is at stake for Arendt is an expression of contempt for necessity, not the disembodiment of the citizen.[20]

Arendt's understanding of the relation of the public sphere to the world of nature is similarly muted in comparison to her sources. What she views with horror is not nature itself but the failure to differentiate oneself from the world of nature, a condition she sees inevitable within the world of work.[21] The construction of the public sphere represents an opportunity for a "second birth," one controlled by the individual himself.[22] And this second birth, unlike the first, carries the potential of immortality. In this, of course, Arendt continues to follow the outlines of the Homeric tradition. At the same time, however, she refuses to take up a position that opposes the world of nature. She writes out of a concern that the modern age might end with the "repudiation of an Earth who was the Mother of all living creatures under the sky," and argues that despite the fact that human artifice separates human existence from the animal world, "through life man remains related to all other living organisms."[23] Thus Arendt has once again redefined and reformulated the ancient sources. She, unlike the Homeric warrior-hero described by Redfield, clearly does not face a "terrifying" (his term) nature, but feels several complex links with and differentiations from this world.

The Arendtian treatment of the series of hierarchial oppositions in which her yearning for a public realm has involved her both mute the antagonism of each of the dualities we have considered and point toward a reformulation in terms that emphasize the proper relation or balance between each term of the pair. This reformulation in relational rather than oppositional terms provides the ground on which Arendt can attempt to translate the radical alterity and opposition of each warrior-hero to every other into plurality, and to redefine heroic action as an effort to gain distinction, or even individuality. Here, too, however, her reliance on ancient sources leads to a variety of ambivalences.

Alterity, Plurality, and Distinction

Arendt argues that "plurality is the condition of human action because we are all the same, that is, human, in such a way that nobody is ever the same as anyone else who ever lived, lives, or will live."[24] To get a sense of the distinctness of this statement compare a similar but profoundly different statement (more in the Hegelian tradition) by Georges Bataille. "Each being is distinct from all others. . . . He is born alone. He dies alone. Between one being and another, there is a gulf, a discontinuity."[25] Arendt emphasizes commonality and uniqueness as opposed to disjunction and separation. Plurality, as Arendt understands it, has the twofold character of equality and distinction.[26] Distinctness requires that the individual express "himself and not merely something—thirst or hunger."[27] On the basis of this definition Arendt puts forward an account of a threefold relation to the world. First, she considers the nature of otherness. The most extreme form of otherness, from the human perspective, occurs in the multiplication of inorganic objects. Organic life differs from these by possessing the quality of variation and distinctness, but only man can *express* this distinction, and does so through his actions in public.

Arendt seems to be involved in a kind of play on the concept of distinction. She treats it as meaning both uniqueness and excellence.[28] Thus, in a number of passages, distinction and the achieving of distinction is best understood as an "initiative from which no human being can refrain and still be human."[29] Distinction, then, for Arendt, can sometimes be interpreted as individuality—a concept of individuality once again surprisingly akin to the Marxian vision of the full flowering of individuality in a world of equals. The competition for dominance essential to the activity of the participants in the Platonic dialogues no less than the warrior-hero becomes in her work an effort to achieve and express one's humanness, a second birth in which "we confirm and take upon ourselves the naked fact of our original physical appearance."[30] Thus, for Arendt, human plurality results in the "paradoxical plurality of unique beings."[31] Political action, if distinction is understood as uniqueness, takes the form of "sharing" words and deeds.[32] Thus, excellence requires the presence of others in a specific realm, the public, where every activity can attain an "excellence never matched in private."[33]

Arendt's other usage of distinction both undermines and enriches her effort to recapture the agonal nature of the *polis*. Thus, despite her efforts to move "distinction" in the direction of individuality, she argues that the "fiercely agonal" spirit of the *polis* meant that everybody had constantly to "distinguish himself from all others, to show through unique deeds that he was the best of all."[34] And she emphasizes the "passionate drive to show one's self in measuring up against others."[35] In these passages she is clearly much closer to the reality of the ancient sources.

In addition, Arendt's account of action in public is muddied by her discussion of the risks to life inherent in it. On the one hand, politics is a "way of life in which speech and only speech [makes] sense and where the central concern of all citizens [is] to talk with each other."[36] And "to be political, to live in a *polis*, meant that everything was decided through words and persuasion and not through force and violence."[37] On the other hand, she recognizes the links between war and political action and emphasizes the need to be willing to risk death in order to act in public. She attempts to dismiss war-making as a central activity of public life by terming the concern with it a "holdover" from the pre-*polis* experience.[38] Given her attachment to the Homeric model of action however, this will not do. Arendt's reworking of the ancient sources is further contradicted by the historically real centrality of talk about war in ancient Athens.[39]

The Nature of the Community

Arendt's reworking of the nature of heroic action can only be clarified by attention to her understanding of the nature of the political community itself. As Arendt understands the *polis*, it is not the fierce and competitive system discussed in the last chapter, but a system that operates both as an equalizing institution and a meaning-creating, immortality-ensuring human construction. If achieving distinction is necessary to being human and if the actions necessary to achieve distinction are more excellent if done in public, then the *polis* can be understood as a construction that can "multiply the occasions to win 'immortal fame,'" by multiplying the possibilities for everyone to "show in deed and word who he was in his unique distinctness," a construction that has as its purpose "to make the extraordinary an ordinary occurrence of everyday life."[40] I see this as her version of my kindred but opposed argument that the *polis* organized the competition for dominance.

The *polis*, for Arendt, has a deeper purpose as well: It operates not only to make immortality possible for the many but to give more permanence to the evanescence of human action and speech by providing witnesses to tell the story. Arendt notes that the chances that a deed deserving fame would actually become immortal were not very good. Human greatness should not, she believes, have to rely on the chance presence of poets.[41] Because the public space transcends the life span of a single generation of men, it can provide the potential of an earthly immortality. This transcendence, Arendt holds, is essential both to politics and the public realm.[42] Thus the *polis* is a guarantee against the futility of individual life, an arena reserved for relative (though not eternal) permanence.[43] The existence of the public realm, then, means that everything that appears in public can be seen and heard by everybody. Arendt holds that this reassurance gives us reality, that it assures us of our reality.[44]

It is only in the context of such a community that the real significance of action can emerge. Only great words and deeds can show the meaningfulness of everyday relations. The meaning of a historical period as a whole inheres in the great events that illuminate it, and perhaps most significantly, the meaning of a life is best shown in the summing up all of one's life in a single deed.[45] Arendt also wishes to claim that although one can think alone, one can act only in concert. She goes on to claim that "real political action comes out as a group act. And you join that group or you don't. And whatever you do on your own you are really not an actor—you are an anarchist."[46] The significance of the deed is self-contained, independent of victory or defeat.[47] Thus, action must be judged only by the criterion of its greatness, to the extent that it reaches into the extraordinary, where what is true of common life no longer applies "because everything that exists is unique and *sui generis*."[48] Arendt is arguing that what is intangible in the form of act or speech becomes tangible only in the *story* of the life, a story that can only be told at the end. The one who aims at leaving a story and an identity that can win immortal fame must choose a short life and a premature death. If one survives one's supreme act, one must face consequences. "How can one live on, having already summed up the meaning of one's life?"[49] In this context, then, the point of achieving preeminence is not simply to savor victory and the defeat of another but to create meaning and establish relations.[50]

Arendt has fundamentally altered the nature of the community as set out in the ancient sources. She has put forward a far more complex and relational account than the dualistic vision present in the ancient sources. She has argued that necessity and freedom, public and private, are not in tension but depend on one another, that they must coexist. Second, she has translated otherness or alterity into plurality and put foward an account of the human relation to both social and natural worlds that envisages not one but three generic relations, the last of them infinitely particular. Third, she has to some extent altered the concept of heroic action. She has shifted it away from an individual competition for dominance and toward action in connection with others with whom one shares a common life and common concerns.

Arendt on Power and Community

Arendt's distinctive understanding of power is part of her effort to reconstruct a more adequate account of community on the basis of ancient writings on politics and community. Several aspects of Arendt's theorization deserve comment, among them her explicit rejection of an understanding of power that sees power as power over others or as domination, her differentiation of power from violence, and her redefinition of power as action in concert. Each of these features of her argument about power are part of her understanding of the possibilities for action in a more humane community. Power is at once (1) the "glue" that holds the community together, (2) the means by which community is constituted, and even (3) the means by which immortality is attained and death overcome. Power, then, is importantly connected to Arendt's understanding of action and its meaning in public life.

Arendt begins her retheorization of power as action in concert by expressing surprise that everyone from Left and Right has understood power as effectiveness of command.[51] She is concerned to reject this understanding because what lies behind it is the mistaken assumption that "the most crucial political issue is, and always has been, the question of Who rules Whom." If this is the issue to be addressed, she holds that one need not distinguish among power, strength, force, authority, or violence.[52] On this view, however, one could not distinguish the power of the policeman from that of the robber. If effectiveness of command is all there is at issue, the man with the gun has it.[53] She adds that this understanding of power would make sense only if one accepted Marx's contention that the state is an instrument for maintaining the domination of the ruling class.[54] But one needs to go beyond the reduction of public affairs to the "business of domination."[55] In order to do this, Arendt proposes to draw on the Athenian and Roman tradition, a political tradition that, as she has interpreted it, did not identify power as command.[56]

The key words in Arendt's account of power seem to be "ability," "potentiality," "empowerment." The community as a whole is as well central to her understanding. Her argument about power can be read as supporting my contention that power and community are closely linked, despite the fact that we differ profoundly as to the precise nature of the linkage.

Against the current definitions of power as forms of domination, Arendt argues that power "corresponds to the human ability not just to act but to act in concert. Power is never the property of an individual; it belongs to a group and remains in existence only so long as the group keeps together. The moment the group, from which the power originated to begin with disappears . . . [the ruler's] power also vanishes."[57] If power were more than the potentiality of being together and did not depend on the inherently temporary agreement of many wills and intentions, omnipotence might be a possibility. Power shares with action the quality of having no physical limitation in human nature or in bodily existence.[58] "Power springs up whenever people get together and act in concert, but it derives its legitimacy from the initial getting together rather than from any action that then may follow."[59] From one perspective, then, given her stress on consent, Arendt can be seen to be involved in the now familiar attempt to redefine coercion as consent. This seems to be the vein in which Lukes interprets her as putting forward a theory similar to that of Talcott Parsons.[60] I argue, however, that the significance of her redefinition of power is quite different. Arendt adds one more qualification for an attribution of power. Power is "actualized" (but, like other potentials, can never be "materialized") where "word and deed have not parted company, where words are not empty and deeds not brutal, where words are not used to veil intentions but to disclose realities, and deeds are not used to violate and destroy but to establish relations and create new realities."[61] Power, then, is benign and operates for the good of the community.

One can in addition begin to see the extent to which exercises of power and political action, especially heroic action, are similar. Arendt distinguishes power from strength, which she defines as the property of an individual, and from force, which she holds should be reserved for reference to the forces of nature or the force of circumstances (i.e., "the energy released by physical or social movements").[62] She also distinguishes power from authority, which she sees as an unquestioning recognition by the one who must obey. Perhaps most important in this context, she distinguishes power from violence, which she argues is close to strength, but is distinguished by its instrumental character. Exercises of power, like action, need no justification because power is an end in itself, whereas violence, because of its instrumental character, does need justification, and "even if justified can never be legitimate."[63]

Arendt makes several important claims about the relations of power and violence: (1) Violence can destroy power; (2) violence and power are opposites; (3) violence and power are most commonly found together. Violence is always capable of destroying power, and this destruction can end in the use of what she terms "terror" to maintain domination—that is, a form of government that, having destroyed all power, all the ability of citizens to come together to act as a group, atomizes the populace and isolates them from each other. Thus, tyrannies are characterized by the powerlessness of subjects who have lost the human capacity to speak and act together.[64] Tyrannies are political systems that have destroyed community. Despite the fact that violence can destroy power, the most common forms of government rest only to some extent on violence, and depend as well on the power behind the violence.[65] Indeed this is one of the reasons for the confusion of power with violence; a special case, the power of government, has been mistaken for the general, and governments do in fact monopolize violence.[66]

Second, violence and power are opposites, and where the one rules, the other does not appear. Violence occurs when power is in jeopardy.[67] Implicit in her claims about the opposition of violence and power are several other oppositions or dualities, among them the fact that power is an end in itself, whereas violence is not; that power is only possible in a community and that violence destroys community; that power is a potential, and can only be actualized in word and deed (perhaps even for the common good), whereas violence can be stored up and unleashed without regard to community and can be the action of a single individual. As Arendt has so tellingly stated, "real political action comes out as a group act."[68]

Third, despite their deep opposition, power and violence are often found together. This argument undermines Arendt's case that the two are in fact opposites, but nothing is less common, she holds, than to find power and violence in their pure forms.[69] Despite her claim that the distinction between the two is not "watertight," and Albrecht Wellmer's suggestion that perhaps these distinctions designate "limiting cases to which nothing in reality corresponds," her general effort to distinguish the two is undermined by this admission.[70] The significance of her effort to distinguish power from violence emerges in her discussion of the close connection between power and community. Violence is a denial of community, and thus, for her, a denial of the possibility of political action. As such, it must be understood as fundamentally opposed to power. Thus, her account of power leads us back to questions of community.

Arendt holds that all political institutions are "manifestations and materializations of power." They exist only so long as the power of the people together exists.[71] There are three separable, though intimately related, claims here: (1) Power is the "glue" that holds the community together; (2) power is co-eval with the constitution of the community; and (3) power is the means by which the inevitability of individual death can be overcome. Power, clearly, has deep connections with Arendt's concepts of both action and community. Arendt's understanding of power, then, supports my own claim that power fundamentally structures community.

First, Arendt holds that power springs up whenever people come together and act and its legitimacy comes from the act of creating a community.[72] Second and related, since power comes into being with, and represents in a sense the end or purpose of, the community, power is also the glue that holds the community together. Thus, power is what keeps the public realm in existence and preserves the public realm, since without being talked about by men, the world would no longer contain the possibilities of immortality and community and would degenerate into a "heap of unrelated things."[73] Without power, the space of appearance constructed by action and speech would fade away as quickly as the speech itself.[74] Finally, power, like the constitution of the *polis* or public space, enables the individual to overcome his individual death.[75]

Arendt insists that death is the certain outcome of the individual life, and represents the "most anti-political experience there is," an experience that is anti-political because it indicates that we shall disappear and leave the community, an experience that is the extreme of loneliness and impotence but that can be transformed by being faced collectively and in action. When faced collectively, the individual death is accompanied by the potential immortality of the group and the species. Arendt comments that "it is as though life itself, the immortal life of the species, nourished, as it were, by the sempiternal dying of its members is 'surging upward,' is actualized in the practice of violence."[76] Despite Arendt's denunciations of the practice of violence, she does recognize what she terms the "dangerously attractive features" of collective violence.[77] She seems to take the contradictory position that on the one hand great words and deeds depend on the ability to act in concert, that is, depend upon the practice of power. Yet on her own account these deeds and words may be dependent on violence or created through violence. Arendt is forced to readmit at least collective violence to the life of the community—violence practiced not against the members of the community itself but against outsiders.

Arendt's understanding of power is characterized by the centrality of community. Her vision of politics ignores self-interested individuals and seems almost to issue in a kind of selflessness or loss of self, a merging with others to create a greater whole. And so, for example, in rejecting a number of moral concepts, she states, "I would say that in the notion of wanting to be good I actually am concerned with my own self. The moment I act politically I'm not concerned with me, but with the world. And that is the *main* distinction." She goes on to argue that what makes Rosa Luxemburg admirable is that she was "very much" concerned with the world and "not at all" concerned with herself.[78]

Summary

Arendt has put forward a very interesting argument about power and community. Her stress on the importance of action in public allows for an understanding of community that depends neither on the mediation of a nonhuman factor nor on the domination of some by others. Her attempt to solve the problem of community and provide a place for human action to take place is both helpful and fundamentally flawed. Some have commented on the dangerous possibility that Arendt holds out for immoral (but in her terms "great") action when she argues that action can be judged only by its greatness.[79] Second, Arendt gives little attention to the erotic dimension of power. She, like most other analysts, simply notes its presence, and passes on without comment. Third, Arendt tends to reduce power to opinion and consent, and gives little attention to real action in the material world. At least one critic has pointed out that despite her preoccupation with noble deeds that stand by themselves, actions do have consequences.[80]

The Significance of Arendt's Theorization of Power

Arendt's argument about the close relation of power, community, and action could be regarded as idiosyncratic.[81] The modifications she makes tend, overall, to reduce tension and opposition and to provide a vision of the political community as a shared and common world in which the individual both merges with others and distinguishes himself. Issues of exercising power over others are redefined in terms of "empowerment," and the exercise of power becomes instead potentiality and capacity. But these modifications of the agonal model of politics and power share some important features with the ideas of several other theorists of power. Let us examine some of the theories of power to which Arendt's work bears some resemblance, despite the fact that they are not ordinarily seen as having much in common: Dorothy Emmet, Hanna Pitkin, and Berenice Carroll. I do not mean to suggest that these theorists agree with each other, for, indeed, they do clearly disagree on many fundamental points. My purpose here is to point to an interesting common thread that links all these theories and distinguishes them from the theorizations of power considered in previous chapters.

Dorothy Emmet: Alternatives to Domination

Emmet argues that power as a key concept of social science should be distinguished from domination, since the production of intended effects need not be the achievement of intended effects through coercing other people.[82] She criticizes Bertrand Russell, among others, because while he attempts to define power as a generic form of energy, he discusses only what Emmet terms domination.[83] Emmet points in particular to the "dislogistic associations of power with domination" which are carried over into discussions of other aspects of power."[84] She, relying in turn on Mary Parker Follett's distinction between "power over" and "power with," or "coercive" and "coactive" power, discusses the advantages of freeing the latter from its association with domination.[85] This in turn allows her to suggest that it might more be helpful in understanding power to notice the variety of meanings of the word. She suggests a rough typology of power as (1) causal efficacy, (2) creative energy, (3) personal influence, (4) ritual power, or (5) legal power. In contrast to giving attention to the varieties of power she has pointed to, Emmet argues that most theorists have devoted attention only to what she characterizes as a subtype of group 1, type 1b— power as psychological pressure, manipulation, and domination by means other than naked force.[86] Emmet carries her case further with an argument that those who have theorized about power are usually so concerned with type 1b that "they hardly notice that there is a distinction between the power some people have of stimulating activity in others and raising their morale and the power which consists in moulding the opinions and practices of others through various forms of psychological pressure."[87] While she recognizes that the two may shade into each other, she holds that they are recognizably different.

She shares with Arendt the sense that political power goes beyond the power of coercion, although she does not go so far as Arendt in her refusal to define power as domination. She does share the conviction that "the power of coercion is only effective when it reinforces the prestige of a general respect for authority" and that if a population is determined to make the power of a government ineffective, it has a good chance of succeeding despite superior forms of coercion available to the state.[88]

In addition, Emmet's discussion of power shares with Arendt's an emphasis on the relation of power and community. Power she too believes is not a thing but a capacity or relation between people.[89] Thus she opposes those who see power as a thing or property and is critical of a number of the writers I criticized in earlier chapters. She is also concerned to discuss the way the exercise of ritual power can make for the coherence of a community. She cites the example of the coronation of Queen Elizabeth as a ritual which "gathered up a number of the aspects of the non-coercive kinds of power."[90] She has hopes for a redefinition of power as a way of referring to "any kind of effectiveness in performance," but also wants to include the aspect of psychological or psychic energy or *mana*.[91] Her expansion/reading out of the meanings of power sometimes goes too far in the direction of reinterpreting power away from coercion or domination. For example, she attempts to define power as something very close to rights when she defines it as the (legal) capacity of a person to take certain actions.

What is important for my purposes here is the emphasis her analysis, like Arendt's, gives to the relation of power to community, to the argument that power is not something possessed or stored up, and to the rejection of power as domination (or, rather, her stress on aspects of power other than domination). Her theorization of power both as creative energy and her stress in more operational terms on the ways it can be manifested—through production of ideas or art, through stimulating productive effort in others, and through a heightening of vitality—coupled with her effort to find terms with which to refer to power as "effectiveness" move her theory beyond Arendt's and lead her to a central focus on effectiveness rather than potential or capacity. Thus, one can, on the basis of Emmet's theory, find a number of interesting common threads of concern in her theory and in Arendt's. Still, Emmet does not downplay effective action or replace it with the capacity to act in concert.

Hanna Pitkin: A Note on "Power To"

Hanna Pitkin, in her discussion of the kinds of contributions a "Wittgensteinian perspective and Austinian tools of analysis" could make to political science, briefly examines the concept of power.[92] She explicitly relies on Dorothy Emmet's suggestion that power is better thought of as a "capacity" word rather than a "thing" word, and shows the linguistic support for the suggestion that "power over" may differ significantly from the concept of "power to." Specifically, she points to the fact that "power over" is inherently relational. This differentiates it from the power to act, since one may have the power to do something alone.[93] Thus, Pitkin too can be said to recognize explicitly the close connection of power to community, and to call our attention to an aspect of power other than domination. In addition, her use of Emmet's argument and Emmet's use of Follett's indicates the existence of a common historical thread linking the few women theorists who have discussed the proper understanding of power.

Feminist Theories of Power

The commonality of these three writers around questions of power has been echoed by more explicitly feminist theorists and has resulted in the widespread adoption of an understanding of power as energy and competence rather than dominance, an understanding referenced by the term "the feminist theory of power." One finds this in a number of works by feminist theorists. This is the context in which Berenice Carroll argues, in a style very similar to that adopted by Emmet, that it is time to say farewell to the understanding of power as dominance.[94] Again, with Emmet, she argues that "to be without the power of dominance is perceived as being very nearly without the power to act at all, or at least as being without the power to act effectively."[95] Carroll's case is more extreme than Emmet's, but, like Emmet, she puts forward an inventory of the "powers of the allegedly powerless." These include (1) disintegrative power; (2) inertial power; (3) innovative power, norm-creating power; (4) legitimizing, integrative power, or socializing power; (5) expressive power; (6) explosive power; (7) power of resistance; (8) collective power, cooperative power; (9) migratory power, population power.[96] Carroll's discussion of the powers of the powerless is offered as "a beginning toward reinterpreting the idea of power in terms of competence instead of dominance,"[97] and she concludes by citing Arendt's argument that the conception of power as dominance is partial and misleading and that one must not take the question of who rules whom to be the most critical political issue.[98]

Conclusion

The common thread connecting the theorizations and tendencies I have discussed is the writers' concern to argue against the understanding of power as dominance or domination; to attempt to point to other meanings of the term more associated with ability, capacity, and competence; and to urge reconsideration of assumptions about power. Theorizations of power such as these have become widespread in the literature of the contemporary women's movement as well.[99] In every case, what has been emphasized are understandings of power that move away from an exclusive focus on domination. These reunderstandings of power, like Arendt's reformulation, are not without difficulties. First, there is a consistent tendency to refuse to confront the problems attendant on acting on or changing the world, the problem of the possibility of doing harm to others by one's actions.[100] Second, by stressing power as energy, capacity, and effectiveness, these arguments have a tendency to direct attention away from relations of domination which must be confronted. This is a fault they share with the exchange theories considered earlier. Finally, all these theories fail to address directly the genderedness of power and its importance in structuring social relations.

Despite these difficulties, I believe it is significant that such a large proportion of the theorists who make these moves and express these concerns are women. Although very few women have addressed the issue of power, I have found none who does not give at least some attention, if not central place, to the understanding of power as energy or ability. A few men have put forward similar arguments, but they represent a minority of the men who have written on the subject.[101] There seems to be a dialogue, or at least some evidence of a series of common concerns and common inclinations among women to shift the discussion away from analyses of domination. What is striking is that the theorists considered here would seem to have little else in common. Both their theoretical interests and their political commitments and inclinations differ profoundly.

If differing life experiences lead to differing world views, the systematic differences between the accounts of power produced by women and men can be taken to be indications of systematic and significant differences in life activity. And since power is an essentially contested concept, and alternative theorizations of power can be expected to rest on alternative epistemological and ontological bases, perhaps the differences in the life activity of women and men have epistemological content and consequences. The question that must be addressed, then, is the nature of this difference. In Chapters 2 and 5 I examined the differences in world view consequent on lives structured by exchange as opposed to production. The question implicitly posed by the differing accounts of power put forward by women and men is whether gender provides a similarly powerful structural experience, that is, whether the experience of gender is world-view structuring.

I propose to explore the feminist suggestion that women's lives differ substantially from men's. I ask whether women's life activity can constitute the base on which a standpoint similar to the standpoint of the proletariat can be constructed, a standpoint that not only makes available a privileged vantage point on social relations but also points beyond those relations in more liberatory directions. If one can discern the outlines of such a standpoint, one might expect that it would operate in ways similar to the standpoint of the proletariat. Adoption of a feminist standpoint, then, should allow us to understand why the masculine community constructed *eros*, and as a result, power, as domination, repression, and death, and why women's accounts of power differ in specific and systematic ways from those put forward by men. Finally, such a standpoint might allow us to put forward an understanding of power that points in more liberatory directions.

NOTES

1. Hanna Pitkin, "Justice: On Relating Private and Public," in *1979 Proceedings of the Conference for the Study of Political Thought* (mimeo), p. 31–32. Pitkin quite correctly notes, however, that "something is wrong with this account," and proceeds to spend the second half of her beautifully argued paper setting the record straight (ibid., p. 36).

2. George Kateb, "Freedom and Worldliness in the Thought of Hannah Arendt," *Political Theory* 5, no. 2 (May 1977): 166. See also Peter Fuss, "Hannah

Arendt's Conception of Political Community," in *Hannah Arendt: The Recovery of the Public World*, ed. Melvyn Hill (New York: St. Martin's Press, 1979), pp. 173–74.

3. I am not alone in noticing the similarity to Marx. See also Mildred Bakan, "Hannah Arendt's Concepts of Labor and Work," in Hill, ed., *Hannah Arendt*, p. 49, who notes that Arendt herself, despite her critique of Marx, seems to see herself as still in the Marxian tradition. See also the statement on Arendt's utopianism in ibid., pp. 325–26.

4. On the *polis* as simply an instrumental community I tend to differ with Pitkin's interpretation in "Justice," p. 32. But since this argument occurs in the section that puts forward an agonal construal of Arendt that she later modifies, I do not want to take issue with it too strongly.

5. These statements occur in Hannah Arendt, *The Human Condition* (Chicago: University of Chicago Press, 1958), pp. 32, 48, 7, 25 respectively.

6. Ibid., p. 73. This would seem to run counter to Kateb's claim that she holds that the distinction between public and private coincides "ultimately" with the opposition of shame and honor (Kateb, "Freedom and Worldliness," p. 144).

7. Arendt, *The Human Condition*, p. 33.

8. Ibid., p. 72. The quoted material within the Arendt quotation is from Aristotle, *Politics* 1254b-25. Arendt sometimes seems to regard woman as excluded from political action by her very biology. There is, however, in contrast her remark that a free woman in ancient Athens did not live among her equals, equals Arendt describes as other free women (though not free men), and so one wonders what political role she can envisage for a woman.

9. Ibid., p. 31. This unusual claim can be better understood once one has understood Arendt's unique distinctions among power, strength, force, and violence. See p. 218 ff.

10. Ibid., p. 36.

11. Ibid., pp. 30, 36.

12. Ibid., p. 59.

13. Arendt seems to accept this as well. See, for example, *On Violence* (New York: Harcourt, Brace, and World, 1967), pp. 67–68.

14. Arendt, *The Human Condition*, p. 292.

15. Kateb, "Freedom and Worldliness," p. 145.

16. "Hannah Arendt on Hannah Arendt," in Hill, ed., *Hannah Arendt*, p. 305.

17. Ibid.

18. See also Simone de Beauvoir's characterization of the male horror of having been engendered. *The Second Sex* trans. H. M. Parshley (New York: Knopf, 1953), p. 135 f.

19. Arendt, *The Human Condition*, p. 36.

20. See also Pitkin, "Justice," pp. 50–51, for a similar reading.

21. See Kateb, "Freedom and Worldliness," pp. 144–45, on the importance of differentiating oneself from nature.

22. Arendt, *The Human Condition*, p. 176.

23. I am indebted to Pitkin, "Justice," p. 50, for directing my attention to this passage.

24. Arendt, *The Human Condition*, p. 8.

25. Georges Bataille *Death and Sensuality* (New York: Arno Press, 1977), p. 12.

26. Arendt, *The Human Conditon*, p. 175.

27. Ibid., p. 176.

28. Pitkin, responding to this same problem, suggests that perhaps Arendt has two understandings of action: action in general and great or heroic action. My own reading indicates a real confusion between the two. See "Justice," p. 20.

29. Arendt, *The Human Condition*, p. 176.

30. Ibid., pp. 176–77.

31. Ibid., p. 176. See also her argument from Genesis that one should understand the creation of male and female as an indication of the fundamental nature of plurality ("On Hannah Arendt," 313). A comparison with de Beauvoir on the otherness of woman could be very instructive.

32. Arendt, *The Human Condition*, p. 197.

33. Ibid., p. 48.

34. Ibid., p. 41.

35. Ibid., p. 194.

36. Ibid., p. 27.

37. Ibid., p. 26.

38. Ibid.

39. Pitkin, "Justice," p. 34.

40. Arendt, *The Human Condition*, p. 197.

41. Ibid.

42. Ibid., p. 55.

43. Ibid., p. 56. The family, in contrast, represents for Arendt only the prolongation or multiplication of one's own position with its attending aspects and perspectives. One wonders whose position in the family she is adopting— that of the citizen with dependents? Or that of the wife, whose perspective might well be different.

44. Ibid., pp. 50–51.

45. Ibid., pp. 42, 194. See also Arendt's more general statement that instead of truth there are "moments of truth," "anecdotes, and they tell in utter brevity what it was all about." See Arendt, "On Responsibility for Evil," in *The Crimes of War*, ed. Richard A. Falk, Gabriel Kolko, and Robert Jay Lifton (New York: Vintage Brooks, 1971), p. 500, quoted in Melvyn Hill, "The Fictions of Mankind and the Stories of Men," in Hill, ed., *Hannah Arendt*, pp. 293–94.

46. Arendt, "On Hannah Arendt," pp. 305, 310 respectively.

47. Arendt, *The Human Condition*, p. 205. The similarity between the position and the Bakunist politics of the deed are striking. See also Kateb, "Freedom and Worldliness," pp. 158, 174.

48. Ibid. These are among Arendt's most controversial claims, and have been widely criticized and rejected. See, for example, Kateb, "Freedom and Worldliness," on the question of the self-containment of the act, p. 174; Fuss, "Hannah Arendt's Conception of Community," pp. 173–74.

49. Arendt, *The Human Condition*, p. 193.

50. Ibid., p. 190.

51. Hannah Arendt, *On Violence* (New York: Harcourt, Brace, and World, 1969), p. 38. This is the context in which she notes, without comment, de Jouvenel's linkage of power with virility.

52. Ibid., p. 43.

53. Ibid., p. 37. (I made a similar point in Chapter 1, p. 29.)

54. Ibid., p. 36.

55. Ibid., p. 44.

56. Some of the strain of this interpretation of the Athenian tradition emerges in Arendt's need to defend herself against the charge that eighteenth-century men *did* talk about obedience to laws. She is forced to state that "what they actually meant" was instead support for laws based on consent (ibid., p. 40).

57. Ibid., p. 44. See also Arendt, *The Human Condition*, p. 200.

58. Arendt, *The Human Condition*, p. 201.

59. Arendt, *On Violence*, p. 52. One can hear echoes here of her argument that the act itself contains the meaning.

60. See Steven Lukes, *Power: A Radical Analysis* (London: Macmillan, 1974), pp. 28–39.

61. Arendt, *The Human Condition*, p. 200.

62. Arendt, *On Violence*, pp. 44–45.

63. Ibid., pp. 51–52.

64. Arendt, *The Human Condition*, p. 203.

65. What Arendt defines as opinion (*On Violence*, p. 49). She holds that even the power of masters over slaves rested on a "superior organization of power—that is, on the organized solidarity of the masters" (ibid., p. 50). She continues that Vietnam showed the helplessness of superiority in means of violence, in the fact that power is of the essence of all government (ibid., p. 51).

66. Ibid., p. 47.

67. Ibid., p. 56. In another context, she argues that what undermines political communities is the loss of power and the substitution of violence (*The Human Condition*, p. 200).

68. Arendt, "On Hannah Arendt," p. 310.

69. Arendt, *On Violence*, p. 47.

70. Arendt, "On Hannah Arendt," p. 325.

71. Arendt, *On Violence*, p. 41.

72. Ibid., p. 52.

73. Arendt, *The Human Condition*, pp. 200, 204.

74. Ibid.

75. Arendt, *On Violence*, p. 27.

76. Ibid., pp. 67–68.

77. Ibid., p. 67.

78. Arendt, "On Hannah Arendt," p. 311.

79. See Kateb, "Freedom and Worldliness," pp. 166–70; and Fuss, "Hannah Arendt's Conception of Community," pp. 173–74, who comments on the ruthlessness of the agonal type, "whose deeds might well destroy the world were it not for the caretakers of the *polis*, those whose boundless capacity for empathetic projection makes them unfit for action in its more dramatic and

decisive forms" (p. 174). These interpretations are supported by such things as her dismissal of questions of justice—of the end of government as possibly leading to "dangerously utopian" answers (Arendt, *On Violence*, p. 51).

80. Kateb, "Freedom and Worldliness," p. 174.

81. Cf. Lukes, *Power*, n. 1.

82. Emmet, "The Concept of Power," *Proceedings of the Aristotelian Society* (London) 54 (1953–54): 4.

83. Ibid., p. 5.

84. Ibid., p. 8.

85. Ibid., p. 9.

86. Ibid., pp. 13. 26.

87. Ibid., pp. 13–14.

88. Ibid., p. 15–16.

89. Ibid., p. 19.

90. Ibid., p. 18.

91. Ibid., pp. 22, 24–26.

92. Hanna Pitkin, *Wittgenstein and Justice*, (Berkeley, Ca.: University of California, 1972), p. 275.

93. Ibid., pp. 276–77.

94. Berenice Carroll, "Peace Research: The Cult of Power," *Journal of Conflict Resolution* 4 (1972): 605.

95. Ibid., p. 607.

96. Ibid., pp. 608–9. The enterprise of Elizabeth Janeway, *Powers of the Weak* (New York: 1980), is very similar as well.

97. Carroll, "Peace Research," p. 614.

98. Ibid., p. 615.

99. E.g., Janeway, *Powers*; Hartsock, "Political Change: Two Perspectives on Power," *Quest: A feminist quarterly* 1, no. 1 (Summer 1974); and Joan Rothschild, "Taking Our Future Seriously," *Quest: A feminist quarterly* 2, no. 3 (Winter 1976).

100. See Kateb, "Freedom and Worldliness," for a discussion of the harmful consequences of this move (pp. 174–77).

101. See, for example, William Connolly, *The Terms of Political Discourse*; Christian Bay, *The Structures of Freedom* (New York: Atheneum, 1968), p. 248 ff.; Bertrand Russell, *Power* (New York: Norton, 1938), represents another contradictory case, since he is in fact investigating domination. Interestingly enough, these theorists would probably describe themselves as socialists.

10

The Feminist Standpoint: Toward a Specifically Feminist Historical Materialism

The different understandings of power put forward by women who have theorized about power implicitly pose the question of the extent to which gender is a world-view-structuring experience. In this chapter I explore some of the epistemological consequences of claiming that women's lives differ systematically and structurally from those of men. In particular, I suggest that, like the lives of proletarians according to Marxian theory, women's lives make available a particular and privileged vantage point on male supremacy, a vantage point that can ground a powerful critique of the phallocratic institutions and ideology that constitute the capitalist form of patriarchy. I argue that on the basis of the structures that define women's activity as contributors to subsistence and as mothers, the sexual division of labor, one could begin, though not complete, the construction of a feminist standpoint on which to ground a specifically feminist historical materialism. I hope to show how just as Marx's understanding of the world from the standpoint of the proletariat enabled him to go beneath bourgeois ideology, so a feminist standpoint can allow us to descend further into materiality to an epistemological level at which we can better understand both why patriarchal institutions and ideologies take such perverse and deadly forms and how both theory and practice can be redirected in more liberatory directions.

The reader will remember that the concept of a standpoint carries several specific contentions. Most important, it posits a series of levels of reality in which the deeper level both includes and explains the surface or appearance. Related to the positing of levels are several claims:

1. Material life (class position in Marxist theory) not only structures but sets limits on the understanding of social relations.

2. If material life is structured in fundamentally opposing ways for two different groups, one can expect that the vision of each will represent an inversion of the other, and in systems of domination the vision available to the rulers will be both partial and perverse.

3. The vision of the ruling class (or gender) structures the material relations in which all parties are forced to participate and therefore cannot be dismissed as simply false.

4. In consequence, the vision available to the oppressed group must be struggled for and represents an achievement that requires both science to see beneath the surface of the social relations in which all are forced to participate and the education that can only grow from struggle·to change those relations.

5. As an engaged vision, the understanding of the oppressed, the adoption of a standpoint exposes the real relations among human beings as inhuman, points beyond the present, and carries a historically liberatory role.

Because of its achieved character and its liberatory potential, I use the term "feminist" rather than "women's standpoint." Like the experience of the proletariat, women's experience and activity as a dominated group contains both negative and positive aspects. A feminist standpoint picks out and amplifies the liberatory possibilities contained in that experience.

Women's work in every society differs systematically from men's. I intend to pursue the suggestion that this division of labor is the first, and in some societies the only, division of labor; moreover, it is central to the organization of social labor more generally.[1] On the basis of an account of the sexual division of labor, one should be able to begin to explore the oppositions and differences between women's and men's activity and their consequences for epistemology. While I cannot attempt a complete account, I put forward a schematic and simplified account of the sexual division of labor and its consequences for epistemology. I sketch out a kind of ideal type of the social relations and world view characteristic of men's and women's activity in order to explore the epistemology contained in the institutionalized sexual division of labor. In so doing, I do not mean to attribute this vision to individual women or men (any more than Marx or Lukács meant their theory of class consciousness to apply to any particular worker or group of workers). My focus is instead on institutionalized social practices and on the specific epistemology and ontology manifested by the institutionalized sexual division of labor. Individuals, as individuals, may change their activity in ways that move them outside the outlook embodied in these institutions, but such a move can be significant only when it occurs at the level of society as a whole.

I discuss the "sexual division of labor" rather than "gender division of labor" to stress, first, my desire not to separate the effects of "nature and nurture," or biology and culture, and my belief that the division of labor between women and men cannot be reduced to simply social dimensions. One must distinguish between what Sara Ruddick has termed "invariant and *nearly* unchangeable" features of human life, and those that, despite being "*nearly* universal," are "certainly changeable."[2] Thus the fact that women and not men *bear* children is not (yet) a social choice, but that women and not men rear children in a society structured by compulsory heterosexuality and male dominance is clearly a societal choice. A second reason to use the term "sexual division of labor" is to keep hold of the bodily aspect of existence, perhaps to grasp it overfirmly in an effort to keep it from evaporating altogether. There is some biological, bodily component to human existence. But its size and substantive content will remain unknown until at least the certainly changeable aspects of the sexual division of labor are altered.

On the basis of a schematic account of the sexual division of labor, I begin to fill in the specific content of the feminist standpoint and begin to specify how women's lives structure an understanding of social relations, that is, begin to follow out the epistemological consequences of the sexual division of labor. In addressing the institutionalized sexual division of labor, I propose to lay aside the important differences among women and instead to search for central commonalities across race and class boundaries. I take some justification from the fruitfulness of Marx's similar strategy in constructing a simplified, two-class, two-man model in which everything was exchanged at its value. Marx's schematic account in volume I of *Capital* left out of account such factors as imperialism; the differential wages, work, and working conditions of the Irish; the differences between women, men, and children; and so on. While all these factors are important to the analysis of contemporary capitalism, none changes either Marx's theories of surplus value or alienation, the two most fundamental features of the Marxian analysis of capitalism. My effort here takes a similar form, in an attempt to move toward a theory of the extraction and appropriation of women's activity and women themselves. Still, I adopt this strategy with some reluctance, since it contains the danger of making invisible the experience of lesbians or women of color.[3] At the same time, I recognize that the effort to uncover a feminist standpoint assumes that there are some things common to all women's lives in Western class societies.

The feminist standpoint that emerges through an examination of women's activities is related to the proletarian standpoint, but deeper-going. Women and workers inhabit a world in which the emphasis is on change rather than stasis, a world characterized by interaction with natural substances rather than separation from nature, a world in which quality is more important than quantity, a world in which the unification of mind and body is inherent in the activities performed. Yet there are some important differences, differences marked by the fact that the proletarian (if male) is immersed in this world only during the time his labor power is being used by the capitalist. If, to para-phrase Marx, we follow the worker home from the factory, we can once again perceive a change in the *dramatis personae*. He who before followed behind as the worker, timid and holding back, with nothing to expect but a hiding, now strides in front, while a third person, not specifically present in Marx's account of the transactions between capi-talist and worker (both of whom are male) follows timidly behind, carrying groceries, baby, and diapers.

Given what has been said about the life activity of the proletarian, one can see that, because the sexual division of labor means that much of the work involved in reproducing labor power is done by women, and because much of the male worker's contact with nature outside the factory is mediated by a women, the vision of reality which grows from the female experience is deeper and more thoroughgoing than that available to the worker.

The Sexual Division of Labor

Women's activity as institutionalized has a double aspect: their contribution to subsistence and their contribution to childrearing. Whether or not all women do both, women as a sex are institutionally responsible for producing both goods and human beings, and all women are forced to become the kinds of persons who can do both. Although the nature of women's contribution to subsistence varies im-mensely over time and space, my primary focus here is on capitalism, with a secondary focus on the class societies that preceded it.[4] In capi-talism, women contribute both production for wages and production of goods in the home, that is, they, like men, sell their labor power and produce both commodities and surplus value, and produce use values in the home. Unlike men, however, women's lives are institutionally defined by their production of use values in the home.[5] Here we begin to encounter the narrowness of Marx's concept of production. Women's production of use values in the home has not been well understood by socialists. It is no surprise to feminists that Engels, for example, simply asks how women can continue to do the work in the home and also work in production outside the home. Marx, too, takes for granted women's responsibility for household labor. He repeats, as if it were his own, the question of a Belgian factory inspector: If a mother works for wages, "how will [the household's] internal economy be cared for; who will look after the young children; who will get ready the meals, do the washing and mending?"[6]

Let us trace both the outlines and the consequences of women's dual contribution to subsistence in capitalism. Women's labor, like that of the male worker, is contact with material necessity. Their contribution to subsistence, like that of the male worker, involves them in a world in which the relation to nature and to concrete human requirement is central, both in the form of interaction with natural substances whose quality, rather than quantity, is important to the production of meals, clothing, and so forth and in the form of close attention in a different way from men's. While repetition for both the wages and even more in household production involves a unification of mind and body for the purpose of transforming natural substances into socially defined goods. This, too, is true of the labor of the male worker.

There are, however, important differences. First, women as a group work more than men. We are all familiar with the phenomenon of the "double day," and with indications that women work many more hours per week than men.[7] Second, a larger proportion of women's labor time is devoted to the production of use values than men's. Only some of the goods women produce are commodities (however much they live in a society structured by commodity production and exchange). Third, women's production is structured by repetition in a different way from men's. While repetition for both the woman and the male worker may take the form of production of the same object, over and over—whether apple pies or brake linings—women's work in housekeeping involves a repetitious cleaning.[8]

Thus the man, in the process of production, is involved in contact with necessity and interchange with nature as well as with other human beings, but the process of production or work does not consume his whole life. The activity of a woman in the home as well as the work she does for wages keeps her continually in contact with a world of qualities and change. Her immersion in the world of use—in concrete, many-qualitied, changing material processes—is more complete than his. And if life itself consists of sensuous activity, the vantage point available to women on the basis of their contribution to subsistence represents an intensification and deepening of the materialist world view available to the producers of commodities in capitalism, an intensification of class consciousness. The availability of this outlook to even nonworking-class women has been strikingly formulated by a novelist: "Washing the toilet used by three males, and the floor and walls around it, is, Mira thought, coming face to face with necessity. And that is why women were saner than men, did not come up with the mad, absurd schemes men developed: they were in touch with necessity, they had to wash the toilet bowl and floor."[9]

The focus on women's subsistence activity rather than men's leads to a model in which the capitalist (male) lives a life structured completely by commodity exchange and not at all by production, and at the farthest distance from contact with concrete material life. The male worker marks a way station on the path to the other extreme—the constant contact with material necessity present in women's contribution to subsistence. There are of course important differences along the lines of race and class. For example, working-class men seem to do more domestic labor than men higher up in the class structure—car repairs, carpentry, and the like. And until very recently, the wage work done by most women of color replicated the housework required by their own households. Still, there are commonalities present in the institutionalized sexual division of labor that makes women responsible for both housework and wage work.

Women's contribution to subsistence, however, represents only a part of women's labor. Women also produce/reproduce men (and other women) on both a daily and a long-term basis. This aspect of women's "production" exposes the deep inadequacies of the concept of production as a description of women's activity. One does not (cannot) produce another human being in anything like the way one produces an object such as a chair. Much more is involved, activity that cannot easily be dichotomized into play or work. Helping another to develop, the gradual relinquishing of control, the experiencing of the human limits of one's actions—all these are important features of women's activity as mothers. Women, as mothers, even more than as workers, are institutionally involved in processes of change and growth, and more than workers, must understand the importance of avoiding excessive control in order to help others grow.[10] The activity involved is far more complex than instrumentally working with others to transform objects. (Interestingly, much of women's wage work—nursing, social work, and some secretarial jobs in particular—requires and depends on the relational and interpersonal skills women learned by being mothered by someone of the same sex.)

This aspect of women's activity, too, is not without consequences. Indeed, it is in the production of men by women and the appropriation of this labor, and women themselves, by men, that the opposition between feminist and masculinist experience and outlook is rooted, and it is here that features of the proletarian vision are enhanced and modified for the woman and diluted for the man. Women's experience in reproduction represents a unity with nature that goes beyond the proletarian experience of interchange with nature. As another theorist has put it, "reproductive labor might be said to combine the functions of the architect and the bee: Like the architect, parturitive woman knows what she is doing; like the bee, she cannot help what she is doing." And just as the worker's acting on the external work changes both the world and the worker's nature, so too "a new life changes the world and the consciousness of the woman."[11] In addition, in the process of producing human beings, relations with others may take a variety of forms with deeper significance than simple cooperation with others for common goals—forms that range from a deep unity with another through the many-leveled and changing connections mothers experience with growing children. Finally, women's experience in bearing and rearing children involves a unity of mind and body more profound than is possible in the worker's instrumental activity.

Motherhood in the large sense, that is, motherhood as an institution rather than an experience, including pregnancy and the preparation for motherhood almost all female children receive in being raised by a woman, results in the construction of female existence as centered within a complex relational nexus.[12] One aspect of this relational existence is centered on the experience of living in a woman's rather than a man's body. There are a series of what our culture treats as boundary challenges inherent in female physiology, challenges that make it difficult to maintain rigid separation from the object world. Menstruation, coitus, pregnancy, childbirth, lactation—all represent challenges to bodily boundaries.[13] Adrienne Rich has described the experience of pregnancy as one in which the embryo was both inside and yet "daily more separate, on its way to becoming separate from me and of-itself. In early pregnancy the stirring of the fetus felt like ghostly tremors of my own body, later like the movements of a being imprisoned in me; but both sensations were *my* sensations, contributing to my own sense of physical and psychic space."[14]

In turn, the fact that women but not men are primarily responsible for young children means that the infant first experiences itself as not fully differentiated from the mother and then as an *I* in relation to an *It* that it later comes to know as female.[15] Nancy Chodorow and Jane Flax have argued that the object-relations school of psychoanalytic theory puts forward a materialist psychology, one that I propose to treat as a kind of empirical hypothesis. If the account of human development provided by object relations is correct, one ought to expect to find consequences—both psychic and social.[16] According to object-relations theory, the process of differentiation from a woman, by both boys and girls, reinforces boundary confusion in women's egos and boundary strengthening in men's. Individuation is far more conflictual for male than for female children, in part because both mother and son experience the other as a definite "other." The experience of oneness on the part of both mother and infant seems to last longer with girls.[17]

The complex relational world inhabited by women has its start in the experience and resolution of the oedipal crisis, cleanly resolved for the boy, whereas the girl is much more likely to retain both parents as love objects. The nature of the crisis itself differs by sex: The boy's love for the mother is an extension of mother-infant unity and thus essentially threatening to his ego and independence. Masculine ego formation necessarily requires repressing this first relation and negating the mother.[18] In contrast, the girl's love for the father is less threatening both because it occurs outside this unity and because it occurs at a later stage of development. For boys, the central issue to be resolved concerns gender identification; for girls, the issue is psychosexual development.[19] Chodorow concludes that girls' gradual emergence from the oedipal period takes place in such a way that empathy is built into their primary definition of self, and they have a variety of capacities for experiencing another's needs or feelings as their own. Put another way, girls, because of female parenting, are less differentiated from others than boys, more continuous with and related to the external object world. They are differently oriented to their inner object world as well.[20]

The more complex female relational world is reinforced by the process of socialization. Girls learn roles from watching their mothers; boys must learn roles from rules that structure the life of an absent male figure. Girls can identify with a concrete example present in daily life; boys must identify with an abstract set of maxims only occasionally concretely present in the form of the father. Thus, not only do girls learn roles with more interpersonal and relational skills, but the process of role learning itself is embodied in the concrete relation with the mother. The male, in contrast, must identify with an abstract, cultural stereotype and learn abstract behaviors not attached to a well-known person. Masculinity is idealized for boys, whereas femininity is concrete for girls.[21]

Women and men, then, grow up with personalities affected by different boundary experiences, differently constructed and experienced inner and outer worlds, and preoccupations with different relational issues. This early experience forms an important ground for the feminine sense of self as connected to the world and the masculine sense of self as separate, distinct, and even disconnected. By retaining the preoedipal attachment to the mother, girls come to define and experience themselves as continuous with others. In sum, girls enter adulthood with a more complex layering of affective ties and a rich, ongoing inner set of object relations. Boys, with a simpler oedipal situation and a clear and early resolution, have repressed ties to another. As a result, women define and experience themselves relationally, and men do not.[22]

Chodorow's argument receives interesting support from Robert Stoller's work on sexual excitement and his search for the roots of adult sexual behavior in infant experience. Attempting to understand why men are more perverse than women (i.e., why men's sexual excitement seems to require more gross hostility than women's) led him to suggest that boys may face more difficulties in individuating than girls.[23] He puts forward a theory of what he terms "primary femininity." Because the male infant is merged with the mother, who is a woman, the boy may experience himself as female. Stoller suggests that it may be that the boy does not start out as heterosexual, as Freud thought, but must separate himself to achieve heterosexuality. The oneness with the mother must be counteracted.[24] Thus, "masculinity in males starts as a movement away from the blissful and dangerous, forever remembered and forever yearned for, mother-infant symbiosis."[25] To become masculine, the boy must separate himself both externally from his mother's body, and within himself, from his own already formed primary identification with femininity.[26] This requires the construction of barriers to femininity directed both inward and outward. The mother may be represented as an evil creature, a witch, to counteract the wish to merge with her. Or the barrier may be constructed and sustained by fantasies of harming the mother.[27] Inwardly, the boy must develop a character structure that forces the feminine part of himself down and out of awareness.[28]

Yet this individuation has a certain fragility, a fragility marked by what Stoller terms symbiosis anxiety—the fear that one will not be able to remain separate from the mother, the desire to return to the original oneness.[29] Symbiosis anxiety in males takes a variety of forms and is memorialized in such things as the fear of changing gender found frequently among male psychotics and infrequently among females; the greater fear of homosexuality among men than women; and *machismo*, an excessive resistance to unacceptable temptations or a great sensitivity about one's masculinity.[30]

Fantasies of harming the mother may help the continual shoring up of these barriers.[31] And Stoller speculates that in erotic fantasies the fetish and its isolation represent the fetishist's efforts to isolate his mother and depict her as no longer being in contact with him, and therefore no longer threatening to merge with him and thus destroy his identity as a separate person. Then he can succumb in scripted and staged form to the temptation to merge again with his mother.[32] Thus, Stoller's account too supports the contention that boys', but not girls', individuation takes place in terms of the building of both inner and outer barriers, barriers sustained in part by making the other (the mother) into a thing.

Abstract Masculinity and the Feminist Standpoint

This excursion into psychoanalytic theory has served to point to the differences in men's and women's experience of self resulting from the sexual division of labor in childrearing. These different psychic experiences both structure and are reinforced by the differing patterns of men's and women's activity required by the sexual division of labor, and are thereby replicated as epistemology and ontology. This differential life activity in class society leads on the one hand toward a feminist standpoint and on the other toward an abstract masculinity.

Because the problem for the boy is to distinguish himself from the mother and protect himself against the real threat she poses for his identity, his conflictual and oppositional efforts lead to the formation of rigid ego boundaries. The way Freud takes for granted the rigid distinction between the "me and not-me" makes the point well: "Normally, there is nothing of which we are more certain than the feeling of ourself, of our own ego. This ego appears to us as something autonomous and unitary, marked off distinctly from everything else." At least toward the outside, "the ego seems to maintain clear and sharp lines of demarcation."[33] Thus, the boy's construction of self in opposition to unity with the mother, his construction of identity as differentiation from the mother, sets a hostile and combative dualism at the heart of both the community men construct and the masculinist world view by means of which they understand their lives.

I do not mean to suggest that the totality of human relations can be explained by psychoanalysis. Rather, I want to point to the ways masculine but not feminine experience and activity replicates itself in both the hierarchical and dualist institutions of class society, in the frameworks of thought these societies have generated in the West, and in our cultural construction of sexuality. It is interesting to read Hegel's account of the relation of self and other as a statement of masculine experience: The relation of the two (unhappy) consciousnesses takes the form of a trial by death. As Hegel describes it, "each seeks the death of the other." "Thus, the relation of the two self-conscious individuals is such that they provide themselves and each other through a life and death struggle. They must engage in this struggle, for they must raise their certainty *for themselves* to truth, both in the case of the other and in their own case."[34]

The construction of the self in opposition to another who threatens one's very being reverberates throughout the construction of both class society and the masculinist world view and results in a deep-going and hierarchical dualism. First, the man's experience is characterized by the duality of concrete versus abstract.[35] Material reality as experienced by the boy in the family provides no model, and is unimportant in the attainment of masculinity. Nothing of value to the boy occurs within the family, and masculinity becomes an abstract ideal to be achieved over the opposition of daily life.[36] Masculinity must be attained by means of opposition to the concrete world of daily life, by escaping from contact with the female world of the household into the masculine world of politics or public life. This experience of two worlds, one valuable, if abstract and deeply unattainable, the other useless and demeaning, if concrete and necessary, lies at the heart of a series of dualisms—abstract/concrete, mind/body, culture/nature, ideal/real, stasis/change. And these dualisms are overlaid by gender; only the first of each pair is associated with the male.

Dualism, along with the dominance of one side of the dichotomy over the other, marks phallocentric society and social theory. These dualisms appear in a variety of forms—in philosophy, sexuality, technology, political theory, and the organization of class society itself. One can, for example, see them very clearly worked out in Plato, although they appear in many other forms.[37] There, the concrete/abstract duality takes the form of an opposition of material to ideal, and a denial of the relevance of the material world to the attainment of what is of fundamental importance: love of knowledge, or philosophy (masculinity). The duality of nature and culture takes the form of a devaluation of work, or necessity, and the primacy instead of purely social interaction for the attainment of undying fame. Philosophy itself is separate from nature, and indeed exists only on the basis of the domination of (at least some) of the philosopher's own nature.[38] Abstract masculinity, then, can be seen to have structured Western social relations and the modes of thought to which they give rise at least since the founding of the *polis*.

The oedipal roots of these hierarchical dualisms are memorialized in the overlay of masculine and feminine connotations. It is not accidental that women are associated with quasi-human and nonhuman nature, that the woman is associated with the body and material life, that the lives of women are systematically used as examples to characterize the lives of those ruled by their bodies rather than their minds.[39]

Both the fragility and fundamental falseness of the masculinist ideology and the deeply problematic nature of the social relations from which it grows are apparent in its reliance on a series of counterfactual assumptions and contentions. Consider how the following contentions run counter to lived experience: The body is both irrelevant and in opposition to the (real) self, an impediment to be overcome by the mind; the female mind either does not exist (Do women have souls?) or works in such incomprehensible ways as to be unintelligible (the "enigma of woman"); what is real and primary is imperceptible to the senses and impervious to nature and natural change. What is remarkable is not only that these contentions have absorbed a great deal of philosophical energy but, along with a series of other counterfactuals, have structured social relations for centuries.

Interestingly enough, the epistemology and society constructed by men, suffering from the effects of abstract masculinity, have a great deal in common with the society and ideology imposed by commodity exchange. The separation and opposition of social and natural worlds, of abstract and concrete, of permanence and change, the effort to define only the former of each pair as important, the reliance on a series of counterfactual assumptions—all this is shared with the exchange abstraction. Abstract masculinity shares still another of its aspects with the exchange abstraction: It forms the basis for an even more problematic social synthesis. Hegel's analysis makes clear the problematic social relations available to the self that maintains itself by opposition: Each of the two subjects struggling for recognition tries to kill the other. But if the other is killed, the subject is once again alone. In sum, then, masculine experience when replicated as epistemology leads to a world conceived as (and in fact) inhabited by a number of fundamentally hostile others whom one comes to know by means of opposition (even death struggle) and yet with whom one must construct a social relation in order to survive.

Women's construction of self in relation to others leads in an opposite direction—toward opposition to dualisms of any sort; valuation of concrete, everyday life; a sense of a variety of connectednesses and continuities both with other persons and with the natural world. If material life structures consciousness, women's relationally defined existence, bodily experience of boundary challenges, and activity of transforming both physical objects and human beings must be expected to result in a world view to which dichotomies are foreign. Women experience others and themselves along a continuum whose dimensions are evidenced in Adrienne Rich's argument that the child carried for nine months can be defined "*neither* as me or as not-me," and she argues that inner and outer are not polar opposites but a continuum.[40] What the sexual division of labor defines as women's work turns on issues of change rather than stasis—the changes involved in producing both use values and commodities, but more profoundly in the activity of rearing human beings who change in both more subtle and more autonomous ways than any inanimate object. Not only the qualities of things but also the qualities of people are important in women's work; quantity becomes peripheral. In addition, far more than the instrumental cooperation of the workplace is required; the mother-child relation and the maintenance of the family, while it has instrumental aspects, is not defined by them. Finally, the unity of mental and manual labor and the directly sensuous nature of much of women's work leads to a more profound unity of mental and manual labor, social and natural worlds, than is experienced by the male worker in capitalism. The unity grows from the fact that women's bodies, unlike men's, can be themselves instruments of production: In pregnancy, giving birth, or lactation, arguments about a division of mental from manual labor are fundamentally foreign.

That this is indeed women's experience is documented in both the theory and practice of the contemporary women's movement and needs no further development here.[41] The more important question here is whether women's experience and the world view constructed by women's activity can meet the criteria for a standpoint. If we return to the five claims carried by the concept of a standpoint it seems clear that women's material life activity has important epistemological and ontological consequences for both the understanding and construction of social relations. Women's activity, then, does satisfy the first requirement for a standpoint.

I can now take up the second claim made by a standpoint: that women's experience not only inverts that of men but forms a basis on which to expose abstract masculinity as both partial and fundamentally perverse, as not only occupying only one side of the dualities it has constructed but reversing the proper valuation of human activity. The partiality of the masculinist vision and of the societies that support this understanding is evidenced by its confinement of activity proper to the man to only one side of the dualisms. Its perverseness, however, lies elsewhere. Perhaps the most dramatic (though not the only) reversal of the proper order of things characteristic of masculine experience is the substitution of death for life.

The substitution of death for life results at least in part from the sexual division of labor in childrearing. The self surrounded by rigid ego boundaries, certain of what is inner and what is outer, the self experienced as walled city, is discontinuous with others. Georges Bataille has made brilliantly clear the ways in which death emerges as the only possible solution to this discontinuity and has followed the logic through to argue that reproduction itself must be understood, not as the creation of life, but as death. The core experience to be understood is that of discontinuity and its consequences. As a consequence of this experience of discontinuity and aloneness, penetration of ego boundaries, or fusion with another, is experienced as violent. The pair "lover-assailant" is not accidental. Nor is the connection of reproduction and death.

"Reproduction," Bataille argues, "implies the existence of *discontinuous* beings." This is so because "beings which reproduce themselves are distinct from one another, and those reproduced are likewise distinct from each other, just as they are distinct from their parents. Each being is distinct from all others. His birth, his death, the events of his life may have an interest for others, but he alone is directly concerned in them. He is born alone. He dies alone. Between one being and another, there is a *gulf*, a discontinuity."[42] (Clearly the gulf of which he speaks is better characterized as a chasm). In reproduction, sperm and ovum unite to form a new entity, but they do so from the death and disappearance of two separate beings. Thus, the new entity bears death with itself.

Although death and reproduction are intimately linked, Bataille stresses that "it is only death which is to be identified with [the transition to] continuity; he holds to this position despite his recognition that reproduction is a form of growth. The growth, however, he dismisses as not "ours," as being only "impersonal."[43] This is not the female experience, in which reproduction is hardly impersonal, nor experienced as death. It is, of course, in a literal sense, the sperm that is cut off from its source and lost. Perhaps we should not wonder, then, at the masculinist preoccupation with death, and the feeling that growth is "impersonal," not of fundamental concern to oneself. Beneath Bataille's theorization of continuity as death lies the conflictual individuation of the boy: Continuity with another, continuity with the mother, carries not just danger but inevitable death as a separate being. But this complete dismissal of the experience of another bespeaks a profound lack of empathy and refusal to recognize the very being of another. It manifests the chasm that separates each man from every other being and from the natural world, the chasm that marks and defines the problem of community.

The preoccupation with death instead of life appears as well in the argument that is the ability to kill (and for centuries, the practice) that sets humans above animals. Even Simone de Beauvoir has accepted that "it is not in giving life but in risking life that man is raised above the animal: that is why superiority has been accorded in humanity not to the sex that brings forth but to that which kills."[44] That superiority has been accorded to the sex which kills is beyond doubt. But what kind of vision can take reproduction, the creation of new life, and the force of life in sexuality, and turn it into death, not just in theory but in the practice of rape and sexual murder? Any why give pride of place to killing? That is not only an inversion of the proper order of things but also a refusal to recognize the real activities in which men as well as women are engaged. The producing of goods and the reproducing of human beings are certainly life-sustaining activities. And even the deaths of the ancient heroes in search of undying fame were pursuits of life and represented the attempt to avoid death by attaining immortality. The search for life, then, represents the deeper reality that lies beneath the glorification of death and destruction.

Yet one cannot dismiss the substitution of death for life as simply false. Men's power to structure social relations in their own image means that women too must participate in social relations that manifest and express abstract masculinity. The most important life activities have consistently been held by the powers that be to be unworthy of those who are fully human, most centrally because of their close connections with necessity and life: motherwork (the rearing of children), housework, and until the rise of capitalism in the West, any work necessary to subsistence. In addition, these activities in contemporary capitalism are all constructed in ways that systematically degrade and destroy the minds and bodies of those who perform them.[45] The organization of motherhood as an institution in which a woman is alone with her children, the isolation of women from each other in domestic labor, the female pathology of loss of self in service to others—all mark the transformation of life into death, the distortion of what could have been creative and communal activity into oppressive toil, and the destruction of the possibility of community present in women's relational self-definition. The ruling gender's and class's interest in maintaining social relations such as these is evidenced by the fact that when women set up other structures in which the mother is not alone with her children, isolated from others, as is frequently the case in working-class communities or the communities of people of color, these arrangements are described as pathological deviations.

The real destructiveness of the social relations characteristic of abstract masculinity, however, is now concealed beneath layers of ideology. Marxian theory needed to go beneath the surface to discover the different levels of determination that defined the relation of capitalist and (male) worker. These levels of determination and laws of motion or tendency of phallocratic society must be worked out on the basis of female experience. This brings me to the fourth claim for a standpoint: its character as an achievement of both analysis and political struggle occurring in a particular historical space. The fact that class divisions should have proved so resistant to analysis and required such a prolonged political struggle before Marx was able to formulate the theory of surplus value indicates the difficulty of this accomplishment.

And despite the time that has passed since the theory was worked out, rational control of production has yet to be achieved.

Feminists have only begun the process of revaluing the female experience, searching for the common threads that connect the diverse experiences of women, and searching for the structural determinants of these experiences. The difficulty of the problem faced by feminist theory can be illustrated by the fact that it required a struggle even to define household labor, if not done for wages, as work, to argue that what are held to be acts of love instead must be recognized as work.[46] Both the revaluation of women's experience and the use of this experience as a ground for critique are required. That is, the liberatory possibilities present in women's experience must be, in a sense, read out and developed. Thus, a feminist standpoint may be present on the basis of the commonalities within women's experience, but it is neither self-evident nor obvious.

Finally, because it provides a way to reveal the perverseness and inhumanity of human relations, a standpoint forms the basis for moving beyond these relations. Just as the proletarian standpoint emerges out of the contradiction between appearance and essence in capitalism, understood as essentially historical and constituted by the relation of capitalist and worker, the feminist standpoint emerges both out of the contradiction between the systematically differing structures of men's and women's life activity in Western cultures. It expresses women's experience at a particular time and place, located within a particular set of social relations. Capitalism, Marx noted, could not develop fully until the notion of human equality achieved the status of universal truth.[47] Despite women's exploitation, both as unpaid reproducers of the labor force and as a sex-segregated labor force available for low wages, then, capitalism poses problems for the continued oppression of women. Just as capitalism enables the proletariat to raise the possibility of a society free from class domination, so too it provides space to raise the possibility of a society free from all forms of domination. The articulation of a feminist standpoint based on women's relational self-definition and activity exposes the world men have constructed and the self-understanding that manifests these social relations as both partial and perverse. More important, by drawing out the potentiality available in the actuality and thereby exposing the inhumanity of human relations, it embodies a distress that requires a solution. The experience of continuity and relation—with others, with the natural world, of mind with body—provide an ontological base for developing a nonproblematic social synthesis, a social synthesis that need not operate through the denial of the body, the attack on nature, or the death struggle between the self and other, a social synthesis that does not depend on any of the forms taken by abstract masculinity.

What is necessary is the generalization of the potentiality made available by the activity of women—the defining of society as a whole as propertyless producer both of use values and of human beings. To understand what such a transformation would require, we should consider what is involved in the partial transformation represented by making the whole of society into propertyless producers of use values: socialist revolution. The abolition of the division between mental and manual labor cannot take place simply by means of adopting worker self-management techniques, but instead requires the abolition of private property, the seizure of state power, and lengthy post-revolutionary class struggle. Thus I am not suggesting that shared parenting arrangements can abolish the sexual division of labor. Doing away with this division of labor would of course require institutionalizing the participation of both women and men in childrearing. But just as the rational and conscious control of the production of goods and services requires a vast and far-reaching social transformation, so too the rational and conscious organization of reproduction would entail the transformation both of *every* human relation and of human relations to the natural world. The magnitude of the task is apparent if one asks what a society without institutionalized gender differences might look like.

Generalizing the human possibilities present in the life activity of women to the social system as a whole would raise, for the first time in human history, the possibility of a fully human community, a community structured by a variety of connections rather than separation and opposition. One can conclude then that women's life activity does form the basis of a specifically feminist materialism, a materialism that can provide a point from which to both critique and work against phallocratic ideology and institutions.

NOTES

1. This is Iris Young's point. I am indebted to her persuasive arguments for taking what she terms the "gender differentiation of labor" as a central category of analysis. See Young, "Dual Systems Theory," *Socialist Review* 50, 51 (March–June 1980): 185. My use of this category, however, differs to some extent from hers. Young focuses on the societal aspects of the division of labor and chooses to use the term "gender division" to indicate that focus. I want to include the relation to the natural world as well. In addition, Young's analysis of women in capitalism does not seem to include marriage as a part of the division of labor. She is more concerned with the division of labor in capitalism in the productive sector.

2. See Sara Ruddick, "Maternal Thinking," *Feminist Studies* 6, no. 2 (Summer 1980): 364.

248 / MONEY, SEX, AND POWER

3. See, for a discussion of this danger, Adrienne Rich, "Disloyal of Civilization: Feminism, Racism, Gynephobia," in *On Lies, Secrets, and Silence* (New York: Norton, 1979), pp. 275–310; Elly Bulkin, "Racism and Writing: Some Implications for White Lesbian Critics," *Sinister Wisdom*, no. 6 (Spring 1980); Bell Hooks, *Ain't I a Woman* (Boston: South End Press, 1981), p. 138.

4. Some cross-cultural evidence indicates that the status of women varies with the work they do. To the extent that women and men contribute equally to subsistence, women's status is higher than it would be if their subsistence work differed profoundly from that of men; that is, if they do none or almost all of the work of subsistence, their status remains low. See Peggy Sanday, "Female Status in the Public Domain," in *Woman, Culture and Society*, ed. Michelle Rosaldo and Louise Lamphere (Stanford: Stanford University Press, 1974), p. 199. See also Iris Young's account of the sexual division of labor in capitalism, mentioned in note 1.

5. It is irrelevant to my argument here that women's wage labor takes place under different circumstances than men's—that is, their lower wages, their confinement to only a few occupational categories, etc. I am concentrating instead on the formal, structural features of women's work. There has been much effort to argue that women's domestic labor is a source of surplus value, that is, to include it within the scope of Marx's value theory as productive labor, or to argue that since it does not produce surplus value it belongs to an entirely different mode of production, variously characterized as domestic or patriarchal. My strategy here is quite different from this. See, for the British debate, Mariarosa Dalla Costa and Selma James, *The Power of Women and the Subversion of the Community* (Bristol: Falling Wall Press, 1975); Wally Secombe, "The Housewife and Her Labor Under Capitalism," *New Left Review* 83 (January–February 1974); Jean Gardiner, "Women's Domestic Labour," *New Left Review* 89 (March 1975); and Paul Smith, "Domestic Labour and Marx's Theory of Value," in *Feminism and Materialism*, eds. Annette Kuhn and Ann Marie Wolpe (Boston: Routledge and Kegan Paul, 1978). A portion of the American debate can be found in Ira Gerstein, "Domestic Work and Capitalism," and Lisa Vogel, "The Earthly Family," *Radical America* 7, nos. 4/5 (July–October 1973); Ann Ferguson, "Women as a New Revolutionary Class," in *Between Labor and Capital*, ed. Pat Walker (Boston: South End Press, 1979).

6. Frederick Engels, *Origins of the Family, Private Property and the State* (New York: International Publishers 1942); Karl Marx, *Capital* (New York: International Publishers, 1967) 1: 671. Marx and Engels have also described the sexual division of labor as natural or spontaneous. See Mary O'Brien, "Reproducing Marxist Man," in *The Sexism of Social and Political Thought*, ed. Lorenne Clark and Lynda Lange (Toronto: University of Toronto Press, 1979).

7. For a discussion of women's work, see Elise Boulding, "Familial Constraints of Women's Work Roles," in *Women and the Workplace*, ed. Martha Blaxall and B. Reagan (Chicago: University of Chicago Press, 1976), esp. pp. 111, 113. An interesting historical note is provided by the fact that Nausicaa, the daughter of a Homeric king, did the household laundry. See M. I. Finley, *The World of Odysseus* (Middlesex, England: Penguin, 1979), p. 73. While aristocratic women were less involved in actual labor, the difference was one of degree. And as Aristotle remarked in the *Politics*, supervising slaves is not a particularly

uplifting activity. The life of leisure and philosophy, so much the goal for aristocratic Athenian men, then, was almost unthinkable for any woman.

8. Simone de Beauvoir holds that repetition has a deeper significance and that women's biological destiny itself is repetition. See *The Second Sex*, trans. H. M. Parshley (New York: Knopf, 1953), p. 59. But see also her discussion of housework in ibid., pp. 423 ff. There, her treatment of housework is strikingly negative. For her the transcendence of humanity is provided in the historical struggle of self with other and with the natural world. The oppositions she sees are not really stasis vs. change, but rather transcendence, escape from the muddy concreteness of daily life.

9. Marilyn French, *The Women's Room* (New York: Jove, 1978), p. 214.

10. Sara Ruddick, "Maternal Thinking," presents an interesting discussion of these and other aspects of the thought which emerges from the activity of mothering. Although I find it difficult to speak the language of interests and demands she uses, she brings out several valuable points. Her distinction between maternal and scientific thought is very intriguing and potentially useful (see esp. pp. 350–53).

11. Mary O'Brien, "Reproducing Marxist Man," p. 115, n. 11.

12. It should be understood that I am concentrating here on the experience of women in Western culture. There are a number of cross-cultural differences that can be expected to have some effect. See, for example, the differences that emerge from a comparison of childrearing in ancient Greek society with that of the contemporary Mbuti in central Africa. See Philip Slater, *The Glory of Hera* (Boston: Beacon, 1968); and Colin Turnbull, "The Politics of Non-Aggression," in *Learning Non-Aggression*, ed. Ashley Montagu (New York: Oxford University Press, 1978). See also Isaac Balbus, *Marxism and Domination* (Princeton: Princeton University Press, 1982).

13. See Nancy Chodorow, "Family Structure and Female Personality," in Rosaldo and Lamphere, *Women, Culture, and Society*, p. 59.

14. Adrienne Rich, *Of Woman Born* (New York: Norton, 1976), p. 63.

15. I rely on the analyses of Dinnerstein and Chodorow but there are difficulties in that they are attempting to explain why humans, both male and female, fear and hate the female. My purpose here is to invert their arguments and to attempt to put forward a positive account of the epistemological consequences of this situation. What follows is a summary of Nancy Chodorow, *The Reproduction of Mothering* (Berkeley: University of California Press, 1978).

16. See Chodorow, *Reproduction*; and Jane Flax, "The Conflict Between Nurturance and Autonomy in Mother-Daughter Relations and in Feminism," *Feminist Studies* 6, no. 2 (June 1978).

17. Chodorow, *Reproduction*, pp. 105–9.

18. This is Jane Flax's point.

19. Chodorow, *Reproduction*, pp. 127–31, 163.

20. Ibid., p. 166.

21. Ibid., pp. 174–78. Chodorow suggests a correlation between father absence and fear of women (p. 213), and one should, treating this as an empirical hypothesis, expect a series of cultural differences based on the degree of father absence. Here the ancient Greeks and the Mbuti provide a fascinating contrast. (See above, note 12.)

22. Ibid., p. 198. The flexible and diffuse female ego boundaries can of course result in the pathology of loss of self in responsibility for and dependence on others (the obverse of the male pathology of experiencing the self as walled city).

23. He never considers that single-sex childrearing may be the problem and also ascribes total responsibility to the mother for especially the male's successful individuation. See Robert Stoller, *Perversion* (New York: Pantheon, 1975), p. 154 and p. 161, for an awesome list of tasks to be accomplished by the mother.

24. Ibid., pp. 137–38.

25. Ibid., p. 154. See also his discussion of these dynamics in Chapter 2 of Robert Stoller, *Sexual Excitement* (New York: Pantheon, 1979).

26. Stoller, *Perversion*, p. 99.

27. Ibid., pp. 150, 121 respectively.

28. Ibid., p. 150.

29. Ibid., p. 149.

30. Ibid., pp. 149–51.

31. Ibid., p. 121.

32. Stoller, *Sexual Excitement*, p. 172.

33. Sigmund Freud, *Civilization and Its Discontents* (New York: Norton, 1961), pp. 12–13.

34. G. W. F. Hegel, *Phenomenology of Spirit*, trans. A. V. Miller (New York: Oxford University Press, 1979), p. 114. See also Jessica Benjamin's very interesting use of this discussion in "The Bonds of Love: Rational Violence and Erotic Domination," *Feminist Studies* 6, no. 1 (June 1980).

35. I use the terms abstract and concrete in a sense much influenced by Marx. "Abstraction" refers not only to the practice of searching for universal generalities but also carries derogatory connotations of idealism and partiality. By "concrete," I refer to respect for complexity and multidimensional causality, and mean to suggest as well a materialism and completeness.

36. Alvin Gouldner has made a similar argument in his contention that the Platonic stress on hierarchy and order resulted from a similarly learned opposition to daily life rooted in the young aristocrat's experience of being taught proper behavior by slaves who could not themselves engage in this behavior. See Gouldner, *Enter Plato* (New York: Basic Books, 1965), pp. 351–55.

37. One can argue, as Chodorow's analysis suggests, that their extreme form in his philosophy represents an extreme father-absent (father-deprived?) situation. A more general critique of phallocentric dualism occurs in Susan Griffin, *Woman and Nature* (New York: Harper & Row, 1978).

38. More recently, of course, the opposition to the natural world has taken the form of destructive technology. See Evelyn Fox Keller, "Gender and Science," *Psychoanalysis and Contemporary Thought* 1, no. 3 (1978).

39. See Elizabeth Spelman, "Metaphysics and Misogyny: The Soul and Body in Plato's Dialogues" (mimeo). One analyst has argued that its basis lies in the fact that "the early mother, monolithic representative of nature, is a source, like nature, of ultimate distress as well as ultimate joy. Like nature, she is both nourishing and disappointing, both alluring and threatening. ... The

infant loves her . . . and it hates her because, like nature, she does not perfectly protect and provide for it. . . . The mother, then—like nature, which sends blizzards and locusts as well as sunshine and strawberries—is perceived as capricious, sometimes actively malevolent." Dorothy Dinnerstein, *The Mermaid and the Minotaur* (New York: Harper & Row, 1976), p. 95.

40. Rich, *Of Woman Born*, pp. 64, 167. For a similar descriptive account, but a dissimilar analysis, see David Bakan, *The Duality of Human Existence* (Boston: Beacon Press, 1966).

41. My arguments are supported with remarkable force by both the theory and practice of the contemporary women's movement. In theory, this appears in different forms in the work of Dorothy Riddle, "New Visions of Spiritual Power," *Quest: a feminist quarterly* 1, no. 3 (Spring 1975); Griffin, *Woman and Nature*, esp. Book IV, "The Separate Rejoined"; Rich, *Of Woman Born*, esp. pp. 62–68; Linda Thurston, "On Male and Female Principle," *The Second Wave* 1, no 2 (Summer 1971). In feminist political organizing, this vision has been expressed as an opposition of leadership and hierarchy, as an effort to prevent the development of organizations divided into leaders and followers. It has also taken the forms of an insistence on the unity of the personal and the political, a stress on the concrete rather than on abstract principles (an opposition to theory), and a stress on the politics of everyday life. For a fascinating and early example, see Pat Mainardi, "The Politics of Housework," in *Voices of Women's Liberation*, ed. Leslie Tanner (New York: New American Library, 1970).

42. Georges Bataille, *Death and Sensuality* (New York: Arno Press, 1977), p. 12; italics mine.

43. Ibid., pp. 95–96.

44. de Beauvoir, *The Second Sex*, p. 58.

45. Consider, for example. Rich's discussion of pregnancy and childbirth, chaps. 6, 7, and *Of Woman Born*. And see also Charlotte Perkins Gilman's discussion of domestic labor in *The Home* (Urbana, Ill.: University of Illinois Press, 1972).

46. The Marxist-feminist efforts to determine whether housework produces surplus value and the feminist political strategy of demanding wages for housework represent two (mistaken) efforts to recognize women's activity as work.

47. Marx, *Capital*, 1:60.

11

Power, Class, and Gender: Questions for the Future

W e are now in a position to begin to answer the several questions posed at the end of Chapter 9, questions of why the masculine community constructed *eros* as domination, and why women's accounts of power differ so systematically from those of men. We can then take up the question of how to construct a more adequate account of power, an account that rests on a feminist standpoint that can both address the irreducibly erotic nature of power and point in more liberatory directions.

Let us begin with the first question: Why are virility and domination so intimately connected? The key structuring experience can now be seen to be fear of ceasing to exist as a separate being, ceasing to exist because of the threat posed by a woman. These fears are expressed clearly in masculine sexual fantasies as these appear in pornography. Intimacy with a woman is so dangerous that she must be reduced to a nonentity or made into a thing. The body, constituting a reminder of loathsome mortality, must be denied and repressed. The whole man is reduced to the phallus; bodily feelings are projected onto the woman, who is reduced to a body without a will of her own. And in sexual fantasy and philosophy about sexual fantasy, creativity and generation take the form of a fascination with death.

These same fears are memorialized in the construction of the agonal political world of the warrior-hero (and later the citizen) as a world of hostile and threatening others, others to whom one relates by means of rivalry and competition for dominance. The other is both necessary and threatening: To guard against the possibilities of fusion and therefore against one's death as a separate being, the other must be forced to submit or be humiliated or killed.

The feelings of the body, because they are reminders of materiality and worse, mortality, reminders that one will one day cease to exist, must be rejected and denied. Thus a philosopher such as Plato attempts to become disembodied to achieve true knowledge and association with the unchanging. And because to be born means that one will die, reproduction and generation are either understood in terms of death or are appropriated by men in disembodied form. Over and over, then, the fear of ceasing to exist is played out. Nowhere is this more prominent than in the search for immortality, whether through the death of the body or the generation of immortal children of the mind.

In contrast, women's stress on power not as domination but as capacity, on power as a capacity of the community as a whole, suggests that women's experience of connection and relation have consequences for understandings of power and may hold resources for a more liberatory understanding. The women, feminist or not, who have written about power tend to assimilate power over others to domination, without providing the analysis that would account for systematic and pervasive relations of power of some over others. They tend to define most exercises of power over others as exercises of domination, a domination they seldom characterize as legitimate. Yet their theories tend toward inadequacies opposite to the masculinist understandings we have discussed. Their theories are dangerously close to the traditional way women's power has been experienced—an energy looking for objects into which to pour itself, even sometimes a demonic possession.[1] It is power bottled up and contained. In addition, these theorists tend to stress connection and relation at the expense of individuality. They describe power in terms that emphasize the submersion of the identity of the individual in the community, thereby falling into a form of the female pathology of loss of self, a fluidity that may submerge individual identity.

Some of Arendt's formulations provide the clearest example of this latter move. She expressly treats power not as the capacity of an individual but of a community. And she heaps contempt on the actions of individuals as not political, as the actions of "anarchists." In addition, the basis of the public world for her is that one is not concerned with oneself but with the common world—thus the praise of Luxemburg, who was not concerned with herself but with the collectivity.

Still, Arendt remains an interesting and important example whose work indicates some of the beneficial theoretical effects women's experience of both connection and individuation may have. This is nowhere more striking than in the relational reformulation Arendt has given to the oppositional and dualistic world view of the ancient Greeks. She has, despite her adherence to the Homeric model, reinterpreted it in ways much more congruent with women's than men's experience. This is the sense in which I interpret her reformulation of the agonal dualisms of ancient Athens as coexistent and mutually cooperative aspects of social being. And this is the sense in which I understand her reinterpretation of the radical alterity that characterized the life and consciousness of the warrior-hero as plurality or individuality. She, unlike the ancient Greeks, is not dealing with a world in which the most important opposition is that between the "me" and "not-me"; she lives in a world in which a variety of relations with others are possible. The plurality of which she speaks, the individuation she sees as necessary and only possible in a public world—these are not the stuff of the striving for distinction *as opposed to all others* so characteristic of the *polis*. Indeed, she holds that it is only through the variety of relations constructed by the plurality of beings that truth can be known and community constructed.

Only when one recognizes the importance she ascribes to plurality and the relational character of her understanding of social life does Arendt's reinterpretation of the *polis* as far more than an instrumental community make sense. The others, as she sees it, are there, not simply as passive beings upon whom one exercises one's power, but as co-citizens *with* whom one acts in common. In the end, it is not distinction but commonality that is primary for Arendt. And this commonality leads to immortality because it is only the action of the community and its preservation as an arena for action that can lead to immortality. While the theorizations of power considered in Chapter 9, then, are flawed, they also hold important resources for more adequate and liberatory understandings. It is to this task that we should now turn.

Toward a More Adequate Theory and Practice

Despite the fact that much remains to be done, we have moved a certain distance toward a more adequate and liberatory understanding of power. An adequate theory would both require and contribute to the development of a specifically feminist historical materialism. Thus, an adequate theorization of power would provide answers for women akin to those Marx's account of class domination provided for workers. It would give an account of how social institutions have come to be controlled by only one gender; it would locate the points at which conflicts between women and men are generated, and make clear the specific relations between individual intentional actions and structural constraints. (A feminist historical materialism, of course, could do far more than ground an adequate theory of power. By locating the sources of women's oppression in history and material life, by encompassing the concrete and varied specificities of women's lives, it could provide the terrain on which both the commonalities of women's situations and differences of race, class, and sexuality could be understood. Perhaps most significantly, a feminist historical materialism might enable us to lay bare the laws of tendency that constitute the changing structure of patriarchy over time. It would add greatly to our understanding of how relations of domination are constructed, maintained, and finally may be destroyed.)

Despite the fact that such a theorization remains to be achieved, it is possible to say something about the outlines of such a theory and to point to a variety of resources that could contribute to its construction. A more adequate and liberatory theory must be located at the episte-mological level of reproduction. Thus it must neither reduce power to domination nor ignore systematic domination to stress only energy and community. Because of the variety of possibilities for both connection and separation available in women's life activity as structured by the sexual division of labor, simple radical alterity can have little part in this theory. Perhaps more important, given the discussion of the last chapter, relocating the theorization of power to the epistemological level of reproduction would put *eros* and its various aspects at the center of an understanding of power. It would enable us to recapture the possibilities Audre Lorde has described as inherent in the mythic personage of Eros—"born of Chaos, and personifying creative power and harmony. When I speak of the erotic, then I speak of it as an assertion of the life-force of women," she states.[2] At the level of reproduction, *eros* not only can take positive forms but can take over and transform the terrain of work. Marxian theory provides some guidance as to what this might mean. His stress on sensuality as well as community suggests that there may be an erotic pleasure available in work itself—in all the various senses in which I have used the term—sensual, bodily, creative, and in community with others.

The Marxian account of unalienated production, quoted at length earlier, includes the erotic joys of work itself—the making of an object that expresses one's life force, or *eros*. This account also stresses the importance of another or others with whom to share the object, and for whom it can be a means to satisfy their needs, and underlines the community produced by this complementary sharing. Thus, one result of the relocation of an understanding of power to the ground of women's lives would be a heightened recognition of the erotic possibilities made available in unalienated work.

It is interesting to note that Audre Lorde has put forward striking-ly similar arguments. She writes: "We are taught to separate the erotic demand from most vital areas of our lives other than sex." As a result, she holds, our work is robbed of its erotic value.[3] She describes the possible empowering erotic nature of work: sharing of a pursuit that can in turn lessen the other differences between the participants, and an acceptance of and "underlining of [the] capacity for joy."[4] In these suggestive statements of the erotic possibilities contained in work, we can begin to see some of the outlines of an understanding of power which stresses both its dimensions of competence, ability, and creativity and does not lose sight of the importance of effective action in the world, action at least in part defined by its sensuality and its variety of connections and relations with others in the community.[5]

A second resource for a theory of power centered on *eros* could be located in a better understanding of women's sexuality. Yet because what our culture has constructed as sexuality expresses masculine experience, we are only at the beginning of the necessary research and discussion. One is struck with the extent to which those who have described the dynamics of conquest and domination in masculine sexuality state that women's sexuality seems to work differently. One finds others as well who note the differences between what is sexually arousing material for men and for women.[6] Two disparate literatures seem particularly promising avenues for further work: research on maternal sexuality, and the current debate about sexuality within the feminist movement; the one concerned with sexuality as it appears in reproduction, the other concerned with sexual excitement and sexual pleasure.

Maternal sexuality is particularly interesting since it has generally been held to be nonexistent and therefore remains culturally constructed as asexual. Perhaps one might say that this is a "feminine" sexuality, since sexuality and maternity, like sexuality and femininity, are generally held to involve a contradiction. Here the work of Niles Newton is very useful. She argues that if one looks at the three "intense interpersonal reproductive acts" available to women—coitus, parturition, and lactation—one finds marked correlations and interrelationships.[7] Yet despite her documentation of a systematic series of similarities between childbirth and sexual excitement, and between breast-feeding and coital orgasm, most women in our culture do not perceive these experiences as sexual. Some of those few women who have reported sexual feelings in nursing also reported feeling guilty about those feelings. In the case of breast-feeding, researchers who probed beyond the conventional answers did find a substantial percentage of mothers who reported that they enjoyed the experience, but described their enjoyment as not specifically sexual, but as feelings of tenderness and closeness.[8]

The inhibition of the sensual pleasures of breast-feeding may, Newton suggests, be similar to those that make birth orgasm seldom found in our culture: Mother and infant are separated in the hospital, and rules about duration and timing of each sucking period are frequently enforced, Newton notes, "by persons who usually have never successfully breast fed even one baby." She concludes that "probably most people in our society would be willing to concede that we would cause coital frigidity if we prescribed the act only at scheduled times and laid down rules concerning the exact number of minutes intromission should last."[9]

The belief is that good mothers have no sexual feelings in relation to children, despite the fact that there is general agreement in the psychological literature that the early mother-child relationship should be erotic for the child.[10] What is less generally appreciated is that breast-feeding can be considered to be a reciprocal or symmetrical erotic activity that does not involve the infant alone, but also the mother. Unlike coitus, this experience can be more persuasively characterized as an "equal opportunity experience."[11]

These experiences—bodily, sensual, creative in the large sense of the term—may be the base for a reunderstanding of power and community. The female relational world can incorporate *eros* without insisting that the only fusion with another is in the death of the other; without, for that matter, insisting that aloneness or fusion are the only options. The female experiences not simply of mothering (but more broadly the general education of girls for mothering, and the experience of being mothered by a person of one's own gender) is one in which power over another is gradually transformed by both the powerholder and the being over whom power is exercised into autonomy and (ideally) mutual respect. The power of the mother over the child, and the sensual and erotic relation with the child, issue (in healthy relations) in the creation of an independent and autonomous being. Thus, the point of having power over another is to liberate the other rather than dominate or even kill her.

Contemporary arguments about the nature of a "feminist sexuality" have so far produced little more than polarization.[12] Yet these arguments both raise the issue of what sexual women might look like and also illustrate how *eros*, even in negative forms, poses different problems for women than for men. Because of masculine hegemony, one would expect that women's sexual excitement too would depend on hostility and transgression, and to some extent this is true. But even among feminists whose sexual excitement has been characterized as deeply structured by masculinist patterns, there is some evidence to support the contention that women are less perverse than men, that is, that women's sexual excitement depends less than men's on victimization and revenge. Thus one finds that the lesbian proponents of sadomasochism hold that "the desire to be sexual and the desire to be combative are complexly intertwined."[13]

Yet in their fiction and autobiographical and political statements, one can see echoes of a different experience. In terms of *eros* one finds that in terms of fusion with another, empathy with the other partner receives far more attention than separation from the other by means of domination and submission.[14] Rather than treat the body as a loathsome reminder of mortality whose needs must be projected onto the body of another, the rejection of the body takes the form of a need for permission to enjoy the pleasures of the flesh without guilt or responsibility.[15] Ironically, given the current controversy, one can compare these dynamics and issues to Anne Snitow's descriptions of the heroine's submission in Harlequin romance novels.[16]

Creativity and generation seem to play small roles in the fantasies described by Samois members. The negative form of this aspect of *eros* appears only indirectly in the separation of sexuality from daily life activity. It is perhaps significant that this aspect too is shared by the sexual dynamics of Harlequin romances.[17] In sum, it can be said that, for women, the cultural construction of sexuality shapes even the negative forms of *eros* in less dangerous ways than for men.

I do not mean to suggest that these echoes of a different construction of *eros* are in themselves liberatory: Denying oneself the sensual pleasures of the body and splitting *eros* off from daily life activity ignore the liberatory possibilities contained in the structure of women's life activity.

Contemporary feminist efforts to understand and remake difference represent a third important area in which to find resources for a more adequate theorization of power. Differences among women have posed difficult problems for feminists since these differences had been treated as radical alterity and used to justify the domination of some over others. The collective effort to recognize and use differences has taken the form of efforts on the one hand to reject claims of commonality and universality, which in fact make invisible women of color or lesbians, and on the other to prevent differences from taking the form of radical alterity. Here, too, Audre Lorde is the source of important advice: "Advocating the mere tolerance of difference between women is . . . a total denial of the creative function of difference in our lives. For difference must be not merely tolerated, but seen as a fund of necessary polarities between which our creativity can spark like a dialectic. Only then does the necessity for interdependency become unthreatening."[18]

In this effort to transform the meaning of difference one can appreciate the feminist significance of Arendt's remaking of the agonal political tradition. In her hands the radical alterity, which constituted community as a death threat for the individual Athenian, becomes a vision in which it is only through the variety of relations constructed by a plurality of people that the richness of community can be constructed. The capacity for a variety of relations with others that grows from the experience of being mothered by a woman may help feminists to develop new understandings of both the differences and similarities among us, and new ways of working with those differences.

The outlines, though not the substance, of an adequate theory of power grounded at the epistemological level of reproduction are now visible, if only hazily. It is an understanding of power rooted in and defined not simply by women's experience but by the systematic pulling together and working out of the liberatory possibilities present in that experience. Such an understanding of power would recognize that relations with another may take a variety of forms, forms not structured fundamentally by alterity but distinction. The body—its desires and needs, and its mortality—would not be denied as shameful but would be given a place of honor at the center of the theory. And creativity and generation would be incorporated in the form of directly valuing daily life activities—eroticizing the work of production and accepting the erotic nature of nurturance.

Given my contention that life activity structures understanding, however, such a theory may remain only a rudimentary vision in a world structured by systematic domination and alienation. Thus, like Marx's brief statements about his vision of the nature of unalienated production, the development of a feminist theory of power must stand as a challenge for action, a challenge to generalize the liberatory possibilities available in the ways the sexual division of labor constructs women's lives by abolishing this division of labor along with the mental/manual division of labor.

Class and Gender: Some Speculations for Further Attention

I have argued for the development of a specifically feminist historical materialism that could adopt Marx's method and take over much of his analysis of class domination. In addition, I have argued that beneath the epistemological level of production, a level defined by workers' experience in contemporary capitalism, one encounters the epistemological level of reproduction defined by women's experience as structured by the sexual division of labor, a level at which a more encompassing and insistent historical materialism may be located. Both these positions can be seen as related to the radical feminist position that the oppression of women gives rise to class society (and to white supremacy). There is a third suggestion that gender underlies class implicit in my comparison of the dynamics that structure communities of rational economic men and agonal, masculine communities. What is the significance of the similarities between the dualisms associated with abstract masculinity and with the exchange abstraction? Why are both characterized by dualities that oppose concrete to abstract, body to mind, nature to society, ideal to material; and why are both communities structured by opposition, distrust, and isolation? We have analyzed exchange as the perspective of the ruling class in capitalism. But perhaps exchange as the mechanism for social synthesis carries gender as well as class.

Marcel Mauss's discussion of gift exchanges among tribal people (among whom one should number the Homeric Greeks) provides several interesting suggestions about the genderedness of exchange as a medium for social synthesis. First, Mauss underlines the "agonistic" character of gift exchange (especially marked in potlatch). Thus he remarks the "spirit of rivalry and antagonism," the motives of "competition, rivalry, show, and a desire for greatness and wealth." And he concludes that "the principles of rivalry and antagonism are basic."[19] To accept a gift is to accept a challenge to one's honor, a challenge to prove oneself worthy by demonstrating not only an ability to repay but one's lack of fear of the challenge. Thus, wealth is as much a thing of prestige as of utility.[20]

The agonistic character of exchange is, as well, related to more open warfare. To refuse to participate operates as "the equivalent of a declaration of war."[21] Yet the exchange itself is sometimes compared to war.[22] In societies structured by this form of exchange, community poses extreme problems. Thus, in the ceremonies that accompany the exchange of gifts, Mauss holds that "there is no middle path. There is either complete trust or mistrust. One lays down one's arms, renounces magic and gives everything away, from casual hospitality to one's daughter or one's property." This is so because "when two groups of men meet they may move away or in case of mistrust or defiance they may resort to arms; or else they can come to terms."[23] Exchange, then, Mauss is suggesting, is a substitute for war. His description of gift exchange and potlatch among peoples who lack a market closely parallels my account of the agonal community characteristic of masculine experience. Themes of rivalry and the defeat and consequent shaming of one's opponent are central to both.

The fact that agonistic interactions of this sort tend to occur in societies in which the sexual division of labor is either the only or the most important division of labor provides a second suggestive support for my speculation about the genderedness of exchange as a means for constructing community. Given the Marxian demonstration of the ways commodity exchange rests on the mental/manual division of labor, one can speculate that gift exchange and the agonistic relations to which it gives rise may be rooted in the sexual division of labor.

A third suggestion of the masculine character of exchange and its possible roots in the sexual division of labor are evidenced in the fact that women are rarely participants and are much more often exchange objects. Thus, Mauss at several points lists women among other items of exchange. He states that "food, women, children, possessions, charms, land, labour, services, religious offices" are all among the things to be given away and repaid. Significantly, he never mentions men in such a list.[24] Claude Lévi-Strauss's arguments about the importance of the exchange of women represent another locus in which to examine the genderedness of exchange. I have discussed some of the issues involved in Appendix 1.

If exchange constructs power and community in specifically masculine ways, that is, if exchange expresses not just the experience of the ruling class but also that of the ruling gender, then a re-examination of exchange theories, in whatever forms they take, is in order. Such a reexamination could help clarify the relation between social systems structured by a sexual division of labor as opposed to those structured by the division between mental and manual labor. Ultimately, such a re-examination could contribute to a better understanding of the social system I have termed the capitalist form of patriarchy.

Conclusion

Clearly a number of large questions have been broached here. I have attempted to demonstrate that theorizations of power are cultural productions in the most complete sense of the word. Those which have been seen as most attractive show the impact of a number of features of the lives and world views of the ruling class and gender. An analysis that begins from the sexual division of labor, understood as the real, material activity of concrete human beings, could form the basis for an analysis of the real structures of women's oppression, an analysis that would not require that one sever biology from society, nature from culture, an analysis that would expose the ways women both participate in and oppose their own subordination. The elaboration of such an analysis cannot but be difficult. Women's lives, like men's, are structured by social relations that manifest the experience of the dominant gender and class. The ability to go beneath the surface of appearances to reveal the real but concealed social relations requires both theoretical and political activity. Feminist theorists must demand that feminist theorizing be grounded in women's material life activity and must as well be a part of the political struggle necessary to develop areas of social life modeled on this activity. The outcome could be the development of a political economy that fully included women's activity as well as men's. It could in addition be a step toward the restructuring of society as a whole in ways that will reflect a generalization of women's activity to all parts of the population. Thus, it could raise for the first time the possibility of a fully human community, a community structured by its variety of direct relations among people, rather than their separation and opposition.

My argument here opens a number of avenues for future work. Clearly, a systematic critique of Marx on the basis of a more fully developed understanding of the sexual division of labor is in order. And this is indeed being undertaken by a number of feminists. A second avenue for further investigation is the relation between the exchange abstraction and abstract masculinity. It may be that the solipsism of exchange is both an overlay on and a substitution for a deeper-going hostility, that the exchange of gifts is an alternative to war. We have seen that the need for recognizing and receiving recognition from another to take the form of a death struggle memorializes only the masculine experience of emerging as a person in a deeply phallocratic world. If the community created by exchange in turn rests on the more overtly and directly hostile death struggle of self and other, one might be able to argue that what lies beneath the exchange abstraction is abstract masculinity. One might then turn to the question whether capitalism rests on and is a consequence of male supremacy. Feminists might then be able to produce the analysis that could amend Marx to read: "Though class society appears to be the source, the cause of the oppression of women, it is rather its consequence." Thus, it is "only at the last culmination of the development of class society [that] this, its secret, appear(s) again, namely, that on the one hand it is the *product* of the oppression of women, and that on the other it is the *means* by which women participate in and create their own oppression."[25]

NOTES

1. Adrienne Rich, *Of Woman Born* (New York: Norton, 1976), pp. 69, 101.

2. Audre Lorde, *The Uses of the Erotic* (New York: Out and Out Books, 1978), pp., 3–4.

3. Ibid., p. 3

4. Ibid., p. 5.

5. I should perhaps note that this interpretation of Marx and of the possibilities for a nonrepressive *eros* shares much with Marcuse's account but differs from his views in some respects. He suggests that the possibility of resexualizing the body and the consequent decline of genital supremacy is located in the fact that the body would no longer need to be a full-time instrument of labor and thus could achieve a certain separation from necessity. The increased play time could serve as the basis for transforming work. See Herbert Marcuse, *Eros and Civilization* (Boston: Beacon Press, 1955), Chap. 11. My view of the possibilities inherent in work itself is more optimistic. In addition, I cannot accept his contention that the reality of a nonrepressive existence is denied by the exist-

ence of death, since timelessness is the ideal for which pleasure strives (ibid., pp. 231–35).

6. See, for example, the articles in the special issues on sexuality published by several journals. *Signs: Journal of Woman, Culture, and Society* 5, no. 4, and 6, no. 1 (Summer and Fall 1980); *Heresies*, no.12 (1980); *Radical History Review*, 20 (Spring/Summer 1979). This last point is especially prominent in Anne Snitow, "Mass Market Romance" *Radical History Review* 20 (Spring/Summer 1979).

7. Niles Newton, "Interrelationships Between Sexual Responsiveness, Birth, and Breast-Feeding," in *Contemporary Sexual Behavior*, ed. Joseph Zubin and John Money (Baltimore: The Johns Hopkins University Press, 1971), p. 95.

8. Ibid., p. 83. The preceding paragraph summarized pp. 80-83

9. Ibid., p. 84.

10. Susan Weisskopf, "Maternal Sexuality and Asexual Motherhood," *Signs* 5, no. 4 (Summer 1980): 770.

11. The quoted phrase is Janice Moulton's, from "Sex and Reference," in *Philosophy and Sex*, ed. Robert Baker and Frederick Elliston (Buffalo, NY: Prometheus, 1975). In addition I am indebted to Sarah Begus for pointing this out to me. See her "Sexual Relations of Domination" (mimeo.), p. 20.

12. See for example Gayle Rubin, "The Leather Menace: Comments on Politics and S/M," in *Coming to Power*, ed. Samois (Palo Alto, Calif.: Up Press, 1981); and for another view, see *Off Our Backs* 12, no. 6 (June 1982).

13. Susan Farr, "The Art of Discipline: Creating Erotic Dramas of Play and Power," in Samois, ed., *Coming to Power*, p. 183.

14. See Pat Califia, "Feminism and Sadomasochism," *Heresies*, no. 13 (1980): 32; Amber Hollibaugh and Cherrie Moraga, "What We're Rollin' Around in Bed With," *Heresies*, no. 13 (1980): 60; Pat Califia, *Sapphistry* (n.e.: Naiad Press, 1980), pp. 124, 125, 128.

15. E.g., Pat Califia's statement that "most of us feel some guilt or shame about being sexual" (*Sapphistry*, p. 131). See also Sarah Zoftig, "Coming Out," pp., 88, 93; Pat Califia, "Jessie," p. 167; Gayle Rubin, "The Leather Menace," p. 215; and Sophie Schmuckler, "How I Learned to Stop Worrying and Love My Dildo," pp. 98–99, all in Samois, ed., *Coming to Power*.

16. Snitow, "Mass Market Romance," p.151.

17. Ibid

18. Audre Lorde, "The Master's Tools Will Never Dismantle the Master's House," in *This Bridge Called My Back*, ed. Cherrie Moraga and Gloria Anzaldua (Watertown, Mass.: Persephone Press, 1981), p.99.

19. Marcel Mauss, *The Gift*, trans. Ian Cunnison (New York: Norton, 1967), pp. 4, 26, 35 respectively.

20. Ibid, pp. 39–40. See also pp. 38, 73.

21. Ibid., p. 11.

22. Ibid., p. 101.

23. Ibid., pp. 79, 80. See also Marshal Sahlins, *Stone Age Economics* (Chicago: Aldine-Atherton, 1972), pp. 172 ff.

24. Mauss, *The Gift*, pp. 11, 79.

25. Marx, *Economic and Philosophic Manuscripts of 1844*, ed. Dirk Stuik (New York: International Publishers, 1964), p.117.

APPENDIXES

He writes that you are currency, an item of exchange. He writes barter, barter, possession and acquisition of women and merchandise.

Better for you to see your guts in the sun and utter the death-rattle than to live a life that anyone can appropriate.

MONIQUE WITTIG, *Les Guèrilléres*

1

The Kinship Abstraction
in Feminist Theory

Like the lives of proletarians as described by Marx, women's lives make available a particular and privileged vantage point on phallocratic social relations and ideology. I propose to use the accounts I have developed of the world views of both the exchange abstraction and abstract masculinity to examine a category central to masculinist ideologies, that of kinship and the family. Claude Lévi-Strauss's work has frequently been used as a starting point for a feminist theory of the patriarchy. This theory, however, emerges from a phallocratic perspective that ignores women's lives and instead treats women as unreal beings who are at bottom simply symbols created by the male mind. Just as Marx's understanding of the world from the standpoint of the proletariat enabled him to get beneath bourgeois ideology, so a feminist standpoint can allow us to see patriarchal ideologies as inversions of real social relations.

A number of feminist theorists have been impressed with Claude Lévi-Strauss's theory that the exchange of women marks the human transition from nature to culture and have credited him with laying the basis for developing a political economy of sex.[1] They are not alone in admiring his work. Lévi-Strauss has been credited with so much by so many that it appears as if his outlook is so amorphous that one sees only. one's own views reflected back from a reading of his work. His elusiveness (and seductiveness) is demonstrated by the fact that a single author can variously characterize him as a return to Rousseau by way of Plato; as having been influenced by geology, Marx, and Freud; and as attempting to synthesize the responsibilities of the anthropologist with both Marxist thought and the Buddhist tradition.[2] Others have suggested that Lévi-Strauss has affinities with Kant; has been influenced by Rousseau; has formulated a Hobbesian social contract; and/or has synthesized Freud, Rousseau, and Marx. He has even been explored as a sociobiologist.[3] Given the diversity—and even oppositions of these commentators to each other—one wonders what to make of this.

On the basis of my own reading of Lévi-Strauss (I begin to think most readings of his work are idiosyncratic), I argue that his theorization of the exchange of women must be set within the context of his more general theory and that far from being an adequate starting point for feminist theory, it leads toward a phallocratic mystification of women's material lives and a location of women's oppression in the sphere of ideology rather than material social relations. If one addresses Lévi-Strauss's work from the insistently materialist vantage point provided by the feminist standpoint, if one reads him with feet firmly planted in the coarsely sensuous ground of female existence, his work can be shown to articulate a series of artificial and ahistorical dualisms: culture/ nature, mind/body, abstract/concrete, science/savage thought, stasis/change, saying/doing, quantity/quality, exchange/use, strangers/kin. An understanding of social life based on these dualisms can posit only a fragile and problematic social synthesis, one that sees contracts and the exchanges constructed by them not as "secondary creations" but as the "basic material of social life."[4] Some of these dualisms have their source in the exchange abstraction analyzed in Part I. Others are more easily located in abstract masculinity. The various faults to which I point are prominent in different areas of his theory—some emerge most explicitly in his discussion of language and symbol systems, others in his discussion of kinship, and still others in his description of the scientific enterprise in which he sees himself engaged. Because feminists have been most influenced by Lévi-Strauss's kinship theory, my attention focuses there, and my attention to other aspects of his thought serves to situate the kinship theory on more general terrain in order to demonstrate the full extent of its perniciousness. I argue, then, that despite his own protestations of being more faithful to Marx than his critics, Lévi-Strauss, because of his search for an eternal and natural human nature, and because of his stress on what he takes to be the creations of the human mind, cannot be considered a Marxist. And despite his sadness at what he sees as the loss of the West's "opportunity of remaining female," and despite his lauding of Buddhism as the hope for the world because it integrates excess by means of "the unifying reassurance implicit in the promise of a return to the maternal breast," his work must be understood as an expression of abstract masculinity.[5]

If this reading of Lévi-Strauss can be supported, it would not only cast doubt on his claims to be carrying on Marxist theory by contributing to the development of a theory of superstructure or by carrying on the work of Lewis Henry Morgan, but also would lay the basis for an overdue rejection of his work as a basis for developing a political economy of sex.[6]

Language, Symbols, and Values

Let us begin with Lévi-Strauss's work on symbol systems, since he sets out from language and linguistics. It is on the basis of his work in linguistics that Lévi-Strauss is able to argue that language, cooking, and the incest taboo represent a series of isomorphisms. All are created by the human mind, and each is what one commentator described as a screen to filter "the anonymous natural world and turn it into names, signs, and qualities. They change the shapeless torrent of life into a discrete quantity and into families of symbols."[7]

As Lévi-Strauss moves through what he sees as three sets of symbol systems sharing a single structure, one can perhaps best describe his trajectory in the terms a feminist poet used to describe the male mind. It is decided, she intones, that "there are three degrees of abstraction, each leading to higher truths. The scientist peels away uniqueness, revealing category; the mathematician peels away sensual fact, revealing number; the metaphysician peels away even number and reveals the fruit of pure being."[8] This is indeed what Lévi-Strauss believes his work does—revealing the underlying categories that structure human thought, developing what one commentator has termed "the rudiments of a semantic algebra,"[9] and finally, by means of an encounter with Buddhism, reaching true being and recognizing that the creations of the human mind are simply "the transient efflorescence of a creation in relation to which they have no meaning, except perhaps that of allowing to play its [destructive] part in creation."[10]

The voyage begins by way of an analogy between anthropology and linguistics. Lévi-Strauss points out that anthropology and linguistics share something fundamental: "*Both* language and culture are the products of activities which are basically similar. I am now referring to this uninvited guest which has been seated during this Conference beside us and which is *the human mind*."[11] The human mind demands order, and this demand for order forms the basis for both primitive and scientific thought. Thus, life is ruled by a universal and unconscious reason, identical for both the savage and the civilized.[12] Both forms of thought center on an insistence on differentiation, on a "logical subordination of resemblance to contrast." In both systems, in cooking rules and in kinship systems built on the model of the incest taboo, one finds, he argues, the dichotomizing activity to be fundamental.[13] All classification proceeds by pairs of contrasts, and the progressive purification of reality by means of abstraction ends in a "final term," which takes the form of a simple binary opposition.[14] Thus, dualism is not only intentionally present in his work but also structures it fundamentally. Dualism forms the basis for a grid that produces meaning itself.[15]

Despite their similar structure, however, the scientific and savage mind proceed along different paths: The one is timeless, the other located in history; the one supremely concrete, the other supremely abstract; the one proceeding from sensible qualities, the other from formal properties; the one producing the neolithic arts, the other, contemporary science.[16] While the savage '*bricoleur*' speaks only through the medium of things, as opposed to the scientist who abstracts, both science and mythic thought are held to operate by reducing multiplicity to a few basic principles.

In both cases, the mind's demand for order follows universal and natural paths dependent on the construction of the human brain, a physicochemical object. The structure then is not historical but natural, and in it resides the real human nature.[17] One critic has pointed out some of the inconsistencies that result from reliance on the assumptions (1) that "what is universally true must be natural," and (2) that "what distinguishes the human being from the man-animal is the distinction between culture and nature—i.e., that the humanity of man is that which is non-natural."[18] Lévi-Strauss's preoccupation with the latter assumption emerges in his claim that language represents the shift from animality and nature to culture. the relation to the natural world is without the symbolization present in every social act.[19] The problem is compounded by the artificiality with which Lévi-Strauss holds that the human mind creates culture by intentional act. Culture, according to Lévi-Strauss, is an artificial creation of the human mind, an activity of creating aloneness out of social being by dichotomizing the world into my tribe and yours, thereby creating strangers who must be made if not kin, relatives by marriage.

This creation of strangers who are made affines on the basis of the universal dichotomizing needs of the human brain is of particular interest here. Lévi-Strauss contends that the study of kinship presents the anthropologist with a situation that formally resembles that of the structural linguist. "Like phonemes, kinship terms are elements of meaning; like phonemes, they acquire meaning only if they are integrated into systems. 'Kinship systems,' like 'phonemic systems,' are built by the mind on the level of unconscious thought."[20] The transformation of raw sound into phoneme is reproduced in the transformation of animal sexuality into a matrimonial system, an operation that selects and combines either verbal signs or signs in the form of women.[21]

Thus he proposes to treat the kinship system as a kind of language, a "set of processes, permitting the establishment, between individuals and groups, of a certain type of communication. That the mediating factor, in this case, should be the *women of the group*, who are circulated between clans, lineages, or families, in place of the *words of the group*, which are *circulated* between individuals, does not at all change the fact that the essential aspect of the phenomenon is identical in both cases."[22] Not only can kinship be treated as a language, but the study of women in the communication system between men may afford an image of the relationship that might have existed at an early period in the development of language between human actors and their words.[23] Lévi-Strauss's interest in kinship, then, can be seen to flow logically (if not historically or biographically) from this interest in the nature of symbol systems. Most particularly, he sees a study of kinship as a means for moving outside history, a means for understanding better the timelessness of the savage mind. The equation is thus posited:

$$\frac{women}{men} = \frac{words}{savage}.$$

Kinship and language, then, both mediate between nature and culture and divide the human from the natural or animal world. Lévi-Strauss holds that matrimonial exchange of women falls midway between nature and culture. Women are "natural products naturally procreated by other biological individuals," as opposed to the goods and services which are "social products culturally manufactured by technical agents."[24] The *system* of women functions, then, as a "middle term between the system of (natural) living creatures and the system of (manufactured) objects."[25]

Let us look a bit more closely at the ways this discussion of symbol systems expresses the perspective of abstract masculinity and the exchange abstraction by exploring the dualisms that emerge from this account. We can then see how these are both replicated and expanded in Lévi-Strauss's account of the exchange of women. The most prominent aspects of the two abstractions appear in his stress on the need to translate concrete, sensual qualities into abstract quantity and symbols, his separation of mind from body, his contradictory separation of natural and social, his opposition of doing to saying, and change to stasis (history vs. myth). These dualisms lead him, like the adherents of the exchange abstraction or the abstract masculinity discussed above, into idealism and into a series of contradictions and counterfactual statements.

Lévi-Strauss's first move toward abstraction is his reduction of the immense variety of societies and histories to a dichotomy—primitive thought vs. civilized or scientific thought. He then, however, discovers that this dichotomy is part of a second opposition, that of nature to culture. He contends that the products of culture—myths, language, kinship, cooking—obey natural laws.[26] Thus, despite the status of language and kinship as intentional human inventions for the purpose of taking control of nature, Lévi-Strauss can also hold that they are themselves "natural," since they result from "objective structure of the psyche and of the brain."[27] Thus, what one commentator referred to as Lévi-Strauss's "formalistic search for binary oppositions and their multiple permutations and combinations" must instead be understood as an effort to uncover natural and universal features of the human mind.[28]

Lévi-Strauss's resolution of the opposition, nature/culture, by means of positing a formal structural commonality, and his location of this commonality in physico-biochemical structure of the brain, forms the base for several further, and ironically idealist, dualisms and counterfactuals. Lévi-Strauss's working out of what one commentator was tempted to call a "transcendent object," as opposed to the Kantian transcendent subject, leads him into a mind/body dualism in which the mind almost disappears and then reemerges as all of reality becomes a metaphor. The mind, which Lévi-Strauss has referred to as an external presence, as the creator of culture, symbol systems, and kinship, is contradictorily defined as a "function of inert matter."[29] Perhaps the most telling statement of the opposition and separation of mind and body, and the subordination of the former to the latter, appears in Lévi-Strauss's description of his own existence as merely a "stake" in "the struggle between another society, made up of several thousand million nerve cells lodged in the ant-hill of my skull, and my body, which serves as its robot."[30] The human subject, in a world of other subjects, has been supplanted by an anthill and a robot! The rigid masculine ego boundaries, the opposition of self and other, here take the form of a rigid separation of and struggle between the mind and body. Further, the activities of the feeling and thinking mind are reduced to the actions of several thousand million uncomprehending and scurrying ants in combat with a robot. And this is so despite Lévi-Strauss's contention that the mind is logically prior to social relations.[31]

The primacy of the physico-chemical object leads Lévi-Strauss away from history. If inert matter is the source of being, then one can recover it only by moving outside of history. This is so because, Lévi-Strauss claims, the meaning given by history is never "*the right one*: superstructures are *faulty acts* which have 'made it' socially. Hence it is vain to go to historical consciousness for the truest meaning."[32] Thus, despite the fact that the scientist is condemned to live in history, he must see it as myth. Episodes in history can be expected to "resolve themselves into cerebral, hormonal, or nervous phenomena, which themselves have reference to the physical or chemical order."[33]

It is mythic thought that can provide a lever to extract oneself from history, mythic thought that provides a "machine for the suppression of time." The machine, however, as Lévi-Strauss describes it, operates without human knowledge or interference. If the human creations of myth, symbols, and kinship merely replicate and work out the inbuilt dichotomous passages of the human brain, he can conclude that nature speaks with itself through man without his being aware, that man is a "moment" in a message that nature sends and receives.[34] Perhaps one can now better understand Lévi-Strauss's contention that the creations of the human mind are simply "the transient efflorescence of a creation in relation to which they have no méaning."

Myths, then, must be understood as a kind of paralanguage; the words of the myth do not express its meaning. The true meaning is unconscious, and not accessible to the group that invented the myth. This group, the originators of the myth, does not know its meaning. The conclusion to be drawn is shocking: "Myths communicate with each other by means of men and without men knowing it."[35] The fetishism of such a position is astounding. Not only have relations between persons vanished as accessible objects of knowledge, but persons themselves have become, directly, the instruments of that which they themselves produced as passive instruments of nature. Man himself now becomes, like goods, words, and women, a sign of exchange.[36]

This is a critical step in the eventual evaporation of matter itself into metaphor in Lévi-Strauss's system. The logic moves from inert chemical reactions toward the use of real human beings by the symbols they themselves originally produced. Nature no longer consists of real trees, animals, and insects; these have been transformed into "equations" and "metaphors." Culture becomes a metaphor of the human mind, which is a metaphor of cellular chemical reactions, which in turn are simply to be understood as another metaphor.[37] As one commentator put it succinctly, for Lévi-Strauss, "the symbols are more real than what they symbolize."[38] Metaphors build on each other and come to relate only to each other. Thus, *Tristes Tropiques* concludes, in the excellent paraphrase of an enthusiastic commentator, with these claims:

> Time is also a metaphor and its passage is as illusory as our efforts to halt it: it neither flows nor stops. Our very mortality is illusory: every man who dies assures the survival of the species, each species which becomes extinct confirms the persistence of a movement which rushes timelessly toward an ever-imminent and always unreachable immobility."[39]

(At this point the ghost of Karl Marx can be heard to exclaim, "What horseshit!")

Lévi-Strauss can now be seen to reproduce a variant of the world view of abstract masculinity: He values the abstract and unattainable over the concrete; devalues material life activity in favor of the production of symbols; holds that the body is irrelevant to the real self, an impediment to be overcome by the mind; and contends that what is real is imperceptible to the senses, is unconscious, and accessible only to a mind detached from participation. The human mind's demand for order leads to a one-sided stress on abstraction, formal properties, and self-moving symbol systems at the expense of concrete, many-qualitied, material life.

The fundamental perverseness of such a vision is apparent in several formulations. For example, the relation of mind to body does not even take the form of the struggle of reason to master the appetites, but is instead a struggle between an ant-hill and a robot; the relation of humans to their own symbolic activity is one in which the signs themselves use human beings, instead of vice versa; material life is evaporated into a series of metaphors; history is abandoned in favor of myth. The masculinist inversion of life into death takes the form in Lévi-Strauss's work of the death of subjectivity both in his contention that myths speak to each other through the medium of men, and without men knowing it, and in his argument that life can in the end be understood as the operation of inert matter.

As I noted above, abstract masculinity has a great deal in common with the perspective imposed by commodity exchange. The separation and opposition of social and natural worlds, of abstract and concrete, of permanence and change, the effort to define only the former of each pair as important, the reliance on a series of counterfactual assumptions characteristic of both structure Lévi-Strauss's work. His work represents still another shared aspect. Both abstract masculinity and the exchange abstraction form the basis for a problematic, fragile, and conflictual social synthesis. The problematic nature of this synthesis, along with the dualism of exchange vs. use and strangers vs. kin, emerges most clearly in the context of Lévi-Strauss's argument that kinship is constituted by the exchange of women.[40]

The Exchange of Women as Social Contract

In *The Elementary Structures of Kinship*, Lévi-Strauss stated that his task was to demonstrate that all kinship systems and types of marriage hitherto excluded from the category of marriage were part of the general classification "methods of exchange."[41] There is, however, a deeper purpose of his work, one to which he frequently alludes: He is concerned with the creation and maintenance of the human group. The exchange of women (and, he notes, "the rule of exogamy which expresses it"), "provides the means of binding men together, and superimposing upon the natural links of kinship the henceforth artificial links—artificial in the sense that they are removed from chance encounters or the promiscuity of family life—of alliance governed by rule."[42] Human society, then, is an artificial creation, separated from the natural world by the intervention of purposeful human will, which replaces chance by organization. The incest taboo, then, can be described as man's "first 'no' against nature," an expression of "the transition from the natural fact of consanguinity to the cultural fact of alliance."[43]

Exchange for Lévi-Strauss is fundamental to purposeful human activity, since it forces natural sentiments and biological relationships into artificial social structures. And purposeful human activity, in turn, is essential, since, as Lévi-Strauss notes, without purposeful intervention, human society might not exist.[44] (One must remind oneself that human society both is and is not artifical for Lévi-Strauss. On the one hand, it requires purposeful intervention; on the other, this intervention can only take the form of imposing a dichotomy, which can then be resolved. The need to impose such a dichotomy is located in the physico-chemical structure of the brain itself.)

Regularized exchange of women results from the scarcity of women, which in turn results from a "natural and universal" feature of human existence—the "deep polygamous tendency, which exists among all men, always makes the number of available women seem insufficient. Let us add that even if there were as many women as men, those women would not all be equally desirable. ... Hence, the demand for women is in actual fact, or to all intents and purposes, always in a state of disequilibrium and tension." Thus, Lévi-Strauss claims, monogamy is not itself an institution "but merely incorporates the limit of polygamy in societies where, for highly varied reasons, economic and sexual competition reaches an acute form."[45] In addition, the social division of labor in primitive societies makes women highly valued members of the family. The human group, then, controls women as a scarce and essential valuable and "institutes freedom of access for every individual [male] to the women of the group." In so doing, the groups create a system in which "all men are in equal competition for all women."[46] In the light of these contentions, it is curious that women but not children are circulating commodities. Indeed, Lévi-Strauss himself notes that pygmy societies, because of their division of labor, consider women *and children* to be the most valuable of the family group.[47] One can only conclude that this is a result of Lévi-Strauss's unwillingness to see any males as commodities.

Lévi-Strauss characterizes the situation as an equal competition, even though few men are allowed to practice polygamy. He argues that the chief's privilege of polygamy is part of a collective bargain, or primitive social contract. "By recognizing the privilege, the group has exchanged the *elements of individual security* which accompany the rule of monogamy for a "*collective security* arising out of political organization." In return for his services, the chief receives several women from the group, which has suspended the "common law" for him. "Polygamy, therefore, does not run counter to the demand for an equitable distribution of women. It merely superimposes one rule of distribution upon another."[48] That is, members of the community exchange individual security, the price of which is the unequal distribution of scarce valuables. Some relinquish their share of these valuables in order to procure an equal share of the collective safety.

Group solidarity, then, based on the exchange of women, represents the "most immediate way to integrate opposition between the self and others," since the transfer of a valuable good makes two separate and opposed individuals into partners.[49] Soical relations, then, take place between men, the only real actors, *by means of* women, or through the mediation of women, who are, in Lévi-Strauss's words, "merely the occasion of this real relationship.[50] The exchange of women in primitive societies does not involve profit in Western terms; it is a total and reciprocal transaction that has the function of creating solidarity. Lévi-Strauss argues that the prohibition against incest is less to prevent marriage with mother or sister than to require that they be given to other men. This is the "supreme rule of the gift."[51] Its role is to establish a community by establishing kin.

The exchange of women as a means for transforming strangers into affines or relatives by marriage prominently carries with it several of the specific dualities present in the exchange of commodities: the separation of exchange from use, quantity from quality, interaction with nature from social interaction, the opposition of participants in the transaction, and the problematic social synthesis. The other features of the exchange abstraction and abstract masculinity analyzed in the context of Lévi-Strauss's analysis of symbol systems are less directly present in his account of the exchange of women. One must remember, however, that language and the incest taboo are isomorphic for Lévi-Strauss: The one simply recapitulates the other.[52]

In the exchange of women the abstract and qualityless character of the commodity appears in Lévi-Strauss's insistence on the need to see women as signs with only two possible values: "same" or "other." He himself underlines the abstractness in this formulation when he adds that in some groups, the same women originally offered in exchange can be exchanged in return: "All that is necessary on either side is the sign of otherness, which is the outcome of a certain position in a structure and not of any innate characteristic. . . ."[53] The exchange of women as described by Lévi-Strauss, then, is characterized by an absence of qualities and differentiation of exchange objects only according to quantity—quantity of other women to be exchange in return, or cows, or cash. The qualitylessness gives them their reality in exchange.

The separation of exchange from use is present in the form of the incest taboo. Here, too, as in the exchange of commodities, the separation of exchange from use results in a separation of mind from action, where the use to which the women will be put is present in the minds and not the actions of the participants. Their minds are focused on the private; their actions are social. The result of this separation is the theoretical weight Lévi-Strauss gives to mind and to abstract and quantitative differences, coupled with his treatment of the activities of mind as profoundly different entities than those of the body.

The separation of nature from society is present, since the woman's change in status is purely social. Yet here, the exchange of women begins to differ from commodity exchange. Lévi-Strauss holds that the exchange of women marks the boundary between nature and culture, and mediates between the two terms. Rather than take place on only one side of the dualities, it brings them together. There is a second difference in the exchange of women from one lineage to the other. Unlike the exchange of commodities, it transforms all participants in the transaction. The buyer or seller of a commodity remains buyer or seller after the purchase/sale, but after a woman is exchanged, those who were strangers are now affines, and the woman herself becomes part of another lineage, a married women, an adult. Every participant occupies a different place afterward. Dualism still reverberates through the transaction, but it is a more complex and contradictory dualism, which transforms not just the social status of the object in question but all other oppositions as well. Yet they remain as oppositions within the social synthesis created by the exchange of women.

The duality contained in the woman herself as both same and other is replicated in the opposition and duality of the separate men exchanging her, although there the opposition is embodied in the dual forms of men and not contained in a simple body. Each recognizes the other as an other who is not yet kin. Each move made by the one must be countered by the other for the exchange to succeed. The needs, feelings, and thoughts involved on both sides are polarized on the basis of whose they are. Not what they think but whose feeling or need will prevail is what shapes the relationship. That is, exchange requires solipsism between the participants. It is a relation between strangers. Lévi-Strauss includes this aspect of the exchange abstraction, too, in his theory. In the societies he describes, he argues, "either a man is a kinsman, actually, or by fiction, or he is a person to whom you have no reciprocal obligations and whom you treat as a potential enemy."[54]

This polar relation represents for Lévi-Strauss a characteristic inherent in any social relation. It represents a "universal situation" in which one is either part of a community formed by reciprocal obligations or else one is an enemy.[55] The fact that when strangers meet, enmity is presumed indicates that, for Lévi-Strauss, communities arise out of what can only be described as a Hobbesian need for security in a hostile world, a need for security so great that the individual will sacrifice his "naturally polygamous tendencies" in return for it.

Hobbes too has given an account of the organization of civil society by means of a covenant setting up a sovereign not subject to the laws of the community. In Hobbes' system, the scarce product is "power," and every man seeks ever more power over others. The war of each against all in the state of nature is changed by the covenant that institutes commonwealth from a situation in which there was equal insecurity of life and possessions to a situation where there was equal insecurity and equal subordination to the market.[56] While initially this may seem an extreme reading of Lévi-Strauss, one should recall his stress on the ways the incest taboo gives rise to alliance. And one should place him in the tradition of anthropological alliance theorists. One of the earliest and most important of these stated the situation in very Hobbesian terms:

> Among tribes of low culture there is but one means known of keeping up permanent alliance, and that means is inter-marriage. Exogamy, enabling a growing tribe to keep itself compact by constant unions between its spreading clans, enables it to overmatch any number of small intermarrying groups, isolated and helpless. Again and again in the world's history, *savage tribes must have had plainly before their minds the simple practical alternative between marrying-out and being killed out.* Even far in culture, the political value of inter-marriage remains.[57]

For Lévi-Strauss, as for Hobbes, community must be artificially yet necessarily always created through the imposition of human will on a natural order. More specifically, community is created through a social contract whereby terms are set for the exchange of valued commodities. Scarce goods, too, make their appearance. Due to the natural polygamous tendencies of men, the community created through the exchange of women is characterized by a scarcity of women, just as the community created through the exchange of commodities is characterized by the scarcity of commodities relative to demand. Men compete for women on equal terms, just as buyers compete with each other for commodities in market. This, Lévi-Strauss maintains, is true even when only a few men are allowed to possess most of the women.[58] Moreover, the men associate with each other for their mutual profit. Lévi-Strauss contends that the individual always "receives more than he gives" and "gives more than he receives."[59] In sum, Lévi-Strauss is arguing that all human groups are composed of the isolated individuals familiar to us from the social-contract theories of the seventeenth and eighteenth centuries. They associate with each other voluntarily, less for gain than for collective security.[60]

Thus, in positing exchange and mutual fear as the explanation for community Lévi-Strauss is suggesting that community, whatever form it takes, illustrates "the various modalities of one primitive need, the need for security."[61] On his account, and given the differences between the exchange of women and the exchange of commodities, it appears that the fragility of the social synthesis follows less from the exchange abstraction itself than from the operation of abstract masculinity. The social synthesis is made poorer by the fact that community is not an end in itself, but arises as a by-product of the search for security in a world seen as populated by hostile others. It is weakened as well by the fact that the integration of the perceived opposition of the self and other takes only indirect forms.

The hostile and combative dualism at the heart of the masculinist world view allows the creation of community with another only through the mediation of things. The Hegelian death struggle between self and other is prevented from occurring by the exchange of recognition carried in a person or object transferred between the two. The relations they construct, then, are only indirect. Lévi-Strauss's claim that this represents an "elemental" and "universal" condition betrays the abstract masculinity of his theory.[62] From a feminist standpoint, in which the self is understood as relationally defined, as constituted by a complex web of interactions with others, it seems perverse to deny a real connection with others and to argue that community can be constituted only indirectly, that men relate only through the mediation of things, that social relations are intentionally created by the act of passing things (most significantly, words and women) back and forth. Lévi-Strauss's work raises the question why even primitive men (at least as understood by Western anthropologists) have to (1) use women as mediators of their relations and (2) socially construct "others" who then must be socially transformed into kin by making the women of one's own clan "other."

The strangeness of all this is only a little compounded by the counterfactual on which the whole theory of the exchange of women rests: Women are not fully human. Why would reasoning, sign-producing beings, possessed of their own needs and desires, consent to becoming rather than possessing valuable objects? To becoming rather than producing signs?[63]

If we begin from the realities of women's lives, it is hard to imagine that women are not humans, but are the means by which humans (men) communicate and establish a social synthesis. On the basis of a division of labor analysis, one can see that the reality is the reverse. Women are not, as Lévi-Strauss would have it, the creation of an intentional act of the male mind, the invention of a symbol by means of which to construct society and to distinguish it from nature. Women are the literal and material producers of men, who in turn like to imagine that the situation is the reverse.

Lévi-Strauss's Marxism

The ridiculousness of Lévi-Strauss's claims to be making a contribution to Marxist theory should now be apparent, although this evaluation flies in the

face of Lévi-Strauss's own claims, as well as those of a number of commentators. Lévi-Strauss argues that he does not intend to question the primacy of the
"infrastructure" or base and that he does not mean to give priority to superstructures, despite the attention he devotes to them. Moreover, he does "not at
all mean to suggest that ideological transformations give rise to social ones.
Only the reverse is in fact true. Men's conception of the relations between
nature and culture is a function of modifications of their own social
relations."[64]

Despite the fact that he does not mean to, Lévi-Strauss parts company
with Marx on a number of fundamental grounds. First, he holds that produc-
tion-based analysis applies only to historical (read Western) societies, and
argues that others are based instead on blood ties and better understood
through myth. He even seems to regret the technical progress Marx held essential to the possibility of communism. Second, he argues that "praxis" and
"practice" are different and must be connected by the mediation of the conceptual framework. This not only runs counter to Marx's contention that theory
and practice imply each other, but also leads Lévi-Strauss to transform the
"mediation" into the primacy of the intellect in opposition to the primacy Marx
gave to concrete human practice. This marks the third difference between Lévi-
Strauss and Marx.

Lévi-Strauss contends that "all social life, however elementary, presup-
poses an intellectual activity in man of which the formal properties cannot,
accordingly, be a reflection of the concrete organization of society."[65] Intellectual activity does not reflect the social organization of society; rather, it emanates from the intellect, the human mind ever the same and located outside
history. Indeed, Lévi-Strauss has been characterized as "the very incarnation of
the structuralist faith in the permanency of human nature and the unity of
reason."[66] Marx, in contrast, had a historical concept of nature and a materialist
concept of history. For Marx, human beings are at once social, historical, and
natural beings. Because Lévi-Strauss rejects this view in favor of a permanent
human nature, his materialism boils down to a positivist faith that humanity
will eventually be understood as a series of chemico-biological processes.[67]
Fourth, Lévi-Strauss's account of kinship as marking the boundary between
nature and culture, as a solution to the opposition of self and other, indicates
his assumption that human beings are not intrinsically social, but must intentionally construct a society. Marx explicitly rejected this assumption.

Finally, Lévi-Strauss parts company with Marx at the level of method.
While he has been credited with employing Marx's method, his own descriptions of anthropology and linguistics make it abundantly clear that his method
has far more in common with contemporary positivism than with Marxism.[68]
Lévi-Strauss, unlike Marx, accepts the dichotomy of natural from social science.
He remarks that "for centuries, the humanities and the social sciences have
resigned themselves to contemplating the world of the natural and exact sciences as a kind of paradise which they will never enter."[69] Linguistics, however,
is crossing the "borderline" into the natural sciences, and is studying language
in a "manner which permits it to serve as an object of truly scientific
analysis."[70] Moreover, he contends that science requires value neutrality in
order to be objective, another very "un-Marxist" contention.

The study of anthropology can only be scientific, he claims, if one "abstains from making judgments" that compare the objectives societies have chosen.[71] The anthropologist faces the dilemma of either contributing to the improvement of his own community, in which case he must condemn social conditions similar to those he is fighting against, wherever they exist, and "in which case he relinquishes his objectivity and impartiality. Conversely, the detachment to which he is constrained by moral scrupulousness and scientific accuracy prevents him criticizing his own society, since he is refraining from judging any one society in order to acquire knowledge of them all." The "thirst for universal understanding," he argues, "involves renouncing all possibility of reform."[72] He attempts to draw back from this dilemma by two means: (1) arguing that all societies contain a residue of evil, and that moderation should be used in considering customs remote from the West; and (2) advocating a Buddhist-inspired contemplation of "that tenuous arch linking us to the inaccessible," in "grasping ... the essense of what it was and continues to be, below the threshold of thought and over and above society."[73] The only means he seems to see of escaping from positivism, then, takes the form of an escape into nonmeaning, and a glorification of the "scent that can be smelt at the heart of a lily [which] is more imbued with learning than all our books."[74]

Lévi-Strauss's thought, then, represents a contradictory amalgam that is at once deeply phallocratic, abstract, antimaterialist, ahistorical, and even mystical. Such a theory poses deep problems for both Marxists and feminists. And the implications of such a theory go far beyond the work of Lévi-Strauss himself and those who have used his work. Lévi-Strauss, after all, based his work on the dualist linguistic theories of Saussure, was a part of the structuralist tradition, and in turn influenced the development of poststructural "deconstructionism."[75] If the ancestry of contemporary deconstructionism is such, then despite the very real feminist commitments of many deconstructionists, one must ask about the effects theories such as Lévi-Strauss's have had on the understanding of symbol systems. How can such a theory be of use to feminist Marxists? One can only expect that those who have taken his theory as a base for their own, or have incorporated his theory into their own, will encounter a number of difficulties in putting forward a materialist account of women's oppression. Let us turn now to see the use two feminist theorists have made of his work and the effects it has had on their own thinking.

NOTES

1. See esp. Gayle Rubin, "The Traffic in Women: Notes on the 'Political Economy' of Sex," in *Toward an Anthropology of Women*, ed. R. Reiter (New York: Monthly Review, 1975); Simone de Beauvoir, *The Second Sex*, trans. H. M. Parshley (New York: Knopf, 1953); and Juliet Mitchell, *Psychoanalysis and Feminism* (New York: Pantheon, 1974).

2. Octavio Paz, *Claude Lévi-Strauss: An Introduction*, trans. J. S. Bernstein and Maxine Bernstein (Ithaca: Cornell University Press, 1970), pp. 133, 63, 5 respectively.

3. Respectively, Paul Ricoeur, cited in Paz, *Claude Lévi-Strauss*, p. 129; Rousseau's influence is mentioned by Edmund Leach, *Claude Lévi-Strauss* (New York: Viking, 1970), p. 35; and Thomas Shalvey, *Claude Lévi-Strauss: Social Psychotherapy and the Collective Unconscious* (Amherst, Mass.: University of Massachusetts Press, 1979), p. 59. Marshall Sahlins credits him with Hobbesianism in "The Spirit of the Gift," in *Stone Age Economics* (Chicago: Aldine-Atherton, 1972); Shalvey, p. 61, credits him as trying to synthesize Freud, Rousseau, and Marx and also devotes a chapter to Lévi-Strauss as socio-biologist.

4. Lévi-Strauss, *Tristes Tropiques*, trans. John and Doreen Weightman, (New York: Atheneum, 1974), p. 315.

5. The quotations come from ibid., pp. 409, 407 respectively. They occur in the course of a more lengthly and very interesting argument that Islam is a barracks religion but also that it resembles Western society. "If one were looking for a barracks room religion, Islam would seem to be the ideal solution: strict observance of rules (prayers five times a day, each prayer necessitating fifty-genuflexions); detailed inspections and meticulous cleanliness (ritual ablutions); masculine promiscuity both in spiritual matters and in the carrying out of the organic functions; and no women" (p. 403). Buddhism, in contrast, is for Lévi-Strauss a female religion. As he discusses the temples of the Burmese frontier, he notes that the sculpture seems to be outside time and space, the sculptors perhaps in possession of "some machine for abolishing time." If any art has a right to be called eternal this is surely it. "It is akin to the pyramids and to our domestic architecture; the human shapes engraved in the pink, closegrained stone could step down and mingle with the society of the living. No statuary gives a deeper feeling of peace and familiarity than this with its chastely immodest women and its maternal sensuality which delights in contrasting mother-mistress with sequestered girls, both of which are in opposition to the sequestered mistresses of non-Buddhist India: it expresses a placid femininity which seems to have been freed from the battle of the sexes, a femininity which is also suggested by the temple priests whose shaven heads make them indistinguishable from the nuns, with whom they form a kind of third sex, half parasitical and half captive.

"If Buddhism like Islam, has tried to control the excesses of primitive cults, it has done so by means of the unifying reassurance implicit in the promise of a return to the maternal breast; by this approach, it has reintegrated eroticism within itself after divesting it of frenzy and anguish. Islam on the contrary has developed according to a masculine orientation. By shutting women away it denies access to the maternal breasts: man has turned the female world into a closer entity. No doubt, by this means he too hopes to attain serenity; but he makes it depend on a principle of exclusion: women are excluded from social life and infidels from the spiritual community. Buddhism, on the other hand, conceives of its serenity as a form of fusion: with women, with mankind in general, and in an asexual representation of the divinity" (p. 407). This characterization seems very much influenced by Rousseau—the return to the modern-day noble savage by way of Buddhism. Note the traditional regional and sexual dichotomies: active/passive; West/East; and the characterization of the latter as female, placid, indistinguishable, and attempting fusion.

6. These two claims occur respectively in Claude Lévi-Strauss, *The Savage Mind* (Chicago: University of Chicago Press, 1966), p. 130; and idem, *Structural Anthropology* (New York: Anchor, 1967) pp. 336–37.

7. Paz, *Claude Lévi-Strauss*, pp. 50–51. He goes on to note that the texture of the screen is death—the need to distinguish between nature and culture contains "the echo and the obsession of knowing ourselves to be mortal" (p. 51).

8. Susan Griffin, *Woman and Nature* (New York: Harper & Row), p. 6.

9. Leach, *Claude Lévi-Strauss*, p. 32.

10. Lévi-Strauss, *Tristes Tropiques*, p. 413

11. Lévi-Strauss, *Structural Anthropology*, p. 70.

12. Lévi-Strauss, *The Savage Mind*, pp. 9–10. See also Paz, *Claude Lévi-Strauss*, p. 133.

13. Lévi-Strauss, *The Savage Mind*, pp. 106, 75, 159.

14. Ibid., p. 217.

15. Ibid., pp. 75 ff. See also Leach, *Claude Lévi-Strauss*, p. 37.

16. Lévi-Strauss, *The Savage Mind*, p. 269. This represents a very interesting argument in favor of Sohn-Rethel's thesis that abstract thought required the previous introduction of exchange. There is also an interesting sexual overlay, since more than one theorist has argued that the inventions of the neolithic period—animal husbandry, pottery, weaving, preparation and conservation of food—were women's inventions, while modern science has been argued to spring from men's rather than women's experience. See Evelyn Fox Keller, "Gender and Science," and Sandra Harding, "The Gender-Politics Structuring the Scientific World View," in *Discovering Reality: Feminist Perspectives on Metaphysics, Methodology, and the Philosophy of Science*, ed. Sandra Harding and Merrill Provence Hintikka (Dordrecht: Reidel Publishing, 1983). See also Paz, *Claude Lévi-Strauss*, p. 117.

17. See Paz, *Claude Lévi-Strauss*, pp. 116, 133.

18. Leach, *Claude Lévi-Strauss*, p. 121.

19. Ibid., pp. 34, 41, 21.

20. Lévi-Strauss, *Structural Anthropology*, p. 32. He notes some difficulties, but hopes that it will be possible (pp. 37 ff).

21. The explicitness of this statement is Paz's. *Claude Lévi-Strauss*, p. 18.

22. Lévi-Strauss, *Structural Anthropology*, p. 60.

23. Ibid., pp. 60–61.

24. Lévi-Strauss, *The Savage Mind*, p. 123.

25. Ibid., p. 128. Put another way, natural species and manufactured objects are two mediating sets "which man employs to overcome the opposition between nature and culture and think of them as a whole" (p. 127). Cooking, too, for Lévi-Strauss is an activity that both separates and unites nature and culture, but discussion of this activity is not essential to my argument here. See Paz, *Claude Lévi-Strauss*, pp. 50 ff, for an account of the significance of the shared forms.

26 Paz, *Claude Lévi-Strauss*, p. 132, makes a part of this case. He, however, writes as an admirer of Lévi-Strauss. In addition, he argues—wrongly, I believe—that the products of culture are not for Lévi-Strauss essentially different

from natural products. This, however, takes as given and correct Lévi-Strauss's dismissal of the concrete in favor of the formal.

27. Lévi-Strauss, *The Savage Mind*, p. 264.

28. See Leach, *Claude Lévi-Strauss*, p. 62, for the description.

29. Lévi-Strauss, *The Savage Mind*, p. 248. This latter phrase occurs as a part of Lévi-Strauss's argument against Sartre, an argument that one may finally understand all of life as a function of inert matter. The argument bears a certain and interesting resemblance to Stalin's deification of the "productive forces" in his *Historical and Dialectical Materialism*. The suggestion of transcendental objectivism occurs in Paz, *Claude Lévi-Strauss*, p. 129 ff.

30. Lévi-Strauss, *Tristes Tropiques*, p. 414.

31. See the discussion in Jean Piaget, *Structuralism*, trans. Chaninah Marchler, (New York: Harper & Row, 1970), pp. 106–7, 112.

32. Lévi-Strauss, *The Savage Mind*, p. 254. This argument occurs in his largely well taken critique of Sartre.

33. Ibid., pp. 255, 257.

34. See Paz, *Claude Lévi-Strauss*, p. 133.

35. Ibid., p. 39. Italics in original.

36. Ibid., p. 132.

37. Ibid. I should make clear that my use of Paz's appreciation of Lévi-Strauss runs counter to his own intentions. He enthusiastically describes Lévi-Strauss's work as Marxism corrected by Buddhism. Of the last chapter of *Tristes Tropiques*, he says that there Lévi-Strauss's thought achieves "a density and transparency which might make us think of statuettes of rock crystal if it were not for the fact that it is animated by a pulsation which does not recall so much mineral immobility as the vibration of light waves" (p. 135).

38. Shalvey, *Claude Lévi-Strauss, p. 62*, in what appears to be a quotation of Lévi-Strauss without a citation.

39. Paz, *Claude Lévi-Strauss*, p. 136. While I confess that I do not find the latter contention so clearly present in the meditations at the end of *Tristes Tropiques*, the overall plausibility of Paz's sensitive reading is supported by Lévi-Strauss's argument that the "great deterministic laws" of the physical universe are "colonizing us on behalf of a silent world of which we have become the agents" (p. 391).

40. The exchange of women has a very interesting place in Lévi-Strauss's theory, since he notes that the exchange of women, unlike the exchange of words, is always "substantive" in part because unlike the illusory status of words as pure signs, women cannot become simply signs without value (see *The Savage Mind*, p. 106, and *Structural Anthropology*, p. 60). The real materiality of women's lives is reflected in Lévi-Strauss's treatment of the connection between marriage rules and eating prohibitions. The connection is not causal, of course, but metaphorical. And the source of the connection is the union of the sexes and the union of eater and eaten because both effect a "conjunction by complementarity," better described as the conjunction of opposites—e.g., the passive food is eaten by the active eater, etc. This leads Lévi-Strauss to take note of the familiar equation of males with "devourer" and female with "devoured or consumed." Interestingly enough, Lévi-Strauss recognizes the signi-

ficance of the *vagina dentata* in mythodology as direct rather than inverted coding (*The Savage Mind*, p. 106).

41. Claude Lévi-Strauss, *The Elementary Structures of Kinship*, trans. James Harle Bell, John Richard von Sturmer and Rodney Needham, eds., (Boston: Beacon Press, 1969), p. 233.

42. Ibid., p. 480.

43. Ibid., pp. 12–20, 30, 32. See also Paz, *Claude Lévi-Strauss*, p. 19.

44. Lévi-Strauss, *Kinship*, p. 490. See also his note in *Tristes Tropiques* (p. 317) that a society reduced to simplest expression is merely individual human beings. Lévi-Strauss notes that men have presented several solutions to the problem of the creation and maintenance of a community. Exogamy is one solution, and language itself is another. But Lévi-Strauss argues that words cannot serve very long the same role as the exchange of women. Words become common property and lose their value, impoverishing perception in the modern world (*Kinship*, pp. 496, 490). This view is no doubt one of the reasons he turns to myth to discover real meaning.

45. Lévi-Strauss, *Kinship*, pp. 37–38.

46. Ibid., p. 42.

47. Ibid., p. 39.

48. Ibid., p. 44.

49. Ibid., p. 84.

50. Ibid., p. 116.

51. Ibid., p. 481.

52. There are some problems with the isomorphisms, however, since if it is the case that the symbols produced by men turn on them and make use of men without their knowing it—myths speaking with each other, nature speaking with herself,—then it might also be the case that Lévi-Strauss has not quite seen that the women exchanged as signs would form the real society, and make use of their exchangers for that purpose. But see note 40 above on the special status of women as material beings in the theory. See also Lévi-Strauss's recognition of the problem of seeing the exchange of words and women as isomorphic. The only way to resolve the contradiction created by the fact that certain terms have value both for the speaker and the listener "is in the exchange of complementary values to which all social existence is reduced" (*Structural Anthropology*, p. 61).

53. Lévi-Strauss,*Kinship*, p. 114.

54. Ibid., p. 482, quoted from E. E. Evans-Pritchard, *The Nuer* (New York: Oxford University Press, 1940), p. 183. See also Lévi-Strauss, *Tristes Tropiques*, p. 315, however, where Lévi-Strauss suggests that the providing of collective security is part of the "fundmental nature of social and political organization."

55. In the community, "one lays down one's arms, renounces magic, and gives everything away, from casual hospitality to one's daughter or one's property." (Quoted from M. Mauss, "Essai Sur le Don: Forme et Raison de l'Echange dans les Societies archaiques," *Annee Sociologique*, 1 (1925): 138., quoted in Lévi-Strauss, *Kinship*, p. 483.

56. See C. B. MacPherson, *The Political Theory of Possessive Individualism* (New York: Oxford University Press, 1962), pp. 84, 269; and Lévi-Strauss,

Kinship, p. 54. I am not alone in seeing Lévi-Strauss as working from a Hobbesian model. See also Sahlins, "Spirit of the Gift."

57. Edward B. Tylor, "On a Method of Investigating the Development of Institutions; Applied to Laws of Marriage and Descent," *Journal of the Royal Anthropological Institute of Great Britain and Ireland* 18, (1888): 267. I am indebted to Kathleen Weston for locating this passage for me. (Her italics.)

58. See Lévi-Strauss, *Kinship*, pp. 39, 45, 37. Also see Sahlins, "Spirit of the Gift," on scarcity (pp. 1–39), in the original affluent societies: hunting and gathering groups.

59. Lévi-Strauss, *Kinship*, p. 30.

60. How ironic that a self-professed disciple of Rousseau should recapitulate the theory of the man Rousseau argues so strongly against!

61. Lévi-Strauss, *Kinship*, p. 86.

62. Ibid., p. 84.

63. One might attempt to say women did not consent but were forced. But this cannot get Lévi-Strauss off the hook, since he has argued that all power "originates in consent and is bounded by it" (*Tristes Tropiques*, p. 314). All feminists who have written about Lévi-Strauss, and Lévi-Strauss himself, have tried to argue that he was not maintaining that women were not human. Yet given his stress on the transaction of the exchange of women as a relation between men, and given the fact that only once in *The Elementary Structures of Kinship*, and in a single sentence, does he make the statement that women might be human, these arguments are unpersuasive. Consider the weight of his general case as I have laid it out in these pages. And consider such statements as the following: "Women are the most precious possession . . . above all because women are *not primarily* a sign of social value, but a *natural* stimulant; and the stimulant of the only instinct the satisfaction of which can be deferred, and consequently the only one for which, in the act of exchange, and through the awareness of reciprocity, the transformation from the stimulant to the sign can take place" (*Kinship*, pp. 62–63).

One must balance statements such as this against his single statement that women are indeed human: "But woman could never become just a sign and nothing more, since even in a man's world she is still a person, and since in so far as she is defined as a sign she must be recognized as a generator of signs" (ibid., p. 496). Can one even say that there is a certain regretful tone about this statement? Would it not be simpler if "woman" (not women in all their empirical diversity but "woman" in all her mysterious splendor, one suspects) were simply a natural stimulant that could be transformed into signs?

64. Lévi-Strauss, *The Savage Mind*, pp. 130, 117. See also Lévi-Strauss, *Structural Anthropology*, pp. 330 ff.

65. Piaget, *Structuralism*, p. 107, quoting Lévi-Strauss, *Totemism* (Boston: Beacon Press, 1963), p. 96.

66. Piaget, *Structuralism*, p. 106.

67. Paz, *Claude Lévi-Strauss*, makes several similar points, but takes this not as a series of fundamentally important departures from Marx, but only as meaning that one would have to "stretch the term 'Marxist' " to cover Lévi-Strauss (pp. 113 ff).

68. Shalvey, *Claude Lévi-Strauss*, for example, holds that Lévi-Strauss employs dialectical materialism as a basis for his account of Bororo village structure since he argues that (1) the apparent structure is not the real one, (2) that understanding consists in reducing one type of reality to another and (3) that the hidden structure is always the diametrical opposite of the visible structure (p. 92). Shalvey also credits Lévi-Strauss with employing Marxist notions of praxis as the core of all the economic practices of society (p. 85). The account he gives of the Marxian notion of praxis, however, makes it clear that he has not understood Marx. Paz, who sees the strategy described above as more closely related to the influence of Freud, is more accurate.

69. Lévi-Strauss, *Structural Anthropology*, p. 69.

70. Ibid., p. 56.

71. Lévi-Strauss, *Tristes Tropiques*, p. 385. For a more complete account of the Marxian meaning of objectivity, see my "Objectivity and Revolution: The Unity of Observation and Outrage in Marxist Theory" (*mimeo.*).

72. Lévi-Strauss, *Tristes Tropiques*, p. 386.

73. Ibid., p. 414.

74. Ibid.

75. See Fredric Jameson's discussion of the tradition in *The Prison-House of Language* (Princeton, N.J.: Princeton University Press, 1972).

2

Simone de Beauvoir: Liberation or Escalating Domination?

D e Beauvoir's pioneering work, *The Second Sex*, is marred by the incorporation of a number of the features of abstract masculinity characteristic of Lévi-Strauss's work.[1] Most generally, the hostile and combative dualism typical of this perspective occupies a central place in her accounts both of the sources for the oppression of women and her suggestions for liberation. The opposition of abstract to concrete, culture to nature, stasis to change, and self to other are all present. On the basis of these dualisms, she is led into an idealist location of the source of women's oppression in permanent and ahistorical male "desire." In addition, in accepting and incorporating Lévi-Strauss's account of the exchange of women she implicates herself in the understanding and reality of a social synthesis that, constructed on this basis, can only be problematic: dependent on solipsism, indirect relations among people, and in which the community itself is only a byproduct of action directed at other ends. Moreover, the characteristically masculinist preoccupation with and valuation of death as opposed to life structures her account of the relation of Spirit to Life. Finally, her adoption of so many aspects of the perspective of abstract masculinity leads her to adopt a number of counterfactual positions—among them, that women are not human, that women cannot contribute equally to society, and that sociality is artificial. I do not mean to suggest that de Beauvoir is an ideologue of abstract masculinity or that her work is useless or even unhelpful. Indeed, her feminism seems to have protected her from some of Lévi-Strauss's worst excesses. I do, however, want to argue that feminist analysis must be rooted in the materiality of women's lives, and to point to the variety of problems that ensue from the adoption of a foreign epistemology.

Dualism, for de Beauvoir as for Lévi-Strauss, is an inbuilt feature of human existence: "Man never thinks of himself without thinking of the other; he views the world under the sign of duality."[2] She cites with approval Lévi-Strauss's claim that "passage from the state of Nature to the state of Culture is marked by Man's ability to view biological relations as a series of contrasts; duality, alternation, opposition, and symmetry, whether under definite or vague forms, constitute not so much phenomena to be explained as *fundamental and immediately given data* of social reality."[3]

This "immediately given" duality replicated itself for de Beauvoir both as the opposition of culture to nature and the opposition of self to other. In her theory, human society itself becomes "an *antiphysis*—in a sense it is against nature; it does not passively submit to the presence of nature but rather takes over the control of nature on its own behalf."[4] The nature of humanity itself is constituted in the attack on nature: The sources both of the technology with which to dominate nature and of the domination of women emerge, on de Beauvoir's account, from the male desire to escape from and control "woman-earth." The source of this desire is located in the nature of humanity itself; "man's design is not to repeat himself in time: it is to take control of the instant and mold the future."[5] This taking control of the future is one and the same act as his escape from woman and his freeing of himself from nature.[6]

Man is able to escape from woman-earth, from his animal nature, from stasis, from repetition of the present, from immanence, into the future, into transcendence, by means of engaging in the privileged activities of hunting, fishing, and war. These activities, rather than the bearing and rearing of children, domestic labor, and the reproducing of the group as a whole, represent the core of what is distinctively human. Woman helps to maintain the life of the group by giving it "children and bread" while man contributes in more "creative" ways. What gives value to the male activities, de Beauvoir argues, is that they were the function "which threw open that society toward nature and toward the rest of humanity."[7] The form in which these activities open a society is, however, one formed by combat, opposition, and the death struggle. Surprisingly, then, humanity in the full sense emerges not from the sensual, many-qualified production of subsistence in interaction with natural and human worlds but is attained only through the male activity of killing—whether killing fish, animals, or humans.

That dealing death rather than giving life is really at the heart of de Beauvoir's theory is confirmed in her explicit acceptance of the Hegelian model central to abstract masculinity. She takes for granted that duality gives rise to conflict, and contends as well that human society cannot be understood as a fellowship based on solidarity and friendship. Following Hegel, she argues that consciousness itself contains a fundamental hostility to every other consciousness. The human subject can only be constituted in opposition to another, an object.[8] "At the moment when man asserts himself as subject and free being, the idea of the Other arises. From that day the relation with the Other is dramatic: the existence of the Other is a threat, a danger."[9]

The combat, whether with nature in the form of hunting or fishing, or with men in the form of war, is essential to the affirmation of Spirit as against mere life. De Beauvoir is quite correct to see that the person of the warrior affirms in most extreme form the primacy of Spirit over Life. The food killed by the hunter, after all, can be eaten and thereby can serve mere life. In risking his life, however, the warrior serves only the cause of Spirit, and contributes nothing to material existence, thereby demonstrating that Life is not the supreme value. She concludes that "the worst cause that was laid upon women was that she should be excluded from these warlike forays. For it is not in giving life but in risking life that man is raised above the animal; that is why superiority has been accorded in humanity not to the sex that brings forth but to that which kills." "Here," she goes on, "we have the key to the whole mystery" of women's oppression.[10]

Thus, it is woman's failure to engage in combat that defines her static and repetitive existence, her maternity that condemns her to give life without risking her life. And because she does not risk her life, woman remains bound to her body like an animal, bound to a life that does not carry reasons for being more important than life itself.[11] De Beauvior has not gone so far in the direction of abstract masculinity as to redefine reproduction as death; she has simply treated it as irrelevant to the human project.

Her insistence on the need for a struggle to dominate either another human being or the natural world emerges once again in her prescriptions for change. She argues that while the devaluation of femininity was a necessary step in human evolution, the time has come to "let [women] have the means to *attack the world* and *wrest from it* their own subsistence, and their dependence will be abolished."[12] That is, the liberation of women requires that they, like men, learn to kill, and participate in the destruction of at least the natural world.[13]

De Beauvoir's theory, then, must be understood as infused with and marred by an abstract masculinity. The hostile and combative dualism that forms the ground on which she constructs her theory memorializes the male rather than female experience of differentiation from the mother, and the male struggle to "achieve" masculinity by escaping the concrete repetition of everyday life. In accepting Lévi-Strauss's contention that man "views the world under the sign of duality" de Beauvoir is implicated in his related contention that the concrete variety of societies can be reduced to a simple, abstract dichotomy. She is implicated in his overvaluation of the abstract, despite her several improvements of his theory. For example, she suggests that there are two distinct forms of duality, rather than a single one. She argues that Lévi-Strauss's theorization of community as constructed between men and by means of women who are not party to it makes it clear that there are two forms of otherness, which are mutually exclusive, since other men are potentially other subjects, while women are not. It is this second form of duality which de Beauvoir holds responsible for the fact that women are not parties to the male bond formed through marriage.[14] In addition, she adds to Lévi-Strauss's argument on exogamy the reasoning that its source must be located in the desire to escape from and dominate "woman-earth," that is, to escape from one's own mother, and to have a wife who is different, not a part of one's own "mana."[15]

In addition to refining Lévi-Strauss's abstract dualism in a more concrete and realistic direction, de Beauvoir draws back from some of his more extreme positions. She explicitly rejects his tendency toward a disembodied mysticism in her argument that "to be present in the world implies strictly that there exists a body which is at once a material thing in the world and a point of view toward this world."[16] Nor does she accept Lévi-Strauss's mechanistic and chemical account of the operation of the human brain. She refuses to take sides "prematurely" in the dispute about the relation of life to consciousness and holds instead that every function implies a project or purpose.[17] Finally, she refuses to believe that symbols either come from heaven or arise mysteriously from the depths and will not treat them as more real than those who produced them.[18]

Her improvements on his theory, however, are not enough to rescue it. The fundamental abstractness of the dualisms he posits reappears in her endorsement of the dichotomy and opposition of Spirit of Life, external subjectivity to the body, and the value put on the former at the expense of the concreteness of the latter. Thus she writes that "man aspires to make Spirit triumph over life, action over passivity; his consciousness keeps nature at a distance, his will shapes her. . . ." As subject, man "poses the world, and remaining outside this posed universe, he makes himself ruler of it; if he views himself as flesh, as sex, he is no longer an independent consciousness, a clear, free being: he is involved with the world, he is a limited and perishable object. . . ."[19]

The dichotomy of abstract to concrete takes different, though related form in both the discussion of the dualist nature of the mind itself, and in Lévi-Strauss's (and later to Beauvoir's) discussion of kinship. The women categorized as Other in the exchange of women have no concrete qualities. Lévi-Strauss, and de Beauvoir following him, indicate that what is significant is not the concrete being of woman, but rather her categorization by men. While this was and is an important and useful insight, which can help to provide an account of how the male mind works out and justifies the oppression of women in a world constructed by men, it cannot form the basis for a theory of women's oppression. If one took de Beauvoir to be formulating the latter, one would have to question its utility, since the abstractness of the categorization tends to locate the oppression of women in the intentional (and universal and timeless) action of the mind rather than in the material relations of embodied beings.[20]

The opposition of nature to culture characteristic of abstract masculinity and central to Lévi-Strauss's theory of kinship makes its appearance in de Beauvoir's work as well. It flows both from her reliance on Lévi-Strauss and from her endorsement of abstract masculinity more generally. She takes over the notion that the achievement of humanity, the passage from nature to culture, is constituted by the adoption of dualism as the fundamental category of social analysis, and even more clearly than Lévi-Strauss posits society as a force against nature.

But because she sees the conceptual links between woman-earth, and because she wishes to argue for the inclusion of women in the human community, and their exit from association with nature, she refuses to accept Lévi-Strauss's contention that women are "natural products naturally procreated" and instead holds that "in human society nothing is natural," and women, like men, are products of civilization.[21] It is, then, de Beauvoir's adoption of a perspective from which humanity must be achieved by dominating nature that leads her to argue that women, like men, must be understood as social, not natural, beings.

The opposition of nature to culture is related to the treatment of stasis vs. change in *The Second Sex*. De Beauvoir's treatment of this dualism demonstrates that abstract masculinity posits two forms of stasis: the one permanent and immobile, the other constituted by cyclic repetition; the one transcendent, the other immanent; the one abstract and inaccessible, the other concrete and ever-present; the one characterized as "human" (read "masculine") the other as female; the one valuable, the other worthless. De Beauvoir's acceptance of these dualisms replicates Lévi-Strauss's one-sided valuation of contemplation of the "tenuous arch linking us to the inaccessible." De Beauvoir's valuation of the male, but not female, contribution to subsistence is marked in opposite ways by her accounts of the importance of male activity and the awfulness of housework. Her account of the achievement of transcendence and humanity by means of hunting, fishing, and fighting recapitulates the boy's struggle to achieve masculinity in opposition to the force of daily life. And her discussion of the grinding and meaningless repetition of housework indicates that this work is not to be confused with more fully human activity. The real opposition that underlies the opposition between stasis and change, then, is the opposition of Spirit to Life, the need to escape from the muddy concreteness of daily life, an escape that Lévi-Strauss finds in contemplation of the inaccessible and that de Beauvoir locates in the activity of killing and risking life.

The social relations de Beauvoir describes form the basis for the problematic social synthesis characteristic of abstract masculinity. Her acceptance of Lévi-Strauss's theory of the exchange of women, coupled with her argument that there are two forms of dualism (the other who is a fellow being to be made a partner in exchange versus the absolute other who cannot be a party to the community), suggests that if, as she proposes, women were to be admitted to a social synthesis constructed on the basis of exchange, the community they could construct would be typified by its dependence on solipsism, indirect relations among people, and the fact that the community is only a by-product of activity directed at other ends.

The other, more Hegelian, model she presents—the death struggle between self and other—presents an even more problematic social synthesis. Real solidarity is impossible, and only relations of domination and submission can emerge from this model. De Beauvoir holds that "when two human categories are together, each aspires to impose its sovereignty upon the other. If both are able to resist this imposition, there is created between them a reciprocal relation, sometimes in enmity, sometimes in amity, always in a state of tension."[22] The community, then, emerges as a by-product of the struggle for recognition/sovereignty for which one must risk one's life. That the community of exchange is simply the outgrowth of the Hegelian death struggle is made clear by Mauss's own account of the development of primitive exchange, an account Lévi-Strauss makes the basis for his own account of women: When two groups of men meet, they may move away, or may resort to arms, or else "they can come to terms." Thus, exchange is a means of avoiding the consummation of the death struggle without modifying the fundamental human opposition posited by Hegel. The community established by exchange, then, has important logical connections with the Hegelian opposition of self and other.[23]

In addition to the problems discussed so far, de Beauvoir's adoption of the epistemology of abstract masculinity leads her into several counterfactual assertions. First, following Lévi-Strauss, she contends that sociality is artificial and must be constructed by intentional action. Second, her description of women as condemned to animality by their biology, and her argument that hunting, fishing, and war "open" society to the future rests on the contention that women's activity is not human activity and that women themselves are not human, since humanity can be achieved only through struggle. A materialist account would give attention to the relations of nurturance and even cooperation among women and children. Third, de Beauvoir suggests that productive work has moved beyond the strength of women. Given what has been said in Part II about the nature and extent of women's contribution to subsistence and childrearing, de Beauvoir's conclusion can only stem from the almost completely negative status she accords housework.[24]

Despite these difficulties, de Beauvoir does not adopt the perspective of abstract masculinity in nearly as extreme form as Lévi-Strauss. Thus, despite her approving citations of Hegel, she refuses to take the position that reproduction is best understood as death; and despite her over-evaluation of risking life rather than giving life, she recognizes that the effort to escape death and mortality is a project of the male mind. Moreover, she, unlike Lévi-Strauss, recognizes that life is lived in embodied form and that history and the production of subsistence are important, if not yet held to be central features of human existence.

Political theorizing must be understood as a historical act structured by and dependent on material social relations. De Beauvoir's theory clearly suffered from the absence in practice of a radical alternative to the masculinist world view. The deficiencies of her theory demonstrate the way a feminist standpoint can emerge only from the historical activity of a radically feminist movement for change. It was only in the context of such a movement that, for example, women's work and activity could be re-theorized and re-valued. Despite the deficiencies, de Beauvoir's work still stands as a descriptive account of the operation of the phallocracy as both ideology and institution. Given her adoption of so many of the perverse features of abstract masculinity, however, it was perhaps fitting that she ended *The Second Sex* with a call for brotherhood. Sisterhood was yet to be discovered.

NOTES

1. I hesitate to say that he is the sole source of difficulties posed by her account, since the points I raise are characteristic also of Sartre and Hegel and these may represent more direct sources of influence. The consequences of maintaining such positions, however, emerged in the discussion of Lévi-Strauss, and that will provide my point of reference.

2. Simone de Beauvoir, *The Second Sex*, trans. H. M. Parshley (New York: Knopf, 1953), p. 63.

3. Ibid., p. xvii; italics mine.

4. Ibid., p. 47. She attributes this view to historical materialism. But the historical materialism with which she is familiar is an inaccurate economic determinist model. See pp. 48, 54.

5. Ibid., p. 60.

6. Ibid., pp. 68-69.

7. Ibid., p. 68.

8. Ibid., pp. xxi, xvii.

9. Ibid., p. 73. It is significant given the deep-going phallocratic values of Greek philosophy described in Part II that de Beauvoir considers that this philosophy has decisively proved the truth of the claim that alterity, otherness, is negation, and is therefore evil.

10. Ibid., p. 58.

11. Ibid., pp. 58–60. De Beauvoir's exclusion of the risks involved in childbirth seems puzzling until one recalls her stress on the need for recognition by another consciousness.

12. Ibid., p. 682; italics mine.

13. De Beauvoir's emphasis on women's role in getting subsistence raises the question whether women should also participate in the killing and dominating of other humans. This is very interesting given the intransitive theories of power developed by theorists such as Hannah Arendt, Dorothy Emmett, Hanna Pitkin, Adrienne Rich, and myself in earlier work. She notes as well that despite the universal dualism and the construction of women as Other, the couple should be regarded as the original *mitsein*, or fellowship based on solidarity. Ibid., p. 32.

14. Ibid., pp. 65–67.

15. Ibid., p. 68.

16. Ibid., p. 5.

17. Ibid., p. 7.

18. Ibid., p. 42.

19. Ibid., p. 151. She notes too that Hegel sees "the birth of children as the death of parents. The ejaculation is a promise of death. . . ." (ibid.).

20. The clarity of de Beauvoir's vision of the male mind is extraordinary. She writes of the male desire to be disembodied, "often man is in revolt against his carnal state." "This fire, this pure and active exhalation in which he likes to recognize himself, is imprisoned by women in the mud of the earth. He would be inevitable, like a pre-Idea, like the One, the All, the absolute Spirit; and he finds himself shut up in a body of limited powers, in a place and time he never chose . . . . Wherever life is in the making—germination, fermentation—it arouses disgust because it is made only in being destroyed; the slimy embryo brings the cycle that is completed in the putrefaction of death . . . man feels horror at having been engendered; . . . through the fact of his birth murderous Nature has a hold upon him" (ibid., p. 135).

21. Ibid., p. 682

22. Ibid., p. 56.

23. Marcel Mauss, *The Gift*, trans. Ian Cunnison (New York: Norton, 1967), p. 79, has described the fundamental rivalry of such a community.

24. See, for example, the research indicating that women are capable of the hard labor involved in homesteading, which indicates that women "proved up" homesteads at a higher rate than men. See Ann Markusen, "Who Were Your Grandmothers, John Hansen," *Quest: a feminist quarterly* 5, no. 2. (1980), Citing Sheryll Patterson-Black, "Woman Homesteaders on the Great Plains Frontier," *Frontiers* 1, no. 2 (Summer 1976).

3

Gayle Rubin:
The Abstract Determinism of
the Kinship System

T he discovery of sisterhood represented a necessary but not sufficient condition for the development of a materialist feminist analysis. Gayle
Rubin's influential essay, "The Traffic in Women: Notes on the 'Political Economy' of Sex," generated a great deal of excitement both before and after its
formal publication. It has been credited as being a kind of "watermark" for a
Marxist feminist methodology, an essay that represented the beginning of a
"much richer, more integrated analytical approach."[1] This essay has been one
of the most widely and favorably cited the contemporary feminist movement
has yet produced. Yet it is marred by the use of categories that locate it at the
epistemological level defined by exchange, and suffers from some of the effects
of abstract masculinity. Because of the importance feminists collectively have
given to this essay, its problems should be regarded as collective ones, difficulties which arise from the fact that it was written and has been used in the
context of a society itself deeply marked by the exchange abstraction. Thus, the
problems to which I point here should be viewed as similar to those discussed
in Chapters 4 and 5 above.

Rubin takes Lévi-Strauss and Freud as dual points of departure in pursuit
of the project Engels "abandoned when he located the subordination of women
in a development within the mode of production."[2] She proposes to take over
his method to identify the "relationships by which a female becomes an
oppressed woman."[3]

Rubin recognizes the inadequacy of Marxism to account for the genesis of
the oppression of women; she rejects both those who subsume questions of
women's oppression under the heading of the "woman question" and those
who point to the relationship between housework and the reproduction of
labor to suggest that women's situation is an artifact of capitalism.[4] To explain
women's usefulness to capitalism is one thing, she argues, but to argue that
utility explains the genesis of oppression is another. She chooses Lévi-Strauss

293

and Freud because she sees in their work the possibility of understanding a "systematic social apparatus which takes up females as raw materials and fashions domesticated women as products."[5] Her project as she describes it is to "isolate sex and gender from 'mode of production,'" in order to counter those who tend to see sex oppression as an outgrowth of economic forces, or, as she has put it to suggest that feminist theory should look for the "ultimate locus of women's oppression within the traffic in women, rather than within the traffic in merchandise."[6]

Rubin recognizes some of the dangers of the project she proposes. She notes that the effort to borrow from structuralism and psychoanalysis in order to carry on Engel's enterprise may lead to "a certain clash of epistemologies," that a "somewhat tortuous argument" is needed to integrate them into feminist theory, and recognizes that her borrowing may have brought in the sexism of the traditions, particularly since she has characterized both psychoanalysis and structural anthropology as "the most sophisticated ideologies of sexism around."[7] Unfortunately, Rubin's reliance on these theorists has indeed distorted her work. In an ironic echo of Lévi-Strauss's contention that signs speak through and use human beings for their own ends, one might even say that Rubin, in attempting to use his theory, has instead been used by it.

Specifically, her use of his account of the exchange of women leads her to accept several of the specific dualities present in commodity exchange. Thus she tacitly endorses the account of reality that grows from the practical separation of exchange from use, of quantity from quality, of interaction with nature from social interaction. She does not question the fundamental opposition of participants in exchange and as a result can provide no alternative vision of a nonproblematic social synthesis.

In addition, like Lévi-Strauss, Rubin gives pride of place to the abstract instead of the concrete and devalues material life activity in favor of the production of symbols. The value she puts on the abstract as opposed to the concrete leads her to reduce the material sexual division of labor to a "taboo," to evaporate concrete social relations into systems of kinship understood as symbol systems, and finally to banish human activity altogether as kinship systems assume the role of the "productive forces" of sex and gender. (This last move is curiously reminiscent of Stalin's doctrine of the primacy of the productive forces.) The concrete activity of real human beings is replaced by the operation of self-moving symbol systems. It is a curious confirmation of Lévi-Strauss's argument that the exchange of signs and the exchange of women recapitulate each other.

The result of the centrality of abstract symbol systems in Rubin's work is (1) acceptance of a gulf between nature and culture, and a stress on the primacy of the social, (2) the location of the oppression of women in the realm of ideology (taboo, convention) rather than in material life activity as structured by the division of labor. (3) Finally, Rubin, in adopting so many features of Lévi-Strauss's system of thought is implicated in several of his counterfactual claims, most specifically, that society is artificial, that women are signs, and that sex and gender are altogether distinct from each other.

Thus, despite Rubin's appropriately jaundiced view of Lévi-Strauss and his project, and despite her efforts to argue explicitly for recognizing sex/gender systems not as products of the human mind but as products of historical human activity, her effort to borrow his account of the exchange of women undermines her stated purpose. I do not mean to suggest that Rubin would endorse all the positions taken by Lévi-Strauss. Indeed, she explicitly rejects his idealism and is appropriately shocked by his treatment of women as words that are misused if not exchanged.[8] The real issues are the extent to which feminists can borrow from phallocratic ideologies without their own analyses suffering in consequence, and the extent to which feminist theory can take place without being relocated onto the ground provided by a specifically feminist epistemology.

Rubin's Reading of Lévi-Strauss

Rubin notes that anthropologists have long considered kinship to mark the discontinuity between semihuman hominids and human beings.[9] She proposes to adopt Lévi-Strauss's account of kinship, an account that rests on both the nature of the gift in primitive societies and the incest taboo. The two of them together, she argues, lead to the exchange of women. Unlike Lévi-Strauss, she does not choose to understand the exchange of women as definitional of culture, nor as a system in and of itself. Instead, she proposes to treat the kinship system as "an imposition of social ends upon a part of the natural world," and thereby define it as production in what she considers to be a Marxian sense: as a "transformation of objects ... to and by a subjective purpose."[10]

Rubin chooses to modify Lévi-Strauss on several points in order to translate his theory of the exchange of women into a theory of the production of gender. First, she leaves out of her summary of his theory the "deep polygamous tendency" that Lévi-Strauss held responsible for creating the scarcity, and thereby the exchange of women.[11] Thus, her account of the exchange of women is detached from the force that set it in motion.

Second, she attempts to read Lévi-Strauss in too feminist a way, a reading that cannot be supported on the basis of her own account of his work. She credits him with positing a gendered human subject, and reinterprets kinship systems as not simply the exchange of women but as the exchange of "sexual access, genealogical statuses, lineage names and ancestors, rights and *people*— men, women, and children—in concrete systems of social relationships".[12] This is clearly contrary to Lévi-Strauss's intent but not a problem given her own purposes. It does, however, run counter to her argument that since it is the women who are being transacted, it is the men who are the partners in the social relation. And she quotes Lévi-Strauss to that effect.[13]

Her defense of women as not simply objects in the transaction only compounds the difficulties: To hold that objects in the primitive world are imbued with "highly personal" qualities indicates that she has accepted Lévi-Strauss's formula: $\frac{women}{men} = \frac{words}{salvage}$. Her acceptance of this formula, however, undermines her outrage at his contention that it is women's dual status as sign producers as well as signs, which explains why relations between women and men have preserved an "affective richness" and "mystery."[14] The imbuing of objects with personal qualities is what he is describing here, a position she has already endorsed. The source of the problem is the difficulty of using a theory that treats women as symbols and objects to analyze and expose systematic domination.

Third, because she wants to treat kinship as production, Rubin attempts to read Lévi-Strauss literally rather than metaphorically. Thus, she argues that "it is not difficult to find ethnographic and historical examples of trafficking in women," and proceeds to cite a number of instances.[15] It is worth remembering that Lévi-Strauss formulated his theory of the exchange of women out of his interest in the nature of symbol systems, most particularly his interest in formulating the laws governing the operation of the primitive mind. Rather than treat them as concrete social relations, Lévi-Strauss held that kinship systems were constructed by the mind at the level of unconscious thought.[16] Thus, each of these moves threatens to pose problems for Rubin.

The effort to treat kinship systems as a form of production is central to Rubin's effort, and this is where I center my attention. This is the means by which her theory is marred by association with Lévi-Strauss's symbol systems. Her explicit strategy is to carry on the series of transformations begun by Lévi-Strauss, from the construction of kinship systems by the exchange of women to the construction of gender by the kinship system. In fact, however, in the end her theory moves in the reverse direction—back to the system she has ignored, the construction of symbol systems by the human unconscious. Let us follow this progression (regression?) by means of which production becomes exchange and theory moves to the epistemological level of exchange, which in turn becomes exchange of women, which becomes the kinship system, which in turn becomes a symbol system, and in which, finally, as in Lévi-Strauss's work, the signs themselves seem to speak through persons.

Capitalist Production from the Perspective of the Exchange Abstraction

Rubin sees Marx's analysis of capitalist production as locating the key to the operation of the working class in the "traffic in merchandise." Her summary of the production and extraction of surplus value in capitalism is marked by an extraordinarily consistent focus on exchange. As a result, the material process of production involving interaction with nature, concentration on concrete qualities of real objects, and cooperation with others, vanishes. Instead, it is "the *exchange* between capital and labor which produces surplus value."[17] And the surplus value belonging to the capitalist no longer inheres in concrete products, but is represented by the purely quantitative difference between the amounts of goods necessary to reproduce labor power and the amounts of goods the labor force can produce.[18]

Even when she addresses production itself, her stress is always on the raw materials, factors of production, and the product, never on the lengthy process by which the one becomes the other. The accumulation of capital is described, then, as if from the perspective of the capitalist, whose world is constituted by a series of transactions, by buying and selling, and for whom the process of production is best conceptualized under the simple heading of "transformation."[19] The process of production, then, becomes "the system by which elements of the natural world are transformed into objects of human consumption."[20] Diverse and many-qualitied human activity in cooperation with others and interchange with nature has been replaced by an abstract "system."

Capital itself is redefined as something that *"reproduces* and augments *itself* by extracting unpaid labor, or surplus value, from labor and into itself."[21] This is a curiously disembodied and self-moving capital, obviously not close kin to the purchaser of labor power striding pridefully toward his factory, or "Moneybags" with whom Marx debates economic theory in the pages of *Capital.*[22] In Marx's analysis, capitalist production took place by means of the actions of specific individuals located in time and space. The capital Rubin describes is better understood as "abstract movement through abstract (homogeneous, continuous, and empty) space and time of abstract substances materially real but bare of sense-qualities, which thereby suffer no material change and which allow for none but quantitive differentiation (differentiation in abstract, non-dimensional quantity)."[23] This capital is not Marx's capital, but our old friend "Exchange" attempting to pass itself off as capital.

That capital should appear as abstract movement of abstract substances is not, of course, unique to Rubin's account. One can find important resemblances between this capital and the "productive forces" of economic determinism. They, like it, seem to need no human help to "select [social] structures according to their capacity to promote development," or even make "demands" and set requirements that humans must meet. For example, "the new productive forces require that the workers in production shall be better educated and more intelligent than the downtrodden and ignorant serfs, that they be able to understand machinery and operate it properly. *Therefore,* the capitalists prefer to deal with wage workers who are free of the bonds of serfdom. . . ."[24]

While one would have to force her analysis too far to claim that Rubin recapitulates economic determinist accounts of the operation of the productive forces, her summary of Marx comes uncomfortably close to doing so. This, then, is the reading of the Marxian account of production that structures Rubin's account of the operation of the kinship system. That the epistemological level of exchange and not production deeply structures Rubin's analysis of Marx as well as her understanding of kinship is underlined by the fact that when she calls for a Marxian analysis of sex/gender systems, she suggests that it should follow the lines of Marx's discussion of the evolution of money and commodities and does not mention his discussion of production.[25]

We have, then, completed the first transition that undermines the value of Rubin's theory: the inadvertent redefinition of production as exchange. Thus, even before she explicitly discusses the exchange of women, Rubin's work is marred by the presence of the exchange abstraction, with the concomitant attention to exchange rather than use, quantity rather than quality, and the opposition of nature to culture. (The transformation of objects by subjective purposes [production] will become in her discussion of the kinship system, the "seizing of control" of biology.) Her eventual destination is prefigured by her vision of a self-moving and disembodied capital which seemingly extracts surplus value without either the complex and many-qualitied processes of production or the intervention of human agents.

The Kinship System and the Production of Gender

Sex is the raw material the kinship system turns out as gender, females the raw material to be made women. But here we run up against a snag in the analogy between the kinship system and the productive forces. Production requires real changes in concrete objects in accord with human purposes and therefore involves both the natural and social worlds; kinship is purely a social phenomenon. This is of course one of the reasons Rubin finds it theoretically attractive, since it enables her to argue against those who would locate the oppression of women in their biological inferiority rather than their socially constructed oppression. This exclusively social character marks the next step, the transformation of exchange of women into kinship. The logic by which humans become the instruments of the signs they orginally produced moves forward by means of the definition of a kinship system as a "system of categories and statuses which often contradict actual genetic relationships," an "invention." Thus, the production done by the system, the producing of gendered beings, is carried on by the operation of the categories of kinship.

Rubin's own discussion of the Nuer custom of "woman marriage" illustrates the purely social nature of kinship, as well as the fact that production of gendered beings is accomplished through the movement of categories. Among the Nuer, Rubin states, "a woman can be married to another woman, and be husband to the wife and father of her children, despite the fact that she is not the inseminator.[26] Her physical being, particular qualities as an individual, talents, and so forth, remain the same of course. Only her social classification has changed. Just as the concrete, quality-laden process of production vanished from Rubin's account of capital's self-expansion, so too women's concrete life activities vanish from the operation of the kinship system. All that matters is their abstract classification most fundamentally as either "same" or "different." All that is necessary for exchange is the sign of otherness. The possibility for persons to occupy statuses that do not reflect genetic relationships serves to underline the abstract and qualityless character of the symbols that constitute the kinship system.

Marx, of course, had encountered theories such as this. He described them as accounts of production "characteristic of philosophical consciousness," "for whom the movement of the categories appears as the real act of production." The system of categories is a "product of a thinking head," and "the real subject retains its autonomous existence outside the head just as before."[27]

We have, then, completed another step in the ascent into abstraction: the transformation of the kinship system into a symbol system. Only the final move remains to be made: the setting of the signs in motion. Rubin's reference to Lévi-Strauss's account of symbol systems as a "chess game" is stunningly apt.[28] We shall see that concrete human actors become instead chess pieces moved about the board by the inexorable forces of kinship. The chess pieces are, moveover, unconscious of the real character of their actions, since the requirements the kinship systems lay down for human beings are met by the oedipal phase of psychic development. "Kinship systems," Rubin states, "require a division of the sexes. The oedipal phase divides the sexes."[29] The kinship system, then (operating analogously to the productive forces of econo-

nic determinists), recruits the oedipal phase to its aid in transforming biologically sexed beings into gendered ones.

The final move has been made. One can perhaps begin to see that the
category of kinship performs the same role in Rubin's theory as myth performed for Lévi-Strauss. For him, myth provides the lever needed to escape
from history; for her, it is kinship. His escape from history rests in part on his
positing of a permanent and universal structure inherent in the human mind;
hers rests on the fact that she sees the exchange of women as operating across
culture and history.[30] For him, myth must be understood as a "paralanguage"
whose true meaning is unconscious; for her, the oedipal phase fulfills this role.
He concludes that the originators of the myths do not know its meaning, that
myths communicate with each other by means of men and without men knowing it; persons not only vanish but become instruments of that which they
themselves produced. She seems to conclude that kinship systems, those human inventions, those socially constructed systems of categories, produce gendered human beings through the "mechanism" of the oedipal phase. For her,
too, persons have become the passive instruments of the symbols they themselves produced. The death of subjectivity inherent in Lévi-Strauss's contention
that myths speak to each other through the medium of men and without men
knowing it here takes the form of the kinship system operating to produce
gendered beings, without their full awareness.

Rubin's theory, then, begins its ascent into abstraction by giving centrality
to the category of exchange. When coupled with the influence of Lévi-Strauss,
the ascent becomes a flight. The myths that loom large over the terrain of Lévi-
Strauss's theory are here replaced by an abstract and self-moving capital and a
kinship system that serves not only as a mechanism for producing gendered
beings but as a machine for the suppression of time and space and materiality.

Rubin's re-creation of Lévi-Strauss's system makes it impossible for her to
give an account of women's oppression located in daily life activity, and instead requires that she locate its source in the purely social and even intellectual
realm of ideology— in taboo, convention, and cultural tradition. Her use of the
taboo on sameness is ambiguous. Whereas Lévi-Strauss indicated that it arose
from the neurological structure of the human mind, Rubin gives no direct indication of the source for such a taboo. The oedipal phase is of course a good
candidate. Rubin's location of the oppression of women in the realm of ideology is not something that must be "read out" of her text in the same way as her
ascent into abstractness. She explicitly located "the entire domain of sex, sexuality, and sex oppression" in what Marx termed the historical and moral element in the determination of the value of labor power.[31] Marx was referring to
the ways in which class struggle could affect the wages actually received by the
worker, by raising or lowering the amount of labor time considered socially
necessary. Rubin translates this as capitalism's "cultural heritage" of gender,
thus seeming to locate this historical and moral element outside the structured
relations of capital and labor altogether. But the question that remains is how
sex oppression is structural rather than dependent on the specific state of the
"battle of the sexes."

Rather than locate the oppression of women in the different activities performed by women and men, and the different consequences these have for

roles in social organization, Rubin, following Lévi-Strauss, translates the division of labor by sex into a "'taboo': a taboo against the sameness of men and women," a taboo that itself creates difference.[32] The taboo is essential to the exchange of women, since they can only be exchanged on the basis of the sign of difference, and thus, "if Lévi-Strauss is correct in seeing the exchange of women as a fundamental principle of kinship, the subordination of women can be seen as a product of the relationships by which sex and gender are organized and produced."[33] Thus, and quite consistently with her intention, the oppression of women is located altogether in society rather than in biology. But Rubin's definition of society ends up locating the source of women's oppression in symbol systems rather than in the structure of material life activity, in systems of meaning rather than in systems of action.

As a result of her location of women's oppression in symbol systems, Rubin is led to posit a gulf between nature and culture, and thereby to implicate herself in the argument that society is artifical and the contention that sex is altogether different from gender. Thus, she seems to have adopted Lévi-Strauss's view that society is artifically constructed by means of a social contract memorialized in the kinship system. This is perhaps why she gives such prominence to "property" in the list of relations that characterize a kinship system. A kinship system, she states, "has its own relations of production, distribution, and exchange, which include certain 'property' forms in people."[34] Her inclusion of property as essential to the system is related to the stress she gives to exchange rather than production in her account of Marxian theory.

Property, after all, marks the separation the market makes of exchange from use.[35] One could read her to say that, given Mauss's and Lévi-Strauss's accounts of the exchange of women as the construction of community, the oppression of women results most centrally from the kind of problematic social synthesis that represents the only community possible on the model of exchange. The difficulty is that she never moves the discussion of the liberation of women beyond the suggestion that women might come to have "full rights to themselves.[36] "Rights" in oneself or to oneself limit one to a community constructed by property owners on the basis of mutual exclusivity of exchange and use, a community that is never anything but a relation between strangers whose creation of a social synthesis is only incidental to their intentional activity. And one must remember as well the fact that, as Mauss described the construction of the gift relation, it was an effort to circumvent the battle that might otherwise have occurred. The choice that led to exchange was that between exchange and war.

Thus, "rights" in themselves would free women to participate, like men, in the construction of a problematic and fragile social synthesis. It is difficult to determine whether this is in fact Rubin's vision of women's role in a more humane society, since her focus is so clearly on the oppression of women. The centrality of exchange in her thought, coupled with her several references to rights and her acceptance of the Mauss/Lévi-Strauss model of community, suggest that this will be so.[37] But real human beings, particularly women, are involved in and even constituted by social relations, and the notion of "rights" enters these relations (such as those between mothers and children) very late, if at all.[38]

Second, Rubin's treatment of sex as opposed to gender divides the two entirely: The one is entirely natural, the other entirely social; the one outside human control, the other subject to it. Kinship is the "seizing of control" of biology, and carries the connotation of making biology subject to human purpose. This overemphasis on the social and on the heterogeneity of society and nature is one source for Rubin's contention that "cultural evolution provides us with the opportunity to seize control of the means of sexuality, reproduction, and socialization, and to make conscious decisions to liberate human sexual life from the archaic relationships which deform it."[39] Given what she had said about the purely social location of women's oppression, and the central role she then seems to give to self-moving symbol systems, one wonders whether it is possible for humans to seize control.

Conclusion

I have attempted to demonstrate the ways feminist theorists can be led into abstraction by adopting theories built either on the categories central to the exchange abstraction or those which constitute abstract masculinity. A historical materialist feminism cannot be developed on the basis of the category of exchange. Nor can we build a materialist theory of women's oppression on the combative dualisms of abstract masculinity. Yet these categories have not only repeatedly proved attractive but have been the basis on which a number of feminist "classics" have been constructed. The high regard in which Rubin's essay "The Traffic in Women" is held indicates that large numbers of feminists hold similar views and have not seen the problems that can grow from taking exchange (whether of commodities, words, or women) as the most basic social relation. I have devoted so much critical attention to this essay in order to make clear the dangers these concepts pose for feminist theory, and to draw attention to their theoretical consequences.

An analysis that begins from the sexual division of labor—understood not as taboo but as the real, material activity of concrete human beings—could form the basis for an analysis of the real structures of women's oppression, an analysis that would not require that one sever biology from society, nature from culture, an analysis that would expose the ways women both participate in and oppose their own subordination. The elaboration of such an analysis cannot but be difficult. Women's lives, like men's, are structured by social relations that manifest the experience of the dominant gender and class. And feminists are not immune to the consequences of this fact.

NOTES

1. Rosalind Petchesky, "Dissolving the Hyphen: A Report on Marxist-Feminist Groups 1–5," in *Capitalist Patriarchy and the Case for Socialist Feminism*, ed. Zillah Eisenstein (New York: Monthly Review Press, 1978), p. 376.

2. Gayle Rubin, "The Traffic in Women," in *Toward an Anthropology of Women*, ed. R. Reiter (New York: Monthly Review Press, 1975), p. 169.

3. Ibid., pp. 169, 158.

4. Ibid., p. 160.

5. Ibid., p. 158.

6. Ibid., pp. 203, 175.

7. Ibid., pp. 159, 203, 208.

8. Ibid., pp. 204, 201.

9. Ibid., p. 170. One wonders why there must be a sharp discontinuity between humans and animals. Is this too an outgrowth of the masculinist project?

10. Ibid., pp. 176–77.

11. See my discussion above, Appendix 1, pp. 274 and n. 63.

12. Rubin, "Traffic," pp. 171, 177. See also p. 179.

13. Ibid., p. 174.

14. Ibid., p. 201.

15. Ibid., pp. 175–76.

16. Rubin's account of the operation of the kinship system and the oedipal phase seem to imply that she too holds the unconscious to be center. But perhaps this simply vitiates her own effort to read kinship systems literally.

17. Ibid., p. 161. (Italics mine.)

18. Ibid., p. 162. Her point, it is true, is to argue that housework is essential to reproducing the labor force. I have no problems with that, but I do have problems with the account of production that is not an account of production at all; rather, it is an account of the exchange of products. Cf. my discussion of production, pp. 116–126.

19. The term implies an instantaneous change, and indeed, from the perspective of the capitalist, it would be better if it were. See, for example, Marx's discussion of the impact of turnaround time on profit.

20. Rubin, "Traffic," p. 165.

21. Ibid., p. 161. (Italics mine.)

22. See, for example, Karl Marx *Capital* (New York: International Publishers, 1967), 1:190 ff.

23. Alfred Sohn-Rethel, *Intellectual and Manual Labor* (New York: Macmillan, 1978), p. 53.

24. Italics mine. Joseph Stalin, "Dialectical and Historical Materialism," in Bruce Franklin, *The Essential Stalin* (Garden City, N.Y.: Doubleday, 1972), p. 325. The earlier quotation is from G. A. Cohen, *Marx's Theory of History: a Defence* (Princeton: Princeton University Press, 1978), p. 162. In fact, Rubin's account of production is perhaps more closely related to Althusser's definition of social practice itself as production—a "process of *transformation* of a determinate given raw material into a determinate *product*, a transformation effected by a determinate human labor, using determinate means (of 'production')." *For Marx*, trans. Ben Brewster (New York: Random House, 1970), p. 185. I have argued that Althusser has misunderstood Marx's account of production and that his understanding of the production of the concrete-in-thought runs directly counter to Marx's own statements. See Nancy C. M. Hartsock and Neil Smith, "On Althusser's Mis-reading of the 1857 Introduction," *Science and Society* 43, no 4 (Winter, 1978–80). Whether these practices are ideological, economic, political, or theoretical, for Althusser, their structure remains the same. Thus, Althusser describes the process of production of knowledge as involving

three "generalities." Generality I is the precondition for scientific labor, the raw material to be transformed into knowledge. Generality II refers to the work done— although Althusser is unclear about whether this is simply the means of production or the labor process itself. Generality III is the knowledge produced through this process of transformation. The stress is on the distinction between Generality I and Generality III. Althusser's lack of clarity about the nature of Generality II marks his real lack of interest in the production process itself.

25. Rubin, "Traffic," p. 205.

26. Ibid., p. 169. See also p. 181.

27. Karl Marx, *Grundrisse*, trans. Martin Nicolaus (Middlesex, England: Penguin Books, 1973), pp. 100–102. Marx here is referring to Hegel.

28. Rubin, "Traffic," p. 171.

29. Ibid., pp. 124, 198. See also p. 199. I do not object to the statement that the oedipal phase divides the sexes. Indeed, this is congruent with my own analysis. Rather, I object to the image of the cooperative oedipal phase racing to the rescue of the kinship system.

30. She draws back from claiming it is universal, but does hold that despite the fact that Lévi-Strauss's data base was non-modern, his description of the exchange of women is correct for modern society as well. In addition, she is attempting to formulate some basic generalities about the organization of human sexuality (ibid., pp. 170, 198, 83). Given the nature of her project, it is perhaps just as well that she wishes to isolate the sex/gender system from the mode of production (p. 198). One should also recognize the political reasons for doing so. When the article was written, it was necessary to respond to those who claimed that women's inferiority was "natural" and not social.

31. Ibid., p. 164.

32. Ibid., p. 178.

33. Ibid., p. 177. One wonders what she means by the organization of sex, as opposed to gender.

34. Ibid.

35. In addition, one should note that her formulation here clearly puts her in the camp of the dual systems theorists criticized by Iris Young in "Socialist Feminism and the Limits of Dual Systems Theory," *Socialist Review* 50–51 (Spring-Summer 1980).

36. Rubin, "Traffic," p. 177. See also her discussion of the strategy of separatism, which she sees as a claim by women of "rights in themselves" (p. 175).

37. If so, it would mean that, ironically, Rubin was back on the terrain she had attempted to avoid, a terrain defined by "the woman question" to which the solution is simply the provision of "democratic rights."

38. On the problematic and conflictual nature of "rights" as a means of organizing social relations, see Richard Flathman, "How Can We Possibly Justify Any Rights Whatsoever?" (mimeo, Department of Political Science, Johns Hopkins University, Baltimore, Md.)

39. Rubin, "Traffic," pp. 199–200. One wonders what the source for cultural evolution may be, as well as about whether there has been progress, since she has already said that Lévi-Strauss's exchange theories describe not only the primitive societies he was studying but Western society as well.

Index